MELVIN J. DUBNICK

BARUCH COLLEGE
THE CITY UNIVERSITY OF NEW YORK

BARBARA S. ROMZEK

UNIVERSITY OF KANSAS

AMERICAN
PUBLIC
ADMINISTRATION

Politics and the Management of Expectations

MACMILLAN PUBLISHING COMPANY

NEW YORK

To Dave and Wallis

B.S.R.

To the Dubnick art colony:
Randi the painter, Heather the writer, and P.D. the musician

M.J.D.

Editor: Bruce K. Nichols
Production Supervisors: Eric Newman and Elisabeth Fleshler
Production Manager: Valerie A. Sawyer
Text Designer: Angela Foote
Cover Designer: Robert Freese
Photo Researcher: Dallas Chang
Illustrations: Reproduction Drawings Inc.

This book was set in Baskerville and Bookman by V & M Graphics, Inc. and printed and bound by R. R. Donnelly & Sons Company. The cover was printed by The Lehigh Press, Inc.

Macmillan Publishing Company
866 Third Avenue, New York, New York 10022

Collier Macmillan Canada
1200 Eglinton Avenue East, Suite 200
Don Mills, Ontario M3C 3N1

Library of Congress Cataloging-in-Publication Data
Dubnick, Melvin J.
    American public administration : politics and the management of expectations / Melvin J. Dubnick, Barbara S. Romzek.
        p. cm.
    Includes bibliographical references.
    ISBN 0-02-330661-0
    1. United States—Politics and government. 2. Public administration—United States.   I. Romzek, Barbara S.   II. Title.
JK411.D83 1991
353—dc20   89-13530
                    CIP

Photo Credits: Hiroshi Hamaya/Magnum (p. 3); UPI/Bettman Newsphotos (p. 23); Atlan Sygma (p. 53); © Kal Muller 1977 (p. 91); Sygma (p. 107); Ashe/Sygma (p. 133); Laura Poracsky (p.157); H. Armstrong Roberts (pp. 189 and 237); © Thomas S. England 1982 (p. 213); © Michal Heron 1981 (p. 271); Gamma-Liaison/ © Cynthia Johnson (p. 347); R. Taylor/ Sygma (p. 379).

Printing: 1 2 3 4 5 6 7   Year: 1 2 3 4 5 6 7

PREFACE

Bureaucrat bashing is a popular pastime in the United States. It gets votes for politicians and sells books for some popular writers. It provides most Americans with an easy answer to the question "What's wrong with our government?"

This is not a bureaucrat-bashing book. Rather, this is a book that stresses respect for those who devote their lives to public service. It is not written as an apology for the negative things that often emerge from the operations of government agencies. There is enough evidence of malfeasance and incompetence to make even the most ardent advocates of public administration doubt their support. Instead, this is a book about the accomplishments of public administration and the pressures facing America's public servants each working day. It is about the responsibilities, obligations, and commitments that constantly challenge those who choose public service as a career. It is also about how public administrators respond to the pressures and challenges they face.

Between us, we, the authors, have more than a quarter century of teaching experience. We have worked with public administrators for years in the classroom and in consulting and have found the vast majority of them to be motivated, hard-working, well-intentioned, and committed professionals. Certainly, as in any profession, there are a few "bad apples" that give the rest a poor reputation. However, we are convinced that most public-service professionals do not deserve the bashing they frequently receive, but rather that they deserve to be understood and appreciated for what they are able to accomplish.

What most students know about public administration is distorted. Their views are often shaped by piecemeal reports and horror stories in the media, by the antibureaucratic rhetoric of political campaigns, and by the general antigovernment tone of our political culture. We feel that students need to know more about who public administrators are and what they do; they also need a better understanding of the complexity and demanding nature of most public-sector jobs. The American public asks public administrators to accomplish the nearly impossible task of satisfying multiple, diverse, and often contradictory expectations. Despite the insurmountable obstacles to succeeding at their jobs, public administrators continue to do them. These dedicated people more often deserve our respect rather than the constant abuse they are more likely to receive from the American public. Such is the theme of this textbook.

Public administration is a wide-ranging and complex subject. Our goal as students of public administration is a greater understanding and appreciation of the subject and what it means to be a public administrator. A necessary first step in achieving this goal is to focus on the essentials of American public administration, including those features that make it such a unique and important part of our political system. This search for the essence of public administration is not new, and in Chapter 2 we survey the various attempts made over the past century to discover the nature of the field. In Chapter 3 we contend that the essence of American public administration rests in the constant efforts of public-sector agencies and workers to live up to the public, professional, and personal expectations and pressures that accompany their roles in the political system. This perspective provides us with the major theme underlying the rest of this book—that public administration is the management of diverse expectations.

In Part II (Chapters 4 through 9), we consider the context within which public administrators operate. Specifically, we explore those features of the physical, social, institutional, and political environments that generate many of those expectations and pressures. Chapter 4 looks at the "ecology" of American public administration and explores how differences in environmental features influence the work of the public sector. In Chapter 5, we focus on the importance of physical, technological, and demographic factors, and in Chapter 6, on the influence of demographic, cultural, and economic conditions. Constitutional and legal institutions are the subject of Chapter 7. In Chapter 8, we consider how the dynamics of the U.S. political and policy-making environment affects the work of public administration. Finally, in Chapter 9, we look at how human needs and the demands of personal lives influence the work of public administrators.

Part III of the text examines the responses of American public administrators to these expectations and pressures. In Chapter 10, we see how they have influenced the organizational and management strategies adopted by public-sector managers. Chapter 11 focuses on the impact of those expectations and pressures on individual behavior within public organizations, while Chapters 12 and 13 consider how they influence public personnel management and public budgeting and finance. In Chapter 14, we consider the future shape and direction of American public administration in light of current and changing expectations and pressures. This final chapter reflects on what we have learned about the field of public administration and discusses how you can further enhance your knowledge and understanding of the subject.

We initially intended this book to be an introductory text for courses in American public administration. Our target audience was the upper-division undergraduate. But as we wrote the book, we discovered that it has a voice and message welcomed not only by our targeted group, but also by both lower-division undergraduates and postbaccalaureate students who have little background in the field but who found our presentation challenging and useful.

The book is also written with the instructor in mind. Despite its thematic nature, the book's general approach serves the needs of different instructors who use various methods of instruction. Our picture of American public administration is painted with broad brush strokes, allowing individual instructors to focus on more detail in lectures or in their use of case studies.

We have made an effort to avoid an overemphasis on any one particular level of government. Most students learn about public administration through textbooks and courses that focus on national government, eventhough most public administration takes place at the state and local levels. Thus, we have peppered the text with examples from all three levels of government.

There is also a tendency among textbook writers to describe the work of public administrators in fairly abstract terms. In order to bring the work of public servants more to life, we have included special Profiles and Insights in Chapters 1–13. The Profiles describe the unique stories of individual administrators, providing students with a personalized link to the world of public service. Similarly, the Insights provide students with additional information and examples that help to illustrate and clarify the ideas discussed in the text. In addition, chapter summaries and study questions are included to enhance the learning experience of students using the book.

It is difficult to define or measure success, but we will risk it here. If, upon completion of this book, readers are better able to make an intelligent assessment of public administration and the efforts of public servants, then we regard our work as a success. Whatever success we achieve, however, is due in large part to the hundreds of students we've taught in introductory public administration courses. Credit is also given to our colleagues at various educational institutions and elsewhere, whose comments and criticisms guided us far along the road leading to this book. Although we each brought unique strengths to this book, the coauthorship contributions have been equal. A special note of thanks is reserved for our colleague and friend John Nalbandian, whose contributions to this coauthorship went beyond mere advice and support.

Should we fall short of achieving our measure of success, however, the responsibility is ours alone.

M. J. D.
B. S. R.

CONTENTS

CHAPTER **3**
LIVING UP TO EXPECTATIONS   53

PART III
THE MANAGEMENT OF
EXPECTATIONS   235

CHAPTER 10
PUBLIC ORGANIZATIONS AND EXTERNAL EXPECTATIONS   237

CHAPTER **13**
MANAGING FINANCIAL RESOURCES   347

CHAPTER **14**
PUBLIC ADMINISTRATION IN THE FUTURE   379

I

UNDERSTANDING

PUBLIC

ADMINISTRATION

The first three chapters of this book are an introduction to the field of public administration and the various perspectives used to understand it. Chapter 1, "The Study and Practice of Public Administration," examines the important role of government in our lives and considers why we should know more about the people who administer government programs. This textbook is intended to enhance your knowledge of public administrators — who they are, what they do, and the constraints within which they operate.

American government is a complex subject to master. It is a constitutional system based on ambiguous divisions of government authority and complicated systems of checks and balances among public institutions. Thus, it is not surprising that public administration presents a challenge to students. However, to understand the subject, it is useful to consider the different perspectives that are applied to it. Chapter 2, "The Search for Public Administration," reviews a variety of the popular perspectives used by scholars, practitioners, politicians, and others to explain public administration. While none of these views is complete, each one contributes significantly to an understanding of government operations and those who work in the public sector.

Chapter 3, "Living Up to Expectations," offers a different perspective on the subject — one that we believe can help you better understand and appreciate the work of public administrators at all levels of American government. In this chapter, we contend that the work of public administrators is greatly shaped by their efforts to respond and react to a wide range of expectations. Thus, to understand the workings of government bureaucracies and civil servants, we must also understand the efforts made by American public administrators to live up to and manage those expectations.

CHAPTER 1

THE STUDY
AND PRACTICE
OF PUBLIC
ADMINISTRATION

The Growth and Pervasiveness of Government

It is surprising how little most Americans know about public administrators and what they do. After all, the work of these government officials is a pervasive force in our daily lives. As they carry out the functions of government, public administrators at all levels of government deal with many of the mundane tasks of community life.

On the local level, we rely on public administrators to provide us with basic goods and services, from the water we drink to the education we receive through high school and sometimes beyond. Local public administrators also arrange for our trash to be collected on a regular basis, and they protect our lives and property by providing police and fire services. At the state level, public administrators help determine the quality of our living and working environments through building, maintaining, and regulating the use of public highways, bridges, and parks. Similarly, administrators working for the national government track our weather, protect our forests, monitor the country's economic health, and oversee the operations of our major airports.

Public administrators also have an impact on less mundane aspects of our lives. They play major roles in defending our nation and negotiating international disarmament. They shape our future by funding and conducting research aimed at finding cures for cancer, AIDS, and other health problems. In the economic sphere, many public administrators actively promote and protect both businesses and consumers in the marketplace. Thus, public administrators are involved in countless activities that affect how we live.

The Expanding Functions of Government

The significance of public administrators in our lives reflects the growing importance of government in American society. Government has not always been so pervasive in the lives of Americans. Traditionally, we have relied on our government for at least three services: security (protection from others who might harm us), welfare (the provision of acceptable standards of living), and law and order (the establishment of fair and just means for settling disputes and making decisions).[1] Furthermore, Americans have always demanded that these services be provided in a manner that does not interfere with their rights and freedoms as individual citizens. These traditional functions of government are so basic that the Constitution's framers used them to justify the newly formed government:

> We the People of the United States, in Order to form a more perfect Union, establish Justice, insure *domestic tranquillity*, provide for the *common defence*, promote the *general Welfare*, and secure the Blessings of Liberty to ourselves and

our Posterity, do ordain and establish this Constitution for the United States of America. (Emphasis added)

This traditional view of government generally limited activities of American governments throughout the nineteenth century. The national government's most important tasks revolved around conducting diplomatic relations with other countries and providing for our national defense needs. Similarly, most nineteenth-century Americans expected state and local officials to maintain law and order in their communities. Providing for the general welfare of the population typically meant governments should keep out of the way of those who sought their riches in emerging industries or on the American frontier.

Although these few traditional functions of government are still regarded as fundamental, Americans today expect a great deal more from their public officials.[2] We expect government to engage in a variety of economic management functions. American governments have always played some role in promoting economic activity, but since the Great Depression of the 1930s this task has become increasingly central to the work of national, state, and local governments. For example, we depend on government agencies to monitor our collective economic health. These agencies issue reports on everything from our productivity at work and the prices we pay at the grocery store to how many of us are employed or unemployed and the number of homes we are building in any given month. We expect the national government to implement policies to stimulate the nation's economy when growth is too slow or to stabilize it when conditions warrant. We call on government to regulate industries that are particularly important to us or whose behavior might pose a danger to its employees or the general public, such as food processing or toxic waste disposal. We seek massive public-sector investments in highways, bridges, ports, dams, and other facilities that seem so necessary to the maintenance and growth of local and regional economies.

We even rely on government to own and operate business enterprises that provide services the private sector is unwilling or unable to supply at a reasonable cost. Thus, in many communities local governments provide electric power and other basic utilities. Sometimes governments provide these services on an even broader scale. During the 1930s, for example, Congress created the Tennessee Valley Authority, a social experiment intended in part to provide economic stimulus to one of the poorest regions of the country.[3] Many years later, Congress formed Amtrak to operate passenger railroad services that were being abandoned by private companies yet critical to many citizens. (See Insight 1.1.)

Americans also rely heavily on government to care for people in need. The social welfare activities of government encompass a wide range of public programs intended to help impoverished people throughout the country. Today our governments provide financial assistance and other kinds of aid

INSIGHT 1.1
SHRINKING PUBLIC ENTERPRISES

The growth in number and size of public enterprises was an issue addressed by President Ronald Reagan during his administration (1981–1989). Arguing that the federal government was too large and needed to be reduced significantly, the Reagan administration attempted to eliminate or shrink a number of federal public enterprises through a variety of methods called *privatization* (see discussion in Chapter 2).

In some instances, the Reagan administration tried to sell some of these enterprises to private companies. In 1987, for instance, it arranged the sale of Conrail, a government enterprise formed in 1976 to operate the Pennsylvania Railroad and six other railroad lines in the northeastern United States that had gone bankrupt that year. Since the system had returned to profitability by 1981 under government ownership, it wasn't too difficult to find willing private-sector buyers. However, administration efforts to sell Amtrak and other major federal assets (e.g., federally owned and operated energy plants and oil fields) were not successful due to the opposition of Congress or to the lack of buyers willing to pay the asking price. Nevertheless, the sale of government enterprises remains an objective of federal officials under the Bush administration.

Another strategy advocated by the Reagan administration toward its goal of privatization was to promote private-sector competition for the services provided by government agencies. The major target of this competitive strategy was the U.S. Postal Service (USPS). By loosening the restrictions that prohibited or weakened competition in postal delivery in the past, federal policymakers eliminated many of the protections that had surrounded the Postal Service for many decades. As a result, United Parcel Service (UPS), a private corporation, had become the number one handler of package deliveries in the nation by the mid-1980s. Similarly, the market for overnight and express-mail deliveries is now dominated by the Federal Express Corporation, Emery Air Freight Corporation, and similar private enterprises. In addition, new innovations such as electronic and facsimile (FAX) mail are making major inroads into the market for postal services.

Through these and other privatization efforts, we see that the growth of government should not be taken for granted. There are signs that the growth in the number and size of public enterprises can be reduced or halted. Nevertheless, public enterprises at all levels of government remain an important part of our lives.

SOURCE: Based on information in Barnaby J. Feder, "Cutting Big Government, Round 2," *New York Times*, Sunday, 12 February, 1989, p. 4F.

to the elderly, disabled, unemployed, and children from broken homes. Those in need of health care or housing now can obtain some assistance from public-sector agencies in times of critical need. The most significant growth in this area has been in Social Security and unemployment insurance programs, which add a preventative dimension to government programs. In addition, our governments manage special programs for veterans, refugees, and other targeted groups with unique needs.

Individually and collectively, we now depend more on governments to help us deal with the many conflicts and risks associated with life in a modern, industrialized society through social management programs. Where possible, we depend on government to take steps to prevent the disruptions to our lives that might come from human-made or natural disasters. For example, today many local governments have action plans for dealing with dangerous chemical spills that might result from trucking or train accidents within their vicinities. In the event of such an accident, we expect our local police to close off the chemical spill area and evacuate the neighborhood if toxic fumes or an explosion was possible. Other kinds of social disruptions also can result in government intervention, such as when government mediators help settle disagreements between corporate managers and labor unions or between landlords and tenants. Similarly, when inclement weather strikes, we expect public officials to help alleviate our distress. A variety of government programs and emergency plans are mobilized when communities are threatened by hurricanes or devastated by tornadoes. Government services can even extend to more routine weather conditions. Each summer, for example, many American cities offer shelter and support to the elderly and poor who might suffer from heat waves. As with many government functions, we are usually unaware of these social management activities until events occur that bring them to our attention.

Over the past century American government has also increased its activities in environmental management. The fight for conservation of America's natural resources began in the late 1800s and led to the establishment of national and state park systems as well as to the management of large tracts of public lands. Many local governments have engaged in the regulation of land use for decades. Regulation of America's air and water has been a major concern of public officials since the late 1960s and early 1970s. The disposal of hazardous and radioactive wastes remains high on today's public-sector agenda.

The growing list of governmental functions does not end here, however. We also expect government to carry out educational and symbolic activities. The public sector provides for our children's education and for the nurturing and support of our cultural institutions (e.g., museums, public broadcasting, and support for the arts). We expect government officials to foster national pride and respect for our national symbols. We take some of these patriotic–symbolic activities for granted, such as Fourth of July celebrations and bestowing medals on soldiers who have served the country in outstanding fashion. Other symbolic activities are much less routine but are important efforts to influence national unity or articulate our national will. For example, President Franklin Roosevelt's address to the nation on December 8, 1941, served to rally our national will as well as announce the country's response to the Japanese attack on Pearl Harbor the day before.

In addition to these varied functions that we expect our governments to perform, we also demand that they accomplish these public-sector tasks (see Table 1.1) in a manner consistent with the basic values of our political system. As a result, we require that governmental activities—traditonal and nontraditional alike—be carried out with efficiency and in a manner consistent with "open" government. We want government programs to maximize citizen participation, guarantee due process of law, and promote fairness in all public-sector endeavors. When we do so we are focusing our attention on that portion of government most directly involved in carrying out those public-sector functions: *public administration*.

The Government's "Black Box"

If the role of public administration is so important in the governing of our nation, why do Americans seem to know so little about it? One reason is that most of us are taught in high school that there are three branches of government: executive, legislative, and judicial. Rarely do discussions of the executive branch provide coverage of those who actually administer public programs. Instead, executive branch coverage usually emphasizes elected chief executives, such as mayors, governors, and the president. The nonelected public administrators who do receive attention are the political appointees of these chief executives, such as cabinet officers and department heads. Chief executives and political appointees, along with legislative and judicial branch officials, provide political leadership to public administrators. These political leaders set the broad outlines of the policies that the bulk of public administrators implement.

In addition, the day-to-day operations of government agencies and administrators attract little attention from the media. News reporters are more interested in what's going on in the White House, the governor's chambers, the mayor's office, the offices of top-level political appointees, the halls of Congress or the legislature, and even the nation's courthouses. Further, many public administrators do not seek media attention. Most view themselves as servants of policy, and politicians and judges as shapers of policy; thus, they say, the shapers should receive the public's attention.

Whatever the reasons, there is no doubt that public administration is the least visible part of our government. For most Americans, it is like the government's "black box"—a necessary piece of governmental machinery operated in mysterious ways by a strange cadre of people whom most of us know collectively as "the bureaucracy." This book is about those people and what they do.

TABLE 1.1   The Expanding Functions of American Government

Type	Examples
Traditional	National security Basic welfare Law and order
Economic management	Monitor economic conditions Stimulate economic growth Stabilize economic trends Regulate important sectors of the economy Build and maintain roads, dams, and other parts of the economic infrastructure Organize and operate government enterprises
Social welfare	Aid to the elderly, disabled, unemployed, destitute Health care Public and subsidized housing Social insurance (e.g., Social Security, unemployment insurance) Job training and relocation Aid to special groups (e.g., veterans, refugees)
Social management	Conflict management and conflict resolution (e.g., mediation in labor disputes) Disaster relief

Environmental management	Conservation of natural resources
	Management of national parks and public lands
	Monitor, regulate, and restore quality of air
	    and water
	Regulate the handling and disposal of hazardous
	    and radioactive materials

Educational and symbolic	Public education Nurture and support of cultural institutions (e.g., museums, zoos, performing arts centers) Promotion of patriotism and national unity

Negative Images of Public Administration

Perhaps it is our ignorance about public administration and administrators that causes most of us to rely on emotional feelings and biased attitudes instead of knowledge and information in our thinking about government. Our views of government rest on negative images, which, in turn, determine how most of us think and feel about bureaucrats.

INSIGHT 1.2
"KAFKAESQUE" ADMINISTRATION

Many of the negative images Americans have about public administration are reinforced by the portrayal of bureaucrats in the media, particularly in popular novels and films. For example, the characterization of bureaucrats as impersonal and cold-hearted individuals who just follow orders is often called "*kafkaesque*," reflecting a view popularized in *The Trial*, a 1925 novel by the German writer Franz Kafka. In one passage from that book, two administrative officials, called "warders," have just arrested the story's protagonist. When the arrested individual protests, one warder responds with a scolding.

> You're behaving worse than a child. What are you after? Do you think you'll bring this fine case of yours to a speedier end by wrangling with us, your warders, over papers and warrants? We are humble subordinates who can scarcely find our way through

a legal document and have nothing to do with your case except to stand guard over you for ten hours a day and draw our pay for it. That's all we are, but we're quite capable of grasping the fact that the high authorities we serve, before they would order such an arrest as this, must be quite well informed about the reasons for the arrest and the person of the prisoner. There can be no mistake about that. Our officials, so far as I know them, and I know only the lowest grades among them, never go hunting for crime in the populace, but, as the Law decrees, are drawn toward the guilty and must then send out us warders. That is the Law. How could there be a mistake in that?

SOURCE: From *The Trial, Definitive Edition*, by Franz Kafka, translated by Willa & Edwin Muir, with additional materials translated by E. M. Butler. Copyright 1937, © 1956 and renewed 1965, 1984 by Alfred A. Knopf, Inc. Reprinted by permission of the publisher.

Many Americans have a stereotyped view of bureaucracy reflecting widely shared images of ineffective and inefficient government. This stereotype includes images of cold-hearted, impersonal, nameless functionaries carrying out their jobs without concern for the needs of individual citizens. (See Insight 1.2.) It perpetuates the widespread idea that bureaucracies employ power-hungry administrators intent on using their positions to enhance their personal wealth.

Public-opinion polls provide evidence of a general and growing mistrust and lack of confidence among Americans in government employees and officials (see Figure 1.1).[4] These feelings are often cultivated by politicians and the media, which frequently publish "horror stories" about bureaucratic errors and editorialize on "waste, fraud, and abuse" in government agencies.[5]

The major goal of this book is to introduce you to the world of American

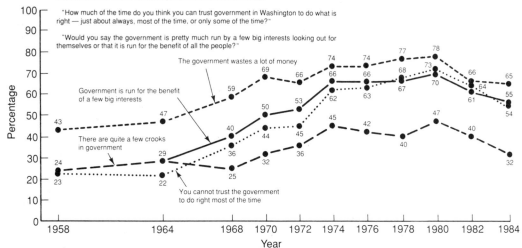

FIGURE 1.1   Confidence in government, 1958–1984. (Source: Seymour Martin Lipset and William Schneider, *The Confidence Gap*, rev. ed. [Baltimore, MD: Johns Hopkins University Press, 1987], p. 17.)

public administration from a nonstereotypical perspective, for there is no greater barrier to knowledge and understanding than stereotypical thinking. Our purpose is not to debunk the negative images about bureaucracy, for some public agencies and administrators may indeed deserve their poor reputations. American public administration is already blessed with some very articulate defenders.[6] Rather, our intent is to offer an introduction to public administration that avoids those negative images and the stereotypes they create.

Studying Public Administration

Our underlying approach in this book is based on an important distinction between the study and the practice of public administration. As a field of study, public administration is a relatively young discipline. In the late nineteenth-century United States, political corruption and a variety of other forces generated an interest in the topic by a growing number of reformers and academicians.[7] As we will see in Chapter 3, the intellectual roots of the field took hold during the era of progressivism and reform, and professional education and training for public servants became a reality.[8] There followed a demand for more theories and greater attention to the systematic gathering of relevant knowledge about public administration. One prominent author in this early movement argued that there "should be a science of administration which shall seek to straighten the paths of government, to make its business less unbusinesslike, to strengthen and purify its organization, and to crown its dutifulness."[9] Out of this emerged the *study of public administration*, which we define as the *systematic examination and analysis of the institutions, agents and processes used in government's efforts to manage the pursuit of publicly defined societal values.*[10]

The study of public administration is unlike the study of most other subjects undertaken in college. In biology or math, for example, instructors have relatively clear ideas about what material to teach and what they want students to learn. The study of public administration is different in that it encompasses a wide range of subjects and can be studied through a variety of approaches. Which particular subjects and approaches the instructor selects depends on several factors, but two stand out: students' motivation and their views on the principal problems of government.

On the issue of motivation, students may engage in the study of public administration for varied personal and civic-minded reasons.[11] Some students approach the subject with several personal objectives in mind. For a few, public administration represents a potential career. Government employment at the local, state, and national levels involves millions of people, and each year several thousands of public-service positions are open to those who qualify and seek to serve. Some government employees are technical experts, such as civil engineers or nuclear physicists who have the special knowledge and skills needed for some unique government jobs. Other government employees have fewer technical qualifications but possess the relevant aptitudes, experiences, or education. (See Profile 1.1.) For a growing number of public sector jobs, however, governments seek employees who have specialized education in public administration.

Each year several hundred American colleges and universities award undergraduate and graduate degrees in public administration and related fields, and each year many of these degree holders enter government service in public management positions. Some seek eventually to become agency heads or policy advisors to legislatures and governors. Others enter the profession with the intention of becoming city managers or the administrators of large-scale public-sector projects. For these people, the study of public administration leads to a career in the field.

Career goals are not the only reasons for taking a personal interest in public administration. Many students are aware of the increasing importance and pervasiveness of government today. They realize that the impact of public administrators is likely to expand still more in the future. These students appreciate the need for the average citizen to learn more about public administration. They understand that the study of public administration can be extremely useful for improving their ability to contend with the possible growth of government influence in the future.

PROFILE 1.1
Climbing to the Top of the Fire Ladder

When he was a teenager, Edward W. Wilson used to visit the fire station in Kansas City, Missouri, where his father worked. The station was one of the all-black firefighter companies that existed during the days when segregated stations were commonplace in Missouri's cities and other areas of the Midwest. Edward Wilson wanted to follow in his father's footsteps, and so in 1943 he sought a position in the Kansas City Fire Department. Because of the shortage of workers created by World War II, Wilson soon found himself alongside his father in the fire station earning less than $30 a week.

But Wilson's dreams went further than just being another firefighter. He not only wanted to join the fire department; he also wanted to become one of the department's leaders. During the 1940s, however, the opportunities for blacks in city fire departments were few, and especially for becoming a fire chief. The chances of Edward Wilson's becoming a driver were slim, let alone his chances of rising to the position of fire chief. Nevertheless, in 1980 Wilson was named acting fire chief, and one year later the "acting" title was removed as he assumed responsibility for that important city agency.

Wilson's four-decade climb to the top of his agency was due in large part to his motivation for agency leadership. When a driver's position opened in the late 1940s, Wilson took the test and passed. He accepted the position even though the new job did not result in any increase in salary at the time. But being a driver made Wilson eligible for a captain's position that opened in 1950—just as city officials were seeking to promote more blacks to managerial positions. He received that position and held it for fifteen years until he was named a battalion chief. By that time the fire department was integrated and Wilson was in a position to move ahead. In 1976, he was named deputy fire chief, a position he held until his appointment as chief in 1980.

Wilson took over the fire chief's position just as the department was emerging from a vicious firefighter's strike that received national media attention. Morale in the department was low, and Wilson's job was to reconstruct a devastated agency. "Anyone you would talk to would tell you that there isn't anyone who could have rebuilt this department the way he has," noted one of Wilson's admirers. "Everything is better."

SOURCE: Based on information in Steve Penn, "Fire Chief Climbed a Long Ladder to Get to the Post at the Top," *Kansas City Times*, 28 August, 1988, pp. E1–4.

Still others pursue the study of public administration with the idea of achieving more civic-minded purposes. Many academicians study the subject because they believe that through scholarship and teaching they can enhance public understanding and control over the way governments work. The study of public administration is also of interest to those inside and outside government who seek to reform and improve the public sector. They believe that a better understanding of how government operates will improve their chances of bringing about the changes they feel are necessary.

In addition to motivation, how students view the major problems of government influences how they approach the subject of public administration. Public administrators face a great many problems in carrying out their complex and wide-ranging tasks, but for most observers these problems fall into two categories: managerial and political.

Many observers of public administration believe that government's problems are primarily managerial. They argue that government can and should operate more efficiently and emulate the practices of successful private-sector businesses. For others the problems of public administration are political. As evidence they cite the pressures that government administrators face as they try to be either more or less responsive and open to the demands of politicians, interest groups, and the general public.

How do these differences in student motivation and student definitions of government problems influence how they approach the study of public administration? Consider the interests of students who are motivated to study the field for personal reasons and who regard the problems of public administration as managerial (see cell 1 in Figure 1.2). These individuals pay special attention to the study of public management techniques. They favor courses and books that stress how to use effectively and efficiently the "nuts and bolts" of public administration. In contrast, those who undertake the study of public administration for personal reasons but who are convinced that the central issues in the field are political (see cell 2 in Figure 1.2) are more attentive to bureaucratic politics and how to obtain and use political power. Students motivated by more civic-minded objectives and who perceive the problems of public administration to be managerial (see cell 3

| | | Problems of Public Administration | |
		Managerial Problems	Political Problems
Motivation for Studying Public Administration	Personal Reasons	1. Learning how to manage public programs effectively and efficiently	2. Learning how to get, retain, and use bureaucratic power
	Civic-minded Reasons	3. Understanding the behavior of public-sector organizations	4. Understanding the role of public agencies in the political system

FIGURE 1.2 Approaches to studying public administration.

in Figure 1.2) have a different emphasis. They seek a greater understanding about public-sector organizations. Such knowledge might someday help improve the design and operation of public agencies. Similarly, the more civic-minded student who believes that the political aspects of public administration are most important (see cell 4 in Figure 1.2) emphasizes exploring and critically assessing the role of bureaucracy in the political system.

Most students fall into one or more of the four categories illustrated in Figure 1.2. Regardless of which category you find yourself in, you share with all students of public administration a desire to know more about what public administrators do and who they are. The knowledge you gain through the study of public administration, however, is bound to be of limited value. What you learn through books, lectures, and discussions can never substitute for the experience of being a public administrator.

The Practice of Public Administration

To study public administration is not the same as experiencing what public administrators do, how they feel, or how they deal with the tasks and pressures that characterize their roles in American government. Therefore, all students of public administration must make a special effort to inform themselves about the *practice of public administration*; that is, *the dynamic reconciliation of various moral, social, political, economic, and technical forces influencing the institutions, agents, and processes used in government's efforts to manage the pursuit of publicly defined societal values.*

In practice, public administration is an ongoing activity through which different and often conflicting demands are accommodated. These demands may emerge from political relationships or budgetary constraints, from personal obligations or standards of ethical conduct, from economic crises or changing technologies. No matter their source, these demands are ever present and invariably create stresses and uncertainties that beg for resolution. They ultimately elicit reactions from among public-sector officials — reactions in the form of efforts to reconcile these demands — that are at the heart of what it means to be a public administrator.

Who are these practitioners of public administration? While stereotypes of "bureaucrats" abound, a look at some facts makes it clear that we are talking about an extremely diverse population that is difficult to characterize in simple terms. For example, not everyone engaged in the practice of public administration (as we define it here) is an employee of a public agency. Many private sector organizations implement government programs through franchises and contracts (see Chapter 2). Many cities contract with private companies to collect trash or to operate waste-disposal facilities. Some governments use private contractors to provide fire fighting services, supply public transportation, and even operate state prisons.[12] Today even the fed-

eral government "contracts out" to private firms to perform work traditionally done by government workers. The armed services, for instance, arrange
for private companies to operate dining halls at some of the larger forts
and bases. Should we count the employees of these private firms among
the population of public administrators? While they are indirectly paid by
the government and are doing the jobs that we normally rely on civil servants
to do, they work under different conditions and constraints than public-sector employees.

Another issue is whether *all* public employees should be regarded as public
administrators for purposes of this text. For example, uniformed members
of the armed forces are certainly public employees, but do the special conditions surrounding their jobs make them unique and distinct from the
general group we call public administrators? Some scholars believe that
military professionals are a special group that should not be included in the
study of public administration.

Few would argue that nonmilitary workers employed by government jurisdictions to carry out public programs are public administrators. According
to Census Bureau statistics (see Table 1.2), in 1986 there were nearly 17
million civilian personnel working for more than 83,000 governmental units.
Federal government employees accounted for just over 3 million of that
work force, while over 4 million workers were on the payrolls of the fifty
states. The remaining 9.8 million were employed by the thousands of county,
municipal, township, school district, and special district governments that
dot this country. All this translated into a monthly public-sector payroll (for
October 1986) of nearly $31 billion, with nearly three quarters of that ($21.3
million) going to state and local employees.

What exactly do these public-sector workers do? This isn't an easy question
to answer, for their jobs cover a wide range of occupations. This is especially

TABLE 1.2 Public Employment and Payroll

Level of Government	Number of Units (1987)	Number of Employees (1986, est.)	Payroll (October 1986; $ billions, est.)
Federal	1	3,019,000	$7.561
States	50	4,068,000	6.810
Local	83,186	9,846,000	16.298
Counties	3,042	1,926,000	3.009
Municipalities	19,200	2,494,000	4.407
Townships	16,691	400,000	0.474
School districts	14,721	4,502,000	7.517
Special districts	29,532	524,000	0.892
Total	83,237	16,933,000	$30.670

SOURCE U.S. Bureau of the Census, *Statistical Abstract of the United States, 1989* (Washington, DC: Government Printing Office, 1989), tables 445, 479.

TABLE 1.3   Public Employment by Level and Function, 1986 (est.)

Function	Number of Employees (in millions)			
	Total	Federal	State	Local
National defense	1,079	1,079	—	—
Space research and technology	22	22	—	—
Postal service	795	795	—	—
Education	7,253	14	1,800	5,439
Teachers	4,079	—	(536)	3,543
Highways	553	4	253	297
Health and hospitals	1,649	260	682	707
Public welfare	443	14	190	239
Police	771	67	79	625
Fire	326	—	—	326
Sanitation	226	—	1	225
Parks and recreation	268	—	36	233
Natural resources	430	235	157	38
Financial administration	449	121	134	194
General control	673	62	140	140
All other	1,996	349	596	1,052

SOURCE   Bureau of the Census, *Statistical Abstract of the United States, 1989* (Washington, D.C: Government Printing Office, 1989), table 480.

true if we consider all levels of American government. In 1985, for example (see Table 1.3), 7.25 million public employees — over 42 percent — were engaged in providing educational services, with most of those individuals serving as teachers. Health and hospital functions were carried out by one in every ten public-sector workers in the United States. Other major areas of federal, state, and local government employment in 1986 involved police protection (4.5 percent), highways (3.2 percent), natural resources (2.5 percent), and financial administration (2.6 percent). In addition, public welfare accounted for 2.6 percent of government employees, fire protection for 1.9 percent, parks and recreation 1.6 percent, and sanitation and sewerage 1.3 percent.

The picture of what public administrators do is quite different when the focus is on the federal government alone. Counting civilian employees only, over one-third of the federal government's employees worked in the national defense sector in 1986. Another one-fourth of the federal work force was employed by the U.S. Postal Service.

In 1986, women made up approximately 41 percent of the public-sector work force, while Blacks, Hispanics, and other minorities accounted for about one in every four public employees. Most women and minority public-sector workers were employed in lower-paying clerical and blue-collar positions. They were least represented in high-level, white-collar managerial positions and better-paid skilled craft jobs.[13]

By far the most visible and studied public administrators in the United States are those employed by the federal government. Although most Americans associate these workers with Washington, D.C., only one of about fourteen federal civilian employees (7 percent) actually work *in* the nation's capital. Another 4 percent work in the metropolitan area immediately surrounding Washington. Other large concentrations of federal employees are found in California (about 11 percent), Texas (6 percent), and New York (5.5 percent). Regionally, the South has the most federal employees (more than 42 percent). Another 22 percent work in the region composed of 13 western states; 17 percent in the north central United States, and 17 percent in the Northeast. Although a great deal of media attention is paid to the activities of federal employees who work outside the country—from state department officials working in foreign embassies to CIA agents gathering intelligence—less than 2 percent of the national government's work force is posted in foreign countries.[14]

Whom do these federal employees work for? In 1987, over 3 million (accounting for more than 98 percent of all federal employees) worked in the executive branch, while about 57,000 were employed by Congress and the federal court system. Most of those working for the executive branch (about 2.05 million) were found in one of the fourteen cabinet-level departments: Agriculture, Commerce, Defense, Education, Energy, Health and Human Services (HHS), Housing and Urban Development (HUD), Interior, Justice, Labor, State, Transportation, Treasury, and Veterans Affairs. An additional 1,553 federal employees worked in the Executive Office of the President (EOP), which includes employees of the White House Office, the Office of Management and Budget (OMB), the Council of Economic Advisors (CEA), the Office of the Vice President, the National Security Council (NSC), and various other presidential staff and support offices. The remainder of the federal government's work force labored in a diverse set of independent agencies, ranging from the U.S. Postal Service (with 797,851 employees) to the Selective Service System (with only 296 employees). Some worked for independent regulatory commissions like the Interstate Commerce Commission (745 workers) and the Securities and Exchange Commission (1,934). Another 5,028 were on the payroll at the Smithsonian Institution, one of the nation's major cultural institutions. These employment patterns have not remained stagnant. The National Aeronautics and Space Administration (NASA) employed fewer people in 1987 (22,950) than it did in 1965 (34,049). Others, such as the Environmental Protection Agency (EPA), employing 15,173 in 1987, didn't even exist in 1965.[15]

It is difficult to draw from this array of statistics a clear picture of who public administrators are. It is also difficult to generalize what they do that makes public administration a distinctive part of American government. To understand public administration—that is, to comprehend and appreciate what it means to practice public administration—calls for a sensitivity to and awareness of the thinking, dilemmas, and feelings of the bureaucrats themselves.

It is argued that only those who experience the practice of public administration can really understand it. For this reason, many degree-granting programs in public administration require students to participate in internships and practicums as part of the curriculum. But it is also possible to get a sense of the practitioner's world through examining some of the day-to-day dilemmas facing public-sector managers. The Insights and Profiles in this book focus attention on some of the basic controversies facing public administrators as they attempt to carry out their mandates. These materials are more than mere examples; they provide close and personal views into the practice of public administration. Only by taking that perspective can students gain some understanding of what it means to be a public administrator.[16]

Summary

1. Public administration is a pervasive force in our daily lives, reflecting the growing influence of government in modern American society.
2. Despite the importance of public administration in their lives, most Americans know little about public administrators and many hold negative images of government bureaucrats and bureaucracies.
3. How you approach the study of public administration depends on your motivation for examining the subject and whether you perceive the central problems of public administration to be managerial or political.
4. The practice of public administration involves the dynamic reconciliation of various forces in government's efforts to manage public policies and programs.
5. It is impossible to fully understand public administration without experiencing it. That experience varies significantly since the work of public administration reflects a wide variety of positions found in many locations.

Study Questions

1. In what capacities do governments have an impact on us from birth to death? What occurs afterward?
2. What makes many Americans so hostile and negative about public administrators? What are your personal views about government bureaucrats and bureaucracies? Are they negative or positive? Why?
3. Think of several events that took place during the past month that caused

you to have *direct* contact with an employee of a public agency. For example, you may have been stopped for a traffic violation, rode a public bus to school or work, or checked a book out of the public library. Were your direct contacts with public-sector workers positive or negative? Explain.

4. Now consider the activities you undertook during the past week that brought you into *indirect* contact with a public agency. For example, you may have driven a car, made a bank deposit, eaten at a restaurant, listened to the radio, watched television, or bought a lottery ticket. How did government agencies influence your activites? Can you think of any activity you undertake that is not indirectly influenced by public administrators? Explain.

5. How you approach the study of public administration depends, in part, on your motivation and whether you view the problems of government as primarily managerial or political. What are your personal motives for studying public administration? How do you see the problems of government?

6. One way to confirm or refute the popular assumption that most federal officials work in or near Washington, D.C., is to find out which federal offices are located near you. Look up "United States Government" in your local phone book. (Some telephone directories have a special "blue pages" section for all government agencies.) What federal offices are listed there? How many are located in your city? In your region? Compare the federal government listings with those of your state and local governments.

Notes

1. See W. W. Rostow, *Politics and the Stages of Growth* (Cambridge: Cambridge University Press, 1971), pp. 11–12.

2. For a detailed discussion of the growth of governmental functions, see Gerald E. Caiden, *Public Administration*, 2d ed. (Pacific Palisades, CA: Palisades Publishers, 1982), chap. 5; and Herbert Kaufman, *Red Tape: Its Origins, Uses, and Abuses* (Washington, DC: The Brookings Institution, 1977), chap. 2.

3. For a classic discussion of the Tennessee Valley Authority, see Philip Selznick, *TVA and the Grass Roots: A Study of Politics and Organization* (Berkeley: University of California Press, 1949); for a critical assessment of the economic impact of TVA after fifty years, see William U. Chandler, *The Myth of TVA: Conservation and Development in the Tennessee Valley, 1933–1983* (Cambridge, MA: Ballinger, 1984).

4. See Seymour Martin Lipset and William Schneider, *The Confidence Gap: Business, Labor, and Government in the Public Mind*, rev. ed. (Baltimore, MD: Johns Hopkins University Press, 1987).

5. For examples of how recent presidents and the media have treated government bureaucracies, see Bernard Rosen, "Effective Continuity of U.S. Government Operations in Jeopardy," *Public Administration Review* 43, (September/October, 1983): 383–386.

6. For an explicit defense of public bureaucracies, see Charles T. Goodsell, *The Case for Bureaucracy: A Public Administration Polemic*, 2 ed. (Chatham, NJ: Chatham House, 1983); and Kaufman, *Red Tape*.

7. The interest of German scholars in the subject had been piqued much earlier. For example, in *Philosophy of Right* (1821), G. W. F. Hegel presented a detailed discussion of the civil service and its role in the modern state. See the discussion of German scholarship on administration in Robert D. Miewald, "The Origins of Wilson's Thought: The German Tradition and the Organic State," in *Politics and Administration: Woodrow Wilson and American Public Administration*, ed. by Jack Rabin and James S. Bowman (New York: Marcel Dekker, 1984), pp. 17–21.

8. See Martin J. Schiesl, *The Politics of Efficiency: Municipal Administration and Reform in America: 1880–1920* (Berkeley: University of California Press, 1977); Alice B. Stone and Donald C. Stone, "Early Development of Education in Public Administration," in *American Public Administration Past, Present, Future*, ed. by Frederick C. Mosher (University, AL: University of Alabama Press, 1975), pp. 11–48; and Robert A. Caro, *The Power Broker: Robert Moses and the Fall of New York* (New York: Vintage, 1974), pp. 60–64.

9. Woodrow Wilson, "The Study of Administration," *Political Science Quarterly*, 2 (1887): 197–222 [reprinted in *Political Science Quarterly* 56 (December 1941): 481–506].

10. The definitions of *public administration* used in this chapter are drawn from Robert Denhardt, *Theories of Public Organization* (Monterey, CA: Brooks/Cole, 1984), pp. 16–17, and extended discussions with John Nalbandian.

11. See Caiden, *Public Administration*, pp. 27–29.

12. The recent trend toward "privatizing" the public sector has gained momentum both in fact and as a popular idea. See E. S. Savas, *Privatization: The Key to Better Government* (Chatham, NJ: Chatham House, 1987).

13. Bureau of the Census, *Statistical Abstract of the United States*, 1989. (Washington, D.C.: Government Printing Office, 1989), table 481.

14. Ibid., tables 512 and 517.

15. Ibid., table 512; Bureau of the Census, *Statistical Abstract of the United States, 1988* (Washington, DC: Government Printing Office, 1988), tables 501 and 502.

16. For additional material, see Nicholas Henry, *Doing Public Administration: Exercises, Essays, & Cases*, 2nd ed. (Boston: Allyn & Bacon, Inc., 1982); and see Robert T. Golembiewski and Michael White, *Cases in Public Management*, 4th ed. (Boston: Houghton Mifflin, 1983).

CHAPTER 2

THE SEARCH

FOR PUBLIC

ADMINISTRATION

Searching for the Essence of Public Administration

To understand and appreciate American public administration, it is necessary to develop some sense of what the subject entails. This calls for more than simple definitions–it requires that we identify the characteristics and qualities that make public administration such a unique and interesting subject.

The search for the essence of American public administration, which has been going on for over one hundred years, has followed three paths of scholarship: (1) the development of concise yet comprehensive definitions of public administration, (2) the appreciation of the relative importance of administration and politics in the public administrator's world, and (3) the understanding of the differences between public and private management.

Seeking a Definition

Students of public administration often attempt to capture the essence of the subject in a definition. Definitions serve to communicate new or important ideas, as in Chapter 1, where the study and the practice of public administration are defined in order to make the distinction between them clear. Similarly, scholarly writers attempt to capture the essence of public administration in short definitions so that their readers can more easily grasp the concept. A clear definition of a complex concept like public administration enhances our comprehension of further discussion of that concept.

There have been nearly as many attempts to define public administration as there have been textbooks and treatises written on the subject. Although the definitions differ in detail, most can be categorized according to their emphasis on executive branch location, policy implementation tasks, or managerial functions (see Table 2.1).

Executive Branch Definitions

By public administration is meant, in common usage, the activities of the executive branches of national, state, and local governments; independent boards and commissions set up by Congress and state legislatures; government corporations; and certain other agencies of a specialized character. Specifically excluded are judicial and legislative agencies within the government and nongovernmental administration.[1]

Executive branch definitions of public administration offer a clear and simple approach to the concept. They define public administration as what takes place in certain government institutions. The approach directs our attention to those agencies and offices that report to the chief executive

TABLE 2.1   Definitions of Public Administration

Type of Definition	Focus	Public Administration Defined[a]
Executive Branch	Where do we find public administration?	"the activities of the executive branches of national, state and local governments; independent boards and commissions . . . ; government corporations; and certain other agencies of a specialized character." (Simon, Smithburg, and Thompson)
Policy Implementation	What purpose or role does public administration fulfill?	"always the servant of policy."(Vieg)
		"all those operations having as their purpose the fulfillment or enforcement of public policy." (White)
		"administration involves the coordination of all organized activity, having as its purpose the implementation of public policy." (Gortner)
Managerial Functions	What do public administrators do?	"the process by which resources are marshaled and then used to cope with facing a political community." (Starling)
		"management of scarce resources to accomplish the goals of public policy." (Williams)
		"organization and management of men and materials to achieve the purposes of government." (Waldo)

[a]See citations in text for sources.

officer—the president, governor, or mayor/city manager—of a government. It focuses primarily on the activities associated with public administration that take place within the executive branch of government.

Although the executive branch perspective is popular among scholars of public administration, it fails to draw attention to those few but critical components of public administration not within the executive branch. As a result, these definitions do not take into account the important administrative functions performed in the legislative and judicial branches of government. Congress, for example, has several major legislative research agencies that help it make laws and oversee the executive branch. The General Accounting Office audits the work of federal agencies and the Congressional Budget Office and helps Congress analyze and respond more quickly to annual budget requests from the White House. State legislatures have similar types of agencies as well.

Administrative activities are also important within the judicial branches of government. Court administrators perform a wide range of tasks from managing court facilities and maintaining court calendars to supervising court personnel and acting as press secretaries for judges. In addition, judicial administration includes the work of clerks, bailiffs, probation officers, juvenile officers, and even enforcement personnel such as U.S. marshals.[2]

Another drawback of the executive branch approach is its failure to recognize the major roles played by nongovernmental agencies in carrying out the administrative duties of government. Literally thousands of private sector companies perform a variety of tasks through contracts with federal, state, and local governments. Their services range from feeding members of the armed forces and providing security for government buildings to operating community hospitals and evaluating public programs.[3] The "contracting out" of government services to private firms is not new to American governments. At the local level, contractors have long been used to collect trash, maintain streets, and provide other basic services.

Policy Implementation Definitions

> Public administration involves the coordination of all organized activity, having as its purpose the implementation of public policy.[4]

[P]olicy implementation definitions of public administration assume that government administration has as its major function the execution of policy made by policymakers and other superiors. The principal task of administrators is to carry out the mandates of the policymakers to whom they report. In the public sector, these policymakers are often elected officials, such as city commissioners, state legislators, members of Congress, mayors, governors, and presidents. The policymakers might also be those appointed by elected officials to policy-making positions. At the federal level, many policies are made by people appointed by the president (with the advice and consent of the Senate) to serve on such bodies as the Interstate Commerce Commission, the Federal Trade Commission, or the Securities and Exchange Commission. Similar types of commissions and policy-making bodies exist at the state and local levels as well, such as state water resources boards and local planning commissions. Policy implementation definitions, then, focus on governmental actions taken after policymakers make policy decisions.

Although the policy implementation approach offers insights into what public administration means, it draws our attention away from some important functions of the public administrator. Public administrators are crucial actors in every stage of the policy-making process. At the federal level, administrators often participate in the formulation of government policies and programs proposed by the White House and adopted by Congress. In some instances, they are even authorized to make policy decisions that others will implement. Congress, for example, authorizes the Environmental Protection Agency and the Occupational Safety and Health Administration to set the standards that private industry must follow. Public administrators also play a central role in bringing issues to the attention of the general public and policymakers. In 1964, for example, the U.S. Surgeon General made cigarette smoking a major public issue by endorsing the research findings that lung cancer and heart disease are directly linked to smoking. During the 1980s, the federal Centers for Disease Control played a key role in placing the AIDS epidemic on the public agenda through its studies and conferences on the illness (see Insight 2.1). In short, public administrators do much more than merely implement public policies. They are often deeply involved in the agenda setting, policy formulation, and other parts of the policy-making process.

Managerial Functions Definitions

[Public administration is] the process by which resources are marshaled and then used to cope with the problems facing a political community.[5]

Managerial functions definitions of public administration stress its role in making government operate more efficiently and effectively through the application of managerial techniques and procedures. They highlight what public administrators do that makes them distinctive actors in our political system.

The managerial functions perspective also has limitations. While we have come to expect the application of management techniques to public-sector problems, few observers would argue that is the *only* task associated with the field. Public administrators engage in politics as much as in management, and some might argue that politics is often more important. Except for some top-level political appointees who head government agencies, the kind of politics administrators most often engage in is not of the partisan (Republican versus Democrat) variety.[6] Rather, the politics of public administration involves mobilizing and maintaining levels of public and political support. Administrators also must deal with the politics of funding to sustain and promote their agencies and programs.[7] Politics remains important in day-to-day agency operations, even in agencies headed by experts, professionals, or career administrators (a typical situation in most local governments). Thus, public administrators within agencies often must be politically sensitive and sometimes use political influence on behalf of the agency and its programs.

Some public administrators become so good at this part of their job that they emerge as important "power brokers" whose influence exceeds those of the elected officials for whom they work. This was the situation in New York City from 1934 to 1968, when Robert Moses exercised effective political control over the city's policymakers. According to one biographer, Moses used his power to reshape the city and its environs. He built bridges and highways, established parks and playgrounds, constructed Lincoln Center for the performing arts, and managed a World's Fair. He helped set New York City's policy priorities for more than three decades and for just as many

INSIGHT 2.1

CONTROLLING HYSTERIA AT THE CDC

The Centers for Disease Control (CDC) is actively involved in the AIDS crisis. In addition to monitoring the spread of the disease and communicating the urgency of the situation to the public, the CDC is engaged in research that could help focus in on the cause—and possibly a cure—for this deadly viral infection.

By July 1983, the CDC was playing yet another role in the AIDS crisis. Randy Shilts, one of the few reporters who followed the AIDS story from its beginnings, notes the growing frustration among CDC researchers who found themselves preoccupied with reducing the growing national hysteria over the epidemic. According to Shilts, more and more reporters came to the CDC's Atlanta labs to find out what the government was doing about the AIDS epidemic. The CDC's public relations office handled these inquiries by allowing the news teams to shoot pictures of activity in a simulated lab (in order to minimize interruptions of the real work being conducted at the CDC) and by issuing press releases of the progress being made in tracking down the viral culprit.

Behind the scenes, however, there was less optimism. Despite all the improvements made in surveilling the disease, the data collected provided no sign that any corner had been turned. The epidemic "was on its way to wiping out the people who had been identified for more than a year as the high-risk groups." Within the agency, only two to three dozen people were assigned to AIDS-related research, and these individuals were unable to follow through on hopeful leads because they were reacting daily to newer leads that developed the world over.

"It seemed," wrote Shilts, "the CDC doctors were always on the phone with one or another local health official, or delivering the same old reassurances to the reporters. Later, dispirited AIDS staffers at the CDC complained they spent more time in July 1983 controlling AIDS hysteria than controlling AIDS."

SOURCE: Quotations and information from *And the Band Played on: Politics, People, and the AIDS Epidemic,* copyright © 1987 by Randy Shilts, St. Martin's Press, Inc. New York.

years wielded significant influence in state government as well. Moses' power was "so substantial that in the fields in which he chose to exercise it, it was not challenged seriously by any Governor of New York State or . . . by any Mayor of New York City" for nearly thirty-four years.[8]

The shortcomings of the various definitions of public administration are not surprising. Dwight Waldo, a preeminent scholar of public administration, argues that "in truth there is no good definition of public administration."[9]

Nevertheless, together the definitions in Table 2.1 reflect three major characteristics of public administration—executive branch location, policy-implementation tasks, and management functions—that help us focus our attention on the field.

The Politics–Administration Dichotomy

The Young Professor's Essay

An alternative path followed by scholars in their search for the essence of American public administration began in 1887. That year a young professor of politics, Woodrow Wilson, published an essay in the *Political Science Quarterly* titled "The Study of Administration."[10] The essay explores the history, conditions, and need for public administration in the United States, and in it Wilson offers a view of American public administration quite different from the European perspective that prevailed during the nineteenth century. The merits of his argument were not really recognized until several decades after the essay's publication.[11]

Since the late 1930s, however, Wilson's essay has been at the center of an ongoing debate focusing on the question of what makes public administration a distinctive part of American government. For Wilson, the distinctiveness of American public administration—its essence—rests in a dichotomy between those portions of government concerned with politics and those concerned with administration.[12] Wilson argues that public administration is unique because the tasks of administration derive from business and can be insulated from the hurry and strife of politics. He argues further that administration

> is a part of political life only as the methods of the counting-house are a part of the life of society; only as machinery is part of the manufactured product. . . . .[A]dministration lies outside the proper sphere of *politics*. Administrative questions are not political questions. . . . .[13]

A great deal has been written about Wilson's essay, particularly the distinction he makes between politics and administration.[14] Some critics believe that Wilson's reform-oriented progressivism caused him to reach the conclusions in his essay. In 1887, corrupt and inefficient behavior by public officials had reached scandalous proportions. Together with other reformers, Wilson sought to gain control of the administrative machinery of government from corrupt political machines and their bosses. Other critics claim that Wilson's politics–administration dichotomy was the product of his admiration for the administrative systems of Germany, France, and other modern European states. He was convinced it was possible to adopt their more efficient means for implementing public programs without having to adopt their autocratic political systems. Wilson argued,

> If I see a murderous fellow sharpening a knife cleverly, I can borrow his way of sharpening the knife without his possible intention to commit murder with it; and so, if I see a monarchist dyed in the wool managing a public business well, I can learn his business methods without changing one of my republican spots . . . .[15]

Regardless of Wilson's reasons for making the distinction between politics and administration, the result is a perspective on public administration that many scholars of American government find convincing. Wilson's perspective places management at the center of government administration while making politics irrelevant and even undesirable. He argues that students of public administration should devote their energies to developing administrative principles that would help public officials meet the challenges of an increasingly complex world. Such problems are the objective of the systematic study of public administration.[16]

Goodnow and the Nature of Public Administration

Does the essence of public administration rest on the administrative side of Wilson's dichotomy? A major contributor to the debate over this question is Frank J. Goodnow, a legal scholar who was among the first to provide an in-depth analysis of the nature of public administration.

In his *Politics and Administration: A Study of Government*, first published in 1900, Goodnow argues that government performs two basic functions: one political and the other administrative. The political function involves the expression of the "state will" while the administrative function involves the execution of the state will.[17] Goodnow contends that while these two spheres of government are *analytically* distinct, in practice the two are not separable. In fact, he argues, they are inevitably linked because they both reflect the state will. Public administration, according to Goodnow, is not distinctive because it is devoid of politics but because in government administration management considerations take priority over political considerations.[18]

Goodnow's analysis gives the impression that public administration has a dual nature. On the one hand, governments are under constant pressure to operate in an efficient and businesslike manner. On the other hand, they face considerable pressure for political control and oversight. The general challenge for public administration, according to Goodnow, is to establish institutional arrangements where the appropriate balance exists between these two forces.[19]

Focusing on the Technical Side of Administration

Despite Goodnow's observation that public administration has a dual (political and administrative) nature, students and scholars of the 1920s and 1930s concentrated on the administrative side of the subject. The political problems of public administration were subsumed under those of administration.

Popular textbooks from that period focus on economy, efficiency, and effectiveness in the actual administration of governmental affairs. They also tend to emphasize technical problems such as organization, personnel, supplies, and finance.[20]

The best-known argument of public administration as a response to purely technical problems came in 1937, with the publication of *Papers on the Science of Administration*, edited by Luther Gulick and Lyndall Urwick. These papers were collected to aid President Franklin D. Roosevelt's Committee on Administrative Management, also known as the Brownlow Committee after its chairperson, Louis Brownlow. The essays argue that the study of administration is synonymous with the study of organizations and their management. Both administration and organizations are regarded as technical problems. In his contribution titled "Organization as a Technical Problem," Urwick contends

> that there are principles which can be derived at inductively from the study of human experience of organization, which should govern arrangements for human association of any kind. These principles can be studied as a technical question, irrespective of the purpose of the enterprise, the personnel comprising it, or any constitutional, political or social theory underlying its creation.[21]

In the same volume, Gulick maintains that political questions are extraneous to the science of public administration. He warns, however, that public administration's emphasis on efficiency will inevitably bring it into conflict with government's political values. The job of the administrator is to strive for technical efficiency within the context of political values, whether those values represent democracy, fascism, or socialism.[22]

The Rediscovery of Politics

While the administrative and technical emphasis dominated during the pre–World War II period, there were other strong voices expressing contrary views. In 1936, Marshall E. Dimock warned that there was a danger

> in going too far in the formal separation between politics and administration. Scholars working in the field of public administration must take care lest by unduly separating the techniques of execution from the content and problems of government they make public administration detached and unreal. In the growing tendency to draw a sharp line between politics and administration there is a constant danger of giving too little weight to the propulsions, policies, and attitudes which run throughout government and which influence administration as well as legislation.[23]

Students of public administration during the 1930s were beginning to sense that there was an underexplored political side to their subject. It became increasingly evident that democratic norms and constitutional structures influence administration, and that administration itself has a significant impact on policy-making institutions and processes.[24] The intellectual pendulum began to swing in the direction of the political problems of public administration, and by the end of World War II they took center stage.

Several writers contributed to the postwar emphasis on the political side of public administration. In the last half of the 1940s, Herbert A. Simon argued that administrative decision making involves questions of value as well as issues of fact. In short, administrative decisions and actions involve both political and technical considerations.[25] Fritz Morstein Marx wrote of public administration as a dynamic social and political process through which policies are made to fit the needs of the people.[26] Similarly, Robert A. Dahl argued in 1947 that public administration does not rest on knowledge of techniques and processes, but on a responsiveness to historical, political, sociological, and economic conditions.[27]

The central figure in the development of a more politically focused study of public administration is Paul H. Appleby. Writing in 1949, Appleby stated that "Arguments about the application of policy are essentially arguments about policy."[28] Thus, public administrators are fundamental parts of the policy-making process and as such they are inescapably involved in politics.

> The great distinction between government and other organized undertakings is to be found in the wholly political character of government. The great distinction between public administration and other administration is likewise to be found in the political character of public administration.[29]

Reforming Government Administration

The acceptance of the political nature of public administration by Appleby and others did not mark the end to the administration–politics debate. Many still believed that the administrative side of the field could be revitalized through governmental reforms. Beginning in the 1950s, people both inside and outside of government began to pursue administrative reforms. These reformers sought to strengthen the administrative dimension of public administration as well as to reduce or control the influence of political factors. Their efforts had the greatest impact at the federal level, where policymakers experimented with a range of decision-making techniques to help make policy choices and public administration more rational. Operations research, systems analysis, planning-programming-budgeting systems, management by objectives, organizational development, and similar tools left their marks on the practice of public administration.

Operations research (OR) was first practiced just before World War II in Great Britain, where military decision makers developed mathematical models of complex weapons systems to help them make the optimal choice when facing different alternatives. These models not only analyzed the technical features of the systems but also included measurements of risk, chance, and error. As it was developed after the war and adapted to private and public sector endeavors in the United States, operations research began to incorporate measures of social and economic factors.

Systems analysis emerged as a broader application of operations research to more general questions, such as policy objectives and political constraints. Thus, while OR was being applied to the design and operations of specific programs, systems analysis was being used to help policymakers choose among alternative programs. *Planning-programming-budgeting* (PPB) systems were a further extension of the OR legacy. Introduced in the early 1960s in the Defense Department, PPB was a means for using the logic of systems analysis to decide on the allocation of scarce resources among competing programs. It was so successful in these initial applications that in 1965 President Lyndon Johnson called for its adoption throughout the national bureaucracy.[30]

Management by objectives (MBO) was a less quantitative approach to administrative reform. Adapted from the private sector and brought to the federal government in the early 1970s, MBO called for joint target setting by supervisors and workers and a performance-evaluation system based on the achievement of agreed on and explicit objectives.[31] *Organizational development* (OD), which developed over several decades, calls for the long-range development of organizational problem-solving capabilities through the application of applied behavioral science techniques.[32]

Individually and collectively, these reforms continue to influence how public administration operates in the United States. Nearly every year new approaches are advocated to enhance the technical capacity of government administration. Underlying each of these efforts is an implied belief in the validity of the politics–administration dichotomy, stressing the differences between what public administrators do and what politicians do.

Attempts to revive the administrative side of public administration have stimulated reactions from those who believe that the political dimensions of the field are eroding. These writers note the need to reintroduce politics and democracy into the operation of government's administrative systems. H. George Frederickson, for example, argues the need for a "new public administration" that actively seeks to "change those policies and structures that systematically inhibit social equity."

> New Public Administration seeks not only to carry out legislative mandates as efficiently and economically as possible, but to both influence and execute policies which more generally improve the quality of life for all. Forthright policy advocacy on the part of the public servant is essential if administrative agencies are basic policy battlefields.[33]

Still others call for equally radical reorientations of the field. Vincent Ostrom, for example, advocates an intellectual revolution in American public administration that would replace the mechanistic and hierarchical view of the field with a philosophy of democratic administration.[34] Instead of a single, uniform system of government administration, Ostrom calls for a system of democratic administration providing citizens with a greater range of choices through a complex arrangement of government agencies and other organizations.

The Dualistic Nature of Public Administration

The century-old debate over the distinctive nature of public administration has generated much controversy but little insight. When we consider the overall theme of that debate, however, we find a common core that is relevant to the search for the essence of public administration. What is clear from discussions arising from the debate is that public administration embodies (and responds to) both administrative and political forces. While some analysts emphasize the administrative side, others stress the political aspects of public administration. Somewhere in the middle stand those like Goodnow who acknowledge the importance of both features.

Goodnow's perspective allows us to see public administration as lying somewhere along a continuum marked by two polar extremes. On the one end are the purely *administrative* aspects of the field. Here the activities of public administrators are carried out in a routine, structured, and impersonal fashion according to orders received from some superior authority. On the other end are *political* activities, involving the sharing of authority and decisions arrived at through the usual political processes of consultation and negotiation for the purposes of reaching some consensus or agreement.[35]

How does Goodnow's perspective help us better understand and appreciate public administration? First, it shows us that public administration has a dualistic nature and that a one-dimensional view is misleading. Second, it reminds us that, since the two sides of that dual nature are often in conflict, public administrators frequently face dilemmas in which they must choose between technical and political responses to issues. Third, this continuum focuses our attention on the potential for tension between politics and administration as the context within which public administrators work. Hence, we enhance our understanding of what makes public administration work by recognizing its dualistic nature and by trying to understand the dynamics of public administration as a function of this nature.

The Public Difference

The Business Executive's Lament

Another path that scholars follow in their search for the essence of public administration focuses on the unique qualities that characterize the *public* nature of governmental functions. Among the strongest proponents of this

view are members of the business community who have held executive positions in both the private and public sectors.[36] A. J. Cervantes became aware
of the differences between business and government affairs when he served
as mayor of St. Louis, Missouri, during the 1960s. A well-known local businessman, Cervantes ran for office on a platform that promised to bring
effective business practices to city government. After two terms in office,
he concluded that it is possible to apply business methods to some functions
of government, but only the common, day-to-day "housekeeping chores" of
city operations. Of course, there is much more to government than basic
housekeeping tasks.

> Government presides over a way of life. And if the government executive
> applies only the priorities and goals of business to the American government
> and to the American people, he will inevitably destroy the purpose of American
> government.[37]

Other executives who have moved from the private to the public sector
echo Cervantes's observations repeatedly, claiming that while their experiences as private-sector managers help them deal with many of the day-to-day
routines of government work, government provides a much different working environment. W. Michael Blumenthal, a former chief executive officer
with the Bendix Corporation and head of the Unisys Corporation, proved
to be an astute observer of those differences while serving as secretary of
the treasury under President Jimmy Carter:

> One of the reasons so many businessmen fail in the government or get frus-
> trated and quit is that they cannot take this system. They say, I'm just sick
> and tired of everybody and his cousin getting in on it. You can't keep anything
> secret, private—anything.[38]

Anthony M. Frank, a former bank executive who was appointed postmaster general in 1988, was impressed with the difference in operating scale
from his previous job.

> "In this job everything is 100 times greater," said Mr. Frank, who headed the
> sixth largest savings institution before coming to Washington. "At First Nation-
> wide [Banks] we had 2 million customers; here [at the U.S. Postal Service] we
> have 200 million. Before we had 400 [office] branches; here we have 40,000.
> We had 8,000 employees; here we have 800,000."[39]

In addition to differences in size, Frank also learned that "they play by
different rules in Government life. . . . In private life you want to earn a
profit, [but] here your objective is to break even." As chief executive of a
private corporation, Frank had two constituencies he had to respond to: the

bank's depositors and its shareholders. At the Postal Service, however, "we have counted 15 different constituencies we are supposed to serve."[40]

The experiences of Cervantes, Blumenthal, and Frank reflect more than just personal frustrations and disappointments. Each came to accept the belief that the public sector differs from the private sector in several important respects. And each came to view the job of the public administrator as unique because of the special conditions characterizing work in the public arena.

Reform Proposals and Reactions

During the late nineteenth century there emerged a flurry of proposals to reform American government at all levels by applying private-sector management techniques to government programs. These proposals reflected the view that government administration should, as Woodrow Wilson and others suggested, run more like a business.[41] If, as Wilson argued, administration is a "field of business," it followed that government should turn to the business world for the tools and technologies that could help improve the operations of public agencies.[42]

The thrust of most of these early reform proposals has been to bring the managerial "genius" of the private-enterprise system into government. In their earliest forms, these reforms called for the application of scientific management methods and widely accepted principles of business organization to the structure and operations of municipal governments.[43] Calls for administrative reform of the federal government have been put forward by almost every president of the twentieth century.[44] In February 1982, Ronald Reagan created the President's Private Sector Survey on Cost Control (PPSS), also known as the Grace Commission after its chairperson, J. Peter Grace. The commission had a 161-member executive committee composed of prominent members of the business community and a staff of more than two thousand. It studied the sources of waste and inefficiency in the federal government and recommended appropriate reforms to the president. The philosophy underlying this effort is stated clearly in the commission's 1984 summary report, *War on Waste*:

> The members of the President's Private Sector Survey on Cost Control . . . believe that the disciplines necessary for survival and success in the private arena *must* be introduced into Government to a far greater degree than previously has been the case. It is that belief which movitated the PPSS effort. A government which cannot efficiently manage the people's money and the people's business will ultimately fail its citizenry by failing the same inescapable test which disciplines the private sector: those of the competitive marketplace and of the balance sheet.[45]

Another group of observers stress the uniqueness of the public setting and criticize the various proposals for government reform based on the

PROFILE 2.1
Going from Public to Private Management

Since 1984, David Greenamyre has served as president of a private corporation specializing in property redevelopment in Leavenworth, Kansas. Prior to going to work in the private sector, however, Greenamyre served thirteen years in government, first as assistant city manager in Leavenworth, then as assistant city manager in Overland Park, Kansas, and finally as city manager of Warrensburg, Missouri. Because he manages a substantial part of city life that is within the private domain, Greenamyre's private-sector activities have been characterized as "the other side of city management."

What difference does he find between the public and private sectors? While cities and private corporations both think in cost-benefit terms, Greenamyre notes important differences in the factors they consider and the ways they operate. In this interview, Greenamyre highlights three dimensions of public and private management: (1) relations with the media, (2) management processes, and (3) return on investment factors.

RELATIONS WITH THE MEDIA

There are some similarities between public and private sectors on relations with elected officials and the media. As a public sector manager you must be concerned about what both of these groups think of your performance. In the public sector we call this the "care and feeding of the elected officials and the media."

This care is equally important for private sector managers because government officials make important decisions that affect your business opportunities in a variety of ways. Besides the obvious zoning decisions, decisions about the location of new streets, schools, parks and the like can affect your business. Similarly, when you do have to deal with the news media in the private sector, you must be as careful as a public sector manager because the business' public image is very important in the community.

In the public sector, you see the news media frequently, if not daily. For example, the press makes a habit of attending weekly city council meetings. Oftentimes you do things a certain way because you anticipate the media's reactions.

In the private sector, managers don't see the press unless the business has had a tremendous success or failure. Unlike the public sector, you don't do things just because of the newspaper. Nor do you avoid doing something just because of the newspaper.

MANAGEMENT PROCESSES

Private sector managers who go into the public sector and complain about "all these people meddling in these affairs" don't understand what they've gotten into. All those people involved in the public's business is the way government is supposed to operate.

Management is less structured in the private sector. It's less formal. In the private sector you sit down with your business associates and decide to do something. You're making the decision.

PROFILE 2.1   *continued*

Once you have the right people around the table and you have enough money to do the project, you can go ahead. You can do whatever you are big enough to do. For the private sector, the consumer is the important reference point. And the relationship with the consumer is a real clear-cut one. "You like my product or you don't like it. I don't care if you like me or not, it's whether you like my product."

In the public sector, with the citizens as a reference group, you can't be that cut and dried about it. It's how you do your job, the process you follow, as much as what you do. How you reach decisions, and whom you involve in the process, is as important to success in the public sector as what you do. In the public sector you find yourself saying, "Well, have you talked to the XYZ group?" and, "We'd better get the office of ABC involved." Since the public manager rarely makes the decision—the elected officials do—you have to pay more attention to the process.

RETURN ON INVESTMENT

To illustrate differences on returns on investment, Greenamyre discusses a proposal made by a volunteer citizens group to increase the visual attractiveness of downtown Leavenworth. Called the Streetscape Project, the proposal calls for planting trees and shrubs, installing new lighting, and laying decorative street brick at the downtown intersections. The costs of such projects are usually financed on a shared-cost basis; that is the city pays half and the private property owners pay the other half. The private property owners are assessed because of the presumed benefit the improvements will bring to their private property and/or businesses. Since a substantial part of Greenamyre's business interests are in commercial and retail property in downtown Leavenworth, this issue had direct bearing on his company. According to Greenamyre,

one way the private sector gets involved in government is when some public improvement is needed. The Streetscape Project in downtown Leavenworth is an example of such an improvement project. The idea was to plant 106 trees, a number of park benches, turn-of-the-century street lights, turn-of-the-century street signs, and decorative crosswalks. The expectation was that the streetscape improvements would make a portion of downtown more attractive and hopefully draw more business downtown.

A volunteer citizens group came up with the Streetscape idea and approached the city. The city decided it would be a good idea and approached the property owners in the benefit district, approximately a 9 square block area. As a property owner in the district, we were very interested in the project, but did not agree with one of the improvements, the decorative crosswalks. We felt that the cost of the decorative crosswalks would never be recouped by the property owners. The city didn't really think in those terms. The economic thinking of the city was in terms of getting the best trees, street lights, and the like for the money spent, not whether there would be any return on investment. We finally told them that we wouldn't join the benefit district if the crosswalks were in there. And the committee that developed the plan got very upset with us. They said that if the city did not do the whole plan, then it should not do anything. But the city agreed to compromise and take out most of the crosswalks. We signed the benefit district petition and the project is going forward.

Governments have scarce resources and must make decisions about how to spend money for competing public activities. Usually in a business you do not face such scarce resource constraints because hopefully what you are doing is generating income that you can use elsewhere. That income in turn will allow you to do other things.

Cities think in terms of cost efficiency; you want to get the most for the money spent. But not that you get it back, necessarily. Now in some instances, such as the water plant, sewers, or refuse operations, a public manager can think in terms of the money a city spends having some return to the city. For example, as more

people hook up to the water system, you receive more fees for this service. But in public improvements like the Streetscape Project you don't get anything tangible back, except maybe indirectly through sales tax receipts. What the city does get is a public improvement and a better community image but not increased revenues. In the private sector you need to think about those things.

In the public sector you don't have to worry about what other people have out there in the market. There's only one police department or one fire department. While it has to be efficient, it's tough being a manager in the public sector because you don't have any competitive benchmarks to use on how well you're doing at managing the public's business. While you can try to measure yourself against the city next door, comparisons are usually tricky. Usually the city next door will have a different tax base or different problems and the like.

SOURCE: Quotes and information from interview with David Greenamyre, March 17, 1989.

private-sector model. These critics add much to our understanding of the differences between the public and private sectors. Their position, summarized in "Sayre's Law," holds that "public and private management are fundamentally alike in all unimportant respects."[46] While not denying that management in the two sectors is similar in some ways, these analysts note that the *differences* are too significant to allow for the free transfer of techniques from one realm to the other.

Peter F. Drucker, a widely cited management consultant who began his career as a professor of government, argues that business is different from government despite certain similarities.

> The Government, the Army or the Church—in fact, any major institution—has to have an organ which, in some if its function, is not unlike the manage-

ment of the business enterprise. But management as such is the management of a *business* enterprise. And the reason for the existence of a business enterprise is that it supplies economic goods and services. . . . The essence of business enterprise, the vital principle that determines its nature, is economic performance.[47]

Drucker calls nonbusiness enterprises "public-service institutions," including government agencies, the armed services, schools and universities, hospitals, and labor unions. These and other public organizations provide services to modern society, but they are not preoccupied with the need to enhance the "bottom line" profitability of their operations. A central difference between these enterprises and business lies in their respective purposes and values. The public-service institution "needs different objectives, and it makes a different contribution to society. Performance and results are quite different in a service institution from what they are in business."[48] After examining the managerial problems and needs of public-service institutions, Drucker concludes that what they need

> is not to be more business-like. . . . But they need to be more hospital-like, university-like, government-like, and so on. In other words, they need to think through their own specific functions, purposes, and missions.[49]

Analyst Paul H. Appleby is even more explicit in his criticism of the view that government and business are alike. He argues that "there is no greater fallacy, and none more hostile to public morality, than the notion . . . that 'government is just a big business.'"[50] In particular, Appleby argues that public administration is unique in the public nature of its functions and in the degree of public scrutiny to which it is exposed.[51] For Drucker, Appleby, and others, it is foolish at best to ignore the differences between the public and private sectors when designing or evaluating the work of public administrators. Indeed, it is the public difference that determines what administrators do and how they do it. And it is that difference that is the essence of public administration.[52]

The Economist's Perspective

Another major group to focus on the distinctiveness of the public sector emerged from the world of economics. Economists rely on Adam Smith's model of the marketplace, which makes a number of key assumptions regarding the goods and services exchanged in society. According to that model, the law of supply and demand decides what goods and services to produce and how to distribute them. It also establishes prices for goods or services in the marketplace. The amount a potential buyer is willing to pay for an item or service and how much a potential supplier is willing to accept determines the price of a good or service. Further, consumers' demands for certain goods and services stimulate production by suppliers if the price consumers are willing to offer is acceptable. Productive activity, in turn, generates jobs and income for workers who, as consumers, then reenter the marketplace with still more demands that further stimulate supply, and so on.

In its simplest form, the economist's model of the marketplace reflects a perfect world in which buyers and sellers are completely knowledgeable about everything that is taking place and where no one is capable of monopolizing the sale or purchase of specific goods and services. Another important assumption of the economist's view is that each good or service offered in the marketplace must be free of externalities. *Externalities* are the costs or benefits of producing or consuming a good or service that specific individuals involved in the exchange process cannot or will not restrict to themselves (see Insight 2.2). In the ideal marketplace, there are no externalities. Those who purchase a good or service are paying the *full* price—a price that includes all the costs and benefits generated through the production or consumption of a good or service.

In the real world, however, we must contend with externalities all the time. We have neither the technology nor the accounting systems that would allow us to allocate the full costs and benefits of goods and services to those who possess them. The challenge, then, is to establish a means for handling externalities, and to do this society generally relies on government. The public sector represents society's principal means for dealing with externalities that the private marketplace cannot handle. For instance, government often regulates or prohibits the production of certain potentially dangerous goods (e.g., drugs and pesticides) that might generate costly externalities. At other times, government offers tax breaks to private individuals who, at their own expense, provide some service that benefits society, such as building and operating a lighthouse. In both instances, government uses its powers to help the marketplace deal with externalities.[53]

A special case for government involvement in the private marketplace occurs with certain goods and services that no individual will manufacture or purchase because they are almost entirely characterized by externalities. Although we all benefit from fire and police protection, most individuals would not be willing or able to pay all the costs of those services. The same is true of national defense or national parks. The term *public goods* is applied to these extreme cases of externalities, and most economists believe that governments must be responsible for providing and paying for them. Economist John Kenneth Galbraith argues that the desire for such goods and services is characteristic of any successful and expanding society.

> Once a society has provided itself with food, clothing, and shelter, all of which so fortuitously lend themselves to private production, purchase, and sale, its members begin to desire other things. And a remarkable number of these things do not lent themselves to such production, purchase, and sale. They must be provided for everyone if they are to be provided for anyone, and they must be paid for collectively or they cannot be had at all. Such is the case with streets and police and the general advantages of mass literacy and sanitation, the control of epidemics, and the common defense.[54]

INSIGHT 2.2
WIDGETS AND EXTERNALITIES

The concept of externalities in the marketplace is inherently simple. For example, suppose I produce a widget and bring it to the marketplace where I intend to sell it. Since I own and possess the widget, it can be assumed that I am the only one who is able to bear the costs and derive the benefits from its use. By offering the widget for sale, I am demonstrating a willingness to give up both the costs and benefits of that product for an acceptable price.

Before coming to the marketplace, I estimated the cost of producing the widget to be $3, including the material and resources needed to manufacture it. Along comes a customer who believes that she needs a widget. She inquires about its price, and I respond by asking how much she is willing to offer. She offers $2, and I respond by suggesting $5. We haggle back and forth until a bargain is struck at $3.50. For that price I am willing to sell the widget, and the customer is willing to purchase it. When I turn over the product to the customer, it is assumed that she now has full and complete possession of the widget; all the costs and benefits associated with its manufacture and use now belong to her and no one else—or so I thought.

Suppose, however, that I was unknowingly careless during the widget manufacturing process and accidentally spilled some of the toxic substances into a nearby creek. I later discovered that my neighbors downstream took ill the next day after having consumed water drawn from the creek just a few hours after the accidental spill. In a sense, they have unknowingly and involuntarily paid part of the costs for the manufacture of that widget. The costs of production have been shared by my neighbors, although they are unlikely to gain any benefit from the sale of the item unless I felt compelled to compensate them for their unintended participation in the widget production process. The costs of production, in other words, have been externalized.

A few days after selling the widget, I am told that the customer who purchased the item used it to fill in a pothole in the street in front of her house that the city had neglected to repair for months. She made the repair herself because her car was taking a beating each time she pulled into her driveway. While not telling her directly, her neighbors were grateful for the street repair, for they also were constantly running into the pothole with their vehicles each time they passed her house. None of them was willing to share the costs of the widget and the other material it took to fill in the pothole, but they all shared in the benefits gained from the repair. Another externality was created in that the benefits gained from the use of the widget could not be restricted to its owner.

According to the economist's perspective, the ability of the public sector to handle problems generated by externalities is the source of both government's distinctiveness and its drawbacks. The public sector is different because it provides mechanisms through which society can allocate the costs and benefits of goods and services that generate large amounts of externalities. Economists see that traditional markets cannot deal with the spillover costs and benefits generated by externalities. In the traditional marketplace, buyers and sellers either cannot or will not restrict access to the costs and/or benefits of the goods and services. In the public sector, however, it is feasible to apply some form of collective decision making to choices surrounding the production and consumption of goods and services with high spillovers. In place of the pricing mechanisms of the open market, public-sector decisions are made through direct voting, legislative deliberation, legal proceedings, or administrative rulings.

Because of the nature of these public goods, the task of administering in the public sector is bound to be quite different from that of working in the private marketplace. Economists emphasize that public-sector decision-making processes do not follow market forces—like the law of supply and demand—but public policies. Therefore, public administrators usually are not informed about whether the goods or services being provided in the marketplace are acceptable or sufficient. This is a central difference between public administrators and their private sector counterparts.[55]

This important difference between private and public administrators has led some prominent economists to argue for using the private-sector marketplace whenever and wherever possible. For them the difference between the public and private sectors is too great and too dangerous. Economist Milton Friedman believes that the use of the public sector is not only less efficient than the marketplace but also poses a danger to freedom because of government's reliance on coercion.

> . . . [G]overnment may enable us at times to accomplish jointly what we would find it more difficult or expensive to accomplish severally. However, any such use of government is fraught with danger. We should not and cannot avoid using government in this way. But there should be a clear and large balance of advantages before we do. . . .[56]

The Unique Tools of Government

We find an odd coalition of business-executives-turned-public-officials, critics of government reform, and economists supporting the notion that the essence of public administration lies in the special demands of the public arena. Implied in their views is the idea that both the dynamics and the tools of governments are significantly different from those found in the private sector. Although in this book we are primarily concerned with the distinctive dynamics of government and public administration, it is also helpful to know the unique tools of government action that reinforce the public difference:

TOOLS FOR PROVIDING PUBLIC SERVICES

- Direct production
- Coproduction
- Intergovernmental agreements
- Contracting
- Franchises
- Subsidies
- Tax Exemptions
- Vouchers
- Volunteer Programs

TOOLS FOR REGULATING

- Prohibition
- Fines and penalties
- Licensure
- Access fees
- Taxes/subsidies
- Marketplace incentives

As this list indicates, public-sector activities are carried out in a variety of ways.[57] Government can provide public services through *direct production*; that is, by using their own employees and facilities. School districts usually provide education by hiring teachers and constructing school buildings for instruction. Some local governments operate city-owned power plants to provide electricity to their citizens. Indeed, government agencies provide most of the public services offered to Americans.

Many governments also rely on *coproduction* arrangements, in which they share the tasks involved in providing public services with those who are receiving the service. In neighborhood watch programs, for example, neighborhood residents help local law-enforcement officials carry out their crime-prevention functions. Similarly, many local governments provide for trash collection, but often require that citizens leave their trash containers near the curb. This coproduction arrangement not only makes sanitation pickup operations much easier and faster but also helps cut down the overall costs of trash collection.

Still another means for the public-sector provision of goods and services is through an arrangement with some third party, sometimes another governmental unit. Under *intergovernmental agreements*, communities arrange for their county government or a nearby city government to provide some specific public service, such as fire or police protection. A community may also contract with another community for its citizens to use the other's libraries, schools, or park and recreation facilities. This approach has long been used, reaching its fullest development in 1954, when the city of Lakewood, California, contracted with the County of Los Angeles for a package of services. The services ranged from animal control and building inspections to traffic-signal maintenance and tree trimming. By the early 1980s, Lakewood was purchasing over forty different services from the county.[58] In other intergovernmental agreements, two governments may enter into a joint venture, such as when the Texas cities of Dallas and Fort Worth agreed to jointly own and operate an international airport. Yet another common arrangement is when local governments agree to aid each other in times of emergency.

Contracting with private firms and nonprofit organizations is another frequently used method for providing public-sector goods and services. The Department of Defense contracts with thousands of private firms to produce the sophisticated weapons systems used by the armed services. State governments rely on private construction companies to build or resurface roads and highways. And some state departments of corrections are now giving serious consideration to using private contractors to run prisons and other penal institutions. On the local level, hundreds of cities use contractors for a variety of services ranging from providing street lighting and engineering advice to collecting trash and maintaining local cemeteries (see Insight 2.3). In recent years, an increasing number of political officials and commentators have advocated the privatization of the public sector; that is, a greater reliance on private contractors to provide public services.[59]

Still another method is the use of *franchise* arrangements. Under this approach, a government gives a private firm a monopoly over the provision of some service if the firm agrees to make the service available to citizens at a reasonable cost. Many local governments use this method to provide electric power, public transportation, water, cable television, and a variety of other services. The franchise agreement typically calls for the service provider to submit to regulation by a government agency.

Other methods used by governments to provide goods and services include cash or in-kind *subsidies* or *tax exemptions* to third parties who can offer a public-sector service. Many local governments give private developers tax breaks, long-term leases on tracts of land at nominal costs, low-interest loans, or some other incentive if they agree to develop a regional shopping center or industrial park. Still another mechanism is the use of *vouchers*, whereby citizens receive from the government coupons that can be applied toward the purchase of some goods or services, such as school tuition or food stamps. Governments also may depend on *volunteer programs*. Many small communities, for example, depend on volunteers to fight fires.

Sometimes the problem facing public administrators is not how to provide goods and services to the community but how to regulate their use. In the case of some drugs, such as marijuana and cocaine, the public sector's regulatory efforts are accomplished through outright *prohibition*. In its most stringent form, these prohibitions make the possession or consumption of some good (e.g., a drug) or service (e.g., prostitution) an illegal act punishable by imprisonment.

INSIGHT 2.3
CONTRACTING
WITH GOVERNMENT

In a turnabout of sorts, there have been a growing number of reports of private-sector firms contracting with government employees for their off-duty services. According to the *New York Times,* in Miami, Florida, more than three hundred off-duty uniformed city police patrol shopping malls, parking lots, and similar locations on weekends. These city employees carry with them their city-issued weapons, badges, radios, and other equipment, which they are free to use while on these private patrols. Further-more, should any trouble arise requiring them to subdue or arrest someone, they are authorized to take the same kinds of actions they would if they were on duty.

The *Times* also reports that similar arrangements exist for police officers in St. Petersburg, Florida, where the police department actually runs a service matching off-duty officers with requests from private-sector firms for these jobs. Not only does this system allow public admin-istrators some degree of control over the contracting process, but it also provides a new source of revenue for the police department, which receives a fee for each placement.

Why is this contracting arrangement so interesting? Haven't off-duty police al-ways taken advantage of part-time em-ployment opportunities? The answer is yes, but with a big difference. By work-ing through the department to hire these officers, the private firms are getting more than a trained police officer. They are also getting individuals who come to the position fully equipped and capable of exercising their legal authority as police if necessary.

Perhaps no group of public employees is as well situated to take advantage of these kinds of arrangements as are police officers. It is less likely, for example, that off-duty firefighters would be allowed to take their equipment to a similar part-time position. Nevertheless, there are other instances of private-sector firms contracting with government to offer services over and above that which is paid for with tax dollars. A private com-pany can rent out city facilities such as auditoriums or parks for concerts, par-ties, or some similar function. Some cities offering regular trash collection to pri-vate residences are also contracted by private firms to pick up their garbage as an alternative to some for-profit com-pany that might provide a similar service. City crews can be hired for snow-removal tasks or to construct private sidewalks or driveways. The possibilities are only lim-ited by the imagination and relevant local laws and policies.

SOURCE: Based on information in Andrew H. Malcolm, "When Private Employers Hire Public Police," *New York Times,* 26 Feb. 1989, pp. 1, 22.

Where regulation is intended to control a behavior rather than prohibit it entirely, public administrators use *fines and other limited penalties.* In its most familiar form, this approach is used to regulate our use of automobiles, particularly where we park them and how fast we drive them. The operation of motorized vehicles is also regulated through the issuance of *licenses*, which allow local officials an opportunity to test individuals before they are able to use public streets and highways.

Sometimes governments rely on *access fees* as a means for regulating the use of some service or facility. For example, in several suburban communities north of Chicago, local residents pay for a card that they must display whenever they use local parks or beaches. In this way local governments limit nonresidents' access to their facilities. Such a system of regulating the use of public facilities is legal if communities do not restrict access on the basis of race, religion, or other criteria that would violate citizens' civil rights.

Finally, governments may rely on *taxation*, *subsidies*, or other manipulations of the marketplace to provide citizens with the incentive to behave in a desired way. For example, many states impose special taxes on the purchase of alcohol and tobacco to discourage their use. Similarly, states might subsidize the cost of mass-transit rides to encourage their use.

The Search Continues

Students and scholars of American public administration have been searching for the essence of their subject for over a century. From their efforts a seemingly clouded image has emerged of what is at the heart of the field. No matter how unclear that image may seem to be, we have learned a great deal from their efforts.

The search for the nature of public administration has produced definitions reflecting its principal place (in the executive branch), primary purpose (policy implementation), and foremost task (management). It has provided us with an awareness of the dualistic nature of public administration as both scholars and practitioners attempt to come to terms with both the administrative and political forces that shape the field. Finally, it has drawn attention to the unique features of public-sector activities that seem to make the jobs of public administrators so different from those of their private-sector counterparts.

When taken together, one common theme arises from the three different searches: American public administration is shaped by—and helps to shape—the many forces that surround it. We may not find the real nature of the field in any one definition, scholarly debate, or difference from the private sector. Instead, the essence of public administration rests in the practitioners' and scholars' responses to the very ambiguities and lack of identity that has made the search for its nature so difficult. Perhaps the essence of our subject manifests itself in the efforts public administrators make to achieve an identity or fulfill a sense of purpose. In Chapter 3, we apply this perspective to our discussion of public administration.

Summary

1. The search for the essence of public administration has followed three major paths over the past century: through the search for a comprehensive definition, through a debate over the dualistic nature of public administration, and through a debate over the differences between the public and private sectors.

2. Some have sought to capture the essence of public administration in definitions that emphasize the location (executive branch), primary tasks (policy implementation), and functions (managerial) of government administrators.

3. Others have sought the essence of public administration in the distinction between the administrative and political tasks of governments. This is reflected in a century-long debate among scholars of public administration over the politics–administration dichotomy.

4. Another approach seeks the essence of public administration in those characteristics that make the public sector different from the private sector.

5. While none of these paths has resulted in a clear image of what public administration is, each has provided interesting leads in our efforts to understand it.

Study Questions

1. A good test of any definition is to attempt to apply it to a particular example. For example, we can test each of the three major definitions of public administration discussed in this chapter by focusing on a specific job of the public administrator and considering how that job fits into the definition. U.S. marshals provide a classic case. Visit your local library and research U.S. marshals. Then apply the executive branch definition, the policy implementation definition, and the managerial definition. How well does each one fit? Now do the same exercise for public school teachers, for someone who works in the Government Printing Office, and for your local sheriff.

2. The division between politics and administration is more of a problem for some public administrators than for others. A person whose job it is to track and report the weather daily is likely to face less political pressure than a person whose job it is to determine whether to recommend keeping

an air force base open ten years from now. Make a list of the government workers who you think have an easy time keeping out of politics. Then draw up another list of the public administrator positions that you believe are more likely to involve politics.

3. Some economists contend that the only function government should perform is the production and delivery of public goods and services. Do you agree or disagree? Why, or why not?

4. Make a list of the services provided by your local government that you think could be effectively provided by the private sector. How much would you be willing to pay for these services? Which (if any) of them would you be willing to do without?

5. Now draw up a list of the services provided by your local government that you think could *not* be effectively provided by the private sector and explain why.

Notes

1. Herbert A. Simon, Donald W. Smithburg, and Victor A. Thompson, *Public Administration* (New York: Alfred A. Knopf, 1950), p. 7. For a discussion of the constitutional legitimacy of public administration, see John A. Rohr, *To Run a Constitution: The Legitimacy of the Administrative State* (Lawrence, KS: University of Kansas Press, 1986).

2. See Felix A. Nigro and Lloyd G. Nigro, *Modern Public Administration*, 6th ed. (New York: Harper & Row, 1984), chap. 19.

3. See Ira Sharkansky, "Policy Making and Service Delivery on the Margins of Government: The Case of Contractors," *Public Administration Review* 40 (March/April 1980): 116–23.

4. Harold F. Gortner, *Administration in the Public Sector* , 2d ed. (New York: John Wiley & Sons, 1981), p. 5. Also see John A. Vieg, "The Growth of Public Administration," in *Elements of Public Administration*, 2d ed., ed. by Fritz Morstein Marx (Englewood Cliffs, NJ: Prentice-Hall, 1959), p. 7; and Leonard D. White, *Introduction to the Study of Public Adminstration*, 3d ed. (New York: Macmillan, 1948), p. 3.

5. Grover Starling, *Managing the Public Sector*, 3d ed. (Chicago: Dorsey Press, 1986), p. 1. Also see J. D. Williams, *Public Administration: The People's Business* (Boston: Little, Brown, 1980), p. 7; and the typical definition of public administration in Dwight Waldo, *The Study of Public Administration* (New York: Random House, 1955), p. 2.

6. On the political management central to the job of high-level political appointees, see Philip B. Heymann, *The Politics of Public Management* (New Haven: Yale University Press, 1987); and Laurence E. Lynn, Jr., *Managing Public Policy* (Boston: Little, Brown, 1987).

7. See, for example, the contrast between political appointees and career administrators in the federal government in Hugh Helco, *A Government of Strangers: Executive Politics in Washington* (Washington, DC: Brookings Institution, 1977), esp. chaps. 3 and 4. For a model built on this view of bureaucratic politics, see Anthony Downs, *Inside Bureaucracy* (Boston: Little, Brown, 1967).

8. Robert A. Caro, *The Power Broker: Robert Moses and The Fall of New York* (New York: Vintage, 1974), pp. 1–21.

9. Waldo, *The Study of Public Administration*, p. 2.

10. Although it was originally published in 1887, not much attention was paid to Wilson's article until the late 1930s. At that time interest in the article led to its reprinting in the early 1940s. See Woodrow Wilson, "The Study of Administration," *Political Science Quarterly* 56 (December 1941): 481–506.

11. For a critical assessment of Wilson's role in the development of American public administration, see Paul Van Riper, "The American Administrative State: Wilson and the Founders—An Unorthodox View," *Public Administration Review*, 43 (November/December 1983): 477–90; and Daniel W. Martin, "The Fading Legacy of Woodrow Wilson," *Public Administration Review* 48 (March/April 1988): 631–36.

12. The European perspective (see Martin, "The Fading Legacy," pp. 631–32) stresses that public administration is at the core of modern government; it is not (as Wilson argues) a separate institutional arrangement. See Carl J. Friedrich, *Constitutional Government and Democracy: Theory and Practice in Europe and America*, 4th ed. (Waltham, MA: Blaisdell, 1968), chap. 19.

13. Wilson, "The Study of Administration," pp. 493–94. Martin and others contend that Wilson's view was the result of a poor translation of some German writers on the subject, and that Wilson himself abandoned his famous dichotomy just a few years later (Martin, "The Fading Legacy," p. 633.)

14. For example, see Jack Rabin and James S. Bowman, eds., *Politics and Administration: Woodrow Wilson and American Public Administration* (New York: Marcel Dekker, 1984).

15. Wilson, "The Study of Administration," p. 504.

16. Ibid., p. 494.

17. Frank J. Goodnow, *Politics and Administration: A Study in Government* (New York: Russell & Russell, 1967), p. 18.

18. Ibid., chaps. 2–4.

19. Ibid., chap. 10.

20. See Leonard D. White, *Introduction to the Study of Public Administration* (New York: Macmillan, 1926); W. F. Willoughby, *Principles of Public Administration* (Washington, DC: Brookings Institution, 1927), pp. viii, 7; and Leonard D. White, *Trends in Public Administration* (New York: McGraw-Hill, 1933), pp. 11–12.

21. Lyndall Urwick, "Organization as a Technical Problem," in *Papers on the Science of Administration*, ed. by Luther Gulick and Lyndall Urwick (New York: Institute of Public Administration, 1937). p. 49.

22. Luther Gulick, "Science, Values and Public Administration," in *Papers on the Science of Administration*, ed. by Luther Gulick and Lyndall Urwick (New York: Institute of Public Administration, 1937), pp. 192–93.

23. Marshall E. Dimock, "The Meaning and Scope of Public Administration," in *The Frontiers of Public Administration*, ed. by John M. Gaus, Leonard D. White, and Marshall E. Dimock (Chicago: University of Chicago Press, 1936), pp. 3–4.

24. See V. O. Key, Jr., "Politics and Administration," in *The Future of Government in the United States: Essays in Honor of Charles E. Merriam*, ed. by Leonard D. White (Chicago: University of Chicago Press, 1942), chap. 8.

25. See Herbert A. Simon, *Administrative Behavior: A Study of Decision-Making Processes in Administrative Organizations*, 2d ed. (New York: The Free Press, 1957 [originally published in 1947]), esp. pp. 52–60.

26. Fritz Morstein Marx, "The Social Function of Public Administration," in *Elements of Public Administration*, 2d ed., ed. by Fritz Morstein Marx (Englewood Cliffs, NJ: Prentice-Hall, 1959), p. 108.

27. Robert A. Dahl, "The Science of Public Administration: Three Problems," *Public Administration Review* 7, (February 1947), 10.

28. Paul H. Appleby, *Policy and Administration* (University, AL: University of Alabama Press, 1949), p. 43.

29. Ibid., p. 12.

30. For background on the emergence of operations research and systems analysis, see E. S. Quade, *Analysis for Public Decisions*, 2d ed. (New York: North Holland, 1982), pp. 21–24. On the adoption of planning-programming-budgeting systems, see Allen Schick, "The Road to PPB: The Stages of Budget Reform," *Public Administration Review* 26 (November/December 1966): 243–58. For a survey and critical assessment of these developments, see Aaron Wildavsky, "The Political Economy of Efficiency: Cost-Benefit Analysis, Systems Analysis, and Program Budgeting," in *Political Science and Public Policy*, ed. by Austin Ranney (Chicago: Markham, 1968), pp. 55–82; and Ida R. Hoos, *Systems Analysis in Public Policy: A Critique*, rev. ed. (Berkeley: University of California Press, 1983).

31. See Grover Starling, *Managing the Public Sector*, 3d ed. (Chicago: Dorsey Press, 1986), pp. 257–59.

32. See Robert T. Golembiewski, *Renewing Organizations: The Laboratory Approach to Planned Change* (Itasca, IL: F. E. Peacock, 1972).

33. H. George Frederickson, "Toward a New Public Administration," in *Toward a New Public Administration: The Minnowbrook Perspective*, ed. by Frank Marini, (Scranton, PA: Chandler, 1971), p. 314.

34. See Vincent Ostrom, *The Intellectual Crisis in American Public Administration*, rev. ed. (University, AL: University of Alabama Press, 1974).

35. See Arthur Naftalin, "Comment on Cleveland's Paper," in *Theory and practice of Public Administration: Scope, Objectives, and Methods*, ed. by James C. Charlesworth (Philadelphia: American Academy of Political and Social Science, 1968), p. 179.

36. This is not to say that students of public administration have ignored the unique characteristics of the public sector in their work. To the contrary, many have devoted a great deal of energy to addressing the differences between public- and private-sector management. The principal theme of their efforts, however, has been the political–managerial dualism surveyed earlier in this chapter. See Laurence E. Lynn, Jr., *Managing the Public's Business: The Job of the Government Executive* (New York: Basic Books, 1981), pp. 114ff.

37. A. J. Cervantes, "Memoirs of a Businessman-Mayor," *Business Week*, 8 December, 1973, p. 19–20.

38. W. Michael Blumenthal, "Candid Reflections of a Businessman in Washington," *Fortune*, 29 January, 1979, p. 36–40.

39. Quoted in Nathaniel C. Nash, "New Postal Chief Looks at the Really Big Picture," *New York Times*, 27 July, 1988, p. 12.

40. Ibid.

41. Historians of the American administrative state argue that efforts to bring business practices to government date back to our nation's founding. Even the Continental Congress, both before and after the adoption of the Articles of Confederation, was constantly attempting to improve the administration of

government. Furthermore, it has been argued that the period of U.S. history most often associated with the extensive use of political patronage and the spoils system — the years of Andrew Jackson's presidency — was also an era when efforts were made to bring private-sector practices into the administration of governmental affairs. See Matthew A. Crenson, *The Federal Machine: Beginnings of Bureaucracy in Jacksonian America* (Baltimore: Johns Hopkins University Press, 1975).

42. For a history of the logic behind government reform in the Progressive period, see Richard Hofstadter, *The Age of Reform: From Bryan to F.D.R.* (New York: Vintage, 1955), esp. pp. 257–71.

43. See Martin J. Schiesl, *The Politics of Efficiency: Municipal Administration and Reform in America: 1880–1920* (Berkeley: University of California Press, 1977).

44. See Herbert Emmerich, *Federal Organization and Administrative Management* (University, AL: University of Alabama Press, 1971).

45. Grace Commission, *War on Waste: President's Private Sector Survey on Cost Control* (New York: Macmillan, 1984), p. 344.

46. The statement is attributed to Wallace Sayre, a renowned political scientist and scholar of public administration. Cited in Graham T. Allison, Jr., "Public and Private Management: Are They Fundamentally Alike in All Unimportant Respects?" in *Public Management: Public and Private Perspectives*, ed. by James L. Perry and Kenneth L. Kraemer (Palo Alto, CA: Mayfield, 1983), pp. 72–92.

47. Peter F. Drucker, *The Practice of Management* (New York: Harper & Row, 1954), p. 7.

48. Peter F. Drucker, *Management: Tasks, Responsibilities, Practices* (New York: Harper & Row, 1974), p. 136.

49. Ibid, p. 166.

50. Paul H. Appleby, *Morality and Administration in Democratic Government* (Baton Rouge: Louisiana State University Press, 1952), p. 44.

51. Cited in Lynn, *Managing the Public's Business*, p. 114.

52. For a unique perspective on the issue of public versus private organization differences, see Barry Bozeman, *All Organizations Are Public: Bridging Public and Private Organizational Theories* (San Francisco: Jossey-Bass, 1987).

53. For a general introduction to the theory of externalities, see E. J. Mishan, *What Political Economy Is All About: An Exposition and Critique* (Cambridge: Cambridge University Press, 1982), part 3.

54. John Kenneth Galbraith, *The Affluent Society* (New York: New American Library, 1958), p. 111.

55. Anthony Downs, *Inside Bureaucracy* (Boston: Little, Brown, 1967), pp. 29–31.

56. Milton Friedman, *Capitalism and Freedom* (Chicago: University of Chicago Press, 1962), pp. 2–3.

57. For a discussion of the various means for providing public sector goods and services, see E. S. Savas, *Privatization: The Key to Better Government* (Chatham, NJ: Chatham House, 1987), chap. 4.

58. Ibid., pp. 67–68. Also see the discussion of the Lakewood arrangement in John C. Bollens and Henry J. Schmandt, *The Metropolis: Its People, Politics, and Economic Life,* 4th ed. (New York: Harper & Row, 1982).

59. The privatization approach is strongly advocated in Savas, *Privatization*.

LIVING UP
TO EXPECTATIONS

The Pressures of Expectations

What We Expect

We all have expectations relating to the behavior of those around us. We expect certain types of commitments and behaviors from our relatives and friends, and we know they have expectations of us. These expectations often influence our relationships with families and friends. If we meet them, the relationships are likely to remain strong. If we do not live up to them, then our family ties and the bonds of friendship are likely to be strained.

Similarly, we all have expectations of government and the officials who run it. If those expectations are high, we hope government will live up to the standards we set for it. If they are low, we hope it will surprise us by exceeding our expectations. In either case, such expectations establish pressures on public officials to live up to or exceed them. Just how much pressure exists cannot be understated: Government officials must respond to the expectations of over 225 million Americans. In this chapter, we explore the many expectations we impose on public officials—and those they impose on themselves. We examine their efforts to live up to those expectations in order to find insights into and a deeper appreciation of public administration.

Expectations and Public Administration

The expectations that influence the practice of public administration address a wide variety of issues and concerns. They include expectations about mundane matters such as how public officials should dress or speak. They focus on how quickly a government agency responds to citizen requests or complaints. Generally, most of us have expectations regarding four areas of government: (1) the purposes of government agencies, (2) the means and instruments used by those agencies, (3) the procedures that agency personnel apply during policy implementation, and (4) their level of performance. Some of these expectations are important to us as individual citizens. Others, such as the appropriate dress of public employees, may not be so important to us. Whether such expectations are high priorities for individual citizens or not, they remain important to many public administrators. They constitute the pressures that public administrators face daily and the demands which they must accommodate as public employees.

Most Americans have expectations about the *purposes* of government agencies. This covers a wide range of expectations, including the general goals of public policies and the specific objectives and missions of government agencies. Most of us have rather broad and ambiguous ideas about the purposes of government officials. We expect our local police to keep the peace and solve crimes, just as we expect the school district to educate our children and the U.S. Coast Guard to patrol our shores. In some instances, there is little or no debate regarding the ends that a particular agency should pursue. If there is broad-based agreement about the ends we expect an agency to achieve, members of that agency can feel secure in their efforts so long as they do not violate other expectations. Where there are significant disagreements over the purpose of a public program, however, agency administrators find their jobs much more difficult.

To illustrate this point, let us compare the situation of the Environmental Protection Agency (EPA) with that of the Central Intelligence Agency (CIA). Although both are independent federal agencies headed by a single administrator and report directly to the White House, each faces a different set of public expectations about its primary mission. The EPA is expected to work toward a cleaner environment as its primary objective. Despite many criticisms about the effectiveness and cost of EPA methods and enforcement priorities (e.g., whether its efforts should be devoted to clean air, clean water, or hazardous waste disposal), the agency faces little debate about its overall mission. In contrast, the CIA is often at the center of national debates focusing on whether its principle purpose is the gathering of strategic intelligence or the conduct of secret ("covert") operations in foreign countries. In this sense, EPA administrators may have a distinct advantage over their counterparts at the CIA in getting support for their projects from Congress and the general public. A good deal of its advantage derives from the consensual nature of the public's expectations of the EPA's goals.

We also have expectations about the *means and instruments* used to carry out government agency objectives. While we may share expectations about the purposes served by our local law-enforcement agency, we may disagree about the methods they use in accomplishing their objectives. A person who believes in law and order may find it quite acceptable for local police to stop and question any suspicious person driving around the neighborhood. Another individual who fears the potential abuses of police authority may argue that such methods are inappropriate and provocative.

While the EPA enjoys a consensus about its general goal of a clean environment, it has been at the center of debates regarding the regulatory means it uses to achieve a cleaner environment. Some expect the EPA to ban pesticides and prohibit the construction of new factories and plants that would increase pollution levels. And they expect the agency to impose heavy fines on persons and corporations who violate legally determined environmental standards. Others advocate a greater reliance on less coercive measures such as consumer discretion, tax incentives, and subsidies to get polluters to change their behavior.[1]

Expectations about means also emerge within agencies. For instance, when Henry Kissinger headed the National Security Council (NSC) staff under President Nixon, he had no qualms about wiretapping the telephones of NSC workers when he suspected one of them of leaking information to the press. People who support wiretapping as a means for protecting our national security expected Kissinger to use wiretaps for that purpose. There were

PROFILE 3.1

"I Couldn't Make It Rain"

There are times when expectations go well beyond the capabilities of any government official. This is especially true when citizens turn to government for help in the face of disaster.

One of the most visible public administrators in the rural areas of the United States is the county agent. Usually an agricultural specialist, the county agent is available to local homeowners and farmers for advice on matters ranging from the hardiest shade trees to plant in the region and the latest pesticide to use on certain crops to the farmer's eligibility for various government agricultural programs.

Eugene Eckrote is a county agent in Bartholomew County, Indiana, an area that harvests a good deal of corn each year. In 1988, however, the corn crop was suffering from one of the worse droughts in over fifty years. By mid-July, nearly $15 million of Bartholomew County's corn crop had shriveled on its stalks and there was no relief in sight. The sweet corn that is usually ready for human consumption on the Fourth of July had about ten kernels to the ear by that Independence day.

As county agent, Eckrote was frustrated with his inability to help the local farmers. "We're not trained to handle a drought like this," he told a *Wall Street Journal* reporter. "We have nothing to go on." Yet that fact doesn't stop the phone calls from those who expect more from the county agent.

The pleas for help keep coming in. Pink telephone messages litter his desk. Farmers he has never heard of call him. "We're getting a lot of calls at home," he says. "The phone is growing out of my ear. Then we go out someplace, and all the people talk about is the drought."

The calls turned angry in June as the drought refused to break. Farmers "were getting impatient with me," he says. "People want me to do something. But I couldn't make it rain." This month, Mr. Eckrote says, many farmers have given up. Gallows humor has replaced the anger. "It's so dry, two trees were fighting over a dog," farmers joke.

SOURCE: Quotes and information from Scott Kilman and Sue Shellenbarger, "As Drought Deepens, Corn Crop Is Ravaged, Hurting World Supply," *Wall Street Journal*, 14 July, 1988, pp. 1, 12.

others, however, including members of Kissinger's NSC staff, who did not expect—and would not accept—the wiretapping.[2]

Public administrators must also face expectations regarding *procedures for implementing programs*. It is not only the means used but also the procedures followed when implementing those means that often concern the American public. For example, a vast majority of those who accept wiretapping for national security purposes, or the use of force by police officers to subdue a criminal suspect, do so with the expectation that investigators will protect the basic constitutional rights of those under surveillance. We expect due process of law and equal treatment under the laws when we have to deal with public officials. We expect fair and equitable treatment and we expect the public administrator not to give special treatment to a relative or friend.

Finally, we hold expectations regarding the *level of performance* provided by public administrators. Regardless of the purposes we expect government to serve, many Americans have a sense of how well they expect public officials to perform in achieving their goals and objectives. At times, our expectations for performance are high—sometimes too high. Thus, in the 1960s, many Americans believed the government's domestic programs could win the War on Poverty while our military forces could secure South Vietnam for non-Communists. At other times, our expectations about government performance are low. More recently, many Americans have had rather low expectations regarding the government's ability to lower inflation or to solve the energy crisis despite the fact that they expect public officials to take action in both arenas.[3] At still other times, we come in right on target, as in 1962, when President Kennedy publicly stated his expectation that the United States would land an American on the moon by the end of the decade. In each of these cases, the expectation is for a certain level of performance by a public agency. (See Profile 3.1.)

The expectations relevant to American public administration come in a variety of forms. They can take the shape of legal requirements imposed by legislatures or a civil servant's personal code of conduct. Expectations may confront the public administrator as a direct order from a supervisor or as advice from a professional colleague. To help us make sense of all these expectations, we need to examine them in terms of two major categories: responsibilities and ethical standards.

Expectations and Responsibility

Among the words most often associated with the expectations that Americans have of public-sector workers is *responsibility*. The word is so overused, however, that it has lost any clear meaning.[4] For our purposes, let us define the *responsibility* of public administrators as *those obligations and commitments that they are expected to assume in their official positions*. In other words, responsibility is that which informs public administrators of what they should do or to whom they should respond in the performance of their tasks.

We can clarify the concept further by distinguishing between responsibilities derived from obligations and those derived from commitments to groups or individuals. Thus, obligations establish a public administrator's *responsibility for* some task or goal, while commitments result in *responsibility to* some person or group (see Table 3.1). For example, as public administrators, city managers are responsible *for* providing city services efficiently and they are

TABLE 3.1   Examples of Responsibilities of Public Administrators

Commitments (Responsibility to)	Obligations (Responsibility for)
Constitution	Upholding of the Constitution and its values
Laws	Obedience to and enforcement of all laws, regulations, and policies
Democracy	Maintaining openness and access to government decision making
Public interest/opinion	Seeking to discover and achieve the public good
Agency	Fulfilling the goals and objectives of the agency as well as protecting or enhancing its position
Profession	Upholding the standards and integrity of the profession
Clientele	Providing services efficiently and effectively
Political leadership	Achieving the programmatic ends of those in power
Supportive groups	Satisfying the demands of active supporters
Personal/self	Achieving personal goals and career objectives

responsible *to* the city commission or council. In both senses, responsibility is a reflection of expectations.

Constitution and Laws

Among the most widely accepted responsibility of American public administrators is their commitment to uphold the U.S. Constitution and, if they work for state or local governments, the constitution of their particular jurisdiction. Americans take this commitment so seriously that many government jurisdictions require public employees to sign a loyalty oath when they join government service. As with all such commitments, the promise to uphold the Constitution carries with it a set of associated obligations. In this case, the public administrator accepts the obligation to uphold the regime and regime values of American government as reflected in the Constitution. Those regime values include the basic principles that are at the heart of our constitutional system — principles such as the rule of law, limited government, guarantees of basic individual freedoms as expressed in the Bill of Rights, and other widely held values of our Republic.[5]

A related commitment expected of all public administrators is to the "laws of the land." This commitment obliges administrators to both obey and enforce laws, regulations, and other legitimately established policies. While this commitment is important to all public administrators, for some it can become an obsession. One inspector from the U.S. Food and Drug Administration (FDA) expressed such an attitude when he declared that the FDA is

> a law enforcement agency, not a service agency. . . .If we go into a factory and see someone picking his nose while he is handling shrimp, we don't say, "Gee, you ought to buy gloves for that guy." We say, "You have violated Section whatever of the Act."[6]

Democracy and the Public Interest

American public administrators are also expected to be committed to the concept and practice of democracy. Political scientist Emmette S. Redford highlights three basic ideals underlying this commitment to democracy. First there is the ideal of individualism, which stresses that individual human beings are "the ultimate measure of all human values." Second is the ideal of equalitarianism, emphasizing that all individuals are worthy of social recognition. And third is the belief that personal worth is "most fully protected and enlarged" through universal participation in the political process.[7]

While it may be impossible to achieve these democratic ideals, Redford and others believe the commitment of public administrators to those tenets obligates them to achieving the "most democracy" that is possible under actual conditions.[8] At minimum, this means maintaining an open and accessible government. At best, it means determining what policies and actions are in the public interest and living up to that standard.

The commitment to the public interest is a laudable one, but it is plagued with problems. Many public administrators enter government service wishing to serve the public, but once in office they discover how difficult it is to achieve that objective. The public interest is an inviting concept in theory but an elusive one in practice. This situation poses a dilemma for the public servant.[9] Despite a strong desire to work in the public's interest, many government administrators find it impossible to discover and articulate just what the public wants or needs.

The frustrations these public administrators face are due to the nature of the public interest. To some degree, the "public" is merely an abstraction — an idea created by academics and politicians that may not exist in the real world of administrators. For example, administrators cannot easily poll the public or communicate with it to discover what it expects of government. And even if administrators were able to communicate with the public, they probably would not be able to understand precisely what the public wants from government. In fact, administrators might discover that the public is generally an uninformed group that is not really aware of what is in its best interest.

Faced with the impracticality of discovering the public interest, some administrators instead turn to some other source for guidance. Many rely on public-opinion polls for insight. These administrators commit themselves to living up to the expectations expressed by a plurality or majority of those polled in some recent public-opinion survey.

There are several problems with relying on public-opinion polls.[10] Although polling techniques have greatly improved over the past several decades, there remains the possibility of sampling errors, problems with the choice of questions, and similar difficulties. There are also many issues that public administrators deal with for which no real public opinion exists. For example, few Americans have an opinion about what should define the job of the Bureau of Standards or the National Center for Atmospheric Research.[11] Similarly, unless there is a catastrophe, like a collapsed bridge,[12] most Americans do not have an opinion about their state's Department of Transportation bridge-inspection program.

Where opinions do exist among most Americans, public-opinion polls provide little more than information about how people feel about a certain issue at a certain time and in a certain place. The results are rarely firm and enduring; in fact, the views of Americans are often volatile and fleeting. Consider, for example, the change in American public opinion regarding consumer protection regulation between 1970 and 1981. In 1970, 55 percent of those polled favored increasing regulations on the manufacture and sale of consumer products, with 14 percent favoring less regulation and 17 percent supporting the status quo. By 1981, however, support for more consumer regulation had declined to 43 percent, while the combined backing for the status quo or less regulation jumped to 45 percent.[13] This pattern is not uncommon when it comes to issues of general concern to the American public.

Finally, there is the critical issue of whether the public's opinion is a valid reflection of the public interest. That is, is it correct to associate that which is popular with that which is appropriate or good for the American public? For some public administrators searching for the public interest, the answer is yes. For others, there is room for doubt regarding the value of polling results as a measure of the public interest.

Agency

Like all organizations, public-sector agencies are social tools used to achieve collective goals and objectives. The achievement of agency goals and objectives is an important measure of success in public administration, and those who work in public organizations are expected to do what needs to be done in facilitating the agency's efforts. The pursuit of these goals constitutes the agency's official mission, which is usually specified in the agency's charter. Employees seek to fulfill these agency commitments through their job performance.

Many agency responsibilities derive from the agency's *mission statements*, publicly stated goals phrased in terms of some ideal objective that the organization's founders sought to attain.[14] Even though they are rarely completely accomplished, mission statement objectives establish an important set of responsibilities for public administrators and at the same time pose interesting dilemmas for them. Sometimes these objectives are so idealistic and far reaching that they set up the public agency for inevitable failure. In 1964, for example, President Lyndon B. Johnson declared an "unconditional war on poverty" and assigned the task for coordinating the war effort to the Office of Economic Opportunity (OEO). Ultimately, the grand assignment of eliminating poverty in the United States proved too much for the OEO. High initial expectations during the mid-1960s were difficult to achieve because the OEO was not able to receive the funding it needed during a period when the government was giving priority to financing the Vietnam War. By the time the Vietnam conflict was winding down in the early 1970s, the OEO faced both a hostile president and opposition from local elected officials displeased with OEO programs. Thus, the agency was slowly dismantled under the Nixon administration and eventually closed its doors.[15] Other antipoverty programs with more realistic and limited missions (e.g., Head Start, Upward Bound) survived a great deal longer.

At other times, mission statements are too vague to provide any sense of what is expected of a public agency's activities. The mission statement of Chicago's police force appears on the side of every patrol vehicle: "To serve and protect." Exactly what does that statement mean? Serve and protect whom? How are those objectives to be attained? Answers to these and other questions depend on how one interprets the statement, and that in turn depends on who you are, what your life experiences have been, and what you value.

At still other times, mission statements act as obstacles to change and must themselves be subject to challenge and change. The U.S. Army, for example, has long operated under the traditional mission of being "responsible for the preparation of land forces necessary for the effective prosecution of war." In short, the army must maintain the capability of controlling the battlefield during times of war. The implications of this broadly stated mission were central to a post–World War II debate within the Army's officer ranks concerning the development of an air-support capability independent of the U.S. Air Force. For many years, top-ranking Army officers relied on a strict interpretation of the mission statement, leaving control of the air to the Air Force. Others within the Army, however, sought to extend their mission to include control of the airspace above the battlefield. After much bureaucratic debate, those who argued for developing an air-support arm finally won in the 1960s. They suceeded in adjusting the Army's mission statement. By the mid-1970s, the Army had established a helicopter force so large that it became the third largest air force in the world, ranking behind the U.S. Air Force and that of the Soviet Union.[16]

Public agencies also adopt goals and objectives reflecting their needs to survive and grow. Called *systemic goals*, these are often as important to agencies as their official missions. Of course, an agency that does not survive will not be able to accomplish its official mission. Organization members believe they have an obligation to protect and defend the organization from threats to its integrity or survival. These threats can take a variety of forms. Sometimes organizations face external threats when budgets are cut or when the political opposition convinces the legislature that the agency's programs should not receive a high priority in its deliberations. At other times, the challenges to an agency can emerge from within because of poor management or the slow deterioration of the organization's ability to deal with changing conditions.[17] Whatever the source of the challenge, public organizations tend to respond by paying more attention to their systemic goals. (See Insight 3.1.)

In some cases, agency employees become preoccupied with organization stability and the minimization of risk for the agency. Such employees may feel obliged to seek long-term legislative authorization for agency programs to assure the organization's survival. They may focus on the agency's budget, perhaps seeking more funds from the legislature, whereas others may be satisfied to maintain their current budgetary positions. Still others may choose to promote growth in the agency's size or power. Finally, agency personnel may even feel personally responsible for maintaining the agency's status or reputation as the "best" or "biggest" operation of its kind.[18]

Profession

Another important commitment made by some public administrators is to professionalism in general and to their profession in particular. The public sector and its employees are becoming increasingly professionalized. Government is becoming more dependent on specialists who have unique training and knowledge. In fact, the trend toward professionalism has gone so far that one prominent observer of the field, Frederick C. Mosher, argues that we have entered the era of the "professional state."[19]

When we use the term profession, the immediate image is of established professions such as medicine and law. These traditional and widely recognized professions have always played a major role in American government. For example, public health agencies have always employed physicians, and members of the legal profession work in a number of capacities throughout government.

There are also emerging professions in the public sector. While not widely recognized as professions, members of these occupations are making efforts to get their respective specialties recognized as professional endeavors. For example, in the public-safety field, police and firefighting departments are encouraging their employees to think of their jobs as lifetime careers and to obtain the relevant advanced training and college degrees. Similarly, spe-

INSIGHT 3.1
COMING TO THE AGENCY'S DEFENSE

The importance of an agency's systemic goals are most clearly evident during periods when program budgets are threatened. During the early 1980s, budget cuts played a major role in the efforts of the Reagan administration to reduce the size and influence of the federal government. David A. Stockman, director of the Office of Management and Budget during that period, recalls how members of Reagan's cabinet—all of them committed to the overall reduction of the federal budget— came to the defense of their individual agencies. In many instances, the cabinet members argued that their agency's work was crucial to national security, an argument they believed worked well with President Reagan.

Attorney General William French Smith did not think his department was a place to start economizing.

"The Justice Department is not a domestic agency," he said. "It is the *internal arm of the nation's defense*. Our budget is less than one percent of [the Department of] Defense's, and dollar for dollar we provide far more actual security to the American people."

Smith then arrived at the gist of his argument. If anything, he said, the Reagan Administration would have to spend more on law enforcement, rather than less. In time I would discover that Smith, a silver-haired, immaculately tailored conservative from central casting, was a sucker for every spending proposal that came along.

But Stockman's most critical observations focus on the Defense Department and its

secretary, Caspar Weinberger. At one briefing before the president, when Weinberger was arguing against Stockman's recommended cuts in the Defense Department's proposed budget, the secretary and his staff used visual effects to enhance their presentation.

Incredibly, Weinberger had also brought with him a blown-up cartoon. It showed three soldiers. One was a pygmy who carried no rifle. He represented the Carter [administration] budget. The second was a four-eyed wimp who looked like Woody Allen, carrying a tiny rifle. That was—me?— the OMB defense budget. Finally, there was G.I. Joe himself, 190 pounds of fighting man, all decked out in helmet and flak jacket and pointing an M-60 machine gun menacingly at—me again? This imposing warrior represented, yes, the Department of Defense budget plan.

It was so intellectually disreputable, so demeaning, that I could hardly bring myself to believe that a Harvard-educated cabinet officer could have brought this to the President of the United States. Did he think the White House was on Sesame Street?

He had even more of these goodies, but someone pointed out that he had almost quadrupled his allotted time.

"Just wanted to be thorough, sir," Weinberger quipped in the President's direction as he sat down.

cialists in public personnel and financial management, purchasing, social work, environmental affairs, education, and a variety of other fields also place greater stress on training for lifetime careers.

Professionals occupy various positions in government. Some help carry out the substantive work of public agencies. The foreign service officer practices diplomacy, just as the Public Health Department physician delivers health-care services. Other professionals play a role as technical staff support for an agency, providing expert advice to those who actually deliver public-sector goods and services. For example, many large public agencies employ a legal counsel to advise them on issues of law related to their jobs. In recent years, the United States has become what one critic calls a "litigious society," in which people are prone to seek relief for their complaints in the courts.[20] As a result, many public agencies have established or expanded their legal staff. While the lawyers who occupy these positions may not be essential to an agency's daily operations, they often play a critical role in the ability of the agency to function in the future.

The emergence of the professional state means that a greater number of public administrators at all levels regard themselves as professionals and try to act accordingly. Through common education and contact with their peers, members of a profession develop a shared sense of responsibility about how they should behave and cultivate a sense of commitment to their profession. Many public-sector professionals have joined together in professional organizations—such as the American Society for Public Administration (ASPA), the International Personnel Management Association (IPMA), and the International City Management Association (ICMA)—through which they can articulate the kind of behavior they expect of their peers. Many of these organizations have adopted an official code of ethics. The ICMA's code of ethics is one of the oldest among the public-service professions, and it has served its members well (see Insight 3.2). In 1985 the ASPA adopted its own code of ethics, outlining the kinds of professional expectations that public administrators should hold (see Insight 3.3).

In the case of ICMA and ASPA, the commitment to professionalism translates into an obligation to uphold the standards and integrity of the profession. Where they differ is in their organizational capabilities to enforce their respective codes. In the case of the ICMA, the professional organization is quite capable of enforcing those standards by investigating and punishing violators (see Insight 3.4). In the case of the ASPA and many other professional organizations, their codes specify professional standards but lack effective enforcement mechanisms.

Clientele and Supporters

Public administrators also face expectations from those groups with whom they work—their clients—and from those who provide political or other forms of support to the agency's efforts. Most public administrators deal on

INSIGHT 3.2
ICMA CODE OF ETHICS

The code of the International City Management Association (ICMA) was first adopted in 1914. This latest version was updated in May 1987.

The purpose of the International City Management Association is to increase the proficiency of city managers, county managers, and other municipal administrators and to strengthen the quality of urban government through professional management. To further these objectives, certain ethical principles shall govern the conduct of every member of the International City Management Association, who shall:

1. Be dedicated to the concepts of effective and democratic local government by responsible elected officials and believe that professional general management is essential to the achievement of this objective.

2. Affirm the dignity and worth of the services rendered by government and maintain a constructive, creative, and practical attitude toward urban affairs and a deep sense of social responsibility as a trusted public servant.

3. Be dedicated to the highest ideals of honor and integrity in all public and personal relationships in order that the member may merit the respect and confidence of the elected officials, of other officials and employees, and of the public.

4. Recognize that the chief function of local government at all times is to serve the best interests of all the people.

5. Submit policy proposals to elected officials; provide them with facts and advice on matters of policy as a basis for making decisions and setting community goals, and uphold and implement municipal policies adopted by elected officials.

6. Recognize that elected representatives of the people are entitled to the credit for the establishment of municipal policies; responsibility for public execution rests with the members.

7. Refrain from participation in the election of the members of the employing legislative body, and from all partisan political activities which would impair performance as a professional administrator.

8. Make it a duty continually to improve the member's professional ability and to develop the competence of associates in the use of management techniques.

9. Keep the community informed on municipal affairs; encourage communication between the citizens and all municipal officers; emphasize friendly and courteous service to the public; and seek to improve the quality and image of public service.

10. Resist any encroachment on professional responsibilities, believing the member should be free to carry out official policies without interference, and handle each problem without discrimination on the basis of principle and justice.

11. Handle all matters of personnel on the basis of merit so that fairness and impartiality govern a member's decisions,

INSIGHT 3.2 *continued*

pertaining to appointments, pay adjustments, promotions, and discipline.

12. Seek no favor; believe that personal
aggrandizement or profit secured by
confidential information or by misuse of
public time is dishonest.

SOURCE: Reprinted with permission of the
International City Management Association, 777
North Capitol Street, Washington, DC 20001.

a regular basis with only a small portion of the American public, and the
work of any particular administrator or agency is likely to be directly relevant
to just a few people. While the Department of Agriculture is important to
us all, its day-to-day functions and responsibilities relate to farmers and
others in agricultural business. The same logic applies to other clientele-
oriented parts of government at the federal, state, and local levels. The
general business community deals regularly with the Department of Commerce and with state government equivalents. Organized labor unions work
closely with the Department of Labor. Educators develop close relationships
with the federal and state Department of Education and local school boards,
depending on the nature of their interest in education and the level of
government that administers the relevant programs. Similarly, administrators
of state and federal prison systems must be sensitive to the concerns of the
law-enforcement community as well as to the expectations of their inmate
clientele groups. In the case of prisons, however, the inmate's expectations
may be very negative and their attitudes quite hostile.

In many instances, the commitment to clients reflects an agency's sense
of obligation to provide effective service. Many public administrators take
pride in lower crime rates, reductions in air and water pollution levels, fewer
traffic accidents, and other indications that their agency has succeeded in
meeting the needs of the community. At a personal level, this commitment
sometimes takes the form of making a special effort on behalf of individual
clients. While this sometimes leads to frustration, it also offers a means for
living up to expectations. One project manager for a city youth employment
training program, for example, felt obligated to help some applicants.

> We've got five or six young people who are burning to get into an automotive
> training program. Everybody says, "It takes signatures, it takes time." I follow
> up on these things because everybody else seems to forget there are people
> waiting. So I'll get that phone call, do some digging, find out nothing's hap-
> pened, report that to my boss, and call back and make my apologies.[21]

INSIGHT 3.3
ASPA CODE OF ETHICS

The code of the American Society for Public Administration was adopted on March 27, 1985.

• Demonstrate the highest standards of personal integrity, truthfulness, honesty, and fortitude in all our public activities in order to inspire public confidence and trust in public institutions.

• Serve in such a way that we do not realize undue personal gain from the performance of our official duties.

• Avoid any interest or activity which is in conflict with the conduct of our official duties.

• Support, implement, and promote merit employment and programs of affirmative action to assure equal employment opportunity by our recruitment, selection, and advancement of qualified persons from all elements of society.

• Eliminate all forms of illegal discrimination, fraud, and mismanagement of public funds, and support colleagues if they are in difficulty because of responsible efforts to correct such discrimination, fraud, mismanagement, or abuse.

• Serve the public with respect, concern, courtesy, and responsiveness, recognizing that service to the public is beyond service to oneself.

• Strive for personal professional excellence and encourage the professional development of our associates and those seeking to enter the field of public administration.

• Approach our organization and operational duties with a positive attitude and constructively support open communication, creativity, dedication, and compassion.

• Respect and protect the privileged information to which we have access in the course of official duties.

• Exercise whatever discretionary authority we have under law to promote the public interest.

• Accept as a personal duty the responsibility to keep up to date on emerging issues and to administer the public's business with professional competence, fairness, impartiality, efficiency, and effectiveness.

• Respect, support, study, and when necessary, work to improve federal and state constitutions and other laws which define the relationships among public agencies, employees, clients, and all citizens.

SOURCE: Reprinted with permission of the International City Management Association, 777 North Capitol Street, Washington, DC 20001. All rights reserved.

INSIGHT 3.4
ENFORCING A CODE OF ETHICS

Among the many professional organizations to which public administrators belong, the International City Management Association (ICMA) has taken exceptional steps to enforce their Code of Ethics (see Insight 3.2). Each year the ICMA examines ethics complaints made against its members. In 1987 and 1988, for example, the organization considered more than thirty complaints and eventually censured several of its members. One member was "publicly censured" when it was found that he allowed his name to be used in a number of questionable investment schemes and had pled guilty to one count of mail fraud as a result. Another member was publicly censured for giving a former employee a $30,000 severance pay check without authority from his city council. Still another was given a similar punishment for having omitted some crucial information on his resumé when applying for a professional position.

In addition, at least seven other ICMA members were privately censured for a wide range of ethical code violations during the 1987–1988 period. Although details of these violations were not released to the general membership, they involved charges of inaccurate resumés and travel vouchers, failure to disclose information about business ties, accepting meals from a company doing business with the city, and similar violations. In each instance, the charge was carefully investigated by a special ICMA committee.

Enforcement of the code was not all the ICMA did, however. The organization has established a program to educate its members through speakers, training programs, and a variety of publications. These activities leave little doubt that the ICMA and its members are serious about their ethical code.

SOURCE: Based on information from International City Management Association Newsletters and interviews with ICMA staff and members.

At other times, responsibility to clients emerges as an obligation to work on behalf of the interests of government-program beneficiaries who cannot speak for themselves. For many years, employees of the federal Children's Bureau, created by Congress in 1912, acted as strong advocates for children's welfare and rights.[22] Similarly, many social service agencies promote the needs of their constituents in the legislative arena.

Many public agencies are sometimes blessed—or burdened—with nonclientele groups, which are nevertheless quite supportive of the agency's work. In some instances, the supportive group has a direct interest in the agency's performance. For example, while local parent groups do not include elementary or secondary students among their members, they are extremely important for school districts and many school administrators feel obliged to listen to them. At the other extreme are groups whose interest in the agency's work is unrelated to their members' circumstances. Local church groups who actively promote prison reform, for example, are unlikely to include incarcerated felons among their membership. Finally, there are groups whose members have some past ties with an agency and who still actively support the agency's programs. Various veterans groups, for instance, are enthusiastic in their support of the Department of Defense and its programs. In each case, the agency usually feels obliged to those groups that provide needed support in the public arena. These obligations, in turn, emerge as agency commitments to the supportive groups and their leaders.

Elected Officials

The political environment of the United States is highly fragmented. Every public agency is susceptible to pressures from the many political actors around it. Frequently, administrators find themselves committed to the policies and priorities of those who occupy political leadership positions. There is, in short, a perceived obligation to serve the interests of those in power.

Public administrators cannot ignore the wishes of elected officials who control the policy-making apparatus of government. In a democracy, public administrators are expected to carry out the wishes of duly elected policymakers. Because the American political system lacks a central political authority, government agencies often develop ties with coalitions of relevant policymakers and other important supporters. The form and power of these political coalitions vary among agencies and sometimes among issues. Some agencies must deal with political coalitions that are at times loose and unstable. The Environmental Protection Agency, for instance, must often deal with short-term political coalitions that emerge when important environmental issues arise. Sometimes, a tightly knit and enduring group of key members of the legislative body and others important to the agency constitute the relevant policy-making coalition. For example, the political coalition relevant to the Department of Agriculture's Forest Service is a relatively stable one. Besides the secretary of agriculture and others in the department to whom the head of the Forest Service reports, the agency is attentive to:

- The six members of the Senate Committee on the Agriculture's Subcommittee on Soil and Water Conservation, Forestry and Environment.
- The thirteen members of the Senate Appropriation Committee's Subcommittee on Agriculture, Rural Development, and Related Agencies.
- The nine members of the Senate Energy and Natural Resources Committee's Subcommittee on Public Lands and Reserved Water.
- The twelve representatives who sit on the House Agriculture Committee's Forest, Family Farms, and Energy Subcommittee.

- The thirteen members of the House Appropriation Committee's Subcommittee on Agriculture, Rural Development, and Related Agencies.
- The eighteen members of the House Interior and Insular Affairs Committee's Subcommittee on Mining, Forest Management, and Bonneville Power Administration.

Of course, not everyone within that group of policymakers is of equal importance to the Forest Service. Some members of the relevant political coalition hold more power than others. For instance, when Congressman Jamie L. Whitten speaks, the Forest Service is likely to listen. As chair of the powerful House Subcommittee on Agriculture, Rural Development, and Related Agencies, Whitten has considerable influence over the agency's funding. Forest Service officials have to be aware of and often anticipate the expectations of Whitten and others who play such strategic roles in the agency's political environment.

There are counterpressures that place limits on how far public administrators can and should go in their deference to the wishes of politicians. Many governmental reforms legislated over the past century — from the establishment of the federal civil service to the adoption of the council-manager form of government at the local level — were intended to help insulate government administration from political interference. Thus, while the American public values democracy, it remains ambivalent about the efficiency and honesty of a politicized public administration. Nevertheless, all successful public administrators must pay at least some attention to the priorities and desires of the politicians who are duly elected or appointed to head their agencies.

Personal Commitments

Finally, there are the commitments that public administrators have to themselves, their families, and their friends.[23] As human beings, public employees try to fulfill their own needs and live up to their own personal values while trying to accommodate the various other expectations mentioned earlier. For example, police officers who strive to protect the general public also face expectations from their families not to take unnecessary risks in the course of their jobs.

In addition to family obligations, public administrators have obligations to themselves as well — to fulfill their needs as human beings, for safety, security, recognition, and the like.[24] They also seek to live in a way that is consistent with their personal value system. Most public employees try to find jobs that allow them to fulfill their needs as human beings and to act out their personal values. Failing that, they try to find jobs that do not require them to act in ways that violate their personal conscience.

Most discussions about the personal commitments of public administrators center on the idea of self-interest. Some students of public administration contend that self-interest represents the principal responsibility of public-sector employees, and that a great many problems in public administration are due to bureaucratic selfishness. Others believe that responsibilities derived from self-interest are not necessarily bad, and that some public administrators are actually well-intentioned and driven to do as well as possible in their jobs. Regardless of which view is correct, there is no doubt that public administrators oftentimes look inward for guidance.[25]

Several students of public administration have developed useful frameworks for examining the role that self-interest plays in government. Economist Anthony Downs, for example, has developed a theory of bureaucracy based in part on the assumption that "every official acts at least partly in his own self-interest, and some are motivated solely by their own self-interest."

> That all officials are partly self-interested does not mean that they never take account of the interests of others in their behavior. Even self-interest narrowly conceived may lead a man to serve the interests of others if doing so advances his own interests. Moreover, self-interested officials have multiple goals, some of which may lead them to sacrifice their own short-run interests to benefit others under certain circumstances. . . .Finally, under normal conditions, men accept certain constraints on their pursuit of self-interest imposed by widely shared ethical values of their own cultures.[26]

Downs offers a typology of officials that reflects some of the different manifestations of self-interest among public administrators. Some bureaucrats, he argues, are *climbers*, motivated by pure self-interest and likely to seek power, monetary rewards, and prestige. Others are *conservers*, who want to make their work and lives as convenient and secure as possible. These individuals are likely to spend their energies protecting whatever power, position, money, and prestige they already possess. There are other administrators whose sense of responsibility derives from less self-centered motivations. *Zealots*, according to Downs, feel committed to the narrowly defined policies and objectives of their agency. An official at the National Aeronautics and Space Administration, for example, may define his or her responsibilities in terms of the successful launch of a space shuttle or lunar probe. The personal needs of that individual are satisfied if the organization's specific programs are successful. *Advocates* also receive personal gratification from the support of agency goals and objectives, but they define those objectives much more broadly. Some workers at the Environmental Protection Agency, for example, may become attached to the overall goals of a clean environment. Finally, Downs notes the existence of *statesmen*, individuals who identify with the society as a whole and who seek personal satisfaction in the promotion of the "general welfare."[27]

Each of these administrator types has a distinctive set of commitments and obligations, derived in part from a unique perspective on self-interest. These mix with other responsibilities to create the priorities and pressures that affect the lives of public administrators and the field of public administration.

Pervasive Responsibilities

The responsibilities of public administrators discussed in this chapter and outlined in Table 3.1 are only a handful of a wide range of possible expectations and obligations that public administrators may encounter. Dwight Waldo, for example, offers obligations to religious values, humanity, and "middle-range collectivities" (e.g., union, church, race) as part of a similar list.[28] Others argue that public administrators have moral responsibilities that transcend or complement even constitutional and legal obligations. H. George Frederickson and David K. Hart contend that "public servants must be both moral philosophers and moral activists" in their pursuit of the humane values that are the foundation of this nation.[29] Still others observe that public administrators may just as easily become committed to a charismatic leader or to a religion and its doctrines, as the Islamic revolution in Iran has shown. The fundamental point, however, is that responsibilities emerge from the variety of expectations that pervade the jobs of public administrators.

Expectations and Ethical Standards

The ethical standards applied to public administration also reflect expectations but of a different sort. For our purposes, the *ethical standards* of public administration are *those norms and standards of behavior that are applied to the work of civil servants for the purposes of guiding and assessing their behavior*. While responsibilities inform public administrators of what must be done, ethical standards inform them of how they are expected to act in their efforts to carry out their responsibilities. Thus, ethics provide public administrators with standards by which they can guide their own behavior, measure their own performance, and judge the behavior and performance of their peers.

Ethical standards represent something more than mere job-performance criteria and something less than widely accepted moral principles. Job-performance standards reflect the wishes of those assessing the public administrator's work under certain conditions. For example, we use the term *efficiency* as both an ethical standard and a standard by which we can assess job performance. As a basis for job evaluation, the efficiency standard gauges how many specific tasks or functions were performed for a given expenditure of resources, such as hours of work. As an ethical standard, efficiency stands independent of the task or function. The ethical standard of efficiency is a general imperative for the administrator to get the most impact for the least expenditure of available resources, regardless of the specifics of the job at hand.

We should also avoid confusing ethical standards with moral principles.[30] Many people use the word *ethics* as if it were synonymous with *morals*. As defined here, ethical behavior is not necessarily the same as moral behavior. To be ethical is to live up to some set of accepted norms and standards of behavior, and there is no guarantee that those standards will be "moral" in the social, theological, or philosophical sense. Morals express what society believes to be "right" behavior for any person under all conditions. Ethical standards express what society believes to be the "correct" behavior for a given group of individuals (in this case, public administrators) under most circumstances. For example, some students of public administration argue that adhering to a technocratic standard such as efficiency may be immoral if it leads an administrator to treat people inhumanely or inequitably. Adolph Eichmann and other members of Hitler's infamous Nazi bureaucracy found gas chambers and crematoriums to be most efficient and effective in their efforts to exterminate the Jews of Europe, but one cannot call their accomplishments moral.[31]

Sometimes ethical dilemmas arise when individuals face circumstances that challenge their personal moral standards. For example, some physicians treating AIDS patients have felt morally compelled to violate traditional medical ethics. In general, medical ethics dictate that the privacy of the patient cannot be compromised by the physician. Thus, physicians have an ethical obligation not to divulge a patient's medical condition to anyone unless the patient has given them express permission to do so. Yet some physicians have felt a moral obligation to violate this ethical proscription when their AIDS patients were unwilling to inform their sexual partners that they had the disease. Doctors who have informed their patients' sexual partners (in some cases, the patients' wives) of the AIDS diagnosis have defended their behavior on moral grounds, arguing that the incurable nature of the contagious disease overrode this particular ethical prohibition. In 1988, the American Medical Association, to deal with this clash between medical ethics and moral responsibilities, voted to change its official code of ethics regarding the privacy of AIDS patients. The change recognized that respecting the privacy of some AIDS patients (those who refuse to inform their sexual partners that they have the disease) can endanger the lives of their sexual partners. Under these circumstances, then, ethical medical behavior includes informing certain individuals without the patient's consent.

Efficiency and Effectiveness

Ethical standards take a variety of different forms, and the range of standards relevant to public administrators is particularly diverse (see Table 3.2). In economics and engineering, the ethical standard of *efficiency* calls for

TABLE 3.2 Examples of Ethical Standards Relevant to Public Administration

Standard	Meaning
Efficiency	Maximize benefits while minimizing costs
Effectiveness	Get the job done!
Responsiveness	Satisfy a specified reference group (e.g., clientele, some politician)
Majoritarianism	Do what the majority wants
Utilitarianism	Do the greatest good for the greatest number of people
Equality	Equal treatment for all who are eligible
Justice as fairness	Violate the strict rule of equality only when everyone gains, especially the disadvantaged members of society

"getting the most out of a given input." In public administration, it means doing the job at hand at the lowest possible cost.[32] As an ethical standard, efficiency requires administrators to carry out their duties in a way that maximizes the benefits being generated while minimizing the costs incurred.[33]

In contrast, the ethical standard of *effectiveness* posits that the administrator should get the job done, sometimes regardless of the costs involved. The concept of effectiveness implies several related standards.[34] For some, being effective means working to achieve agency goals; for others, it calls for making the maximum effort in carrying out the agency's mandate. In recent years, many government officials have advocated a standard of cost-effectiveness which stresses the need to be concerned with making the most efficient use of available resources while remaining attentive to the achievement of desired objectives.[35]

Responsiveness, Majoritarianism, and Utilitarianism

The ethic of *responsiveness* is associated more with the public sector than with the private sector. According to one definition, it is "the taking of nonarbitrary, pertinent, and timely action by a decisional body in reply to expressed preferences by clients, constituents, or some segment of the public."[36] As an ethical standard of behavior, to be responsive is to seek out those preferences with the intent of providing an appropriate response.

Majoritarianism, a related ethic, calls on the public administrator to be responsive to the wants of the majority of those being served. Administrators adhering to this standard are likely to look to public-opinion polls or some other indicators of the public's wishes to guide their behavior. In contrast, the *utilitarian* standard requires administrators to do the greatest good for the greatest number of people. Thus, the public administrator's actions are based on what will benefit a majority of the people, even though those actions may not be favored by a majority and despite the possibility that they may be costly to a few individuals. An example of this is the 65-mph speed limit on interstate highways in rural areas. Although intended to benefit the majority by curtailing accidents, saving lives, and reducing auto insurance premiums, interstate truckers and others who earn their living by transporting goods must pay a higher price for these social benefits. The utilitarian ethic justifies imposing those costs.[37]

Equality and Justice-as-Fairness

More widely known in the United States is the ethical standard of *equality*, which holds that a public agency should treat all its clients the same. In economic terms, equality calls for minimizing disparities among individuals or families.[38] In administrative terms, it typically calls for minimizing differences in the way public agencies treat people.

Finally, there are more elaborate ethical standards based on the idea of social justice. In recent years, a standard of *justice-as-fairness* has gained the attention of students of public administration. As articulated by philosopher John Rawls, this ethic is based on two principles: (1) a strict adherence to the need for equality in the distribution of rights and duties, and (2) acceptance of social and economic inequalities only if they result in benefits for everyone, especially the disadvantaged members of society.[39] For public administration, the justice-as-fairness ethic translates into a standard of behavior that calls for treating all citizens alike, except in cases where unequal treatment benefits all citizens, and especially the most needy. One example of this is the government tax collector with limited resources who has a list of citizens whose tax payments are delinquent. The people on the list may range from the wealthy to the impoverished. How should the tax collector proceed? Under the first principle of Rawls's justice-as-fairness doctrine, the tax collector should treat each of the delinquent taxpayers equally, regardless of the individual's economic situation. Further, tax collection should proceed according to some arbitrary standard, such as alphabetical order or age of the delinquent taxpayer. This strategy for tax collection may not be possible with limited resources, and so the tax collector must decide from whom to collect first. Under the second principle, however, the tax collector should start with the wealthier individuals on the list while making the collection of back taxes from the others on the list a much lower priority. This procedure means treating the wealthy and the poor differently, a justified choice under this principle. The result is greater revenues to help pay for more public services that benefit everyone in the community. And the impoverished delinquent taxpayer receives special advantages by getting access to more public services and additional time to pay the government what is owed.

The examples covered here are only some of the potentially relevant ethical standards. Some people place equity, fairness, and justice high on the list, while still others give greater emphasis to values like patriotism and loyalty. Regardless of the forms they take, each represents a manifestation of the many expectations that characterize American public administration.

The Need for Accountability

By surveying the different expectations that affect American public administrators, we get a sense of some of the pressures they face daily. The resulting picture shows a group of individuals and agencies constantly being pushed and prodded by expectations taking the form of shifting commitments, obligations, and ethical standards. Not only are there a great many expectations, but they also often pull public administrators in several different directions at once. It may be that the essence of public administration rests in this very situation.

Following this line of thought is a unique definition of public administration offered by Robert Denhardt and John Nalbandian. For them, public administration is the dynamic interaction among "institutions, agents and processes used in government's efforts to manage the pursuit of publicly defined societal values."[40] If these values are the bases from which expectations derive, then this definition may indeed get to the heart of American public administration.

For both public administrators and those interested in how public policies and programs are pursued by government agencies, the *management of expectations* is a major issue. For public administrators, the question is how to deal with the many demands and other pressures they face daily. For those with an interest in the work of government agencies, the question is how to get public administrators to pay exclusive or particular attention to certain expectations. From both perspectives, the principle method for managing expectations is through systems of accountability.

What Is Accountability?

Accountability is another of those widely used terms that we hear so often and in so many different contexts that it is difficult to define. For some, it is merely a means by which a superior is able to check on the performance of a subordinate. For others, accountability is "the link between bureaucracy and democracy" that makes the modern administrative state work.[41] For our purposes, we define *accountability* as *those methods and relationships that determine which expectations will be reflected in the work of public administration.*[42]

Defined in this way, accountability takes a variety of forms. Over the past two centuries, however, four major types of accountability have emerged in the United States. These systems for managing expectations differ from each other along two dimensions. First, accountability systems differ according to whether the people managing those expectations are situated within or outside the agency. Internally based accountability systems allow government administrators to control their own situations, whereas externally based systems rely on individuals or groups outside the agency to control. Second, accountability systems also vary in the degree of control they afford. Some forms of accountability rely on a high degree of control. In such a system, many of the activities of public administrators are scrutinized with considerable frequency. Where there is a low degree of control, the depth and frequency of accountability is much less.[43]

Based on distinctions made along those two dimensions, we can point to four major types of accountability systems: bureaucratic, legal, professional, and political (see Figure 3.1). In their most ideal forms, each of the four types is characterized by (1) either an internal or external source of control and (2) the imposition of either a high or low degree of control over the activities of public administrators.

Bureaucratic Accountability Systems

Bureaucratic accountability is a widely used approach for managing expectations. It narrows and defines the expectations facing public-sector employees by focusing their attention on the priorities of those at the top of the oraganization hierarchy. At the same time, it is applied intensively to a wide range of public administration activities. Thus, it provides for accountability involving a high degree of control from within the organization.

Bureaucracies exist because the person or persons at the top of the organization hierarchy have a job to get done but do not have the time, skills, or inclination needed to accomplish the required tasks. Therefore, they delegate the required tasks to hired subordinates who, in turn, may delegate even more detailed tasks to their subordinates, and so on down the hierarchy. Bureaucratic accountability systems rest on this kind of hierarchical relationship.[44]

		Source of Control	
		Internal	External
Degree of Control	High	1. Bureaucratic	2. Legal
	Low	3. Professional	4. Political

FIGURE 3.1   Four types of accountability systems.

In its most basic form, the ideal functioning of a bureaucratic accountability system involves two simple ingredients: (1) an organized and legitimate relationship between a superior and a subordinate, and (2) close supervision. The first ingredient is essential because it clearly and explicitly establishes *who is accountable* and *to whom they are accountable*. Organizational superiors and subordinates are clearly delineated. The superior has direct authority over the subordinate and the ability to reward or punish the subordinate. The second ingredient, close supervision, is the fundamental method used in a system of bureaucratic accountability, although it is not the only one applied. The use of close supervision assumes that the superior and subordinate are in close proximity and that an intense, face-to-face relationship is possible. This method is often not feasible because there may be too many people to supervise or impractical because of long distances between the supervisor and supervised individual. Consequently, the relationship may be based on the establishment of *standard operating procedures* (SOPs) or the enforcement of rules and regulations intended to govern the work of subordinates.[45]

We are most familiar with this form of accountability in the military services, although it exists in public agencies at all levels of government. It functions most often in large-scale organizations involved in the processing of claims and other forms. For example, the bureaucratic accountability system is found in the Social Security Administration, the Internal Revenue Service, and even the local county clerk's office. When frustrated or angered at the service we are receiving from these agencies, we know to "ask for the supervisor" in the hope of getting something accomplished.

Legal Accountability Systems

Legal accountability, similar to the bureaucratic form in that it involves the frequent application of control to a wide range of public administration activities, differs in three fundamental ways. First, there must be a relationship between a controlling party outside the agency and those inside the organization. In bureaucratic accountability, the controller is someone within the organization who has a supervisory position. In legal accountability, however, the controller is an outsider. But that outside party is not just anyone; it is the individual or group that is in a position to impose legal sanctions or to assert contractual obligations on the administrator. In policy-making terms, these controllers make the laws and other policy mandates that the public administrator is to enforce or implement. In other words, the outsider is the lawmaker, while the public administrator is the law enforcer.

Second, the relationship between the controller and the controlled is different in the two accountability systems. In the bureaucratic accountability system, the superior has direct authority over the subordinate; the supervisor has the ability to reward or punish that subordinate. In legal accountability, the relationship is between two relatively autonomous parties: those who make the law and those who enforce it. Some examples include a state legislature that passes laws and holds a state agency accountable for its implementation; a federal district court that orders a school board to desegregate its classrooms and holds members of the board accountable; and a local city commission that passes a sign ordinance and holds the city staff accountable for its enforcement. In a sense, the relationship between the two parties involves a binding contract between the public administrator and whoever is playing the role of lawmaker.[46]

Finally, while bureaucratic accountability relies on methods like close supervision and rules and regulations, legal accountability depends on monitoring, investigating, auditing, and other forms of "oversight."[47] An outside controller can require an agency to submit reports to the controlling party on a regular basis. At other times, Congress or some other legislative body may hold hearings to investigate the activities of an agency. In many jurisdictions, requirements mandate regular audits of agency operations. Sometimes the agency audits itself and submits a report to the controlling party. At other times, specially designated agencies conduct such audits. In 1921, for example, Congress created the General Accounting Office (GAO) for just such activities. Similar agencies exist in many states: In Kansas, the Department of Legislative Post-Audit conducts audits for the state; in New York State, it is the work of the Legislative Commission on Expenditure Review. Where such agencies are not available, private firms often perform formal audits under contracts issued by the interested outside party. City councils (the law makers) often hire private accounting firms to audit the financial operations of their cities.

Oversight need not be as formalized as an annual audit. Sometimes it takes the form of legislative staff work, an unofficial request for information, or some other informal means. Oversight occurs when a legislator responds to a constituent's complaint about how an agency is dealing with a specific problem by calling the agency administrator. It occurs, for instance, when a city commissioner decides to visit the local public works office to inspect the facilities. No matter its specific form, oversight is the primary method used in legal accountability systems.

Professional Accountability Systems

Government often deals with technically difficult and complex problems, and it must therefore rely on skilled and expert employees to provide appropriate solutions. Professional accountability systems can work well in such situations. They are characterized by the controlling party — usually the head of the agency — deferring to the employee who has the expertise or special skills to get the job done.

In a professional accountability system, the central relationship is similar to that found between a layperson and an expert, with the public administrator taking the role of the expert. As noted earlier in the chapter, professionalism is spreading throughout the public sector as more and more government workers claim to have special skills and knowledge that make them valuable to their agencies. As experts, these workers are not likely to need or readily welcome close supervision. They tend to view close supervision and oversight as interferences in their work. Rather, they expect considerable freedom to act as they see fit. They take responsibility for their actions and expect that the agency head trusts them to do the best job possible. If they fail to do their job, or do it in a less-than-satisfactory fashion, they can be fired. Otherwise, they expect to exercise the necessary degree of discretion they need to get the job done.

This kind of relationship may exist even if the head of the agency is also a professional by training. During World War II, for example, the American government brought together a group of atomic physicists to work on the development of the first atomic bomb. Gathered together in Los Alamos, New Mexico, they were part of the Manhattan Project headed by J. Robert Oppenheimer, a well-respected physicist. For the most part, Oppenheimer was able to get these world-renowned scientists to work together. But Edward Teller, a brilliant Hungarian-born scientist who would later be called the "father of the H-bomb," noted how his relationship with Oppenheimer reflected the kinds of problems that can emerge under a system of professional accountability.

> From the start he [Teller] felt betrayed by Oppenheimer. The goal-oriented discipline of the . . . [project] offended him, especially since its goal was not his. Oppenheimer's troops were obsessed with the uranium and plutonium bombs, which failed to challenge Teller sufficiently. . . .
> "It was a shock to work in a machine-like organization," he remembered later. "I refused. It was not my style." It was not his style, in short, to accept any boss.[48]

Of course, few public-sector professionals have the kind of egos that characterized Teller and the other brilliant scientists at Los Alamos. Nevertheless, many expect to exercise a great deal of freedom in doing their jobs, and they are just as willing to accept the responsibility that comes with it.

Political Accountability Systems

Responsiveness is the term most appropriate for describing political accountability systems. Here the relationship is similar to that between a representative (the public administrator) and his or her constituents (those to whom he or she is accountable). Under most circumstances in a democratic society, we expect a representative to be responsive to the needs and wishes of his or her constituents. That is the implication of adopting this system of accountability for public administrators. We expect administrators to reflect the interests of their constituents and be responsive to their demands and requirements.

Given this perspective, the primary question is, "Whom does the public administrator represent?" The list of individuals and groups that the administrator could represent is long, including those with specific roles in the hierarchy of political institutions, such as members of the legislature, the elected chief executive (president, governor, or mayor), and the head of the agency. It can also include groups and individuals outside the official hierarchy but nonetheless important, such as the leaders of the political party in power, the agency's clientele, the attentive public, some special interest group, and future generations. Each of these groups is a potential constituency for the public administrator under the political accountability system. Regardless of which is adopted, administrators operating under this system feel a need to be responsive to that group's policy priorities and programmatic needs.

The most explicit use of political accountability occurs in governments where administrators owe their positions to patronage appointments by elected officials. Perhaps the best-known example of a patronage system is that which existed in Chicago under Mayor Richard J. Daley (1955–1978). According to one account:

> By two o'clock . . . [Daley was] back behind his desk and working. One of his visitors will be a city official unique to Chicago city government: the director of patronage. He brings a list of all new city employees for the day. The list isn't limited to the key employees, the professional people. All new employees are there — down to the window washer, the ditch digger, the garbage collector. After each person's name will be an extract of his background, the job, and most important, his political sponsor. Nobody goes to work for the city, and that includes governmental bodies that are not directly under the mayor, without Daley's knowing about it. He must see every name because the person becomes more than an employee: he joins the political Machine, part of the army numbering in the thousands who will help win elections. They damn well better, or they won't keep their jobs.[49]

Less explicit is the political accountability that develops in agencies where the emphasis is on service to a specific clientele. We noted earlier the close relationship between the Department of Agriculture (DOA) and America's farmers. According to one observer, "more than any other federal agency, the DOA has been the major protagonist for farm interests."[50] Administrators at the Department of Labor, state Departments of Social and Rehabilitative Services, and county Health Departments are also likely to feel the same need for responsiveness to their relevant clientele groups.

While political accountability often seems to promote favoritism and even corruption in the administration of government programs, it may also serve as the basis for a more open and representative government. For example, in response to pressures exerted by consumer-oriented interest groups, the Federal Trade Commission (FTC) established an "openness policy" in 1974, which allowed the general public greater access to the work of that agency.[51]

TABLE 3.3   Relationships within the Accountability Systems

Type of Accountability System	Analogous Relationship (Controller/Administrator)	Basis of Relationship
Bureaucratic	Superior/Subordinate	Supervision
Legal	Lawmaker/law enforcer	Contract
Professional	Layperson/expert	Responsibility
Political	Constituent/representative	Responsiveness

Similar actions by other agencies at all levels of government are becoming commonplace. Statutes passed by federal and many state and local governments, such as legislation mandating open meetings, freedom of information, and "government in the sunshine," reflect a trend toward greater openness. Further, pressures exerted by the media and public interest groups have increased the openness of government. Even the agencies themselves have moved toward greater openness and citizen participation. Underlying all these efforts is the belief that a political accountability system is a legitimate means for managing the expectations that public administrators face.

Table 3.3 summarizes the relationships that characterize the four types of accountability systems outlined in this chapter. Each reflects a different approach to the management of the many expectations that affect public administrators, and each plays a role in the operations of American government at all levels. In bureaucratic accountability systems, expectations are managed through the development of supervisory relationships within a hierarchical structure. In legal accountability systems, the relationship is represented by a contractual agreement between lawmaker and law enforcer. Within professional accountability arrangements, the expert (public administrator) is supposed to act responsibly in his or her relationships with laypersons (elected officials, citizens). Finally, responsiveness is the central relationship in political accountability systems, where administrators act as responsive agents to the demands and needs of their constituents.

The Challenges of Public Administration

We began this chapter seeking to understand and appreciate public administration by focusing on the multitude of expectations that characterize this arena. In pursuing this objective, we discussed how the many responsibilities and ethical standards that characterize the operation of American government reflect those diverse expectations. Finally, we examined how accountability systems have emerged as a means for making these responsibilities and ethical standards more manageable.

Putting the lessons of this chapter together with those of Chapter 2, what can we conclude about the essence of American public administration? The conclusions we reach will obviously be complex. From those who have sought to define the field, we have learned that public administration is primarily (although not exclusively) an executive branch activity that focuses on bringing managerial rationality to the implementation of value-based public policies. From the century-old debate among students of public administration, we have learned about the dual themes of politics and administration that constantly shape and direct the work of the public sector. From administrators, critics of administrative reform, and economists, we have learned that there are differences between the private and public sectors that make public administration distinctive. Finally, we have learned the important role that responsibilities, ethics, and accountability play in the lives of public administrators. In short, we have a picture of public administrators as individuals who face the challenge of managing diverse expectations from a variety of groups within the political system.

Summary

1. The practice of public administration is influenced by a variety of expectations that range from the purposes of government agencies and the means and procedures they use to their level of performance.
2. Expectations of American public administrators frequently take the form of responsibilities emphasizing the obligations and commitments we demand of government employees.
3. Expectations also take the form of ethical standards that are intended to guide and assess the work of public administrators. As with responsibilities, ethical standards reflect a wide diversity of views on what public administration should accomplish.
4. The management of diverse expectations is central to the conduct of American public administration and is accomplished primarily through systems of accountability.
5. Accountability involves those methods and relationships that determine which expectations should be reflected in the work of public administrators. In the United States, four major accountability systems—bureaucratic, legal, professional, and political—have emerged to shape the practice of public administration.
6. At any point in time, an agency may find itself operating under more than one system of accountability, and administrators may find it necessary to shift among the systems as different expectations are thrust upon them. The ability to adapt to changing expectations is at the heart of American public administration.

Study Questions

1. To understand the role that expectations play in the work of public administrators, consider your own expectations for the people around you — your parents or spouse, your instructor, the college's registrar, yourself. Each of these individuals faces expectations from you and perhaps dozens of other persons each day. Choose one of these individuals or some other person with whom you have contact and list the expectations they face each day. Is your list short or long? Are all the expectations consistent? Are any contradictory?

2. Public administrators often face conflicting or contradictory expectations, in part because they must live up to many different types of responsibilities and ethical standards. Consider how you would react if faced with two clearly distinctive sets of responsibilities. What if you were a minor administrator in Nazi-occupied France or Holland who has been ordered to find and arrest a Jewish family and to put them on a train that you know will send them to certain death? What are your responsibilities? How would you deal with them?

3. There are four major systems of accountability in the United States. In many cases, public administrators are subject to all four, but usually only one is stressed within a specific agency. Which accountability system do you think is best suited for your college? For your local police department? The Marine Corps? The administrative office of the mayor?

4. Select some controversy about government administration that has been covered extensively in the media. Identify the different expectations that shaped the behavior of the public administrators involved in the controversy. Do you see evidence of accountability systems at work? Which one(s)?

5. Draft a code of ethics for faculty and students in a state-supported university. What accountability systems would be useful for enforcing the code?

Notes

1. See Alfred A. Marcus, *Promise and Performance: Choosing and Implementing an Environmental Policy* (Westport, CT: Greenwood Press, 1980); and Charles Schultze, *Public Use of the Private Interest* (Washington, DC: Brookings Institution, 1977).
2. Henry Kissinger, *Years of Upheaval* (Boston: Little, Brown, 1982), p. 119.
3. This lower level of expectations is associated with a confidence gap in government institutions. See Seymour Martin Lipset and William Schneider, *The Confidence Gap: Business, Labor, and Government in the Public Mind* (New York: The Free Press, 1983), pp. 61–66.

4. For an in-depth discussion of the concept of responsibility in government, see Herbert J. Spiro, *Responsibility in Government: Theory and Practice* (New York: Van Nostrand Reinhold, 1969).

5. Dwight Waldo, *The Enterprise of Public Administration: A Summary View* (Novato, CA: Chandler and Sharp, 1980), pp. 103–104. See also John A. Rohr, "The Study of Ethics in the P.A. Curriculum," *Public Administration Review* 36 (July/August 1976): 398–406; John A. Rohr, *To Run a Constitution: The Legitimacy of the Administrative State* (Lawrence: University Press of Kansas, 1986); and H. George Frederickson and David K. Hart, "The Public Service and the Patriotism of Benevolence," *Public Administration Review* 45 (September/October 1985): 547–53.

6. Quoted in Eugene Bardach and Robert A. Kagan, *Going by the Book: The Problem of Regulatory Unreasonableness* (Philadelphia: Temple University Press, 1982), p. 73.

7. Emmette S. Redford, *Democracy in the Administrative State* (New York: Oxford University Press, 1969), p. 6.

8. Ibid., pp. 197–204.

9. David Mathews, "The Public in Practice and Theory," *Public Administration Review* 44 (March 1984 [Special Issue]): 120–125.

10. For a general discussion on public-opinion polling and its limitations, see Herbert Asher, *Polling and the Public: What Every Citizen Should Know* (Washington, DC: CQ Press, 1988).

11. See Kenneth J. Meier, *Politics and the Bureaucracy: Policymaking in the Fourth Branch of Government*, 2d ed. (Monterey, CA: Brooks/Cole, 1987), pp. 55–58.

12. See Jonathan D. Salant, "Who Will Keep America's Aging Bridges from Falling Down?" *Governing* 1 (May 1988): 52–57.

13. Lipset and Schneider, *The Confidence Gap*, p. 254.

14. Richard N. Osborn, James G. Hunt, and Lawrence R. Jauch, *Organization Theory: An Integrated Approach* (New York: John Wiley & Sons, 1980), p. 46.

15. On the passage of the War on Poverty, see James L. Sundquist, *Politics and Policy: The Eisenhower, Kennedy, and Johnson Years* (Washington, DC: Brookings Institution, 1968), Chap. 4. On OEO programs, see Daniel P. Moynihan, *Maximim Feasible Misunderstanding: Community Action in the War on Poverty* (New York: The Free Press, 1970). On the inability of the OEO to undertake its mission, see Michael Harrington, *The New American Poverty* (New York: Penguin, 1984), pp. 20–22. On the relative success of War on Poverty programs, see John E. Schwartz, *America's Hidden Success: A Reassessment of Public Policy from Kennedy to Reagan*, rev. ed. (New York: W. W. Norton, 1988), esp. chap. 2.

16. See Frederic A. Bergerson, *The Army Gets an Air Force: Tactics of Insurgent Bureaucratic Politics* (Baltimore: Johns Hopkins University Press, 1980).

17. See the discussion of challenges to public organizations in Charles H. Levine, "Organizational Decline and Cutback Management," *Public Administration Review* 38 (July/August 1978): 318–319.

18. See Charles Perrow, *Organizational Analysis: A Sociological View* (Belmont, CA: Brooks/Cole, 1970), pp. 144–158; Talcott Parsons, *Societies: Evolutionary and Comparative Perspectives* (Englewood Cliffs, NJ: Prentice-Hall, 1966); and Osborn, Hunt, and Jauch, *Organization Theory*, pp. 39–40.

19. Frederick C. Mosher, *Democracy and the Public Service* (New York: Oxford University Press, 1968), chap. 4. Much of the following discussion on government professionalism draws heavily from this source.

20. See Jethro K. Lieberman, *The Litigious Society* (New York: Basic Books, 1981).

21. Studs Terkel, *Working* (New York: Avon Books, 1974), p. 449.

22. See Barbara J. Nelson, *Making an Issue of Child Abuse: Political Agenda Setting for Social Problems* (Chicago: University of Chicago Press, 1984), chap. 3.

23. See Barbara S. Romzek, "Work and Nonwork Commitments: The Search for Linkages," *Administration and Society* 17 (November 1985): 257–282.

24. See the various human needs theorists: Abraham Maslow, *Motivation and Personality*, 2d ed. (New York: Harper & Row, 1970); Clayton P. Alderfer, *Existence, Relatedness and Growth: Human Needs in Organizational Settings* (New York: The Free Press, 1972); Frederick Herzberg, *Work and the Nature of Man* (Cleveland: World Publishing, 1966); and David McClelland, *The Achieving Society* (Princeton, NJ: Van Nostrand Reinhold, 1961).

25. For an overview of the various theories on the behavior of individuals in public and other organizations, see Robert D. Denhardt, *Theories of Public Organization* (Monterey, CA: Brooks/Cole, 1984), esp. chap. 5.

26. Anthony Downs, *Inside Bureaucracy* (Boston: Little, Brown, 1967), pp. 83–84.

27. Ibid., p. 88.

28. See Waldo, *The Enterprise of Public Administration*, chap. 7.

29. See Frederickson and Hart, "The Public Service and the Patriotism of Benevolence," p. 551; and Louis C. Gawthrop, *Public Sector Management, Systems, and Ethics* (Bloomington: Indiana University Press, 1984), chap. 6.

30. For a different perspective, one that views ethics as the application of moral principles, see Dennis F. Thompson, "The Possibility of Administrative Ethics," *Public Administration Review* 45 (September/October 1985): 555–61. Waldo defines ethical behavior as "right behavior" that has been examined and reflected upon; see his *The Enterprise of Public Administration*, p. 99.

31. For an insightful and controversial analysis of the Nazi "administration" of the death camps, see Hannah Arendt, *Eichmann in Jerusalem: A Report on the Banality of Evil*, rev. ed. (New York: Penguin, 1964).

32. See George W. Downs and Patrick D. Larkey, *The Search for Government Efficiency: From Hubris to Helplessness* (New York: Random House, 1986); and Robert C. Fried, *Performance in American Bureaucracy* (Boston: Little, Brown, 1976), pp. 67–70.

33. For a defense of efficiency as an ethical principle, see Robert E. Goodin and Peter Wilenski, "Beyond Efficiency: The Logical Underpinnings of Administrative Principles," *Public Administration Review* 44 (November/December 1984): 512–17.

34. See Fried, *Performance in American Bureaucracy*, pp. 55–76.

35. See Henry M. Levin, *Cost-Effectiveness: A Primer* (Beverly Hills, CA: Sage, 1983).

36. On the concept of responsiveness in government, see Richard Claude, "The Supreme Court Nine: Judicial Responsibility and Responsiveness," in *People vs. Government: The Responsiveness of American Institutions*, ed. by Leroy N. Rieselbach (Bloomington: Indiana University Press, 1975), p. 131; and Fried, *Performance in American Bureaucracy*, pp. 48–55.

37. See Nicholas Henry, *Public Administration and Public Affairs*, 3d ed. (Englewood Cliffs, NJ: Prentice-Hall, 1986), p. 350.

38. Arthur M. Okun, *Equality and Efficiency: The Big Tradeoff* (Washington, DC: Brookings Institution, 1975), p. 3.

39. John Rawls, *A Theory of Justice* (Cambridge, MA: Belknap Press, 1971), esp. pp. 11–17.

40. See Robert B. Denhardt and John Nalbandian, "Teaching Public Administration as a Vocation: A Calling for Theorists," *Southern Review of Public Administration* 6 (Summer 1982): 151–162.

41. On accountability as control systems, see James W. Fesler, *Public Administration: Theory and Practice* (Englewood Cliffs, NJ: Prentice-Hall, 1980), pp. 312–318; and Douglas Yates, *Bureaucratic Democracy: The Search for Democracy and Efficiency in American Government* (Cambridge, MA: Harvard University Press, 1982), chap. 6. On the role of accountability in democracy, see Michael Lipsky, *Street-Level Bureaucracy: Dilemmas of the Individual in Public Services* (New York: Russell Sage, 1980), p. 160.

42. See Barbara S. Romzek and Melvin J. Dubnick, "Accountability in the Public Sector: Lessons from the Challenger Tragedy," *Public Administration Review* 47 (May/June 1987): 227–238. Among extant definitions of accountability, this one comes closest to the approach used in Herbert A. Simon, Donald W. Smithburg, and Victor A. Thompson, *Public Administration* (New York: Alfred A. Knopf, 1950), pp. 513–14.

43. On control in organizations, see Philip M. Marcus and Dora Marcus, "Control in Modern Organizations," *Public Administration Review* 25 (June 1965): 121–27.

44. For a brief history of bureaucratic accountability, see Spiro, *Responsibility in Government*, pp. 84–89. For a defense of bureaucratic accountability systems, see Victor A. Thompson, *Without Sympathy or Enthusiasm: The Problem of Administrative Compassion* (University, AL: University of Alabama Press, 1975); in contrast, see Frederick C. Thayer, *An End to Hierarchy and Competition: Administration in the Post-Affluent World*, 2d ed. (New York: Franklin Watts, 1981).

45. See Alvin W. Gouldner, *Patterns of Industrial Bureaucracy* (New York: The Free Press, 1954), chap. 9.

46. See Barry M. Mitnick, *The Political Economy of Regulation: Creating, Designing, and Removing Regulatory Forms* (New York: Columbia University Press, 1980).

47. Most discussions on oversight methods focus on legislative controls. See, for example, Fesler, *Public Administration*, chap. 10; Lawrence C. Dodd and Richard L. Schott, *Congress and the Administrative State* (New York: John Wiley & Sons, 1979), chaps. 6–7; James Hamilton, *The Power to Probe: A Study of Congressional Investigations* (New York: Random House, 1976); and Mathew D. McCubbins and Thomas Schwartz, "Congressional Oversight Overlooked: Police Patrols versus Fire Alarms," *American Journal of Political Science* 28 (February 1984): 165–79.

48. Peter Wyden, *Day One: Before Hiroshima and After* (New York: Warner Books, 1985), p. 101.

49. Mike Royko, *Boss: Mayor Richard J. Daley of Chicago* (New York: E. P. Dutton, 1971), p. 17.

50. Wesley McCune, quoted in Peter Navarro, *The Policy Game: How Special Interests and Ideologues Are Stealing America* (New York: John Wiley & Sons, 1984), p. 115.

51. Robert A. Katzmann, *Regulatory Bureaucracy: The Federal Trade Commission and Antitrust Policy* (Cambridge, MA: MIT Press, 1980), pp. 161–64.

PART II

THE SOURCES OF

EXPECTATIONS

Our search for the nature of American public administration in Part I took us down a number of different paths through which we explored various perspectives. In the balance of this book, we hold that the essence of public administration rests in attempts to manage and respond to the expectations generated for the public sector. It is crucial, then, that we understand the *sources* of those expectations.

In Chapter 4, "The Ecology of Public Administration," we begin with a discussion of the general environment of public administration and its different dimensions. Chapter 5, "Physical and Technological Ecology," emphasizes how these parts of the environment pose problems and offers some solutions. In Chapter 6, "Demographic, Cultural, and Economic Factors," our focus turns to the influence of social settings, value systems, and economic conditions on the work of government administrators.

The next two chapters consider the influence of America's political system on public administration. Chapter 7, "Governmental Institutions," considers the impact of government's basic structures on public administration, while Chapter 8, "The Policy-making Ecology," considers the influence of the dynamic processes and interactions that create public policies. Finally, in Chapter 9, "The Personal Dimension," we describe some of the personal factors that help to shape the activities of American public administrators.

Taken together, the chapters in Part II show how various ecological factors have both direct and indirect effects on the challenges facing public administration. In short, public administrators encounter those indirect effects in the expectations generated by the ecological factors.

THE ECOLOGY

OF PUBLIC

ADMINISTRATION

The Concept of Ecology

Effects of Ecology

It is not easy to understand or appreciate public administration out of its context. Public administration is not some solid object with impermeable boundaries that exists in isolation from its surroundings. Rather, it is a set of dynamic social interactions and relationships undertaken in pursuit of publicly defined values. These values manifest themselves in the variety of expectations discussed in Chapter 3. If we accept this view, then knowledge about the environment of American public administration is necessary to an understanding of the field. In this chapter, we begin our exploration by considering how the surroundings of public administration influence how governments operate.

Public administration encounters two kinds of effects from its ecology: (1) *direct* and (2) *indirect*. The first kind occurs as public administrators directly confront the ecology. The second type occurs when public administrators contend with the indirect impact of the ecology on expectations for government action. (See Figure 4.1) For example, the state government of Colorado faces demands for highways and rapid communication suitable for a mountainous terrain. Its terrain also generates indirect effects, such as residents' expectations for reasonably passable roads. These expectations become the benchmarks for the public administrators responsible for the state's road maintenance.

To the extent that such direct and indirect effects motivate and shape the work of government officials, then American public administration is a creation of its surroundings. This is not to say that what goes on within public agencies is unimportant, but that internal agency activities are also significantly influenced by external factors. Further, by "surroundings" we

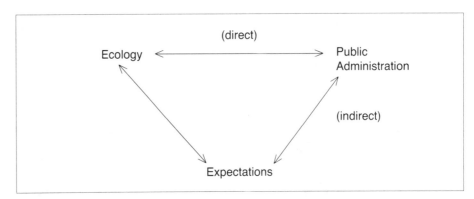

FIGURE 4.1   The direct and indirect effects of ecology on public administration.

mean the environment of public administration. The term *environment* conveys a broad range of factors surrounding American public administration. In fact, by definition it is a residual concept; that is, it includes everything that is not directly part of American public administration.

In a complex world of growing interdependencies, we are increasingly aware of just how interrelated people, places, and events have become. What happens today in Moscow, the Persian Gulf, Manila, Prague, or Managua can have considerable impact on our lives tomorrow morning or next week or next year. Yet the concept of environment is often too inclusive to be of any real help in the study of American public administration. There are certain parts of the environment that are more relevant to the work of public administrators than others. For this reason, we focus our attention on a narrower concept—the *ecology* of public administration, that portion of the general environment with which government's administrative systems are "inextricably intertwined."[1]

John Gaus was the first to apply the concept of ecology to public administration. Writing in the 1940s, Gaus argued that public administration is built

> quite literally from the ground up, from the elements of place—soils, climate, location, for example—to the people who live there—their numbers and ages and knowledge and ways of physical and social technology by which from the place and in relationships with one another, they get their living. It is within this setting that their instruments and practices of public housekeeping should be studied so that they may better understand what they are doing, and appraise reasonably how they are doing it.[2]

Gaus's view of American public administration, called the *ecological perspective*, has given many students insight into the functioning of the public sector. For our purposes, there are eight important dimensions of the ecology of public administration (see Figure 4.2). At the center of our model is public administration as it is practiced in the United States. Surrounding the core subject is its ecology, represented by eight concentric circles reflecting its (1) physical, (2) technological, (3) demographic, (4) cultural, (5) economic, (6) governmental, (7) policy making, and (8) personal dimensions. Each of these ecological dimensions is a major source of the challenges and expectations that drive American public administration today.

Physical Ecology

At the outer edges of our model are those features of the *physical* environment that are most relevant to American public administration. Gaus wrote of this in terms of "the elements of place," referring to factors like geographic region, climate, soil conditions and topography. In addition, we can include human-made settings such as the workplace, the location of a school, and the site of a military encampment. In the private sector, we use the term

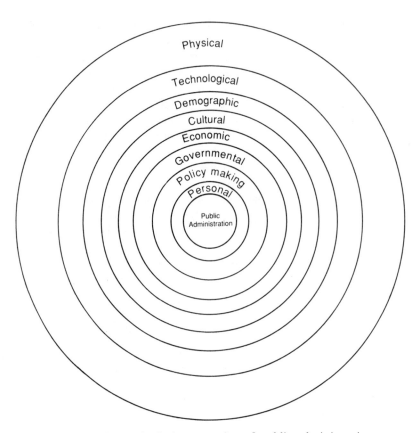

FIGURE 4.2   The ecological perspective of public administration.

plant to describe the physical features of a business setting or factory created to produce the company's goods or services.[3]

Of course, physical settings themselves cannot articulate or communicate expectations. Rather, it is the influence of the physical ecology on human behavior and social conditions that generate different expectations of governments. The physical environment also has an impact by setting limits on how public administrators can respond to various expectations. The story of County Agent Eugene Eckrote in Chapter 3 (see Profile 3.1) illustrates this—Eckrote responded to pleas that he do something about the drought by noting that he "couldn't make it rain."

Whether it includes the "elements of place" or human-made settings, the physical portion of the public administrator's ecology too often is taken for granted. For some government agencies, the physical environment is extremely important. And while the environment is less important for others, we must still be aware of its actual and potential impact on the work of public administrators. (We examine the physical aspect of the ecology more closely in Chapter 5.)

Technological Ecology

Also important is the impact of *technological* factors on public administration. Technological ecology includes the means and methods we use in our daily lives. Both physical and social technologies have been a mixed blessing for American public administration. On the one hand, technological growth has created major problems and challenges for America's bureaucracies. On the other hand, technological advances have made it easier in some ways for public administrators to meet those challenges.

However, there is little doubt that technological factors significantly influence the quality and quantity of expectations facing public administrators. As technology advances, so do expectations that government develop new and more effective solutions to old public problems. In contrast, there are expectations that government not use its current or potential technological capabilities to abuse the public trust. Thus, while government may be quite capable of monitoring our daily mail and conversations, we expect it not to misuse this power. (Technological ecology is discussed further in Chapter 6.)

Demographic and Cultural Ecology

Demographic and *cultural* factors also affect public administration. First and foremost, public administration is a social activity. It involves people working together to carry out a set of tasks or to accomplish some goals. It is also a social activity in terms of the challenges it faces as a result of serving an extremely diverse population. The size, composition, and distribution—the demographics—of the American people are key factors shaping public administration. The structure and dynamics of American population changes and movements affects the work of government.

In addition, cultural factors influence the work of public administrators. We are especially interested in the impact of values on the operations of government. Governments usually reflect the values of their people—what they desire, the kinds of behavior they are willing to accept, and the types of actions they are unwilling to sanction. Our understanding of American public administration is enhanced by examining American values.

How do demographic and cultural factors influence the challenges and expectations facing government? Shifts in demographic patterns and values have been as frequent in the past century as in any other time in history. As populations change, so do the quantity and quality of services demanded of government. Similarly, as cultural priorities change, so do the public's views of what government does. (Demographic and cultural ecology are examined more closely in Chapter 6.)

Economic Ecology

Important as well is the relationship between *economic conditions* and the work of public administration. Like most Americans, government officials concern themselves with questions about resource availability. Operating government agencies during times of affluence is quite different than operating under periods of economic recession or stagnation.

The effect of economic conditions for public administrators, like those of the physical environment, is not always direct. Public administrators feel these impacts through the changing expectations of people who feel the influence of shifting economic circumstances. (Chapter 6 discusses economic ecology in further detail.)

Governmental Ecology and Policy Making

The *governmental* ecology of public administration includes those constitutional and legal institutions with which public administrators interact on a regular basis. In this part of the ecology, there are two major types of relevant governmental institutions: (1) *intragovernmental institutions*, which are found within the same legal jurisdiction as the public administrator's agency, and (2) *intergovernmental institutions*, which are outside of the public administrator's immediate jurisdiction. Both types of governmental institutions help to shape and direct the work of American public administration. (Governmental ecology is the focus of Chapter 7).

Similarly, the *policy-making* ecology of American public administration is also influential. More administrators today are playing a greater role in the policy-making process, and that process involves more than government officials. The immediate policy-making environment of public administration includes all the actors, relationships, and procedures central to American politics. In our examination of the policy-making ecology in Chapter 8, we focus on three key factors: (1) the organization of the policy arena within which policy-making takes place, (2) the stages in the policy-making process, and (3) the types of policy actions and issues being considered.

The policy-making processes of American government are, of course, directly linked to the rules and procedures of our governmental institutions. These institutions are built on long-standing expectations regarding how government should operate in both legal and policy-making terms.

The Personal Dimension

Finally, we focus attention on the *personal* dimension — the lives, attitudes, and aspirations of those who work for public agencies. Individual employees bring with them various needs and values, which they seek to pursue as they also fulfill their responsibilities as public employees. These personal factors can influence the challenges and expectations that public agencies and administrators must face. Public employees' expectations about wages or retirement benefits, for example, can affect an agency's labor expenses. Personal factors also can influence the reactions of the agencies and administrators to the wide range of expectations they face. In one sense, the personal dimension of public administration acts as a filter through which the expectations generated by other dimensions of the environment pass. (Personal factors are examined in detail in Chapter 9.)

The Challenge of the Ecology

Our environment is largely what we make of it, both physically and mentally. Physically, anyone who has walked along the banks of a polluted river or driven in the brownish-green air that hangs over the cities of Denver, Birmingham, and Phoenix realizes how much damage we can do to our most precious natural resources. Yet as human beings we know that we cannot remain completely oblivious to what is taking place in our physical surroundings. When the stench is too strong to ignore, when our eyes begin to tear as we sit in a city's traffic gridlock, when we can wipe dust particles from our front-porch railings, then we are able to understand the impact of our actions on the environment.

Our environment is also in part a creation of our minds—that is, what we make of it mentally. There are so many things occurring around us that if we attempted to be aware of all this physical and social activity, the result would be sensory overload and mental exhaustion. For this reason, we have developed the ability to be selective in how we perceive and deal with our surroundings.

Since we are surrounded by a multitude of situations, issues, and problems, we tend to pick and choose among them. Thus, there are some parts of our environment we choose to ignore, perhaps because we really don't see them or because we've concluded they're too insignificant to warrant our attention. There are other parts of the environment that we perceive as hostile, and in response to this we may choose to fight, flee, or surrender.

In contrast, for circumstances regarded as helpful or friendly, we are more likely to adapt short-term strategies that take advantage of the situation. Similarly, we adapt long-term strategies to make full use of predictable trends. Finally, we focus attention on those parts of our environment that we can control and alter.

Thus, how we act toward our surroundings depends to a great extent on how we perceive them (see Figure 4.3). As a human endeavor, public administration deals with its surroundings in a similar way. Depending on how they perceive the environment, public administrators may choose to ignore, resist, adapt to, use, or alter their surroundings. To illustrate these points, the remainder of this chapter looks at several examples.

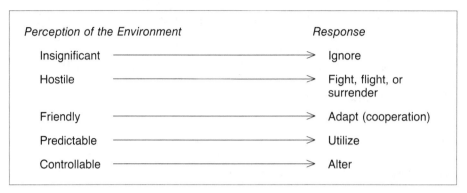

FIGURE 4.3   Responses to environmental perceptions.

The *Challenger*: The Price of Indifference

On January 28, 1986, the National Aeronautics and Space Administration (NASA) launched the space shuttle *Challenger* from Kennedy Space Center in Florida. Shortly after liftoff from the launch pad, the booster rocket assembly exploded, resulting in the deaths of seven astronauts. Extensive investigations conducted by both NASA and the specially appointed Presidential Commission on the Space Shuttle *Challenger* Accident (also known as the Rogers Commission) pointed to a technical flaw in the design of an O-ring seal used for joints in the booster rocket. NASA and its subcontractor, Morton Thiokol, had known for years about the limitations of the design seal. Yet, because NASA had successfully launched several space shuttles with the same type of seal in the booster rockets, the agency decided that the problem was not significant enough to warrant further attention before launch. In the months immediately preceding the January 1986 launch, the agency had consented to removing the O-ring problem from a list of critical problems needing resolution.[4]

On the issue of the rocket-seal design, NASA acted as though its environment was insignificant to the agency's success in the January 28 mission. That is, NASA acted as though it could ignore design flaws of the O-rings without affecting the outcome of that particular launch. The reality of the situation was that the environment was potentially hostile. When the O-ring seal failed on that cold January morning, the rocket exploded and resulted in the space shuttle's plunging to the ocean.

The *Challenger* accident illustrates an important point about how public agencies and public administrators can be wrong in their perceptions of their environment. In the case of NASA, it was wrong in its perception of the O-ring problem as insignificant, and therefore, something it could ignore. When administrators wrongly perceive the environment, there is potential for serious failure. In the instance of the space shuttle *Challenger*, the failure resulted in the deaths of seven people.

McCarthy and the Army: Facing Hostility

During the late 1940s and early 1950s, a number of congressional committees and subcommittees investigated the loyalty of government employees, especially those working in the U.S. State and Defense Departments. One of the most prominent congressional investigators was Senator Joseph McCarthy, a Wisconsin Republican who headed the Investigations Subcommittee of the Senate Government Operations Committee. During 1953 and 1954, McCarthy and his top aide, Roy Cohn, turned their attention to senior officers in the U.S. Army who, they implied, were guilty of disloyalty at worst and incompetence at best.

At the outset, Secretary of the Army Robert T. Stevens cooperated with McCarthy and his staff, hoping to appease the senator and thus avoid a major confrontation that might do more damage to an already demoralized military. McCarthy, however, took advantage of this appeasement approach and held more hearings and dug deeper into the army's files. As a result, both army officials and the Eisenhower administration decided to adopt a more defensive strategy. They charged Roy Cohn with trying to get preferential treatment for an enlisted serviceman who once served on the Investigations Subcommittee staff. When McCarthy sought to look into the source of this charge, President Eisenhower issued a directive to the Defense Department forbidding employees of the army from testifying about any aspects of the Pentagon's decision-making procedures.[5] It was a fighting response to the hostile environment created by McCarthy, and it eventually won the day for the army and administration officials.

Friends of the TVA: Adapting through Co-optation

The passage of the Tennessee Valley Authority Act in 1933 marked a major event in the development of American public administration. It established a relatively new type of federal agency, the autonomous public-sector corporation. The Tennessee Valley Authority (TVA) was a unique organization for its time. In the words of President Franklin Roosevelt, the TVA was a government agency "clothed with the power of government but possessed of the flexibility and initiative of private enterprise."

The TVA stood out among federal agencies in two important respects. First, it remained outside of and unconstrained by executive departments, Washington's civil-service laws, budget offices, and the General Service Administration (the government's "landlord" and chief source of supplies from paper clips to entire buildings). The TVA was unique as well in that when first established it tended to generate more opposition than support among state and local officials as well as the area's farmers.

A three-member board governed the TVA. The first chairman of that board, Arthur E. Morgan, came into office ready to implement a broadly defined mission to develop the Tennessee Valley socially and economically in spite of any opposition from local interests. During the first three months in office, Morgan alienated many people in the region as well as his co-directors, Harcourt A. Morgan and David Lilienthal, and others working for the agency. From the beginning, A. E. Morgan viewed the opposition from local interests as hostile and threatening and treated them accordingly.

TVA's other directors took a more positive view of local interests. Together H.A. Morgan and Lilienthal eventually established the agency's goals in terms of grass-roots democracy as well as development. By outvoting A. E. Morgan on key issues, they made one of the agency's central missions the cultivation of good relations with local groups. The strategy used to accomplish this goal was to involve local groups in agency decision making as much as possible. These codirectors believed that whatever opposition existed was superficial at best. TVA officials hoped that if they included state and local officials and local farmers in the policy making and operations of the agency, then the TVA would gain their confidence, cooperation, and support.[6]

In the early 1940s, A. E. Morgan was removed from the agency and the success of the TVA's grass-roots approach was evident. The key to this success was a strategy called *co-optation*, in which parts of the environment that might otherwise prove unfriendly are made participants in the policy-making system. The TVA worked with state land-grant colleges and local chapters of the powerful American Farm Bureau Federation to sponsor local cooperatives and municipal improvement projects. In addition, the agency entered into numerous contractual arrangements with local schools, municipal power cooperatives, planning commissions, and similar bodies. The grass-roots approach was a victory for those who felt a federal program could adapt to and work with local people.

However, in gaining co-optative support, the TVA soon became identified with the interests of local power structures and governments. It had adapted itself to the local situation and in the process made itself part of that locality and its dominant interest groups. For many of the TVA's programs, the agency's interests became those of the clientele groups it was serving. This situation continued until the late 1960s, when it became evident that the TVA was losing touch with the very same grass roots it fought so hard to cultivate thirty years earlier.

Predicted Trends: Demographics and Education

During the 1970s and early 1980s, information on population trends had a significant impact on the behavior of public agencies. Looking toward the future, analysts at the Social Security Administration (SSA) became increasingly concerned about the nation's ability to meet its old-age and disability pension needs in the early twenty-first century (see Insight 4.1). Similarly, public school districts and state-supported institutions of higher education

INSIGHT 4.1
MULTIPLE FUTURES FOR SOCIAL SECURITY

Government agencies like the Social Security Administration (SSA) must consider their future needs in addition to their current operations. The bulk of Social Security outlays go for old-age and survivor's benefits. Following the practice of the private-sector insurance industry, the SSA uses demographic projections and actuarial statistics to predict many of its future needs. However, unlike the private insurance industry, the SSA must also rely on projections about specific economic conditions. For example, since some Social Security program benefits are tied to cost-of-living estimates, predictions about future inflation rates are very important. Furthermore, since many programs are funded through payroll taxes, projections about unemployment and wage-growth patterns are also extremely significant.

None of these important variables can be predicted with any great certainty, however. As economists testify, it is difficult enough to forecast next month's unemployment rate or next year's inflation rate. The SSA simply cannot predict with any degree of certainty the inflation rate in the year 2010 or the wage growth by the year 2050. But these difficulties do not stop the SSA from looking into the future. What it does to compensate for the uncertainty of the future is develop several different forecasts, each based on a distinct set of assumptions about future economic conditions. In 1982, for example, the SSA worked up four alternative future scenarios. One was optimistic and saw a low-inflation, high-growth economy continuing into the twenty-first century. Another scenario

was only mildly optimistic about future economic conditions, while the remaining two projected pessimistic and very pessimistic conditions, respectively.

The SSA's projections are not merely for the agency's internal use. The White House and Congress depend on the forecasts for determining whether Social Security programs need to be modified. This has been the case since the Social Security system was modified in 1972, when increases in benefits were indexed (made automatic) to reflect inflation increases. This posed a challenge for SSA actuaries, for they had to decide which set of projections to forward to Congress and the White House. "Because the system was now on automatic pilot," notes Paul Light, "[the SSA actuaries were expected] to pinpoint any coming crisis. Then they would have to tell Congress and the president what to do." Realizing the degree of uncertainty they faced, the actuaries at the SSA were not willing to put forward only one projection.

In 1983, a critical year for reassessing the future of Social Security, the SSA sent all four projections to Capitol Hill. The choice of which scenario of the future to believe was left to the White House and Congress. What resulted was that Congress, the White House, and others spent much of that year engaged in what Light terms "the politics of assumptions"— arguing over program reforms based on the equally possible alternative scenarios developed by the SSA.

SOURCE: Based on information in Paul Light, *Artful Work: Politics of Social Security Reform* (New York: Random House, 1985), chap. 5.

looked at projections of dwindling numbers of children and wondered how they would sustain their levels of service.

Demographic patterns make it possible for public educational institutions to develop effective long-term strategies for dealing with predicted population shifts. In some public school districts, for example, a number of elementary schools were closed and their personnel dismissed or transferred. Some public universities have sought changes in the formula used for state funding of higher education so that the projected loss in student enrollments will not have a significant negative impact on the quality of education. During the postwar baby boom of the 1960s and 1970s, when each fall term brought a greater number of students to campus, public-supported colleges and universities argued for a formula based on a given ratio of faculty or operating funds to the number of full-time equivalent students enrolled at the school. Thus, as the baby boomers came to campus in record numbers, the financing of state universities and colleges increased. As population figures indicated a sharp downturn in student enrollments during the 1980s, higher education officials went before their governing boards and legislatures to argue for a change in the formula—one that would protect them from losing any current funding or at least place a floor on funding under which the state would not go. In some states this approach succeeded, and in some it failed.

The approach succeeded in one midwestern state. A funding formula was created in one state that allowed allocations to remain unchanged over a three-year period unless the number of students enrolled increased or decreased significantly during that time. At one of that state's two major universities, a large drop in student enrollment in the mid-1980s led to a funding decrease of more than $1.25 million. At another university, however, consistent increases in student enrollment did not result in increases in funding because the increases were not significant. Such are the risks of basing one's actions on so-called predictable environments.

Control: The "Good Old Days" at the CAB

On September 30, 1985, the Civil Aeronautics Board (CAB) permanently closed the doors to its Washington headquarters. The CAB was created in the late 1930s by Congress to help promote and regulate the growing passenger airline industry. Its termination was part of a seven-year process, beginning in 1978 with the passage of the Airline Deregulation Act.

For most of the years between its birth and death, however, the CAB was in control of interstate airline operations—that is, air travel that occurs across state lines. With the exception of companies that specialized in air travel within large states like Texas and California, the CAB determined how the nation's major airlines and regional carriers competed against each other. Since an airline needed to have a CAB certificate to conduct interstate passenger service between any two points, the agency was in full control. It certified only those lines found "fit, willing, and able" to provide interstate service. Rights to serve a particular route or market were given only where the added service would not harm the airlines currently offering service on the same route.

Just how much in control was the CAB? Consider the agency's commitment to having only the most modern equipment to service air travelers in the United States. Those working at the CAB during the 1950s believed that the agency's mission of promoting the airline industry meant making flying as desirable as possible. That was the setting when, in 1955, Alaska Airlines asked the CAB for permission to charge a lower fare than Pan American for similar flights because it used DC-4s instead of the newer and more costly DC-6Bs used by its competitor. Alaska Airlines argued that because it was using older and less costly equipment, it could afford to charge a lower fare to passengers willing to accept DC-4 service. The CAB turned down the airline's request for lower fares because it believed that to do otherwise would only lower the incentive for airlines to operate the most modern equipment. The constant modernization of airline fleets during the 1950s and 1960s was a result of the CAB's capacity during that period to alter the competitive conditions of the airline industry.

The CAB was so much in control that it was able to increase or decrease competition among the airlines almost at will. During the 1950s and 1960s, the CAB kept pricing competition low by restricting new airline entry into the interstate air passenger market and by minimizing the number of airlines permitted to fly given routes. During the middle 1970s, however, the CAB decided there wasn't enough competition among the airlines. The agency started to loosen its restrictions on price competition as well as open up access to popular routes. By the time the Airline Deregulation Act passed in 1978, the CAB had brought about major changes in the airline industry.[7]

Perceptions and Responses

Each of the preceding case studies illustrates how different perceptions of environmental conditions tend to generate certain types of responses among public administrators. In the case of the *Challenger* disaster, would the seven astronauts be alive today if NASA administrators had paid more attention to the conditions of the space shuttle's O-rings? How much longer would the McCarthy era have gone on if the army and President Eisenhower had not decided to fight his tactics? Would the TVA have survived very long if it had not adopted a co-optation strategy in dealing with the people of the Tennessee Valley? What would have been the effect on public higher education if universities had ignored the demographic patterns of the 1980s? And how much better or worse would air travel in the United States be today if the CAB had not controlled effectively the airline industry? How much better or worse is air travel today in the absence of CAB control?

It is not just the nature of the direct effects of ecological conditions that can affect the jobs of public administrators; the indirect effects of those administrators' perceptions of their environment can also influence how they perform their jobs. Central to those perceptions are the expectations for government action generated by the environment. The expectations of administrators facing hostile environments are bound to differ from those who perceive their surroundings as friendly.

Summary

1. Public administration is best understood in terms of the different dimensions characterizing its surroundings. These dimensions help to shape the expectations and work of public administrators.
2. The ecology of public administration is that part of the general environment with which government's administrative systems are intertwined.
3. The ecology has many dimensions, including the physical, technological, demographic, cultural, economic, governmental, policy making, and personal.
4. The challenge of the environment varies, as does the public administrator's approach to each challenge.

Study Questions

1. Using the definition of *ecology* given in this chapter, describe the most important features of your environment. How are they similar to or different from the factors discussed in this chapter?
2. In your daily reading of the newspaper, you are certain to come across stories about how government actions are influenced by the type of ecology defined in this chapter. Select two stories from today's newspaper as examples, and then determine which of the ecological dimensions is relevant to the public administration activities being described. Explain your choices.

Notes

1. See Richard J. Stillman, II, *Public Administration: Concepts and Cases*, 3d ed. (Boston: Houghton Mifflin, 1984), pp. 74–76. For a brief overview of the ecological perspective of public administration, see Ivan L. Richardson and Sidney

Baldwin, *Public Administration: Government in Action* (Columbus, OH: Merrill, 1976), pp. 23–26.

2. See John Gaus, *Reflections on Public Administration* (University, AL: University of Alabama Press, 1947). p. 1.

3. See Chester I. Barnard, *The Functions of the Executive* (Cambridge, MA: Harvard University Press, 1938/1968), pp. 66–67.

4. Rogers Commission, *Report of the Presidential Commission on the Space Shuttle Challenger Accident* (Washington, DC, Government Printing Office, June 6, 1986).

5. See James Hamilton, *The Power to Probe: A Study of Congressional Investigations* (New York: Random House, 1976), pp. 167–69.

6. On the story of the TVA, see Philip Selznick, *TVA and the Grass Roots: A Study of Politics and Organization* (Berkeley: University of California Press, 1949/1984); William U. Chandler, *The Myth of TVA: Conservation and Development in the Tennessee Valley, 1933–1983* (Cambridge, MA: Ballinger, 1984); and Annmarie Hauk Walsh, *The Public's Business: The Politics and Practices of Government Corporations* (Cambridge, MA: MIT Press, 1978), pp. 45–47.

7. See Alfred E. Kahn, *The Economics of Regulation*, Vol. 2, *Principles and Institutions* (New York: John Wiley, 1971), pp. 209–20.

PHYSICAL AND

TECHNOLOGICAL

ECOLOGY

Reactions and Expectations

The image of public administrators as desk-bound clerks who spend most of their time creating red tape and pushing paper from stack to stack is a popular but false view of what the public service is all about. Public administrators, whether out in the field or in an office, contend with the problems and challenges of America's diverse physical environment. They also must contend with the rapid changes occurring in America's technological infrastructure. The physical ecology directly affects the job challenges that public administrators face and indirectly affects the expectations that we have of them.

How do the physical and technological elements of the ecology affect our expectations of public administrators? Consider the way that elements of the physical environment such as climate and weather shape the expectations you have of your state highway department. If you live in a state that experiences harsh winters, you expect the state highway agency to have the appropriate snow-removal equipment to deal with snowstorms in your region. If you live in a state like Florida, however, you would have no such expectations. Further, it would be difficult for citizens of a snowbound state to forgive the highway department administrator who failed to maintain snow-removal equipment in top-notch condition. At the same time, it would be hard to feel the same way about a Florida highway department official who had not prepared for an unusual quarter-inch snowfall that might hit the northern area once every decade or so.

Technology also influences our expectations of government. For example, the existence of new technologies that can improve air-traffic safety or crime detection is often enough to lead to public calls for their adoption by the relevant government agencies. In contrast, the fact that government agencies possess technologies that can be abused (e.g., wiretapping) can lead to expectations that public officials establish rules and procedures to protect the general population from their misuse.

As we will see in this chapter, the relationships between public administration and the physical and technological dimensions of the environment are complicated. Physical ecologies tend to vary from place to place and technological ecologies tend to change over time. The physical and technological environments do not generate expectations; rather, the people who feel the daily influence of whatever occurs in these environments generate expectations for administrators. Different people react differently in the face of similar physical conditions or when dealing with a particular technology. How these differing reactions translate into expectations of government is the central issue addressed in this chapter.

The Physical Setting

Physical surroundings are obviously more important to some public administrators than to others. Weather conditions, for instance, are relatively unimportant to the job of civil servants who process disability claims at the Social Security Administration. The fact that it may be raining outside their Baltimore office may affect how administrators dress for work, but in most cases that is all; weather is not likely to influence the nature of their job tasks. Atmospheric conditions, however, are extremely important to meteorologists at the Severe Storms Forecast Center, who constantly monitor changing weather patterns. Because their agency tasks involve monitoring and forecasting changes in the weather, the weather is more than just something for them to talk about over coffee in their Kansas City offices.

The job of the forest ranger is an interesting but difficult one. Among other duties, a forest ranger is responsible for preventing, detecting, and, when necessary, fighting forest fires. The Forest Service provides its rangers with training and equipment for accomplishing these tasks. But when it comes time to act, it is the individual ranger who deals with the situation at his or her specific location. Forest rangers in the western part of the United States face different conditions than their colleagues in the East. The physical setting of their jobs has a significant impact on how they carry out their assigned tasks. Location does make a difference, especially when the rangers are attempting to coordinate the fighting of major forest fires:

> The men on the fire lines must be fed and sheltered. It is up to the Rangers to see that they are. East of the Mississippi, this may mean nothing more than bringing coffee and sandwiches to them; the men designated by the Rangers as fire dispatchers . . . handle this, placing orders with local storekeepers and restaurants with whom prior arrangements have been made. As crews are relieved, they return to their homes for rest, and reassemble if the fire is still not under control when their next tour of duty comes around. In the West, where distances are too great and fire fighters too scattered to permit such a mode of operations, fire camps are set up. In such cases, merchants and food suppliers are furnished with lists of provisions in advance, and they simply put the packages together and turn them over to truckers for delivery to the camps, where they are cooked and served camp style. Equipment—tents, blankets, field kitchens, and the rest—must be on hand for hurried establishment of the camps.[1]

The physical ecology affects the jobs of many other American public administrators as well. The city manager of Butte, Montana, is no doubt going to face a different situation this winter from the one the city administrator in Tampa, Florida, will face. Similarly, a supply officer at a naval station in Hawaii must meet different demands from those of the air force supply officer located on a base in Alaska. In each case, the climate, weather, and terrain of their physical locations affects the nature of the challenges they face as administrators and how they carry out their respective jobs. Physical surroundings can and do make a difference!

Several characteristics of the physical ecology are especially important to the work of many public administrators. These include (1) spatial factors; (2) terrain, topography, and geological features; (3) climate and weather conditions; (4) the physical dimensions of our human-made surroundings; and (5) natural and human-made disasters.

Spatial Factors

Physical distance and space make a difference to public administrators. We have already seen how these factors influence the job of the forest ranger. National forests in the eastern United States are relatively small and usually located near populated areas. Consequently, firefighting personnel and supplies are relatively close at hand. In the West, however, national forests cover large tracts of land that are often far from populated towns or cities. Hence, the logistics of firefighting are much different in western forests.

Spatial factors are extremely important for the performance of many government functions. Whether it's police protection, educating children, or delivering the mail, the question of organizing government services to cover large geographical areas is usually an important one. Traditionally, three distinct approaches have been taken to deal with the problem of delivering such services throughout the country: (1) general service jurisdictions, (2) special service districts, and (3) field service offices.[2]

General Service Jurisdictions. The type of governmental unit known as general service jurisdictions frequently administers a variety of public service functions, including providing police and fire protection, collecting trash, providing social services, and maintaining local streets and roads. These governments take three major forms. Some are counties, others are townships, and most are municipalities. In 1987, there were approximately 39,000 general service governments operating in the United States (see Table 1.2 in Chapter 1). Each is responsible for providing a variety of services to its citizens.

Every state except Rhode Island and Connecticut uses *county governments*. There are over three thousand counties in the nation, and they come in almost every imaginable shape and size. New York City, for example, encompasses five densely populated counties: New York (Manhattan), Kings (Brooklyn), Queens, Richmond (Staten Island), and the Bronx. At the opposite extreme, is one county in Nevada that has no residents at all! In many metropolitan areas, counties provide the services and amenities that we usually expect from local governments. In other areas, mostly rural ones, county government offers its citizens just a few basic services. Despite this diversity, county governments typically house a sheriff's office, a judicial system, and other offices that maintain roads and parks, provide social services, and the like.

In 1987, the Census Bureau reported that there were 16,691 *townships and towns* operating within only twenty states (see Table 1.2). Historically, townships played an important role in the Northeast, but today they are on the decline as general service jurisdictions. As with counties, towns and townships come in every conceivable form. Some are large government organizations that offer citizens a wide range of services, whereas others are merely anachronisms that continue to exist despite having few real public functions to perform.

The most common form of general service jurisdiction is the *municipality* or city government. In 1987, the Census Bureau counted more than nineteen thousand municipalities ranging in population from a few hundred to the millions (see Table 1.2). Municipalities, like counties and townships, are legal creations of state governments. Municipal charters granted by the state legislatures determine the number and types of services these governmental units provide. Some municipal governments offer their constituents just a few basic services such as law enforcement and fire protection, while others offer a wide range of public services from sanitation to museums and other cultural facilities.

Special Service Districts. Another form of government organization, often called special service jurisdictions or special district governments, also provides limited government services. The Census Bureau reported the existence of over 44,000 of these governments in 1987. Special service districts stand as autonomous and independent governments, just as their general service counterparts. The key difference is that they perform only one major function for the geographical area they serve.

More than a third of the special service jurisdictions found in the United States are school districts. Another six thousand are classified as natural resource districts, which deal with such specialized functions as soil and water conservation. Fire protection is the only service provided by over 4,500 fire districts, while public housing and local economic development programs are the primary purposes of over 3,000 housing and community development special districts. A unique special district government operates in Reedy Creek, Florida. Formed in 1967, its special purpose is "to promote and create favorable conditions" for its one and only property owner—the Disney World entertainment park.[3]

Field Service Offices. Many government services are provided through branch offices of some central administrative office located in city hall, the state capitol, or in Washington D.C. Public library agencies in large metropolitan areas usually establish branches throughout their cities to serve their citizens. In recent years, many state governments have taken over the administration of social service programs and other welfare programs that were once the concern of counties and townships. To implement these new responsibilities, states have opened regional offices to deal directly with the needs of local recipients.

Perhaps the most familiar example of the field-office approach for organizing the administration of public services operates at the federal level. The delivery of the mail in the United States is exclusively a national government function run out of Washington, D.C. The performance of this crucial government activity involves almost daily face-to-face encounters between public employees and citizens at the local level. The U.S. Postal Service (USPS) accomplishes this enormous task by using local field offices (post offices) located in or near every community in the country. The system is so vast and its job so immense that its smooth and effective operation depends on a scheme requiring everyone to use the Postal Service ZIP codes that designate the specific field office to which they are sending mail.

Organizing the Spatial Dimension.   What factors determine the spatial organization of a particular government function or service? In an ideal world, we might assume that the spatial organization of government administration is based on factors such as cost-effectiveness and efficiency. In reality, the spatial organization of a government service depends on a number of factors, including natural features of the environment, relevant constitutional and legal provisions, political conditions, and a variety of emotional factors.[4]

The impact of natural environmental factors is obvious in those administrative areas having some unique geographic feature. Thus, although public administrators working for the state of Hawaii deal with a relatively small land mass, they cannot ignore the unique administrative problems generated by the need to deliver public services throughout a chain of islands.

Constitutional authority and legal boundaries also play a role in determining the area being administered. Our national constitutional system is designed on the principle of *federalism*. The founders of our Republic faced a difficult problem when they met in Philadelphia in 1787. On the one hand, there were demands from the individual states for maintaining the independence and autonomy they enjoyed under the Articles of Confederation. On the other hand, there were advocates for a strong central government who wanted to make the states subservient to a unitary national government. As on many other issues, the constitutional framers struck a compromise. State governments retained some of their authority while establishing a central government that has the authority to deal with many national issues, such as foreign and defense policies. This federal system has evolved over the past two centuries into a complex arrangement of government authority and responsibility. It is not uncommon, for example, for Congress to design and fund national policies that state and local officials implement (see Insight

5.1). Such arrangements make the spatial dimension a challenging one for public administrators at all levels. The Washington, D.C.–based administrator makes every effort to have the program implemented in a way that is consistent with congressional intent. In contrast, the state or local administrator tries equally hard to adapt the national program to meet local needs.

The operation of the federal system is sometimes complicated by legal boundaries between state and local governments. Legal boundaries often get in the way of cooperation, creating arbitrary barriers to the efficient organization of administrative areas. While it may be useful and reasonable for neighboring cities such as St. Louis, Missouri, and East St. Louis, Illinois, to cooperate in resolving mutual problems, they are in different states. Consequently, such intercity cooperation is awkward if not unlikely.

Political and community loyalties may also play an important role in determining the spatial organization of public services. For example, while the U.S. Postal Service (USPS) needs most of the individual post offices it maintains throughout the country, there are some offices it keeps open because of political pressures applied by local community leaders and members of Congress. Whenever the USPS proposes closing a particular office as part of its efforts to become more efficient, the community and its elected representatives mobilize their political influence to stop the action. The same kind of opposition arises when any major federal or state government facility is a candidate for being closed or moved.

Similar factors emerge at the local level whenever communities consider spatial reorganizations of their local governments. American urban areas have grown enormously over the past century, and in most cases this growth has been accompanied by a proliferation of general service and special district governments. In the early 1970s, the average number of governments in large metropolitan areas of over a million inhabitants was nearly 270. Faced with such numbers and the fragmentation of government services, reformers in different parts of the nation have argued for what they call "metropolitan consolidation," in which all government jurisdictions are consolidated into a single, large, and unified governmental unit. Advocates of consolidation believe that the elimination of fragmentation among local governments would result in improved public services that could be delivered more equitably for all citizens and at less cost. Consolidation movements have encountered opposition from individuals who believe that smaller governments enhance citizen participation and choice while maintaining community identity.[5] Those who advocate reorganization have often found it difficult to overcome these opponents of change. Thus, the specific form that a government administration (spatial) area takes results as much from politics and public debates as it does from any rational design based on the desire for administrative efficiency.

In many instances, then, the administration of government programs and services often occurs within geographic areas organized to promote princi-

INSIGHT 5.1
ROADWORK AND BOTTLENECKS

A proposal to build a "debottlenecking" bypass around the city of Lawrence, Kansas, illustrates the diversity of different legal entities at different levels of the federal system that must cooperate to get something done. The objective of this effort was to build a relatively short (14.3-mile) bypass around the community of 50,000 located west of Kansas City and east of Topeka. National, state, and local authorities each played a separate role in the process.

The national government was involved in several ways. First, the Federal Highway Authority was authorized by Congress to allocate $7.2 million for the project. Second, the U.S. Army Corps of Engineers controlled all the bottom land along the river that runs near the area because of a dam that the Corps built upriver. Third, the Environmental Protection Agency reviewed the environmental impact statement prepared by private consultants and paid for by the city and county.

Several state actors were involved in the planning, approval, and construction of the proposed highway project. The Kansas Fish and Game Commission reviewed the environmental impact on fish and game in the marshland where the proposed highway would be built. There was a great deal of controversy over whether a rare frog was inhabiting the marshland that the roadway would bisect. In addition, the Kansas Department of Health and Environment reviewed the environmental impact of the project. This agency's concern was a rare prairie

orchid that grows in the area. Then, of course, the state legislature had to decide how much money (if any) it would allocate to the project. The state Department of Transportation was involved because the proposal included designating the bypass as state highway K-10. Even if the highway was built without state funds, Kansas still had to give its approval to the state designation and agree to maintain the bypass as a state highway.

In addition to these mainline state agencies, the Kansas Turnpike Authority (a special service district chartered by the state) was involved in the project. Proponents of the bypass wanted the authority to build a new turnpike interchange at the junction of the Lawrence bypass and the Kansas Turnpike that touches the city on the north. The authority agreed to spend up to $1.2 million to do so.

At the local level, the governmental actors included Douglas County, the City of Lawrence, and their joint City-County Planning Commission. The Planning Commission endorsed the project and the city and county commissions each voted to contribute $4 million to the project.

Thus, this relatively small project involved legislative bodies at all three levels of government, three federal agencies, three state agencies, the staff of a state-chartered authority (the Kansas Turnpike Authority), the staffs of the city and the county, and the joint planning commission working on the project.

Cooperation and agreement among such a diverse group of actors is difficult at best. Public administrators who successfully operate in this kind of arena must be skilled in interpersonal, interagency, and intergovernmental operations. They must be able to work with (or around) the diversity of expectations generated by the various government actors, special interest groups, and citizens.

SOURCE: Based on information from an interview with Buford Watson, city manager of Lawrence, Kansas, April 27, 1989.

ples other than administrative efficiency. Few government administrators have the luxury of shaping the spatial dimensions of the geographic area within which they must work. Instead, they must often shape their jobs to the jurisdiction.

Terrain, Topography, and Geology

Public administrators also have little power over the terrain, topography, or geology with which they must contend on a daily basis. Although these features of physical ecology are not of interest to all public administrators, some find such factors to be extremely important in doing their jobs.

Soil conditions and geological features of the land are obviously important for county-extension agents and other public officials who serve in federal and state agricultural agencies. County-extension agents, who work throughout the United States (see Profile 3.1), advise local farmers on the latest developments in agricultural research, especially as they relate to local conditions. The success of these county agents depends on their familiarity with local soil and geological conditions as well as on their knowledge of the latest technical developments to enhance farm production or reduce losses. Similarly, forest rangers and National Park Service employees cannot be effective unless they understand the unique characteristics and problems of the geographic areas they serve.

Another group of public employees directly concerned with terrain, topographical, and geological conditions are those who build or maintain America's streets, roads, highways, and other public facilities. Consider, for example, the different tasks facing snow-removal crews on the flat plains of midwestern states such as Illinois or Minnesota and their peers working on mountain passes in Colorado. While each may have to deal with similar amounts of snowfall after a winter storm, their jobs are quite different because of the different types of land surfaces they must plow.

Some public administrators are faced with the task of attempting to change or minimize the impact of terrain or topographical features. For example, a major public sector accomplishment since World War II has been the construction of more than 40,000 miles of multilane, limited-access roads that make up our interstate highway system. Wherever possible, these highways were built to minimize the impact of the surrounding terrain on high-speed motor-vehicle traffic. Americans no longer had to travel across the country on two-lane roads built on the contours of the land they traversed. Nor did they have to go around—rather than through or over—significant physical obstacles such as mountains and rivers.

Feats of modern highway engineering, however, have also generated some problems. By slicing through and changing the natural contours of the land, highway builders have often disturbed the natural ecology by cutting off the access of wildlife to feeding areas or destroyed its scenic beauty by blasting through hills and mountains. In recent years, highway designers have been required to consider these factors when proposing highway projects (see Insight 5.1). Newly built sections of the interstate highway system reflect these concerns. For example, when Colorado's Vail Pass was made part of a four-lane interstate highway in the early 1970s, highway engineers designed the project so that it actually enhanced the beauty of the area and minimized interference with the wildlife habitat along the route.

Climate and Weather

A well-known cliché claims that everyone talks about the weather but no one does anything about it. For some public administrators, however, this situation is a challenge rather than a truism. Obviously, the weather is a concern to those working for the government's Weather Bureau, but public-sector meteorologists aren't the only government workers who must contend with climates and changing weather conditions. Climate and its effects on the terrain are also a major concern for Defense Department administrators who supply our armed forces with clothing and equipment suitable for the varied locations where American troops operate. They cannot afford to ignore the climate where American military personnel carry out their work.

Consider what happens when climate and related factors are overlooked. When the first teams of American military advisors went to South Vietnam in the early 1960s, they found that their standard radios would not work under local conditions in Southeast Asia. In addition, the tropical weather and jungles of Vietnam proved too much for their standard issue clothing, particularly footwear, which literally fell apart after a few routine patrols. The Pentagon worked quickly to develop and ship new radios and boots— equipment that would be adopted as standard issue for most military personnel within a few years.

Climate has an important influence on how public administrators spend their funds and prepare for the future. A city located in America's Sun Belt is not likely to spend its time, energy, or precious finances on snow-removal plans or equipment; but city administrators in Denver, Chicago, or Buffalo must. In cities that have harsh winters, a good deal of government's resources are expended in anticipation of snowfall. Each summer and autumn they contract for private snowplows and begin stockpiling sand and other material needed to deal with the effects of a potentially severe winter. Similarly, administrators in Wichita Falls, Texas, or New Orleans, Louisiana, are likely to prepare for potential tornadoes or hurricanes.

There are other public officials who are not preoccupied with the weather or climate but who find such factors playing an important role in the success of their missions. NASA, for example, must consider weather conditions when deciding whether to proceed with a scheduled launch. Cape Canaveral, Florida, was selected as NASA's primary launch site in part because of the suitability of the area's climate. Even so, since the late 1950s, many scheduled launches from the Kennedy Space Center have been delayed due to poor weather conditions either at the Cape or somewhere down range of the launch site. The concern of NASA officials over weather conditions is justifiable. There is evidence that the tragic loss of the space shuttle *Challenger* in January 1986 was due in part to the unusually cold weather conditions that prevailed the day of the tragic launch.

Unusual climatic conditions often highlight the impact of the physical surroundings on a public agency's ability to deliver a service. In July 1988, for instance, New York City's ambulance service suffered an unusually high rate of out-of-service ambulance vehicles. While typically 24 percent of the ambulance fleet is out of service at any point in time, 40 percent of the city's ambulances were out of service during the week of July 16, 1988. First Deputy Mayor Stanley Brezenoff attributed much of the problem to the "summer's exceptionally high temperatures and mounting demand." Brezenoff noted that "many of the city's 237 ambulances were very heavy vehicles that did not run well in extreme heat."[6]

Human-made Surroundings

Not all of the physical features of the ecology relevant to public administrators are "natural"; some human-made elements are equally important. We often create or significantly alter the environments in which we work and live. Factories, construction sites, underground mines, housing units, shopping malls, and other physical settings can pose unique challenges and problems. Some of these challenges take the form of potential or actual disasters that threaten human lives, while others are much less dramatic.

Human-made environments can be threatening, particularly when they directly affect the health and safety of workers or the general public. A poorly constructed coal mine can result in hundreds of worker deaths, a fact attested to by the history of American coal mining. State and federal governments have responded to such dangers by establishing regulations for operating underground mines and creating agencies to monitor compliance with those rules. On a more general level, this concern for worker safety and health led to the creation of the Occupational Safety and Health Administration (OSHA) in 1970.

The workplace is not the only location where the human-made environment poses a potential problem. There are many people concerned about the quality and safety of residential and public buildings, especially in large American cities. Almost every local government regulates building construction through the issuance of permits and visits by building inspectors.

The problems and challenges posed by human-made environments are not always dramatic or life-threatening. At times, they focus on issues of service and life-style or aesthetics. The construction of new buildings or residential developments, for example, may call for adjustments in the delivery of public services. Utilities have to hook up lines to the new development, cities must pave streets and extend police and fire protection, and so on. Many cities respond to these pressures by requiring builders and developers to arrange and pay for these additional services through special property-tax assessments.

New buildings and residential developments may also be perceived as a threat to the life-styles of current residents of a city. The proposed construction of a factory or warehouse in the middle of a residential neighborhood is likely to generate opposition from area citizens. In some areas, the particular design of a proposed building may face opposition because it doesn't blend into the commonly accepted neighborhood norms for a structure. These issues are typically addressed through city land-use plans and zoning laws.[7]

Dealing with Disasters

A special and important area of interaction between public administration and the physical environment is in how governments deal with natural and human-made disasters. *Natural disasters* range from the common snowstorm to the less common flood, earthquake, tornado, hurricane, or drought. And after decades of abusing the environment, we are now faced with the need to develop solutions for *human-made disasters* — problems we've created with our own hands in our own backyards. We have buried our radioactive and toxic wastes near our homes and drilled for oil off the pristine shores of California and the Gulf of Mexico. In the process, we have created considerable potential for disasters that are no less devastating than tornadoes and hurricanes.

More and more government resources are being devoted to dealing with emergencies that arise because of natural and human-made hazards. Public-sector efforts have focused on four objectives: mitigation (reducing the possibility or risks of such disasters); preparedness (planning effective responses if disasters should strike); response (implementing those plans); and recovery (providing aid and support in the disaster's aftermath).[8]

Mitigation.   There are some types of disasters that government can help prevent through mitigation programs. Flood-control projects (e.g., dam construction and water diversion) have been undertaken by the Army Corps of Engineers, the Soil Conservation Service, and other agencies in regions where flooding is common. In addition, the federal government established a floodplain regulation program in 1968 to help more than 17,000 local communities manage areas susceptible to flooding. Government programs regulating dam safety, building construction in earthquake-prone areas, hazardous waste disposal, nuclear power plant operations, and other potentially dangerous activities are also examples of mitigation policies.

Preparedness.   Although mitigation programs can help reduce the risks of some disasters, none is likely to be 100 percent effective. Furthermore, some potential disasters are simply not preventable, such as earthquakes, hurricanes, and tornadoes. For these reasons, preparedness programs are an important government activity.

Central to the federal government's preparedness efforts is the Federal Emergency Management Agency (FEMA).[9] President Jimmy Carter created the FEMA in 1979 through an executive order, which combined the emergency management functions and personnel from several different agencies. These included:

- The Civil Defense Preparedness Agency, formerly located in the Department of Defense.
- The Federal Disaster Assistance Administration and Federal Insurance Administration, both formerly in the Department of Housing and Urban Development.
- The Federal Preparedness Agency, formerly associated with the General Services Administration.
- The National Fire Prevention and Control Administration, formerly located in the Department of Commerce.

Among the FEMA's many functions is the important task of promoting and helping to fund the development of local emergency preparedness plans (see Insight 5.2). Under the provisions of the 1977 Earthquake Hazards Reduction Act, the FEMA works closely with communities in earthquake-prone areas to draw up plans to deal with emergencies should they arise. Workshops, simulations of emergency situations, and so on are all part of the efforts that the FEMA promotes. In the early 1980s, the FEMA helped fund the Southern California Emergency Preparedness Plan (SCEPP), which provides an integrated plan of action for nearly five hundred local governments in the region. The SCEPP model has been used in other locations as well.[10] One such plan was activated during the October 1989 earthquake that hit northern California. While many lives were lost in the San Francisco–

INSIGHT 5.2
BEING PREPARED

Among its other requirements, the Federal Emergency Management Agency (FEMA) asks participating cities to engage in two emergency response exercises each year. These exercises proved valuable to the people of Brownsville, Texas, on July 7, 1988. Having practiced for disasters like hurricanes, chemical spills, and airplane crashes, local personnel found they were well prepared to handle the challenge of a store collapsing during a severe storm. While fourteen people died immediately in that tragedy, those who were trapped alive under the rubble were quickly rescued. "That's as good a record as you can get," observed Ignacio Garza, Brownsville's mayor.

Much of the credit for that effort was given to the city's preparedness. The success of the rescue effort, claimed Garza, "stemmed from allowing knowledgeable people to do their jobs. . . .

Nobody played God. No egos came into play. I let the people with a special area of expertise do their jobs." Through preparedness plans and briefings, Garza and other city leaders had learned to avoid the turf battles that can emerge in such situations. The problem had been getting all public officials to take preparedness seriously. "You don't realize the impact of it until it happens to you," noted Mayor Richard L. Berkley of Kansas City, Missouri. He knew of the value of preparedness. In 1981, a skywalk filled with people fell on a dance floor of a Kansas City hotel, killing 114 people and injuring another 201. "It's extremely important to be prepared."

SOURCE: Based on information in Ellen Perlman, "Managing to Survive Disasters: Officials Urge More Planning," *City & State*, 18 July 1988, pp. 1, 26.

Oakland area as a result of that quake, many more were spared because public officials were prepared for such an event.

Response and Recovery.   In the face of disaster, Americans are more than willing to come to the aid of their neighbors. We expect government agencies to take the lead when disaster strikes. Too often in the past, however, there have been times when responses made the disasters worse because government officials were unable to take charge of rescue and relief operations. For example, when a tornado overturned a crowded dinner showboat in Lake Pamona, Kansas, in 1978, nearly eighty public, volunteer, and private-sector organizations responded to the rescue scene. Of these eighty groups, twenty played significant roles in the rescue effort. Efforts to coordinate the work of the organizations failed, and the resulting confusion and lack of coordination made a tragic situation even worse.[11]

Governments have also established special programs to help victims recover from disasters. Immediately after a hurricane or tornado strikes, FEMA sets up assistance centers to help victims get grants, loans, economic advice, and even psychological counseling. People expect those centers to be up and operating within a day or two of the disaster, and in most cases FEMA is able to meet those demands. In September 1989, however, FEMA came under severe criticisms when it failed to respond quickly to the destruction caused by Hurricane Hugo in South Carolina, Puerto Rico, and the Virgin Islands.[12]

To deal with environmental disasters such as the contamination of entire communities at Love Canal, New York, and Times Beach, Missouri, Congress created a special "superfund" devoted to toxic-waste cleanups. Some states and local communities have passed ordinances requiring compensation for victims of disasters caused by another's negligence. Even better known are the many low-interest loan plans and outright grants that go into effect for residents and businesses who live in a declared disaster area. A variety of federal, state, and local agencies administer these programs. The nature of the programs and agencies depends on the type of disaster being faced. For example, after the Midwest was hit by a drought in the summer of 1988, Richard Lyng, secretary of the Department of Agriculture, designated 1,231 counties (40 percent of the nation's counties) in 30 states as suffering from drought disaster. This designation made farmers in those areas eligible for a variety of aid and relief programs.[13]

The Importance of Physical Factors

The importance of the physical ecology depends on both the specific public administrator's job and the conditions in the environment surrounding that job. Where an individual works and the kind of job he or she performs is obviously important in determining the influence of the physical ecology on that public administrator. When determining the type of training and equipment needed by local firefighters, for example, we must know whether they work for the City of New York or Ponca City, Oklahoma. When buying uniforms for local law-enforcement personnel, we need to know whether they serve the citizens of Phoenix, Arizona, or Anchorage, Alaska.

In many instances, public administrators cannot control or change their physical surroundings. Under such circumstances, the best administrators can do is adapt to their surroundings and hope that the expectations they face do not exceed their capabilities to deal with the physical ecology. With the exception of our emergency-preparedness agencies, most American public agencies are designed to deliver services under normal conditions. Extreme events, such as droughts, hurricanes, earthquakes, chemical spills, or nuclear power plant accidents, often highlight the nature of our expectations for these agencies as well as the limits of their administrative capacity.

The Impact of Technology

The kinds of technologies present within public administrators' environments greatly influence their jobs, both positively and negatively. Although we usually think of technologies as machines or computers that help us do our work, they are much more than that. By *technologies* we mean those *standardized physical and social means that society uses to achieve some predetermined results.*

Every community has problems it seeks to resolve and goals it seeks to achieve. Some communities tackle their problems and goals through methods and means specially designed for the specific challenge at hand. Most, however, rely on some methods or tools—technologies—that are already available to them. A city administrator in Minneapolis doesn't have to rethink how to conduct snow-removal operations after each major winter storm. The technology for accomplishing snow removal—the snowplows and the personnel who operate them—are already in place with instructions and orders in hand.

The technological ecology of American public administration has two distinct facets, physical and social. *Physical technologies* are those standardized inanimate tools and other forms of equipment that we count on to help solve some problem or achieve some objective. By *social technologies* we mean those standardized social means and methods that help us accomplish certain problems or reach predetermined goals. Social technologies are not inanimate objects but standardized human behavior patterns. Since social technologies depend on people rather than on machinery, the degree of standardization involved is hardly what we might expect from physical technologies. Nevertheless, there are patterns of human behavior that are regularized to the point that they constitute technologies in our sense of the term.

Physical Technologies

We live in a world of rapid technological change. Such changes have a tremendous impact on our daily lives, so much so that many Americans would find life without them intolerable. This is most obvious in the areas of physical technology. In just two generations, we have witnessed major advances in everything from telecommunications and information processing to genetic engineering, organ transplants, and space exploration.

The wide range of technological innovations poses both challenges and opportunities for public administrators. Not only must government officials be knowledgeable about the latest technology and adapt it to the public's needs (see Insight 5.3), but they must also recognize that the very existence of that technology creates administrative dilemmas. Following the space shuttle *Challenger* accident in 1986, for example, there was much administrative investigation and soul-searching about whether NASA had used the best

INSIGHT 5.3
PLASTIC WELFARE

Many Americans now carry credit cards for making everyday purchases. Behind the wide use of credit cards is a growing technology that is being adapted by government agencies for use in the delivery of social services.

In 1988, the federal government made funds available to states that wanted to start using plastic-card technology for the delivery of social services. The hope is that this "electronic benefits transfer" system, as it is called, will ultimately allow governments to distribute an array of social services—"from food stamps to child-support payments"—to eligible recipients.

A pilot project for testing the system was set up in Berks County, Pennsylvania, in 1988. The area's six thousand welfare recipients receive their welfare payments at automatic-teller machines and use their cards in lieu of food stamps at the grocery checkout counter.

While the new technology is convenient and effective in many ways, its overall cost remains an issue. While the paperwork associated with the standard means for distributing food stamps amounts to a monthly cost of $2.92 per recipient, the monthly costs of the electronic system is $27.23 per recipient. Officials hope that expanded use of the technology in the future will make the program more cost-effective.

SOURCE: Based on information in Georgina Fiordalisi, "States Endorsing Automated Services," *City & State*, 18 July 1988, pp. 2, 25.

---

available technology. Specifically, investigators probed whether the agency had used the best design available for the joint seals on the booster rockets that launched the shuttle into space.

Other administrative questions arise in decisions about the introduction of new technologies, such as the irradiation of produce as a food preservative. In deciding whether to allow the sale of irradiated foods in this country, the Food and Drug Administration (FDA) must determine the health effects of the widespread use of irradiation in the food supply.

In the transportation field, perhaps no technological innovation has had a greater impact on public administration than the automobile and associated inventions. As a result, the public sector has become responsible for a wide variety of services, ranging from building and maintaining streets and highways to regulating traffic and operating parking garages. In many major urban areas, the public sector also plays a key role in providing mass-transit facilities such as bus lines and subway trains.

During the 1800s, the infant railroad industry was nurtured by governments at all levels. Today, the public sector remains the major provider of rail-passenger service in the United States as well as a regulator of rail-freight services. Similarly, government is also significantly involved in air transportation. At one time or another, government has assumed responsibility for the safety of air travel as well as the economic health of the airline industry. Furthermore, nearly every major metropolitan area has constructed and maintained airports. As the technology of air-passenger transport evolved, those facilities have undergone substantial changes.

Changes in telecommunications have also had wide-ranging impacts on governments. New technologies in this area have extended or improved human sensory capabilities and have linked us closer together as a nation. Technological advances like cable television have diminished the amount of effort citizens must exert to keep informed about the functioning of their government administrators. Now residents can watch city commission meetings on television rather than having to attend those meetings.

Technology has undoubtedly enhanced the capabilities of our governments to serve us. Advances in communication have made police and fire protection more accessible and effective. In particular, the establishment of the 911 emergency telephone number in most local communities has speeded up the response time of police, fire, and emergency medical teams. At the same time, however, advances in communication have created new areas for government regulation and new concerns about potential government intrusion. For example, the widespread use of cordless telephones in homes, cars, and airplanes has made it much easier to eavesdrop on phone conversations. There is some concern about the limits of privacy of communication channels that can be so easily monitored by public agencies and private citizens.

We often use the term *automation* to focus on those areas where technology has changed the way we accomplish physical tasks of production. Sometimes these changes have reaped gains for society in general and other times they have resulted in losses. On the one hand, the automated delivery of some basic public services is much more efficient. The U.S. Postal Service, for example, can now process mail faster because of new optical scanners that sort ten thousand letter-size items in the time it takes highly trained postal clerks to sort eight hundred! In many cities and towns, trash collection costs less and uses fewer workers because of recent technological innovations. (See Insight 5.3.) On the other hand, though, technology has had its costs. Some innovations have resulted in the loss of many traditional jobs. Some believe that the loss of the personal touch once associated with some government services is also a result of technology.

Public-sector agencies today can handle a great deal more data because of advances in information processing. Again, this has benefits and costs. For example, we can receive our Social Security and income-tax refund checks much more quickly when all systems are working well. Such speed depends, in part, on public officials keeping their records and solving their problems more efficiently through modern computers. But there are potential drawbacks to having extensive computerization in government (see Profile 5.1). Widespread computerization can result in the depersonalization of government services. Other drawbacks relate to citizen privacy. Computerization affords government the opportunity to collect and store a great deal of information on its citizens. This potential leads many critics of government to predict that the public sector's increasing computerization may lead to the kind of society described in George Orwell's chilling novel *1984*. Efforts to minimize the potential for government abuse of information have resulted in legislation protecting individuals' privacy. The rights of Americans to privacy is an established principle of U.S. law, particularly through the 1974 Privacy Act. Nevertheless, the challenge of maintaining those rights in the face of technological advancement is obviously difficult.

Advances in the biological and physical sciences also pose opportunities and challenges for the public sector. Discoveries in these fields have brought about significant changes in American life, particularly in medicine, the economy, and the typical American life-style. We can now save and extend more lives with expensive medical technologies. Government has been directly or indirectly involved in the development and provision of almost every major medical and scientific endeavor undertaken within the past fifty years. Advances in chemistry allow us to grow more food through the use of pesticides and manufacture more durable and useful products. Technological advances allow us shorter work weeks and improved conditions in the workplace. In short, advances in the biological and physical sciences enable us and our governments to do things that would have been impossible for our ancestors even to imagine less than a century ago. Many of these advances help the public sector serve American citizens more effectively.

Many scientific advances have been as costly in the long run as they were beneficial in the short run. Because we feel torn between the positive and negative qualities of these technologies, we frequently turn to government to promote or regulate their use and impact. For example, we ask government to try to control rising hospital costs and to investigate decisions regarding the medical care of children born with deformities. We expect government to monitor programs to develop new pesticides that protect crops and to regulate the production, distribution, and disposal of harmful chemicals. In each of these areas, the role of government in technological development and use is considerable and is growing every year. So has the challenge to make certain that the technology does not become an end in itself.

Some technological changes have created new administrative challenges for public administrators, such as in the areas of organ transplants and human reproduction. Now that we know how to transplant human organs successfully, hospital administrators, physicians, and patients grapple with the hit-and-miss nature of our organ-donor supply system. The ability to transplant organs has generated pressure for an administrative solution, such as a national organ bank, to handle distribution problems. Similar legal

PROFILE 5.1

Unscrambling Eggs at Social Security

In December 1989, Gwendolyn S. King had the unenviable task of telling 33 million Americans that the agency she headed—the Social Security Administration (SSA)—would be temporarily and unavoidably borrowing (at no interest) more than $1 billion from them for a few months. She tried her best to prevent this from happening, but without success. Her agency was trapped by the very computer technology that made it operate so effectively.

King was appointed by President George Bush in 1989 to serve as commissioner of the SSA. Although she hadn't worked at SSA before assuming the position, King did have a wide-ranging background in public service. After graduation from Howard University in 1962, she went to work for the Washington, D.C., Board of Education. Her experience in the federal government began in 1976 when she accepted a management internship at the U.S. Department of Health, Education and Welfare; and by 1978 she was head of the Division of Consumer Complaints at the U.S. Department of Housing and Urban Development. In 1979 she moved from the administrative bureaucracy to a position as legislative assistant to Senator John Heinz, a Pennsylvania Republican. She served in that capacity for seven years, eventually moving over to the White House, where she worked in the Intergovernmental Affairs office.

Her "technological" problems at SSA began early in September 1989, when members of Congress were discussing the need to modify or eliminate a catastrophic illness insurance program they had passed in 1988. SSA had operated this insurance program as part of Medicare. The coverage it provided was funded through premiums collected from Medicare-eligible Americans. The premium was deducted each month from the Social Security pension checks sent to the elderly.

On November 22, 1989, Congress voted to end the program as of January 1, 1990. King's problem was that her agency could not reprogram the SSA computers in time to comply with Congress's order to end the program on that date. To make matters worse, the computers were programmed to implement a premium *increase* on the very day that the coverage was to end. Her hands were tied. Her agency would "have to put people to work almost around the clock to straighten things out by April or May."

King had warned Congress that this might happen, telling them on October 3 that this situation would arise if they waited too long in deciding whether to continue or terminate the program. Congress, however, was unable to make the necessary decisions on time. A majority of the House of Representatives wanted to repeal the entire program, whereas members of the Senate wanted to curtail the coverage provided under the program. The debate raged on until just before Thanksgiving, but by then it was too late for King and her colleagues at SSA.

The problem was rooted in the computer programs that SSA uses to issue pension checks and arrange for premium deductions. The checks are actually printed and mailed by the Treasury Department based on programmed computer tapes it receives from SSA. Those computer programs are developed months in advance and reflect the fact that there are different payments made to pensioners throughout the country depending on a great many factors. There are at least 276 different premium structures for Medicare deductions alone. The complex process of reprogramming is at best extremely difficult.

Eventually, all the deductions— amounting to more than $1 billion— would be refunded. In this case, the technology had to catch up with the policy-making machinery of government. As for King and her agency, they wanted it made clear that they were doing their best under the circumstances. "Social Security will have to unscramble this egg," King told a *New York Times* reporter, "but I have to make it clear that we did not lay it."

SOURCE: Based on information in Martin Tolchin, "U.S. Will Continue Medicare Charges," *New York Times*, 5 Dec. 1989, pp. A1, A29.

and administrative dilemmas arise over the issue of surrogate motherhood. Over the years, adoption agencies have developed strict screening criteria and procedures to protect the natural and adoptive parents as well as the child in traditional adoptions. As the celebrated late 1980s custody trial of "Baby M" in New Jersey illustrated, the area of surrogate parenthood does not lend itself to tidy administrative criteria.

Social Technologies

There are two types of social technologies, traditional and designed. *Traditional social technologies* are widespread social arrangements that evolved over time and provided some particular societal function. They are technologies to the extent that they help people solve problems or achieve desired goals and objectives. Traditional social technologies include such familiar institutions as the family, schools, churches, and everyday racial, ethnic, and gender relationships.

The family, as a social technology, performs a variety of functions in all societies. Besides reproduction, sexual gratification, and kinship, families traditionally supply economic security, socialization, companionship, and social control. To the extent that the typical family unit performs these functions, the role of the general community and the public sector in particular is minimal.

As we have become less dependent on traditional social institutions for carrying out basic economic, political, and even social functions of society, we rely more on *designed social technologies*. When there is no traditional social technology that can handle a new social problem, we often create one. These technologies, which are created expressly to meet today's social, economic, and political needs, tend to be more specialized than traditional ones.

In earlier times, for example, families and friends were relied on to take care of the elderly, young, and incompetent. As patterns of family structure and friendship networks have changed, people now rely on designed social technologies, such as nursing homes and day-care centers, to provide services that families and friends are no longer willing or able to provide. Many of these designed social technologies have proven transferable from arena to arena. Other examples of designed social technologies include corporations, consumer advocacy groups, special interest groups, and the media. We learn more about these in our discussions of organizations and management in Chapters 10 and 11.

Technologies and Change

A common theme throughout our discussion of both physical and social technologies has been the impact of change and innovation. Technological change has been the subject of many recent commentaries on American society. These changes are occurring today at a pace that was unheard of just fifty years ago.

According to Alvin Toffler, a popular writer on social change, our lives are so different from our predecessors' "because of the astonishing expansion of the scale and scope of change." Technological advances have made it possible to translate ideas into action within extremely short time frames. Toffler believes that America is overwhelmed by this "accelerative thrust" of technological and related changes. He coined the term *future shock* to describe what he sees as a "disease of change" plaguing American society. For Toffler, "it will take drastic social, even political action" to alleviate the problems caused by that disease.[14] As a result, the technological environment of American society often seems turbulent and somewhat unpredictable to some observers.

For others, however, technological change is much less disturbing. They view these changes as broad patterns of long-term change that are emerging from within American society. As John Naisbitt notes in his book *Megatrends*, Americans are no longer denying the future. Instead, they are facing up to—and taking advantage of—the challenges such changes create.[15] Where Naisbitt sees the pace and direction of technological and demographic change as opportunities, Toffler and others see them as potentially destructive.[16]

While we can debate whether such changes are positive or negative, the fact that America's public administrators face an unstable and unpredictable technological ecology is indisputable. For example, the trend in American family life has been away from the traditional extended family structures (in which grandparents and other relatives are as important as parents, brothers, and sisters) and toward the nuclear family structure (in which anyone outside the immediate household is considered a distant relative). The increase in divorce rates and a greater tolerance of nontraditional life-styles reflect a further extension of this trend. As a result, we have seen in recent decades an increase in the number of single-parent families. As these trends continue, people increasingly rely on government rather than their relatives when some crisis or need arises. Consequently, there are even greater demands for the kind of social and supportive services that government provides. Now we expect government to remind divorced parents of their child-support obligations. In Missouri, for example, the newly established Division of Child Support Enforcement is responsible for making sure that absent parents meet their child-support obligations. When parents fail to make their payments, the state can withhold wages and other income, intercept unemployment compensation benefits, and even obtain liens against real and personal property.[17] The trend toward two-paycheck families who live in the suburbs with fewer children also has affected demands for government services. These families demand after-school programs and public facilities to meet their distinctive life-styles.

A similar pattern has developed as our reliance on another traditional social technology—churches—has declined. The local church was once the center of community and political life, especially in ethnic areas of large cities and in small rural communities. Today church membership among Americans remains high, but we are less likely to turn to religious organizations to meet our secular needs and more likely to go to government first. In fact, while the dependence of Americans on organized churches has declined, their religiosity has not. In the past, religious institutions performed most general social functions, such as dispensing charity and caring for the needy. As religious institutions continue to withdraw from this area, government agencies increasingly assume these functions.

In the area of physical technology, a major technological trend has been the shift from an industrial society based on manufacturing and production to an information-based society in which knowledge and services dominate.[18] The implications of this trend for the public sector are substantial. On the positive side, American governments are strikingly well suited for adapting to an information-based society in that they have provided services and knowledge to their constituencies for decades. It should be noted that public administrators played a central role in promoting the initial development of computer and other information-processing technologies. Many of the primary inventions that transformed our technologies have their roots in government programs. These programs range from Social Security, which generated demands for data-processing innovations, to the effort to land an American on the moon by 1970, which stimulated a vast array of technological breakthroughs and inventions. On the negative side, many of the problems generated by the current trend toward an information-based society will fall on government officials to resolve.

Adapting to Change

In this chapter, we considered the impact that physical and technological factors have on the operations of American public administration. Even something as simple as the location of a government agency can affect the nature of its operation. Geography, climate, available technologies, and related factors influence how public administrators go about their tasks in two major ways.

First, physical and technological factors have a direct influence on public administrators' abilities to perform their jobs. For example, advances in sanitation and water-treatment technology now make it easier for cities to provide clean drinking water and handle sewage. At the same time, both physical and technological ecologies can impose severe constraints on the capacity of public administrators to do their work. Droughts, acid rain, noisy aircraft engines, and the like can all make life more difficult (and challenging) for the government worker. How physical and technological ecologies influence public administration depends on the specific circumstances surrounding a governmental function or task.

Second, physical and technological factors have indirect effects on the jobs of public administrators. Parts of the ecological landscape help shape the expectations the American population has for public administrators. It is through these expectations that public administrators get a sense of how the public is reacting to their physical and technological surroundings and what they might want government to do in response. This can take the form of specific demands on government for everything from more efficient snow removal to increased regulation of airline safety. Or it can help set the general tone of public expectations about the role and responsibility of government in general. Americans expect their government to be in the forefront of the use of technology (as in space exploration) to solve physical and social problems. Under some conditions, the public administrator may develop new and innovative means for meeting the challenges posed by physical and technological ecologies. Under other circumstances, the administrator might rely on old and proven ways for handling those challenges. In either instance, the bottom line is for public administrators to adapt to and work with the physical and technological ecologies that surround them. Under normal conditions, the adaptation is likely to be fairly smooth and go unnoticed by the average citizen. Under extreme conditions or in the face of unusual events, the impact of physical and technological ecologies on the jobs of public administrators becomes more obvious to the average citizen.

Summary

1. The relationship between public administrators and their physical and technological surroundings is complicated because various publics and individuals react differently to these features of the ecology.
2. Important physical characteristics of the public administration ecology include spatial factors, terrain, climate, and the human-made environment.
3. Most governments meet the challenge of spatial factors by creating general service jurisdictions, special districts, and field offices.
4. Terrain, climate, and human-made surroundings often provide special challenges for American public administration in the form of disasters.
5. Technologies, both social and physical, can challenge public administration as well as make it easier to accomplish the tasks of government.
6. Public administration has learned both to adapt to and work with its physical and technological ecologies.

Study Questions

1. How do the physical surroundings in your hometown affect the work of local government officials?
2. How have technological innovations (e.g., automobiles, shopping malls, and cable television) influenced the operations of local government in your hometown?
3. Describe the challenges and opportunities to public administration of (a) the jumbo jet (Boeing 747, DC–10), (b) personal computers, (c) air conditioning, and (d) the use of pesticides on produce.

Notes

1. Herbert Kaufman, _The Forest Ranger: A Study in Administrative Behavior_ (Baltimore: Johns Hopkins University Press, 1967), p. 54.
2. For a classic discussion of the relationship between geographical area and public administration, see James W. Fesler, _Area and Administration_ (University, AL: University of Alabama Press, 1949).
3. Rodd Zolkos, "Disney's Clannish District: Magic Kingdom Clashes with Neighboring Counties," _City & State_, February 1987, p. 14.
4. See Fesler, _Area and Administration_, chap. 2.
5. For a brief overview of the debate between consolidationists and their opponents, see Thomas R. Dye, _Politics in States and Communities_, 6th ed. (Englewood Cliffs, NJ: Prentice-Hall, 1988); and Nicholas Henry, _Governing_

at the Grass Roots: State and Local Politics, 2d ed. (Englewood Cliffs, NJ: Prentice-Hall, 1984), pp. 254–61.

6. "Ambulance Problems Linked by Deputy Mayor to Heat," *New York Times*, 26 July 1988, p. 12.

7. On the use and misuse of zoning laws, see Richard F. Babcock, *The Zoning Game: Municipal Practices and Policies* (Madison: University of Wisconsin Press, 1966). Also see case studies of planning in Alan A. Altshuler, *The City Planning Process* (Ithaca, NY: Cornell University Press, 1965).

8. See William Petak, "Emergency Management: A Challenge for Public Administration," *Public Administration Review* 45 (January 1985 [Special Issue]): 3–6.

9. For information on the FEMA, see Peter J. May and Walter Williams, *Disaster Policy Implementation: Managing Programs under Shared Governance* (New York: Plenum Press, 1986).

10. Ibid., chap. 7.

11. See Thomas E. Drabek, "Managing the Emergency Response," *Public Administration Review* 45 (January 1985 [Special Issue]): 85–92.

12. On the criticisms facing FEMA during the fall of 1989, see Michael Wines, "U.S. Relief Agency Seeks Relief from Criticism," *New York Times*, October 25, 1989, p. A-29.

13. See Keith Schneider, "Drought Disaster Hits 1,231 Counties in 30 States," *New York Times*, 23 June, 1988, pp. 1, 11.

14. See Alvin Toffler, *Future Shock* (New York: Bantam Books, 1971), pp. 15–16.

15. John Naisbitt, *Megatrends: Ten New Directions Transforming Our Lives* (New York: Warner Books, 1984).

16. See Toffler, *Future Shock*, pp. 428ff; and Richard D. Lamm, *Megatraumas: America at the Year 2000* (Boston: Houghton Mifflin, 1985).

17. "Missouri Tracking Down More Child Support," *Kansas City Times*, 26 July 1988, p. B-1.

18. Harlan Cleveland, "The Twilight of Hierarchy: Speculations on the Global Information Society," *Public Administration Review* 45 (January/February 1985): 185–95.

CHAPTER 6

DEMOGRAPHIC, CULTURAL, AND ECONOMIC FACTORS

Problems in Lancaster County

State and local officials face a difficult situation in Lancaster County, Pennsylvania. They want to build new roads and expand existing ones to help relieve the bottleneck traffic that has plagued the area for several years. This once-rural county, the center of the Pennsylvania Dutch community, has become a major focus of regional development. Since 1970, the number of acres approved for development has increased nearly tenfold. The population of Lancaster County has risen from fewer than 260,000 people in 1964 to more than 400,000 in 1988. More significant has been the growth of business and commercial activity, especially in the tourism industry. A tourism official estimates that between 3.5 and 5 million visitors come through the county annually. All objective analyses support the call for a major highway construction effort in Lancaster County.

The problem is that this economic and population growth in Lancaster is in direct conflict with the beliefs of the county's long-time residents—the Amish. Indeed, these demographic and economic changes not only challenge their beliefs but threaten their very existence. The 10,000-member Amish community has been in Lancaster County for 250 years. A religious sect that clings to an old world life-style and strict community standards of behavior, the Amish have provided the area with its distinct identity and are (unintentionally) the primary tourist attraction in the region. For them, the proposed highways and increased development pose a threat to the community's values and life-style. And while they are not usually vocal on issues outside their community, the Amish have shown up by the hundreds at state highway department hearings to silently protest that agency's plans. Their concerns have already led to the cancellation of one superhighway proposal, and in 1988, they challenged several other proposals considered by public officials.[1]

The ongoing story of Lancaster County is one example of how demographic, cultural, and economic factors influence the decisions of government and the work of public administrators. In this chapter, we turn our attention to those demographic, cultural, and economic conditions that help shape the work of American public administration. Included among these factors are population patterns, value systems, and economic circumstances, which many government administrators must face each day. Ranging from the growth or decline in the number of city residents and the priorities of the citizenry to the existence of affluence or poverty in the community, together these are called *social* or *demographic factors*. Each imposes constraints on what government agencies can do, and each can provide an opportunity for better public service.

As is the case with physical and technological ecologies, the actual impact of demographic, cultural, and economic factors varies from agency to agency.

Nevertheless, it is difficult for any national, state, or local agency to escape their influence. This is especially true when social factors shape the general public's expectations. For it is not only the distribution of populations or the values of people or the existing economic conditions that stimulate and direct government activity. To these features of public administration's ecology must be added the indirect effect; that is, how each influences the expectations that public administrators face.

The Demographics of American Society

At its most basic level, public administration involves service to people by people. What characterizes the people being served—who they are, where they reside, what they do for a living, and what kind of life-style they have—is an important concern of American public administration. Consequently, it is important that we understand the characteristics of these people—that is, the *demographics* of the population—if we are to improve our understanding of public administration.

Different public administrators deal with different types of people, some rich and some poor, some young and some old, some healthy and some ill. A public school administrator deals with young people (or their parents) all the time. In contrast, a nursing home administrator serves the needs of a much older age group, elderly people (and their children). Each local government administrator must deal with the unique characteristics of the area's residents. These demographic features of the ecology—both population patterns and changes in population characteristics over time—can have direct impacts on the nature of the job challenges facing public administrators. These same characteristics also can have dramatic impacts on the public's expectations for government administration (see Profile 6.1).

Being an administrator in a homogeneous community, in which most residents are alike in terms of age, race, and income, is much different from holding a similar position in a city with a more diverse population. In both kinds of cities, administrators provide basic services; but the differences in the diversity of the populations affect the administrative tasks. When the population is relatively homogeneous, most public policies are not controversial. In Santa Barbara, California, where all residents are relatively comfortable financially, the city council had no trouble passing an ordinance in 1986 that banned sleeping overnight in the parks. The ordinance was passed to discourage homeless people from staying in Santa Barbara. The community ultimately retracted the ordinance, but only after advocates for the homeless from outside Santa Barbara threatened to organize protests to embarrass the city.

Consider also the age factor as an influence on public administrators' jobs. The public administrator cannot ignore the influence that different age groups

PROFILE 6.1
The Keeper of the Numbers

One way that changing demographics can influence the work of public administration is in creating a demand for government to establish a means for monitoring demographic trends. On the national level, this task is undertaken by a number of federal agencies, the best known of which is the Department of Commerce's Census Bureau. Equally important, however, is the Department of Labor's Bureau of Labor Statistics.

Samuel M. Ehrenhalt is a regional commissioner of the U.S. Bureau of Labor Statistics. With a staff of one hundred and a budget of $5 million, Ehrenhalt is charged with conducting statistical research on the economies of New York, New Jersey, Puerto Rico, and the Virgin Islands. He serves as "the keeper of the numbers" for a region that includes one of the nation's largest metropolitan areas and the world's most important financial centers.

To the uninformed outsider, collecting and reporting on economic statistics may seem mundane and unexciting work. But those who look to Ehrenhalt for information wouldn't agree. His numbers can influence payrolls on Wall Street and rents for apartments and homes throughout metropolitan New York. "He can help the Transit Authority make its trains run on time (by pointing out the shortage in railway maintenance workers) or cause an upheaval in the planning office of the Brooklyn Union Gas Company (by forecasting a move of bank computer operations from Manhattan to the other boroughs). . . ."

The impact of such economic statistics, however, is not limited to the detailed decisions of specific companies and agencies. Ehrenhalt's numbers can also influence the policy-making activities of entire governments. Although he tries to keep out of politics, his statistical reports sometimes make that impossible. Throughout the 1980s, for example, he warned New Yorkers that the city "was placing too many of its eggs in one basket by allowing the financial services industry to overwhelm manufacturing as the largest segment of the local economy." City officials, he argued, needed to do more "to preserve balance and diversity" in the city's economy. While reflecting Ehrenhalt's informed judgment on the trends he was monitoring, these conclusions directly conflicted with the forecasts and policies of the city. "Mayor Koch kept sending me letters that started, 'I can't believe you were quoted correctly,'" Ehrenhalt told a *New York Times* reporter.

Ehrenhalt started with the Bureau of Labor Statistics in the mid-1950s, gradually working his way up the ladder. He is well respected in his profession and has often been given the opportunity to assume an even higher position at the bureau's Washington headquarters. In the late 1970s, he decided to accept one such offer. His two high school–age children were equally excited for him. "They told me how happy they were for me and how exciting it would be to live in a new place. I could go to Washington, they said, and they would find a family to move in with here." Ehrenhalt changed his mind and remains in New York as the keeper of the economic numbers for that region.

SOURCE: Quotes and information from Albert Scardino, "Keeper of That Statistical Song and Dance" *New York Times*, 2 May 1988, Business section, pp. 1, 27.

make on government. The relative mix of city services is different in cities with relatively young and relatively elderly populations. In Hollywood, Florida, for example, where one in every four residents is sixty-five years or older, city administrators face much different demands and problems from those in El Paso, Texas, which has the highest proportion of residents under eighteen years old among all major American cities. A younger population calls for more schools, more sports-oriented programs, and a greater emphasis on traffic safety issues like school crosswalks, school crossing guards, and speed-limit enforcement. In contrast, an older population generates demands for senior citizen centers, recreation programs tailored to more diverse interests and oftentimes sedate life-styles,[2] and the traffic safety issues are more likely to revolve around retesting drivers for vision and driving skills. Further, in a city where many residents are no longer able to drive, public transportation is likely to be in high demand.

The ethnic and racial composition of a community also can have an effect on public administration. City administrators in El Paso, Texas, cannot ignore the fact that nearly two-thirds of the city's residents are of Latino origin. Similarly, administrators in Los Angeles County, California, cannot pretend that the growing ethnic diversity of its population does not affect the city's daily operations.[3] Such factors do make a difference. Communities that have diverse ethnic populations pose a challenge to the public administrator, who must be sensitive to the special concerns and needs of minority groups. Population diversity brings with it the need for public administrators — whether ambulance drivers or teachers in the local school system — to be sensitive to cultural and language differences.

In areas where language factors are important, public services are also affected. Public facilities and services must minimize the potential barriers that language can create for citizens of the community. Citizens who cannot read English still need government services. In many communities in the southwestern United States, governments post forms and signs in Spanish as well as English. In some communities with a high proportion of recent emigrés, emergency service agencies have on staff people who can speak the various languages of the population. Thus, when life-threatening emergencies arise, ambulance drivers and emergency room personnel do not have to take the time to seek out an interpreter. The increasing bilingualism of many American communities has caused voters in some jurisdictions to pass statutes making English the official language. It is difficult to predict what impact such laws will have on the work of government officials who must contend with the facts of cultural life in their communities.

The stability of the population can also make a difference to public administrators. When we examine demographic migration patterns, we see reasons for dramatic differences in demands for government services. For example, the job of public administrators changed considerably prior to World War II, when Americans moved in great numbers from rural areas and small cities to metropolitan areas. From the end of World War II until the early 1970s, the population shifts were from central cities to suburbia. More recently, the shift has been toward "exurbia," those areas outside the suburban ring that typically surrounds a city. Each of these population shifts has created new opportunities and challenges for local administrators. The nature of the effect depends on whether the administrative area gained or lost population.

While some communities have gone through periods of boom and bust, others have remained demographically stable. In Colorado, for example, small towns in the mountains have been through cycles of population gains and losses over the past 125 years. These boom-and-bust cycles were caused by on-again, off-again efforts to mine the region's riches. In the 1800s, it was gold and silver mining. Throughout the twentieth century, it has been mining of coal, uranium, and other scarce ores. During our national energy shortage in the early 1970s, projects aimed at producing oil from shale rock created population explosions in some Colorado cities. By 1986, most of those oil projects had been abandoned.

Public administrators must adapt their public-service activities to these boom-and-bust cycles. As communities boom, the demand for services is intense. When the demand goes bust, the local government must cut back its services. When populations decline, governments must cope with the problems generated by having excess capacity, such as too many city garbage trucks given reduced demand. Should the city sell those garbage trucks or put them in storage as spares? Government officials face extreme challenges as they try to adapt to the boom-and-bust swings in demands for public services.

Historically, the American people have been moving westward for nearly two centuries (see Figure 6.1). On a national and regional level, the movement of the U.S. population has been consistent over the past several decades. Between 1950 and 1987, however, that trend increased in strength. States in the northeastern United States contained 26.1 percent of all Americans in 1950, but by 1987 only 20.5 percent of Americans resided in that region. In the meantime, states in the western United States counted 13.3 percent of all Americans among their residents in 1950. By 1987, just over 20 percent of all Americans lived in the West—almost as many as in the Northeast.[4]

These trends are even more dramatic if we consider what happened in specific parts of the nation. During the late 1970s, Texas was gaining nearly

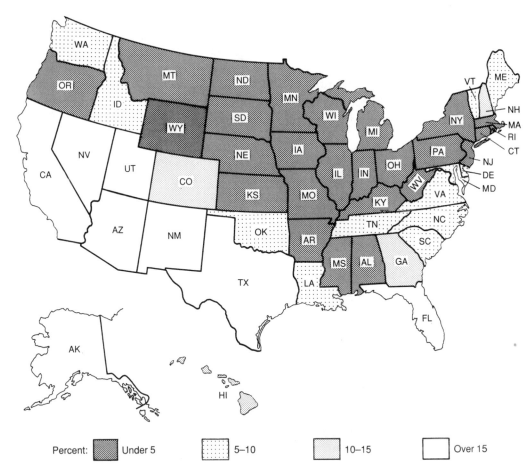

FIGURE 6.1   Changes in state population, 1980–1986 (in percentages).   (Source: *Statistical Abstract of the United States*, 108th ed. [Washington, DC: Government Printing Office, 1987], pp. 6, 21.

400,000 new residents each year. Other states, such as Massachusetts, Pennsylvania, and Iowa, were recording losses or minimal population gains during that same period. By 1986, the huge population shifts had tapered off; the migration patterns were less dramatic. Nevertheless, between 1980 and 1986, the Northeast suffered a net loss of nearly 1 percent of its residents, and the Midwest lost nearly 3.4 percent of its population base to other regions. While these figures may seem small, consider that 1 percent of the Northeast's population in the mid-1980s amounted to about 386,000 people, many of them productive taxpayers. In Iowa alone, nearly 166,000 (or 5.7 percent) of its 1980 population had left the state by 1986![5]

Shifts in population present public administrators with major challenges in building and maintaining physical and social infrastructures, such as roads and schools. The exact nature and impact of these changes on public administration depends on whether there is a net gain or loss due to the migration. Cities like Houston in the late 1970s found themselves strained to the limits of their capacity to provide needed services as new residents moved to the area. In contrast, government units in areas of population decline found themselves with unused facilities to maintain and excess capacity to deliver unneeded services.[6]

Public administrators' jobs are also affected by the density or concentration of the population with which they must deal. Densely populated communities pose problems different from those of communities with relatively dispersed residents. Consider the differences between tasks undertaken by a Wyoming county sheriff's department and the Los Angeles County police department. In addition to distinct physical surroundings, the two law-enforcement agencies must deal with completely different levels of population concentration. In general, the high density of Los Angeles' population will result in a higher rate of serious crimes than that in Wyoming. While a Wyoming sheriff's department may face one homicide in a decade, the Los Angeles Police Department is likely to face this problem about every 12 hours or so.

The population's socioeconomic status also affects the expectations for public administrators and the nature of their jobs. A poorer population generates greater demands for social welfare services and related government functions, whereas wealthier areas of America tend to put pressure on their governments to provide social amenities such as tree-lined streets and concerts in the park. Hence, we expect public administration in Newark, New Jersey (with a 1985 per-capita income of $6,494), to differ from administration in Seattle, Washington (with a 1985 per-capita income of $12,919).[7]

These are just some of the demographic features that shape the character of a community or region and thereby help shape the job of American public administrators. We need to be aware of demographic patterns in the ecology of America's public administrators. The composition of the population affects the job challenges and expectations public administrators face in their jobs. In turn, shifts in population impact on the jobs of public administrators. Administrators must adapt government operations to the changing circumstances.

American Culture and Social Values

The Concept of Culture

In addition to the composition of the American population, public administrators find their jobs influenced by the society's culture and those values held in common by the American people. By American culture we do not mean symphony orchestras or Bruce Springsteen concerts. Rather, we mean America's collective worldview. This collective worldview affects what we think is possible and, in turn, what we think is reasonable to expect from government administration.

For example, our collective worldview does not hold that human beings can control most natural geological forces. Hence, we do not expect public administrators to prevent earthquakes. However, we do expect them to monitor the construction standards for buildings and bridges in earthquake-prone areas. We expect public administrators to make sure these structures are as safe as the law requires. When a major highway bridge in Oakland, California, collapsed during the October 1989 earthquake, there was a public outcry about the design of that structure. Modifications were soon made to prevent a recurrence of the problem.

Similarly, we do not believe human beings can control or adequately predict the weather. Hence, we do not blame public administrators for droughts or torrential rainstorms. But we do expect the Weather Bureau (the National Weather Service) to monitor weather patterns and to inform us of the upcoming weather and to advise us about what to do in case of a weather emergency. We also look to other agencies, such as the Federal Emergency Management Agency (FEMA), to have contingency plans for handling weather-related disasters (see Insight 5.2).

Added to our worldview — that is, to what we believe we can control — are our value systems, which reflect what we think is appropriate and desirable for government to do. *Values* are those conditions or behaviors that individuals or groups desire and are willing to expend effort to attain. Values play an important role in determining how people act and their reactions to others' behavior. Although we may not always behave according to the mandates of our value systems, we judge our own behavior and the behavior of others according to the ethical standards derived from those values (see Chapter 3). In this sense, then, the values society holds affect all aspects of American life, including the work of public administrators.[8] This is particularly true in regard to social and political value systems.

Social Values

Social values reflect how society expects individuals to act and to relate to other people. They have an important influence on public administration because they reflect our fundamental expectations for the behavior of others in society. Social values prescribe how individuals in society should behave toward other members of society. Students of social values have attempted to analyze them by focusing on the role they play in performing some critical social functions.[9] For example, social values help specify how to harness individual needs and desires, how to harmonize social and private interests, the norms for applying rules and regulations, and the standards for evaluating others. These four dimensions of America's basic social values reflect our collective judgment about how individuals should behave. Each represents a type of human behavior with which society must contend

1. Harnessing individual needs and desires: *immediate gratification versus deferred gratification.*
2. Harmonizing social and private interests: *individual interest orientation versus collective interest orientation.*
3. Norms for applying rules and regulations: *particularistic versus universalistic.*
4. Standards for evaluating others: *ascription versus achievement.*

The first dimension relates to what society prescribes as desirable approaches to *harnessing individual needs and aspirations.* Does society value behavior that seeks the immediate gratification of individual needs and desires or does it reward those who defer their desires and needs to some future time? The role of government and the behavior expected of public officials vary according to where a community falls on this continuum. For example, in a community that values immediate gratification, there are bound to be fewer restrictions on social behavior and less pressure on government to enforce laws dealing with such things as sexual activity, drinking alcoholic beverages, and the use of dangerous drugs. In a community that values deferred gratification, however, government officials are more likely to be pressured to formulate and implement policies that place restrictions on social behaviors (see Insight 6.1).

The second dimension of the American value system is concerned with how to *harmonize social and private interests.* When faced with a conflict between individual and community needs, does society value the interests of the individual or those of the group? Communities that value the individual are likely to limit the role of government, whereas those that value the group or some collective interest are likely to expect government's role to be more active and visible.

The third dimension of our value system addresses the *norms or standards used to apply society's rules and regulations.* Does the community frown upon the use of favoritism or nepotism in the application of rules, or does it overlook violations of regulations under some conditions? That is, do the rules and regulations apply universally or particularistically? Are speeding tickets always given to drivers caught exceeding the 55-mph speed limit on a local highway, or are there some times of the day (e.g., after midnight) when police tolerate speeding up to 70 mph? Communities that value the universalistic application of standards expect their public officials to avoid and actively prevent favoritism. Those that take a more particularistic approach permit people to plead their special cases and tolerate public officials who "give a break" to offenders.

The fourth dimension of social values addresses the *standards for evaluating others.* Does an individual's standing in a community depend more on who

INSIGHT 6.1

ENFORCING "ANTISMOKING" POLICIES

In January 1988, New York City Mayor Edward I. Koch signed the Clean Indoor Air Act. Under the provisions of this legislation, described as "among the toughest of its kind in the nation," cigarette smoking is restricted in most public places in the city. Businesses can set aside an area for their employees who wish to smoke, and restaurants with seating capacities greater than fifty must provide nonsmoking and smoking areas. To help enforce the legislation, the city set up a complaint hot line for reporting violations, hired inspectors, and established a system of fines for violators. The policy was successfully implemented in phases starting in April 1988 and ending in mid-July of that year.

The fact that New York's antismoking policies are working so well is a surprise to many observers. Jane Gross, a reporter for the *New York Times*, notes that New York "is a city not known for environmental awareness or good manners, a city that even its boosters say has more than its share of foul air and foul mouths." So why is the Clean Indoor Air Act working so well? Gross reports that many believe its success is due to "a profound social change that has transformed the way people live and work."

The law has been accepted, according to health experts, public officials, smokers and nonsmokers, because it reflects these widespread changes in attitude, which have left many smokers ashamed of their habit and compliant to the wishes of nonsmokers.

Gross points out that smokers feel isolated, almost like criminals. "When you have to slink off to have a cigarette, there's a sense of shame that attaches to that," reports one smoker. The areas set aside for smokers in offices are often in designated restrooms or vacant offices filled with the haze of smoke and ashtrays filled with cigarette butts. "Smokers describe these as demeaning places," reports Gross, "that contribute to their sense of being pariahs."

Thus, although New York City has spent little to enforce the Clean Indoor Air Act, it is working quite well. The secret in this case is the support for the policies generated by today's antismoking social values and attitudes.

SOURCE: Quotes and information from Jane Gross, "New York's No-Smoking Law: Echoing Society's 'No More!'" *New York Times*, Sunday, 24 July 1988, pp. 1–14.

he or she is than on what he or she has accomplished? An ascriptive society evaluates individuals based on criteria over which they have little or no control, such as family ties, race or ethnic group, and gender. Such a society looks with favor on those people who have the right family ties, attend the right church, or have the right skin color. Favoritism is inherent in any society that gives some of its members status based on personal characteristics as opposed to an individual's level of achievement. Thus, favoritism is more likely to be tolerated in an ascriptive society. In contrast, public officials in an achievement-oriented society focus their attention on those who have earned their status in the community. In an ascriptive social setting, the son or daughter of a mayor may get a summer job because of who he or she is. In an achievement-oriented society, however, it does not matter who you are so long as you score high on relevant examinations or performance tests.

These four dimensions of the American value system are only a few among many that have an impact on the administration of government. Generally, Americans tend to favor deferred gratification, individual interests, the universalistic application of standards, and rewards for achievement. In most instances, these are the values that administrators follow.

Beyond these nationwide values, however, state and local administrators must be sensitive to the values of their particular communities. A city manager who agrees to provide a stand-by fire truck during the local college's homecoming bonfire may find that policy decision is consistent with the local community's standard of harmonizing social and private interests. Imagine the controversy engendered if that same manager also agreed to provide a stand-by fire truck while the local Ku Klux Klan burned a cross at a local rally.

How important are basic social values to the way American government actually operates? Some sociologists and other students of American culture argue that America's traditional social values are irrelevant and even ignored in practice. More and more studies point out a growing gap between America's social values and the reality of social behavior in the United States.[10] Daniel Bell, for example, argues that in the 1920s and 1930s, a form of materialistic hedonism took hold in the United States. According to Bell, this trend reflects a greater willingness of Americans to seek immediate gratification. Others argue that Americans have replaced their individualism with a collective-oriented social ethic that is manifested in the modern corporation.

Nevertheless, we still see the basic social values of American life reflected in some important issues. Consider, for example, the federal government's commitment to *equal employment opportunity* (EEO). As a public policy, EEO reflects the basis of our social value system in its call for equal treatment of each individual regardless of race, sex, color, religion, national origin, or physical condition. Specifically, it prohibits arbitrary discrimination against an individual on any of these grounds.

Programmatically, government efforts to prevent discriminatory behavior in hiring and other personnel practices now extend beyond a simple prohibition against discrimination. Under provisions of various civil rights legislations, government efforts also include *affirmative action* programs. Unlike antidiscrimination programs, affirmative action calls for positive "actions appropriate to overcome the effects of past or present practices, policies, or other barriers to equal employment opportunity." In one sense, affirmative-action policies are a logical extension of EEO and are arguably in line with America's social values dating back to the Civil War. In fact, many Americans support such programs because they are a means for compensating minorities for past discriminatory practices.

Nevertheless, affirmative-action programs have been the focus of much controversy in recent years. Some critics argue that the programs are poorly designed or administered. Others claim that they are associated with preferential treatment. Critics of affirmative action argue that it is in conflict with individual achievement and other core values of American life. The hostility against affirmative action increased as the U.S. economy slipped into recession during the 1970s and the job market became tighter for many Americans. Thus, as public administrators continue to implement affirmative-action programs as forcefully as possible, they find themselves in an awkward position—implementing legislation that is perceived by some as contrary to America's basic social values.[11]

Political Values

Americans have a value system relating to American government and politics as well. *Political values* embody the standards by which people evaluate government and orient themselves within the political system. The American public's political values fall into three categories: the public ethos, political ideologies, and public attitudes. The most basic group of political values is the *public ethos*, which represents those widely shared political values over which there is little disagreement. At a more concrete level are several major *political ideologies*, which represent conflicting orientations toward the role of government in American society. Finally, there are general *public attitudes*, which reflect how the American people feel about government and politics at any particular time.

Public Ethos.   Of all the parts of the social ecology described in this chapter, perhaps none is more difficult to grasp than that of the American public ethos. Our public ethos reflects such basic and fundamental assumptions about political life that most of us take it for granted. As a result, discussions of beliefs that are part of the public ethos almost never occur. Tenets of the public ethos are most noticed when some behavior or suggestion violates those basic assumptions; then discussion of these beliefs may occur. The American public ethos includes these five basic tenets about the role of government in American society:

1. *Individualism*
2. *Equality*
   - Of opportunity
   - Political
   - Under the law

3. *Limited Government*
   - Civil liberties
   - Rule of law
4. *Private Property*
   - Rights of ownership
   - Capitalism
   - Priority of marketplace
5. *Self-rule*
   - Democracy
   - Local sovereignty

Individualism is related to the social value that emphasizes giving priority to the interests of the individual.[13] In the political arena, individualism stresses the rationality of individual ideas. As a tenet of our political ethos, individualism justifies a political system that operates on the assumption that every person acts in his or her own self-interest. As a political value, individualism implies an instrumental view of the state, in which government exists to serve the needs of the individual participants in the political system, rather than the interests of the system as a whole. Individualism also provides a justification for the American pluralistic system, in which individuals are free to pursue their narrow and limited interests through joining with others in alliances called pressure groups. Most important, individualism places a strong emphasis on the rights of individuals in their relationships with government—rights against intrusions and arbitrariness as well as rights to receive public services.

The American public ethos also includes *equality*, a political value expressed in three distinct ways. First, it takes the form of equality of opportunity, which emphasizes freedom from government-supported interference in the choices a citizen can make. According to this notion of equality, government may even be expected to increase the options people have in everyday life. Second, it oftentimes emerges as political equality, in which each individual is to have equal access to influencing government matters. The third manifestation is equality under the law, in which government is expected to treat each individual the same under similar circumstances.

The American public ethos also reflects the view that government is a necessary evil that must be restrained. From this political value of *limited government* comes the American stress on fundamental liberties. Americans' belief in their fundamental liberties is the basis for the limits we impose on our government's abilities to intervene in our private lives. These limits may take the form of prohibitions on certain types of government actions (as expressed in our Constitution's Bill of Rights) or guarantees of due process of law. Also associated with this value is the "rule of law" doctrine, which posits that America is a nation of laws, not people. Consequently, no one individual is above the law.

As a political value, the right to hold *private property* is more highly valued in the United States than just about anywhere else. Thus, the American political ethos stresses the rights of ownership, the capitalist economic system, and the value of using market mechanisms rather than government in dealing with problems.

Self-rule is another widely shared value that serves as the basis for two strongly held American beliefs. First, Americans value the idea of democracy. They hold to a belief in consent of the governed through a system of majority rule, minority rights, citizen participation, and representative government. Second, self-rule promotes a belief in the value of localism, which means that problems are best solved at the level where they occur. In turn, this belief leads most Americans to favor local sovereignty and governmental decentralization.

How does the American public ethos influence the world of public administration? The public administrator's contact with the public occurs within the context of these widely shared values we call the public ethos. In some instances, the nature of the contact is likely to create tension or conflict for the values of public administration. For example, while providing due process of law may take additional time and resources, public administrators must be careful not to take an action that may violate or challenge some fundamental liberty laid out in the public ethos, no matter how trivial the action may seem at the time. This is especially true in law enforcement, where the failure to inform a suspect of his or her rights or the arrest of the wrong person can prove very costly. In addition, the administrative values of efficiency, expertise, and bureaucratic control are not easily reconciled with the democratic principle of self-rule. Hence, acceptable administrative mechanisms sometimes seemingly contradict those of American democracy (see Insight 6.2). There is little doubt that the public administrator must contend with the real or potential dilemmas posed by the public ethos.

The public ethos of self-rule is also notable for another implication it has for the operations of government. Self-rule includes strong bias in favor of democratic approaches to decision making. Hence, public administrators face continuous pressures for citizen participation in government decision making. Many agencies must hold public hearings regarding some upcoming decision. In many cities and counties, the adoption of a new zoning regulation can occur only after the local planning agency has provided local residents with notification of the forthcoming change and given them an opportunity to address the changes in an open forum. While desirable in many respects, such citizen participation does have its costs. Not only may increased citizen participation lead to additional time and resources being devoted to decision making, but it may also not result in any better or different decisions. Nevertheless, the public ethos of self-rule demands that public agencies provide such notification and hold such hearings.

Political Ideologies. In contrast to the public ethos, political ideologies are specific, action-oriented belief systems reflecting differing perspectives

INSIGHT 6.2
BUREAUCRACY VERSUS DEMOCRACY

Some students of American government argue that there exists an inherent and irreconcilable conflict between the social and political values of public administration and the public ethos of democratic self-rule. Ralph P. Hummel, for example, contends that the bureaucratic organization of public-sector agencies shapes the way people interact with one another. In place of "ordinary *social interaction*, in which individuals act by mutually orienting themselves to each other," bureaucracy calls for "*rationally organized action*, in which individuals orient themselves to

created a new society in which social, psychological, cultural, linguistic, cognitive, and political norms are being distorted. The emergence of bureaucracy is, in short, a direct challenge to the fundamental values of American society.

A similar assessment is provided by David Nachmias and David H. Rosenbloom in their analysis of American government. They see an "inherent tension" between the requirements for democracy and bureaucracy. The contrasts between the two organizational forms are starkly outlined here:

Democracy Requires	Bureaucracy Requires
Plurality	Unity
Equality	Hierarchy
Liberty	Command
Rotation in office	Duration in office
Openness	Secrecy
Equal access to participation in politics	Differentiated access, based on authority
Election	Selection

goals and meanings defined from the top down" in some organization. Furthermore, an individual's actions are no longer evaluated on the basis of their social meaning, but instead are assessed according to their functionality for the bureaucratic system. The impact of bureaucracy is felt on the psychological level as well, for personal identity is replaced by organizational identity as the individual ego is subsumed under the pressure of bureaucratic demands.

Hummel's analysis covers other aspects of social life. He contends that bureaucratic approaches to governing have

These contrasts are made even more significant by the fact that they reflect bureaucratic challenges to some of the most fundamental dimensions of the American public ethos. It is little wonder that many Americans feel threatened by the growth of government.

SOURCE: Based on information in Ralph P. Hummel, *The Bureaucratic Experience*, 3d ed. (New York: St. Martin's Press, 1987), chap. 1, esp. pp. 3–10; and David Nachmias and David H. Rosenbloom, *Bureaucratic Government, USA* (New York: St. Martin's Press, 1980), chap. 2, esp. p. 31. Copyright © 1980 St. Martin's Press, Inc.

on government. Ideological differences may exist within the context of the general consensus embodied in the public ethos. Thus, while most Americans adhere to the public ethos of fundamental liberties, they may disagree about the degree to which an individual's freedom should be given priority over the interests of others or the good of the entire community. In recent years, for instance, the individual's right to privacy has been challenged by the community's desire to prevent the spread of AIDS. Under previous circumstances, a person diagnosed with a disease could expect that information to remain confidential. However, a great many people today argue that those with whom the AIDS victim has had sexual contact also have a right to know. Often these differences in opinion become linked to other beliefs about how the public ethos should be put into action. In short, they become part of ideological differences.

American political ideologies, unlike those found in most European and Third World countries, are rather ambiguous, inconsistent, and loose in form. They are better described as relatively consistent points of view rather than a coherent set of clearly articulated ideas. There are four major political ideologies in the United States: liberal, conservative, libertarian, and populist. These major ideologies reflect differences in views on two important issues: government intervention in economic affairs and the expansion of personal freedoms (see Figure 6.2).[14]

Traditionally, Americans have fallen into two broad ideological categories: liberal and conservative. The *liberal ideology* represents a set of beliefs favoring government intervention in the economy while opposing government interference in the basic civil liberties of American citizens. The national Democratic party since the Great Depression usually has liberal party agendas. In contrast, *conservatives* are more likely to favor maintaining government's role in regulating individual behavior while opposing increased government intervention in the economy. Conservative ideologies usually support laws against so-called victimless crimes, such as gambling and prostitution, as well as the enforcement of society's moral codes regarding pornography, drug use, abortion, and other individual behaviors.

| | | Government Intervention in the Economy | |
		Support	Oppose
Expansion of Personal Freedoms	Support	Liberal	Libertarian
	Oppose	Populist	Conservative

FIGURE 6.2 American political ideologies. (Source: William S. Maddox and Stuart A. Lilie, *Beyond Liberal and Conservative: Reassessing the Political Spectrum* [Washington, DC: CATO Institute, 1984], p. 5.)

In recent years, two other ideologies have gained a major foothold on the American political scene. *Populism* combines the liberal's desire for increasing governmental activity to deal with economic problems with the conservative's willingness to permit government intervention in the private lives of the American public. The *libertarian* ideology takes the opposite stand by opposing government intervention in either the general economy or the private life-styles of citizens.

The specific content of the major political ideologies is constantly changing as conditions change and new issues arise. It is possible for one ideology to dominate at any particular point in time. Liberalism was dominant during the 1960s, under the administrations of John F. Kennedy and Lyndon B. Johnson. Conservatism was preeminent under the presidency of Ronald Reagan and remains so under the Bush administration. There is no question, however, that the dominance of one ideology is a temporary phenomenon and challenges are likely to arise at any time.

The implications of this ideological instability for public administration are considerable. Ideologically, the liberal and populist perspectives are most conducive to the support and expansion of government. The conservative and libertarian views oppose increasing or continuing government action. Thus, shifts in the dominant ideology are likely to influence how public-sector programs and workers fare in any given period of time.[15] For example, although liberal President Johnson established the Office of Economic Opportunity (OEO) during his administration, conservative President Nixon later abolished the agency. Administrators at the OEO saw several years of their efforts undone as a result of a change in political ideology.

Ebbs and flows of political ideologies are not at all unusual. The staff of the Environmental Protection Agency (EPA) under the Carter administration was mandated to take positive steps toward protecting the quality of our air, water, and land. During the early years of the Reagan administration, however, the EPA took a much less activist approach toward environmental protection. Imagine the challenge to EPA administrators of having to serve two administrations with such disparate political ideologies! This is just one example of how public administrators must adapt to substantial changes in policy direction that accompany changes in the political ideologies of their elected leadership.

Public Attitudes.   Another dimension of American political values involves public attitudes toward government. Over the past two decades the American public's attitude toward government has been far from stable. Over time, it has swung from positive to negative and back again. Typically, when asked about their personal experiences with government programs and administrators, Americans respond favorably. However, their assessment of government in general is negative. Each year public-opinion polls indicate that an increasing number of Americans believe that government is wasteful, is run for the benefit of a few special interests, and cannot be trusted to do the right things most of the time.[16] For nearly thirty years, the Gallup Poll has been asking a sampling of the American public which institution they think poses the greatest threat to the country: big labor, big business, or big government. In 1959, only 14 percent of those polled thought it was big government; by 1969, that figure had climbed to 49 percent. In 1977, about 39 percent of the respondents thought government was the primary threat; in 1983, that figure reached 51 percent and in 1985 it remained high at 50 percent. In short, public attitudes toward government vary over time. Such variation creates constantly shifting public attitudes with which public administrators must contend.

Typically, the general public attitude toward government is difficult to pinpoint because it reflects the unstructured feelings of the citizenry. Historically, these feelings have ranged from viewing government as a necessary evil to seeing it as a positive virtue.[17] If the public attitude toward government is extremely negative and distrustful, people are likely to hold the job of the public administrator in fairly low regard. If the public attitude toward government is positive, the position of government administrators becomes more desirable in the public's eye and the level of trust and discretion allowed them increases greatly.

The Challenge of Values

American culture generates a wide range of social and political values that influence the work of government officials and public administrators in particular. Oftentimes these values represent the fundamental views of Americans about basic social and political relationships. At a less fundamental level, such as political ideologies and public attitudes, there is a tremendous degree of change and tolerance for diversity. This change presents public administrators with an ongoing challenge in their quest to be responsive to the wishes of their ultimate superiors—the citizens in their communities.

Economic Conditions

Public administration is influenced by the economy in two ways: (1) through the level of economic development and (2) through current economic conditions.

The *level of economic development* is an important factor for public administrators in several respects (see Figure 6.3). First, the level of economic development affects the capacity of a society or community to support the public sector. Logically, the greater the level of economic development of a community, the more capacity it has to fund government operations. Higher levels of economic development mean there are more resources and wealth available for government to tax. For example, suburban areas with high per-capita incomes find it much easier to generate the funds they need

FIGURE 6.3   The influences of economic development on public-sector activity.

for good schools and the finest parks and recreation programs. Since local property values are probably high, the tax rate they apply to the holdings of local residents need not be high to raise the level of revenue they need. In less economically developed areas, the same level of services will require higher tax rates. There is no doubt that a higher level of economic development can be extremely helpful.

The level of economic development also has an impact on the level of demand for public-sector services. Communities with relatively high or relatively low levels of economic development make greater demands on government than communities with moderate levels of economic development. Middle-income populations tend to make fewer demands on government than do low-income and high-income populations. A society that has many poor, unemployed, or underemployed citizens is likely to face increased demands for programs to improve the economic circumstances of those in need. Contrary to popular belief, wealthy populations do not demand less of government. Affluent communities place the same high level of demand on their governments, but they expect different types of government programs and services, such as parks and recreational facilities, tree-lined streets, and other amenities.

Finally, the level of economic development also influences the quality of the demands for public-sector services. The demands of the low-income society are different from those of the affluent society. After World War II, the United States developed into what John Kenneth Galbraith calls "the affluent society." Galbraith argues that this condition of general affluence was a new experience. "Nearly all throughout all history have been poor," and the role of governments reflected that. With affluence, however, came different attitudes toward government and expanded opportunities to solve public problems and provide public services.[18] Improvements in economic conditions generated demands for a different and more expansive role for government.

Regardless of the overall level of economic development, *current economic circumstances* as perceived by the population have an impact on the day-to-day activities of public administrators. In a period of economic growth and expansion, the public attitude is likely to be positive toward the public sector. Such attitudes are likely to result in the expansion of government programs, particularly those that serve the needs of the most economically active members. At the same time, there is likely to be less concern and pressure for the efficient operation of public agencies and more emphasis on achieving program objectives.

In contrast, during a period of recession, public attitudes are likely to turn more negative. Program cutbacks and taxpayer revolts are more common during tough economic times and issues of government efficiency and wastefulness take center stage.

"Economic growth is a powerful solvent for the problems that trouble governments," notes Charles H. Levine. "Each increment of real growth in national income can enhance the take-home pay of citizens or can be used to create new public programs without accelerating the rate of inflation or forcing politically divisive tradeoffs between old programs and new demands." This was the situation facing American governments throughout the 1950s and 1960s. When economic growth rates declined in the 1970s and 1980s, these same governments were forced "to confront some politically sensitive tradeoffs" that are "largely ignored during periods of rapid growth."[19] The continued funding and administration of government programs became increasingly problematic. The political strain this situation caused posed a serious challenge to both political and administrative officials at all levels of government.[20] The challenge of expanding government programs without economic expansion has had considerable influence on how American public administration has operated in the 1980s.

Conclusions

Just how relevant are demographic, cultural, and economic factors to the work of American public administrators? The anecdotal evidence indicates that all three factors are very important. There is, however, some direct empirical evidence to show just how important this part of the ecology is to the work of public officials. One study indicates that the quality of public-sector administration is higher in urbanized and more affluent states (such as California, Wisconsin, and Pennsylvania) than in more rural and less affluent states (such as Alabama, Mississippi, and Wyoming).[21] This finding is supported by numerous other studies indicating that socioeconomic factors are extremely important in shaping the politics and policies of state and local governments as well as their administration.[22]

Thus, if we are to understand American public administration, we must improve our knowledge of its demographic, cultural, and economic ecologies. In many respects, the connections are quite clear. Shifting populations bring shifting responsibilities for public-sector workers. There are considerable pressures, as well, on public programs reflecting whether the people being served are old or young, poor or wealthy, or growing or declining in numbers.

The same is true for changes occurring in American culture. Some social and political values are stable and change only gradually if at all. Other values are constantly changing. The result is likely to be even more pressures on public administrators, sometimes challenging basic ethical standards of behavior. For example, over the past century American attitudes toward racial minorities has changed significantly. Where once segregation was acceptable in some parts of the country, today we have laws prohibiting discrimination and social values discouraging such behavior. Thus, where once public administrators were expected to enforce segregation laws, today we expect them to enforce desegregation policies and promote integration where possible.

Further, the influence of changing economic conditions on public administration is clear. Since 1975, the U.S. economy has seen ups and downs, and many public programs have been at the mercy of these changes in economic fortune. Thus, when discussing the economic parts of the ecology that help shape public administration, we cannot underestimate their direct impact.

In addition, these factors have an indirect influence on public administration through public expectations. Population changes generate changes in attitudes among the population. As a population ages, so does its views of government and how it should operate. As values change, so does the public's definition of what is right and wrong behavior by government officials. As economic circumstances become less stable, so do the expectations we have of government services and the people who provide them. For American public administration, the constant changes in our society—whether demographic, cultural, or economic—pose a continuing challenge.

Summary

1. The social factors of the ecology—demographics, cultural values, and the economy—have significant impacts on the work of public administration.
2. Population characteristics and trends—demographics—are relevant to almost every public administrator's job, although their influence varies from place to place and from task to task.
3. Cultural values help shape the work of public administration by reflecting fundamental expectations regarding the behavior of others (social values) and how we feel about government (political values).
4. The economy influences public administration in two ways: through the level of economic development and through the public's perceptions of current economic conditions.

Study Questions

1. How have the demographic characteristics of your hometown changed over the years? Consider how these changes have influenced the kinds and quality of public services provided in the area.
2. American values have gone through major changes during the past two centuries, most of them reflecting a shift from a rural to an urban society. What impact do you think that shift has had on our social and political values? What kinds of impacts have these value changes had on the work of government administrators?
3. Given the way Americans react to shifts in the economy, what would be the consequences for government services if the United States experienced a period of unprecedented economic growth over the next decade? What would happen if we instead suffered another Great Depression?
4. Can you think of any public administration job that is not influenced by the social factors discussed in this chapter?

Notes

1. John G. Falcioni, "County Mulls New Growth, Amish Values," *City & State*, 18 July, 1988, pp. 1, 25.
2. See William W. Lammers, *Public Policy and the Aging* (Washington, DC: CQ Press, 1983).
3. See Clarence N. Stone, Robert K. Whelan, and William J. Murin, *Urban Policy and Politics in a Bureaucratic Age*, 2nd ed. (Englewood Cliffs, NJ: Prentice-Hall, 1986), esp. chap. 3.
4. Bureau of the Census, *Statistical Abstract of the United States, 1989* (Washington, DC: Government Printing Office, 1989), table 22.
5. See William K. Stevens, "Census Report Finds a Return to Normal in Population Shifts," *New York Times*, 1 October 1987, pp. 1, 16. There is some evidence that the trend has not only returned to normal but that it may in fact have shifted entirely. By 1986, for example, there was a noticeable shift in economic and population growth toward the Northeast, especially in the New England region. See "A Tale of Two States," *Time* magazine, 26 May 1986, pp. 14–18. Also see Robert Reinhold, "Texas in a Tailspin," *New York Times Magazine*, 20 July 1986, pp. 22–25, 50–52, 57.
6. Both population growth and population decline have political as well as administrative consequences. On the politics of growth, see Paul E. Peterson, *City Limits* (Chicago: University of Chicago Press, 1981). On the politics of decline, see Terry Nichols Clark and Lorna Crowley Ferguson, *City Money: Political Processes, Fiscal Strain, and Retrenchment* (New York: Columbia University Press, 1983).
7. Bureau of the Census, *Statistical Abstract of the United States, 1989* (Washington, DC: Government Printing Office, 1989), table 732.
8. For a general discussion of values, value systems, and their implications for public administration, see Geoffrey Vickers, *Value Systems and Social Process* (Middlesex, Engl.: Penguin, 1968).

9. See Talcott Parsons, *The Social System* (Glencoe, IL: The Free Press, 1951), pp. 4–23

10. See Daniel Bell, *The Cultural Contradictions of Capitalism* (New York: Basic Books, 1978), pp. 74–76; William H. Whyte, Jr., *The Organization Man* (Garden City, NY: Doubleday-Anchor, 1956), chap. 2; David Riesman, with Nathan Glazer and Reuel Denny, *The Lonely Crowd: A Study of the Changing American Character*, abridged ed. (New Haven, CT: Yale University Press, 1969); Gunnar Myrdal, *An American Dilemma* (New York: Harper & Row, 1944); and Samuel P. Huntington, *American Politics: The Promise of Disharmony* (Cambridge, MA: Belknap, 1981).

11. See Felix A. Nigro and Lloyd G. Nigro, *The New Public Personnel Administration*, 2d ed. (Itasca, IL: F. E. Peacock, 1981), p. 191; and Thomas Sowell, "'Affirmative Action' Reconsidered," *The Public Interest* 42 (Winter 1976): 47–65. For a discussion of how affirmative action fits into the fundamental value scheme of public personnel administration, see Donald Klingner and John Nalbandian, *Public Personnel Management*, 2d ed. (Englewood Cliffs, NJ: Prentice-Hall, 1985), chap. 5.

12. For a recent study of the American public ethos, see Herbert McClosky and John Zaller, *The American Ethos: Public Attitudes Toward Capitalism and Democracy* (New York: Harvard University Press, 1984).

13. On the pervasiveness of individualism in America today, see Robert N. Bellah, et al., *Habits of the Heart: Individualism and Commitment in American Life* (Berkeley, CA: University of California Press, 1985).

14. See William S. Maddox and Stuart A. Lilie, *Beyond Liberal and Conservative: Reassessing the Political Spectrum* (Washington, DC: CATO Institute, 1984).

15. For an interesting case study on the policy implications of changes in the ideological perspectives of our national leaders, see David A. Stockman, *The Triumph of Politics: How the Reagan Revolution Failed* (New York: Harper & Row, 1986).

16. See Seymour Martin Lipset and William Schneider, *The Confidence Gap: Business, Labor, and Government in the Public Mind* (New York: The Free Press, 1983).

17. The idea of government as a "necessary evil" is, of course, from the pen of Tom Paine; the view of government as a positive virtue is an observation made by Theodore J. Lowi, *The End of Liberalism: The Second Republic of the United States*, 2d ed. (New York: W. W. Norton, 1979).

18. See John Kenneth Galbraith, *The Affluent Society* (New York: New American Library, 1958).

19. Charles H. Levine, "The New Crisis in the Public Sector," in *Managing Fiscal Stress: The Crisis in the Public Sector*, ed. by Charles H. Levine (Chatham, NJ: Chatham House, 1980), p. 3.

20. See B. Guy Peters and Richard Rose, "The Growth of Government and the Political Consequences of Economic Overload," in *Managing Fiscal Stress: The Crisis in the Public Sector*, ed. by Charles H. Levine (Chatham, NJ: Chatham House, 1980), pp. 33–51; and ed. by Richard Rose, *Challenge to Governance: Studies in Overloaded Polities* (Beverly Hills, CA: Sage, 1980).

21. Lee Siegelman, "The Quality of Administration: An Exploration in the American States," cited in Richard C. Elling, "State Bureaucracies," *Politics in the American States: A Comparative Analysis*, 4th ed., ed. by Virginia Gray, Herbert Jacob, and Kenneth N. Vines (Boston: Little, Brown, 1983), chap. 8.

22. See Thomas R. Dye, *Understanding Public Policy*, 6th ed. (Englewood Cliffs, NJ: Prentice-Hall, 1987), chap. 12.

GOVERNMENTAL

INSTITUTIONS

The Governmental Stage

Governmental institutions constitute another arena that can influence public administrators. These institutions represent the constitutional and legal factors in our ecology of public administration. They usually have much more direct and pervasive consequences for public administration than any of the ecological factors discussed in earlier chapters. The principal reason is that public administration is a part of the general government framework established through constitutional and legal institutions. Thus governmental institutions provide the stage on which public administrators and other policymakers play their roles.

Extending this theatrical metaphor, we can say that the ecological factors described in Chapters 5 and 6—physical, technological, social, economic—represent the theater building. The theater's stage sets limits on the performers' movements, and with the help of a stage director, the actors shape their performances to fit within those limits. Further, the scenery on the stage of public administration is important to both the actors and members of the audience—that is, the general public. As the curtain is drawn, the audience gets its first look at the setting for the performance. What audience members see at that moment has an impact on what they expect. If what they see is a nineteenth-century English drawing room, they will expect the actors to dress a certain way and to speak with British accents. However, if the scene is one of the mountainous outdoors, then their expectations will be quite different. Thus, the stage setting not only directly influences what the actors do, but it also indirectly affects them through shaping the expectations of those in the audience.

Two Dimensions of Governmental Institutions

When discussing the constitutional and legal ecology of American public administration, our focus is on those long-standing institutional structures within which all government activity takes place. Our primary concern is with those basic principles and enduring behavior patterns in American government relevant to political representation, public policy making, and public administration. For our purposes, governmental institutions are classified as either *intra*governmental or *inter*governmental. This distinction is used here as a means for describing the scenery on the stage on which public administrators perform.

Intragovernmental institutions are those within the same government level or jurisdiction as the administrator. For the public administrator working in the national government, for example, Congress, the courts, the White

House, and other federal agencies are the basic components of the intragovernmental ecology. For a city administrator, other city departments comprise the intragovernmental ecology.

Intergovernmental institutions are those outside of the administrator's primary jurisdiction but still relevant to the work of that administrator. Thus, for the national government administrator this would include any state and local institutions he or she must interact with in conducting agency business. For a state prison administrator, the relevant intergovernmental institutions would include the federal courts because such courts may rule on the civil rights of prisoners.

Intragovernmental Institutions

At the *intragovernmental* level, the institutions relevant to each public agency take a variety of forms. Among the most important are constitutional institutions, peer agencies, and administrative management structures.

Constitutional Institutions

Constitutional institutions include those fundamental structures established in the basic legal instrument that set up the governmental jurisdiction. At the national level, this legal instrument is the U.S. Constitution. At the state and local levels, the basic legal instruments are state constitutions and local charters.

These documents or constitutional instruments perform a number of functions. First, they establish the legitimate basis of governmental authority. For example, the preamble to the U.S. Constitution confirms that the source of national governmental power is the consent of the general population. The opening phrase of that section reads, "We the People. . . ." Second, these documents also set forth the formal powers of government institutions and forge limits on governmental powers; that is, they specify what governments can and cannot do. In addition, constitutional documents arrange for the formal exercise of three basic governmental functions: the power to pass laws (legislative power), the power to execute laws (executive power), and the power to settle disputes arising under the laws (judicial power).

In studying public administration, it is important to understand the institutions assigned responsibility for the legislative, executive, and judicial functions of government. A fundamental concern of public administration is the relationship of the public bureaucracy to these different government institutions: How does the bureaucracy "fit" into the relationships among the different institutions at each level of government? Sometimes the relationships among the major governmental institutions make it easier for public agencies to accomplish their tasks. Other times the relationships among the different institutions make it more difficult for a particular agency to operate.

Local Governments. Although each local government in the United States has its own distinctive characteristics, there are three general types into which most can be classified: council/mayor governments, council/manager forms, and the commission type.

In *council/mayor governments*, the local charter establishes an elected council or commission to carry out the legislative functions of government. A popularly elected mayor is the chief executive official of government. Under this kind of arrangement, the public administrator usually reports to the mayor's office directly. In turn, the mayor answers to the council—and ultimately to the voters—for the actions of the city's bureaucracy. In its purest form, often called the *strong mayor government*, the mayor is clearly in charge. In contrast, there are *weak mayor government* forms in which voters directly elect other executive officials, such as the city treasurer or city assessor. Under the weak mayor form, the council actively participates in the appointment and oversight of the city's administrative officials (see Figure 7.1).

In *council/manager governments* (also called the *city manager plan*), the bureaucracy is under the control of a professional manager or chief administrative officer (CAO). The popularly elected council hires the manager to administer the city's affairs. Under this system, the council itself usually selects the mayor from among its members. The mayor's obligations typically include chairing council meetings and performing many of the symbolic duties of the city, such as greeting special guests and signing official documents on behalf of the city. The manager or CAO is usually a professional administrator who serves at the will of a majority of the council. The manager usually has full control over the day-to-day operations of government, including the hiring and firing of administrative employees (see Profile 7.1). While under this system the professional manager responds directly to the council, all other administrative officials report directly to the CAO (see Figure 7.2).

In the *commission government* form, different administrative departments are under the supervision of one of several popularly elected city commissioners who together function as a legislative body. The entire commission

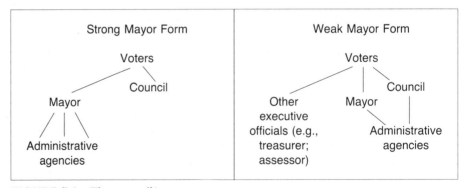

FIGURE 7.1   The council/mayor government.

PROFILE 7.1

Tucson's Native Son

Joel D. Valdez, city manager and lifelong resident of Tucson, Arizona, sometimes wonders if he would have succeeded elsewhere. It is not that he didn't have the opportunity to relocate; other cities sought to recruit his services. But today Valdez remains in his hometown.

In a 1988 interview, Valdez reflected on his fourteen years as city manager of Tucson, describing the position as a "responsible" and "important" job. He was appointed to the position at the age of thirty-nine by a 4–3 city council vote. The selection was controversial because Valdez did not have as much experience and education as the other candidates seeking the position. But the man who cast the deciding vote in Valdez's favor—then-Mayor Lew Murphy—never regretted doing so.

Valdez's fourteen-year tenure as city manager of Tucson is impressive, considering that the national average for city managers is just under four years. Although there have been a couple of instances when he nearly lost his job, his opponents had not been able to muster the four council votes needed to fire him.

Valdez is the only Hispanic city manager of a U.S. city with over 300,000 inhabitants. This is quite an accomplishment considering the fact that Tucson's large Hispanic community still remains outside of the inner circle of powerful social and economic leaders. Valdez is all too aware of this. He wonders whether he would still be invited to the prestigious Skyline Club if he wasn't city manager.

"Would I be treated differently? Not by the people I grew up with, who I cultivated friendships with, based on trust. I'd still have a drink with them, play golf with them. But," he adds in a streetwise slang, "the new guy who comes in, he don't know me. Hell, I'm just another brown guy. Fact of life. Hey, the key is, it don't bother me. I just feel sorry for him."

Valdez's long tenure in Tucson is impressive as well in view of the major changes that have occurred in the social, economic, and political composition of the city. Tucson's metropolitan population has increased to over half a million residents in recent years. Nearly 30 percent of its residents weren't living there just five years ago. Further, there has been increased controversy over municipal services, the city's use of federal grant monies, economic development, social service policies, and a variety of related issues. In the face of all this, Valdez survives, often by leading rather than by following. In fact, many regard him as the city manager "who owns Tucson." "I hear that I'm 'the most powerful man in Tucson,'" Valdez says. "That's a bunch of bunk. If you really start believing that you're that potent, you're dead. You're dead."

SOURCE: Quotes and information from Norma Cole, "Joel D. Valdez: The City Manager Who Never Takes No for an Answer," *Governing* Vol. 2, no. 1 (October 1988): 45–49.

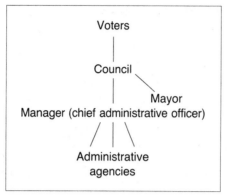

FIGURE 7.2   The council/manager
government.

usually deals with the appointment and firing of all administrative employees.
They hire individuals to manage the day-to-day operations of each major
department (e.g., revenue and finance, streets and public works, public
safety). The entire commission then votes to assign each commissioner the
responsibility of overseeing the operations of a specific administrative agency.
Thus, the administrator who supervises the operations of a particular department reports directly to a single commissioner. This commissioner can make
departmental (executive) decisions while sharing legislative powers with other
commissioners (see Figure 7.3).

In each of these three major types of local government, there is a relatively
clear picture of where the public administrator fits into the constitutional
framework. This is especially true for both the strong council/mayor and
council/manager forms of government, where there is a single, clear line of
authority under which the typical administrative agency operates. In the
weak council/mayor and commission forms, there is greater ambiguity as to
who has constitutional authority over administrative agencies.

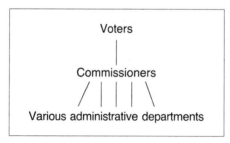

FIGURE 7.3   The Commission
Government.

State Governments. At the state level, the place of bureaucracy varies. In some states, the governor has strong executive powers and is constitutionally in complete control of the state bureaucracy. In other states, however, the governor shares executive responsibilities with other, competing elected officials, such as the attorney general and secretary of state. Table 7.1 summarizes type and number of elected executive officials found in the fifty state constitutions.

Similarly, a powerful and active legislature may limit the governor's responsibilities. According to one study of the 1,992 major administrative officials serving in American state governments in 1985, 299 (15 percent) were elected directly by the people and 761 (38.2 percent) were appointed by some body in the state government other than the governor. Since over half of the major administrative officials in state governments are independent of the governors, this tends to weaken the executive powers of these officials.[1]

TABLE 7.1   Separately Elected State
Officials, 1988–1989

Elected Official	Number of States
Governor	50
Lt. Governor	42
Secretary of State	36
Attorney General	43
Treasurer	38
Auditor	25
Controller	10
Education Commissioner	18
Agriculture Commissioner	12
Labor Commissioner	4
Insurance Commissioner	8
Mining Commissioner	1
Land Commissioner	5
Elections Commissioner	1
Highway Commissioner	1
Tax Commissioner	1
Adjutant	1
University Regents	5
Board of Education	12
Public Utilities Commission	11
Executive Council	2
Railroad Commission	1
Corporation Commission	1

SOURCE   *The Book of the States, 1988–89*
(Lexington, KY: Council of State
Governments, 1982), p. 53–57.

The conclusion drawn from these facts is that the place of administrative agencies in the states is not clear-cut. Historically, states have constitutionally dispersed executive powers among a variety of elected officials and other actors. In recent years, however, the trend is toward enhancing the executive authority of state governors. In 1955, for example, there were nineteen states in which voters directly elected seven or more executive officials; by 1981, this number dropped to twelve states. Further, the powers of the governor's office have also strengthened in regards to its ability to reorganize government agencies. In 1955, only two states gave broad authority over administrative reorganization to their governors. By 1981, there were sixteen states in which such gubernatorial powers existed.[2]

Federal Government.   At the national level, the Constitution has little or nothing to say about the administrative aspects of government. However, it does establish a system of separation of powers and checks and balances among the three branches of government. This system has an impact on the role that bureaucracies play at the national level.

For example, the president clearly possesses the executive powers of government. Article II of the Constitution explicitly states the responsibility of the president to "take care that the laws be faithfully executed." What has that grant of executive powers meant over the past two centuries of constitutional government? It definitely implies presidential control over the administration of the national government. In addition, almost every organizational chart of American bureaucracy indicates that the president is the chief administrative officer of government (see Figure 7.4). Yet, as one presidential scholar notes, executive power has emerged as "a term of uncertain content." Instead of exercising control over the federal bureaucracy, the White House is constantly *trying* to assert presidential power over many public agencies.[3]

At the heart of the debate over the role of the president in administering national government programs is the degree to which a president can control the operations of agencies that formally report to him. This debate dates back to the very first Congress of 1791, which made special provisions for the secretary of the treasury to report directly to Congress on certain matters. In fact, Congress tended to dominate the bureaucracy until Andrew Jackson asserted presidential authority over many public agencies during the 1830s through strong political leadership.

Congress attempted to modify presidential control during the 1880s. It reduced the patronage powers of the White House by establishing the Civil Service Commission and by creating new agencies that were formally independent of the president. The Interstate Commerce Commission was the first of several independent regulatory commissions created by Congress. The debate continued well into the twentieth century, as presidents argued for more control over the bureaucracy in the face of congressional efforts to rule the bureaucratic domain.[4]

THE GOVERNMENT OF THE UNITED STATES

THE CONSTITUTION

LEGISLATIVE BRANCH

CONGRESS

Senate   House

Architect of the Capitol
United States Botanic Garden
General Accounting Office
Government Printing Office
Library of Congress
Office of Technology Assessment
Congressional Budget Office
Copyright Royalty Tribunal
United States Tax Court

EXECUTIVE BRANCH

THE PRESIDENT

Executive Office of the President

White House Office
Office of Management and Budget
Council of Economic Advisers
National Security Council
Office of Policy Development
Office of National Drug Control Policy

National Critical Materials Council
Office of the U.S. Trade Representative
Council on Environmental Quality
Office of Science and Technology Policy
Office of Administration
National Space Council

THE VICE PRESIDENT

JUDICIAL BRANCH

The Supreme Court of the United States

United States Courts of Appeals
United States District Courts
United States Claims Court
United States Court of Appeals for the Federal Circuit
United States Court of International Trade
Territorial Courts
United States Court of Military Appeals
United States Court of Veterans Appeals
Administrative Office of the United States Courts Federal Judicial Center

Departments

DEPARTMENT OF THE INTERIOR
DEPARTMENT OF AGRICULTURE
DEPARTMENT OF JUSTICE
DEPARTMENT OF COMMERCE
DEPARTMENT OF LABOR
DEPARTMENT OF DEFENSE
DEPARTMENT OF EDUCATION
DEPARTMENT OF ENERGY
DEPARTMENT OF HEALTH AND HUMAN SERVICES
DEPARTMENT OF HOUSING AND URBAN DEVELOPMENT
DEPARTMENT OF STATE
DEPARTMENT OF TRANSPORTATION
DEPARTMENT OF THE TREASURY
DEPARTMENT OF VETERANS AFFAIRS

INDEPENDENT ESTABLISHMENTS AND GOVERNMENT CORPORATIONS

ACTION
Administrative Conference of the U.S.
African Development Foundation
American Battle Monuments Commission
Appalachian Regional Commission
Board for International Broadcasting
Central Intelligence Agency
Commission on the Bicentennial of the United States Constitution
Commission on Civil Rights
Commission of Fine Arts
Commodity Futures Trading Commission
Consumer Product Safety Commission
Environmental Protection Agency
Equal Employment Opportunity Commission
Export–Import Bank of the U.S.
Farm Credit Administration

Federal Communications Commission
Federal Deposit Insurance Corporation
Federal Election Commission
Federal Emergency Management Agency
Federal Home Loan Bank Board
Federal Labor Relations Authority
Federal Maritime Commission
Federal Mediation and Conciliation Service
Federal Mine Safety and Health Review Commission
Federal Reserve System, Board of Governors of the
Federal Retirement Thrift Investment Board
Federal Trade Commission
General Services Administration
Inter-American Foundation
Interstate Commerce Commission

Merit Systems Protection Board
National Aeronautics and Space Administration
National Archives and Records Administration
National Capital Planning Commission
National Credit Union Administration
National Foundation on the Arts and the Humanities
National Labor Relations Board
National Mediation Board
National Science Foundation
National Transportation Safety Board
Nuclear Regulatory Commission
Occupational Safety and Health Review Commission
Office of Personnel Management
Office of Special Counsel
Panama Canal Commission

Peace Corps
Pennsylvania Avenue Development Corporation
Pension Benefit Guaranty Corporation
Postal Rate Commission
Railroad Retirement Board
Securities and Exchange Commission
Selective Service System
Small Business Administration
Tennessee Valley Authority
U.S. Arms Control and Disarmament Agency
U.S. Information Agency
U.S. International Development Cooperation Agency
U.S. International Trade Commission
U.S. Postal Service

FIGURE 7.4 Organization chart of the federal government. (Source: *U.S. Government Organization Manual, 1987–88* [Washington, DC: Government Printing Office, 1987], p. 21.)

One major issue concerns the power of the president to remove government administrators from office. Some of the framers of the Constitution initiated this debate. On the one side was Roger Sherman, author of the Connecticut Compromise at the Constitutional Convention of 1787. Sherman argued that just as the president cannot appoint individuals to office without the advice and consent of the Senate, so the president must obtain the Senate's advice and consent to remove an appointed official. On the other side was James Madison (known as the "father" of the Constitution), who argued that the president should have total discretion to remove appointed officials. Madison felt that such power is necessary for the president to carry out executive obligations. The debate over the president's power to remove appointed officials continued for many years. Today, under provisions of civil service legislation that covers a vast majority of federal government employees, the president cannot dismiss a public employee for merely political reasons. Even in the case of some political appointees, such as regulatory commissioners, the president has only limited removal powers.

Another issue is the power of the president to prohibit administrative officials from providing information to or testifying before Congress. George Washington was the first president to exercise this power, called *executive privilege*. He refused to share with Congress information about a treaty with England that Congress had formally requested. In more recent times, President Eisenhower used executive privilege to block Senator Joseph McCarthy's access to military records during his investigation into the influence of communists in the Defense Department. Presidents have also used executive privilege to refuse Congress' requests for material on sensitive policy decisions and background checks of political appointees. For its part, Congress still tries to obtain relevant information from the bureaucracy by claiming that federal agencies are as much an arm of Congress as they are an arm of the presidency. It has even succeeded in overturning executive privilege when it needed information to conduct an investigation of corruption or malfeasance in office.

Similar issues surround other administrative roles of the president. During the early 1970s, for example, President Richard Nixon impounded (refused to spend) congressionally authorized funds for the construction of sewage-treatment plants opposed by his administration. The federal courts eventually overturned Nixon's impoundment, and Congress later passed legislation to limit presidential impoundment powers.

The White House is obviously an important actor in the ecology of federal public administrators. The executive power of the presidency, however, is constantly changing as relationships between the president and Congress change. This continually changing relationship generates uncertainty among federal administrators, which in turn has a significant impact on the behavior of many agencies.[5]

Central to this sense of uncertainty is the fact that Congress has many potential means for influencing the work of federal agencies.[6] Congress' most obvious sources of influence include its power to establish public agencies, authorize public programs, and appropriate funds for agency and program operations. Congress has always been the formal creator of public-sector agencies. Although many agencies were established on the recommendation of the White House, the final word always rested with Congress. In recent decades, Congress has passed laws that allow the president to create and modify public agencies without obtaining preliminary approval from either the House of Representatives or the Senate. Thus, in 1970, President Nixon established the Environmental Protection Agency (EPA) through an executive order. The EPA was formed out of other agencies found in the various other departments (e.g., Interior; Agriculture; and Health, Education and Welfare). As with many other reorganizations, the creation of the EPA met with congressional approval.

Other reorganization plans have met with congressional opposition. In 1971, for example, the Nixon Administration's proposal to create four "superagencies" out of seven cabinet departments was not well received by Congress and never materialized. After the Watergate affair (which eventually led to President Nixon's resignation), Congress significantly reduced the reorganization powers of the president; they were partly restored when Jimmy Carter came to office in 1977.[7]

The creation of public programs (i.e., program authorization) is almost entirely a congressional prerogative. The president has played an increasing role in recommending programs, but it is Congress that determines the formal shape of most federal efforts. The same is true for funding government agencies and programs. The president can recommend a budget, but it is Congress that passes it, subject to White House veto. During the budgeting process, Congress holds hearings in which it asks administrative officials about their programs. Many members of Congress use these opportunities to make their views known about the operations of the federal bureaucracy.[8]

In addition to its authorization and appropriation powers, Congress can influence American public administration through its power to establish federal personnel policies and to conduct audits and formal investigations of federal agency operations. Any member of Congress, for example, can request that the General Accounting Office conduct an audit and report on the efficiency and effectiveness of any federal program.

Congress also has the power to change specific administrative decisions through legislation. Members of Congress do this by addressing specific administrative regulations through "riders," which are attached to major pieces of legislation, or through "private bills." For example, Senator Robert Dole of Kansas once sponsored successful legislation to have the Census Bureau change the boundaries it used to define the Wichita, Kansas, statistical metropolitan area. The proposed redefinition extended those boundaries to a small rural community many miles to the north of the city. Dole's action was taken at the request of two Kansas hospitals in the community, which sought to take advantage of the more generous Medicare reimbursement schedules offered to health-care facilities located in places officially designated as "metropolitan" by the Census Bureau.[9]

Members of Congress can also influence the work of administrative agencies through the casework they and their staffs perform for constituents. Most casework activities involve facilitating the processing (or "cutting through the red tape") of a constituent's claim or case under consideration at some public agency. When a person contacts a member of Congress about a federal grant he or she has applied for, a federal check he or she hasn't received, or any other concern about the operations of the federal bureaucracy, the congressional office begins to make contacts on that constituent's behalf. Public administrators cannot ignore such casework inquiries by elected officials, especially if the senator or representative sits on a committee that directly affects the agency's authority or appropriations.

These are just some of the ways that Congress can influence the work of federal public administrators.[10] As implied in our discussion of the presidency, the relationship between Congress and the president affects public administrators. The degree of congressional influence on the federal bureaucracy depends to a great extent on the relationship between the legislative and executive branches of government. Another important factor is the role played by the federal judiciary.

The relationship between the federal courts and the federal bureaucracy is a unique one. Unlike the president and Congress, who can point to direct constitutional bases for their authority over federal agencies, the courts have no direct constitutional claim on federal bureaucracies. In addition, the federal judiciary is, by its very nature, passive—that is, the courts typically do not act until some real controversy or injury is brought to their attention. In fact, it can be argued that the judicial branch of our federal government is perhaps the least likely to exercise influence over the federal bureaucracy. Yet, as one authority on the subject notes, over the past several decades the federal judiciary has managed to force the federal bureaucracy to "respond to its direction and values."[11]

One reason for the major role played by the federal judiciary is the ongoing dispute between the executive and legislative branches over which is really in command of the bureaucracy. The courts often hear cases that arise out of this jurisdictional debate. For instance, in one famous case a president fired an Oregon postmaster after the postmaster had served three years in that position. The postmaster challenged his firing because the Senate had confirmed him for a four-year term in office. In its 1926 decision on the issue, the U.S. Supreme Court held that the president's power to remove individuals from office was unrestricted. Yet just nine years later, in an equally famous case, the Court held that the president's removal power was restricted in the case on appointees to regulatory commissions.[12]

A closely related reason for the judiciary's growing influence over federal agencies is our tendency to resolve policy disputes in the courts. Often disputes between the executive and legislative branches result in policy vacuums. When neither side chooses to act, litigation may mandate some resolution. In 1978, for example, Congress enacted a coal-mining reclamation act that required strip-mining companies to pay for the clean up of areas after they were finished mining them. A provision in that law exempted mine operators whose mines covered two acres or less. The larger strip-mining companies used this loophole in the law to avoid clean-up costs by subcontracting with small operators to work on two-acre plots. Under the influence of the Reagan administration's deregulation policies, federal administrators made little effort to deal with this problem until environmental groups filed lawsuits against the federal government for not treating the subcontractors as agents of the larger companies. As a result of such lawsuits, the federal government eventually forced the larger companies to clean up the mining areas.[13]

Most important among the reasons for judicial influence over public administration is the federal bureaucracy's growing independent impact on the lives of most Americans. Under ideal circumstances, federal bureaucrats could act as agents of the president or Congress and it would not be necessary to try to exercise direct control over the bureaucracy. Instead, the behavior of the bureaucracy could be controlled by making the White House or Congress more accountable. However, David H. Rosenbloom argues that this is a "naive and inaccurate" view of the way things actually operate in government. "Legislatures and elected executives influence the actions of public agencies," notes Rosenbloom, "but the agencies are not controlled or held accountable by them in any simple sense."[14] Thus, the courts have taken on the task of making certain that the federal bureaucracy is accountable legally (if not also politically) for their actions.

What are the different ways the courts can influence the operations of American public administration? Given the complex nature of the American legal system, the answer depends on the specific type of dispute involving a government agency. Actually, it is misleading to speak of *the* American legal system, for there are at least five legal systems that have implications for the work of American public administrators. These include those dealing with constitutional law, statutory law, administrative law, equity law, and specialized legal concerns (see Table 7.2). The differences among these systems rest in the types of legal disputes with which they deal as well as the kinds of issues raised in each. The types of legal disputes include:

- *Private:* Disputes between citizens over property, civil damages, and the like.
- *Civil:* Disputes between citizens, or between citizens and government, involving contracts (voluntary agreements) or torts (obligations imposed in civil society).
- *Criminal:* Disputes over laws protecting the public order, in which the government is always the plaintiff.
- *Public:* Disputes over government powers and citizen rights, in which the government is always the defendant.

TABLE 7.2   The American Legal Systems

Legal System	Type of Disputes Handled	Issues Raises
Constitutional	Public	Questions of citizen rights and obligations; powers of government
Statutory	Criminal and civil	Issues or jurisdiction derived from specific laws, codes, and so on
Administrative	Public	Cases dealing with the jurisdiction, powers, and procedures of specific agencies and officials (Administrative Procedures Act)
Equity	Private and civil	Handles claims for damages or civil relief beyond that recoverable under other systems (e.g., statute, common)
Specialized	Private, civil, and criminal	Handles disputes in civil and other areas through unique rules and procedures (e.g., military, maritime, small claims, bankruptcy)

Public administrators are most often directly concerned with issues that arise under systems involving public disputes (constitutional and administrative law). These are the legal systems that set the stage for government activity. *Constitutional law* deals with the authority of government and the limitations on what government officials can do. *Administrative law* establishes the standards and procedures for bureaucratic behavior. Constitutional law derives from the Constitution itself, but it is defined in greater detail through decisions of the U.S. Supreme Court (see Insight 7.1). It is constitutional, for example, for government welfare agencies to refuse further aid to a recipient who refuses to allow inspectors into his or her home. It is unconstitutional, however, for government inspectors to enter someone's home without obtaining the occupant's permission or a search warrant from the courts.

Administrative law derives from statutes like the Administrative Procedures Act (APA) of 1946 and from court decisions. The APA requires that agencies provide sufficient notice of public hearings and publish any proposed rules and regulations in the *Federal Register* prior to adopting them. In addition, federal agencies must maintain open records and make them accessible to the public, including any agency decisions, procedures manuals, and the like.[15] The courts have established other requirements as well, perhaps the best known of which are outlined in the Supreme Court's ruling in *Miranda v. Arizona*. In this case the Court ruled that government officials must inform all suspects in criminal investigations of their rights—the "Miranda warning."

INSIGHT 7.1
LIVING WITH A "LIVING CONSTITUTION"

The influence of constitutional law on public administration is demonstrated by the way the U.S. Supreme Court has recently shifted its interpretations of the Tenth Amendment to the Constitution. The Tenth Amendment is usually regarded as part of the Bill of Rights, which was passed by the first Congress and ratified by the states in 1791. It states that "The powers not delegated to the United States by the Constitution, nor prohibited by it to the States, are reserved to the States respectively, or to the people." According to constitutional scholars, the Tenth Amendment gives "reserved powers" to the states and the public.

As many historians have noted, one of the enduring qualities of our legal system is the vagueness of our Constitution, which allows Americans to adjust the meaning of its various provisions to changing conditions. In short, ours is a "living Constitution" rather than a rigid one that can only be interpreted one way. This adaptability has helped policymakers over the past two centuries reinterpret those parts of the Constitution that concern the powers of the national government. The "necessary and proper" clause (Article I, section 8, paragraph 18) has been used so often to justify expanding national powers that it is also commonly called the "elastic clause." In the face of this elasticity, the meaning of the Tenth Amendment has been unclear for many decades. Since we cannot specify what constitutional powers have been "delegated to the United States," it is almost impossible to specify just what powers are "reserved" to the states and the people.

Thus, it came as a surprise in 1976 when the U.S. Supreme Court handed down a decision based on the Tenth Amendment, which asserted that there are areas where states (and localities) can exercise their powers without national government intervention. Specifically, the Court held in *National League of Cities (NLC) v. Usery* that certain 1966 amendments to the Fair Labor Standards Act, which made state and local governments susceptible to national minimum wage and hour requirements, were unconstitutional. In the 5–4 decision, the Court stated that the Tenth Amendment protects the rights of state and local governments to determine how they will conduct their traditional governmental functions. They argued that the 1966 amendments were a direct and unconstitutional infringement on that right.

The potential significance of the *NLC* decision on the operations of state and local administration cannot be underestimated. Most immediately, the decision had an impact on public-sector wage and hour policies. More important, the Court has established a precedent for the meaningful use of the Tenth Amendment. For many years, the national government used its financial leverage over states and localities (i.e., its grants-in-aid programs) to get recipient governments to design their public-sector programs in specified ways. Funding for highways, for example,

INSIGHT 7.1   *continued*

called for eliminating political patronage from highway departments, professionalizing those agencies, and standardizing the design of federally funded roads. In recent years, however, the federal government used more direct approaches by passing regulatory legislation in the areas of environmental protection, civil rights, and labor law that treated state and local governments like private corporations.

It wasn't long, however, before the Supreme Court qualified its position. In the 1981 case, *Hodel v. Virginia Surface Mining and Reclamation Association*, the Court established a three-part test for applying the Tenth Amendment to federal legislation: (1) Does the national policy directly interfere with state or local actions? (2) Is the state or local action one in which state governments have indisputable jurisdiction? And (3) does implementation of the federal policy impair the state's or the locality's ability to conduct its traditional governmental functions? Then, in the 1983 case of the *Equal Employment Opportunity Commission v. Wyoming*, the Court went even further by noting that even if those three tests could

be met, there still could be a significant "federal interest" in a national policy that would lead the Court to justify the direct regulation of state activities by Washington.

Finally, in 1984, the Supreme Court all but abandoned its *NLC* decision. In *Garcia v. San Antonio Metropolitan Transit Authority*, it held that more recent federal regulations (developed under the Fair Labor Standards Act) aimed at regulating wages and hours in "nontraditional" state and local government activities are constitutional. The message to state and local governments is clear: Don't count on using the Tenth Amendment to justify being excluded from national government policies and regulations.

The story of the Supreme Court's handling of the Tenth Amendment from 1976 to 1984 gives us some insight into what public administrators face in the areas of constitutional and administrative law. What may be constitutional and legal today may be deemed unconstitutional by the Court tomorrow. Having to operate within this "living Constitution" has its drawbacks for public administrators.

If constitutional law and administrative law set the stage for the operations of public administration, *statutory law* is the legal system through which public-sector bureaucrats play out their roles. Statutory law establishes what the government sees as the basic requirements of public order. Under this legal system, the public sector carries out specific criminal or civil mandates by enforcing the provisions of legislative statutes. Thus, state statutory law declares that it is criminal to murder someone and illegal to drive while under the influence of alcohol and other drugs. The role of the public administrator is to enforce both statutes when they are violated. Similarly, it is a civil offense to exceed the speed limit on interstate highways and public authorities may impose fines for violations.

Public administrators, like all Americans, are subject to *equity law* systems. Under the law of equity, individuals can be accountable for damages that go beyond those recoverable under other forms of law (e.g., in criminal or civil actions). Traditionally, many legal authorities held that government officials, like governments, should be immune from such suits. Although there were never any explicit grants of immunity granted to either the government or public administrators by Congress, the courts generally followed a long-standing tradition in Anglo-Saxon law of protecting governmental actions and actors from litigation. One of the strongest statements of this position came in 1896, when the Supreme Court held that public administrators should be immune from lawsuits resulting from the conduct of their official duties. In a sense, the Court threw a blanket of absolute immunity over all administrative behavior.

By the 1960s, however, the support for this position was substantially weakened as the courts took a closer look at their grants of immunity to government agencies. In 1971, the Supreme Court explicitly altered the tradition in a case involving actions of federal narcotics agents, *Bivens* v. *Six Unknown Named Narcotics Agents*. In that case, the agents were charged with entering a suspect's home without a warrant or probable cause, handcuffing him, threatening his family, using excessive force, and subjecting him to a strip search. The Court held that victims of such mistreatment do have the right to sue individual federal administrators because such behavior violates basic constitutional rights.[16]

Since 1971, both the courts and Congress have made it easier for the public to bring civil or private suits against governments and public officials who they believe have acted in a maliciously irresponsible and unreasonable manner. Today, all governments have "limited immunity" from tort and liability claims, meaning that governments possess immunity only for acts committed under certain conditions (e.g., during a state of emergency or war). Public administrators and other officials, however, have "qualified immunity," which means they are vulnerable to litigation when the actions they take are malicious or unauthorized. In addition to these legal doctrines, Congress (in 1976) amended sections of the Administrative Procedures Act to allow citizens to file suit against the federal government.[17]

Finally, some administrators work in areas of government that are subject to a *specialized legal system*. For example, the Internal Revenue Service (IRS) must contend with the existence of special procedures and courts. When a dispute arises between a taxpayer and the IRS, it is settled in federal Tax Courts. Similarly, the federal government has established bankruptcy courts, small-claims courts, maritime courts, and special military courts. In each case, public administrators must deal with a distinctive set of procedures and other ground rules.

Taken together, the relationships between public administrators and the constitutional institutions with which they work can be extremely complicated. This is especially true in those government jurisdictions where the distribution of constitutional powers and political power is unclear. Obviously, the federal government and many state governments fall into this category. Yet even in many local governments, there is uncertainty about just who is—or ought to be—in charge. Under such conditions, administrators must inevitably serve several leaders over a period of time.

Peer Agencies

Although the constitutional branches of government are the best-known parts of the intragovernmental ecology of American public administrators, there are a variety of other public agencies in the same jurisdiction with which public administrators of any given agency must contend. These are called *peer agencies* because they share their constitutional and legal contexts.

Peer agencies exist in government jurisdictions that have more than one agency implementing public-sector programs. On the local level, there are thousands of general service governments that provide their constituents with a variety of public services. In most cases, these general service jurisdictions contain several public agencies. At the state and national levels, peer agencies are more common because each government implements hundreds of distinct public-sector programs. As we will see in Chapter 10, these agencies come in a variety of shapes and sizes.

The relationships among peer agencies can range from indifference to cooperation to competition. The national government, for example, is so large that it is possible for administrators operating in one agency to be indifferent to the work going on in another. For example, a forest ranger stationed in the mountains of Colorado is not likely to cross paths with an employee of the Federal Trade Commission. While both receive their paychecks from the U.S. Treasury, their tasks and concerns are not at all connected. At other levels of government, however, indifferent relationships among government agencies are less common. While state troopers may have little or no contact with state librarians, they are likely to share common concerns about how the legislature and governor are handling this year's budget requests or proposed sales-tax increases.

Competitive relationships among peer agencies are certain to develop when they have similar missions or rely on a common resource base. At the same time, such conditions may call for cooperation and coordination of efforts to accomplish the common objectives of the peer agencies. Perhaps the most obvious example of such mixed relationships among peer agencies on the federal level exists among the U.S. Armed Forces. In providing for the national defense, Washington has established three major branches of the military: the Army, the Navy (including the Marine Corps), and the Air Force. While each branch of the military functions as a distinct public-sector agency, none can ignore the activities of the other two. In one sense, the relationship among the three services is competitive, with each trying to outdo the other in terms of prestige, assignments, funding, and other matters. At the same time, the national security of the United States depends on a coordination of the policies and decisions of these three agencies. For this reason, the general activities of the armed services are administratively coordinated through the Defense Department and the Joint Chiefs of Staff.[18]

A less visible but no less significant example of the relationships among peer agencies exists in almost every local government where different agencies are responsible for protecting their constituents. Public safety is obviously a job for law-enforcement officials. In turn, the police need to work with firefighters, ambulance drivers, public health officials, and others to offer the citizenry the comprehensive type of protection expected of government. No police department can operate in a vacuum. What its peer agencies do can either enhance or hinder its own activities. This is why peer agencies form an important part of the intragovernmental ecology of American public administration.

Administrative Management Structures

Administrative management structures are special peer agencies established by constitutional institutions to help support and/or control the work of public administrators in a specific jurisdiction. Included in this category are three types of public agencies: control agencies, oversight agencies, and housekeeping agencies.

Control agencies are used by chief executive officials as a means of clearing and coordinating agency actions. At the national level, for instance, the Office of Management and Budget (OMB) provides the president with the means for managing the vast bureaucracy under White House control. Every agency reporting to the president must clear its budget requests and all legislative testimony through the OMB. This power has made the OMB a pivotal institution in Washington when a strong president seeks to make major policy changes. The control orientation of the OMB was especially evident to David A. Stockman, the agency's controversial director during the early years of the Reagan administration. In his memoirs, Stockman notes that "the six hundred OMB career staff were dedicated anti-bureaucrats. They weren't in the business of giving things away. They were in the business of interposing themselves between the federal Santa Claus and the kids and saying, 'Whoa. . . . '"[19]

The president also uses other control agencies to help manage the national bureaucracy; together with the OMB, these agencies make up the Executive Office of the President (EOP). The EOP contains the White House Office, which includes the president's personal aides and assistants, many of whom are responsible for coordinating federal programs and policies. It also includes the Council of Economic Advisors (CEA), the National Security Council (NSC), the Office of Science and Technology, and a variety of other agencies. Each agency in the EOP has as its principal task assisting the president in the management of federal programs and policies.

Similar types of control agencies operate on the state level. More and more governors are using budget or planning offices as means for coordinating the agencies under their control. At the local level, finance officers and comptrollers perform similar functions.

Oversight agencies are involved in investigating and reporting on the activities of public organizations. At the national level, the major oversight agency is actually an arm of Congress—the General Accounting Office (GAO). Headed by a comptroller general who is nominated by the president for a fifteen-year nonrenewable term (and who can be removed only by Congress), the GAO acts as Congress' watchdog over the entire federal bureaucracy.[20] At the state level there is usually a *legislative audit agency* similar to the GAO in form and function. In addition, there are states in which a state auditor or comptroller is either popularly elected or appointed by the governor to perform oversight functions.

Housekeeping agencies exist to perform basic support and other services for government agencies. These agencies acquire and manage government facilities, establish and maintain government personnel records, and provide for some of the common needs of all agencies. For example, most national agencies rely on the General Services Administration (GSA) for supplying everything from paper clips and file cabinets to buildings and janitorial services. Many state and local governments have central purchasing agencies that perform similar functions. In the area of personnel, the Office of Personnel Management (OPM) helps coordinate human-resource management functions for most national agencies, just as many state and local governments depend on similar agencies that specialize in personnel matters. There are even agencies specializing in the printing and dissemination of reports and other information generated by public agencies. At the national level, this is the Government Printing Office (GPO). At the state level, there are usually similar agencies.

Housekeeping agencies have emerged for several reasons. First, they reduce duplicative efforts by government agencies within the same jurisdiction. That is, each agency does not need its own personnel to oversee building maintenance when a central administrative unit such as the GSA can accomplish the same task more efficiently. Second, centralized housekeeping agencies can operate at a scale that can lead to greater efficiency and cost-savings to the agency. The volume of government purchasing is staggering. In 1987 alone, state and local governments purchased $225 billion in goods and services—nearly equal to the national government's expenditure of $238 billion.[21] Given its overall purchasing power, a state's central purchasing unit can order thousands of computers, automobiles, and boxes of paper clips at significant discounts in price compared to the money that a single agency might have to spend to acquire dozens of these items.

Centralized housekeeping units also allow high-level decision makers to establish and maintain a government-wide set of quality and other standards. For example, when the GSA seeks rental space for federal government offices, it sends out a set of requirements specifying certain minimal conditions (the "specs") the rental property must possess. These common standards assure all federal workers that government offices will have certain features, such as fire alarms and sprinkler systems. The same kind of approach is used for computers, desks, and other supplies.

Finally, by centralizing housekeeping agencies, policymakers can enhance their ability to oversee the operations of government that are susceptible to wastefulness and even fraud. In addition, housekeeping agencies have the potential of being used as control agencies in jurisdictions where the centralized agencies report directly to the chief executive officer. Thus, if the work of the Environmental Protection Agency or a state regulatory unit is adversely affecting some presidential or gubernatorial policy, then the White House or state house can use its leverage over housekeeping functions as indirect pressure to bring the agency back in line.

Intergovernmental Institutions

The American constitutional system is a complex arrangement of governments. There are more than eighty thousand individual government jurisdictions in the nation, and they come in a variety of forms. Obviously, this fragmentation of government poses a challenge to the effective governance of the United States. The major question is how to get public programs successfully implemented despite this fragmentation.

The framers of the Constitution faced a similar challenge on a much smaller scale in 1787. As noted in Chapter 5, the constitutional framers had to develop mechanisms for governing a country comprised of thirteen states and the new national government they were designing. To accomplish this task, they created the distinctly American institution of federalism.

The Federal Solution

The constitutional framers had two possible approaches from which to choose. On the one hand, they could follow the centralized "unitary" model found in Great Britain, making the national government the primary level of government and subordinating the states to the authority of the newly formed Congress. On the other hand, they could continue under the highly decentralized "confederal" arrangement they had under the Articles of Confederation. Instead, they developed a middle course that eventually came to be known as *federalism*.

Under a federal arrangement, the people of the United States are governed (at least in theory) simultaneously by two governments, the national government and the state government where they reside. The national government and the individual state governments each have authority over certain separate functions of government. If this arrangement is to work smoothly, it requires a clear delineation of which functions the national government is to perform and which functions the individual states are to handle.

Unfortunately, the Constitution's framers did not provide a clear definition of which public-sector functions are to be carried out by each governmental level. The framers specified the powers of the national government in Article I, section 8 of the Constitution, including the powers to borrow money, regulate commerce with foreign nations and among the states, establish uniform laws on bankruptcy, establish post offices and post roads, declare war, and provide for and maintain a navy. At the end of this list of powers, however, they added a phrase that gives the national government the authority to "make all laws which shall be necessary and proper for carrying into execution the forgoing powers. . . ." This "necessary and proper" clause offsets whatever clarity the preceding list of explicit powers provides. In contrast, the Constitution has hardly a word about what powers are to be held by the individual states. American federalism is unlikely to run smoothly given all these ambiguities about which government level is to perform which government functions.

Hence, the checkered history of American federalism is quite understandable. From the very outset, the distribution of governmental authority in the United States was an open question. Debates over that question raged on the floors of Congress and eventually spilled over onto the battlefields of the Civil War. In the midst of all this debate and confusion, national and state administrators—from the postal clerk to the local land assessor—tried to conduct the business of government as best they could.

Emergence of Intergovernmental Relations

This situation did not improve very much until the 1930s. The Great Depression forced national and state policymakers and administrators to consider the benefits of cooperating with each other to provide some public services. By the late 1940s, this cooperation included local governments as well. Furthermore, the spirit of cooperation went beyond the relationships of the three hierarchical levels of government (national, state, local) and extended to the relationships among governments at the same level—that is, among states and among local communities. These recent developments have radically expanded and almost completely restructured the original federal solution. In place of traditional federalism, we now have a system of *intergovernmental relations* (IGR).

Deil S. Wright notes five major characteristics of IGR that distinguish it from federalism. First, IGR involves all governmental units, not just relationships between the national and state governments or among the states. Second, IGR relies more on human relationships than the more formal, impersonal, and legalistic relations that characterized federalism. Third, it emphasizes the establishment of regular contacts among public officials rather than the infrequent contacts that were typical of federalism. Fourth, IGR involves a great many more actual and potential public officials than federalism did in its heyday. In fact, while elected officials dominated federalism, Wright points out that public administrators are the most numerous and active participants in intergovernmental relations. Finally, while the primary concerns under federalism were over which government had jurisdiction over what functions, under IGR the focus is on the formulation and implementation of public policy.[22]

While rooted in cooperation, the emergence of IGR has not been without difficulties. The cooperative attitudes that had triggered the development of the IGR system in the 1930s had faded by the late 1960s. At that time, state and local officials became aware of just how dependent they had become on the national government. National policymakers began to use their financial domination of intergovernmental relationships to impose cumbersome and costly requirements on state and local governments. In addition, many IGR participants began complaining about the red tape and the complexities involved in the elaborate maze of several hundred federal grant-in-aid programs. Elected officials were especially concerned about the extent to which they were being left out of decisions regarding the design and distribution of IGR programs.

It is within this setting of intergovernmental relationships and institutions that many public administrators find themselves today. It is a setting that poses different challenges to the public-sector worker.

Vertical Relationships

Many of the challenges facing public administrators today are a result of a system of *vertical* intergovernmental relations that has developed in recent years. These vertical relationships most directly reflect those established under the formal federal system, which divides powers between the national and state governments. The key difference between today's intergovernmental relationships and the formal arrangement of federalism is the prominent role of local governments.

Counties, municipalities, townships, special districts, and the like have no formal status or legal standing under the U.S. Constitution. They are regarded as legal creations of the states and therefore a part of state government. As a result, there were few contacts between national and local governments prior to the development of IGR in the first half of the twentieth century. In 1932, for example, the only U.S. city to receive any direct federal aid was Washington, D.C., which is under the direct authority of the national government. By 1940, however, the national government was providing nearly $300 million in grants to selected cities for housing and public-works programs. Over the years, the political clout of local officials and the strength of the American public's attachment to local government have made local governments important actors in the intergovernmental arena.

Vertical intergovernmental relationships are primarily fiscal in nature; that is, they revolve around grants-in-aid programs. In fact, over the years federal grants-in-aid programs have become the key to understanding national–state–local relations.

The most common of these programs are the more than four hundred *categorical grants* that provide funds to states and localities for specific, narrowly defined purposes (see Table 7.3). There are several types of categorical grants. Recipient governments receive *formula grants* on the basis of criteria set forth in authorizing legislation. In the case of funding for some education programs, for example, Congress has mandated that per-capita income or the number of federal government employees who live in a school district should be used to determine how much funding is provided. *Project grants* require potential recipients to apply formally for funding by submitting a program proposal. There are also *open-ended reimbursement grants*, in which Washington promises to pay a portion of state and local costs for a federally desired program. Under the Social Security Act of 1935, for example, Congress authorized the federal government to reimburse state governments for a portion of the cost of providing services to the dependent poor.[23]

At the opposite extreme of categorical grants are *general revenue-sharing programs*, in which the federal government provided funding to state and local governments with few or no strings and conditions attached. General revenue sharing was first enacted in 1972, and for many years it provided

TABLE 7.3   Federal Aid to State and Local Governments, 1970–1988

Government Function	1970 ($ millions)	1988 (preliminary) ($ millions)
Administration of justice	$ 42	$ 336
Agriculture	604	1,751
Commerce/housing credit	4	2
Community/regional development	1,781	4,498
Education/training/employment/social services	6,417	21,336
Energy	25	414
General government	479	1,956
Health	3,849	32,846
Income security	5,795	31,494
National defense	37	210
Natural resources/environment	411	3,864
Transportation	4,599	17,854
Veterans' benefits/services	8	106
Total	24,065	116,666

SOURCE   Bureau of the Census, *Statistical Abstract of the United States, 1989* (Washington, DC: Government Printing Office, 1989), table 451.

several billions of federal dollars to thousands of local governments. By the mid-1980s, however, support for general revenue had declined in Congress and the program was phased out completely in 1987.

A third type of federal program involves *block grants*, which provide state and local governments with funds that they can spend in some broadly defined functional area. The recipient governments can decide the details of where and how to spend the funds. The number of federal block grants has increased in recent years, covering a wide range of policy areas from law enforcement to community development:

• Social Services
• Low-income Home Energy Assistance
• Community Services
• Alcohol, Drug Abuse, and Mental Health
• Preventative Health and Health Services
• Maternal and Child Health
• Elementary and Secondary Education
• Community Development

How important are these vertical fiscal relationships to the work of American public administration? The answer depends in large part on the level of government. For the federal administrator, grant programs provide an opportunity to use state and local agencies and workers to implement national policy goals. This is especially true in the case of project-based categorical grants, since such programs often give federal officials considerable influence over the recipient government. At times this means being able to exercise direct control over the specific program being funded. At other times it means providing federal officials with considerable indirect leverage over other matters. Many states and localities, for example, have become so financially dependent on federal monies that they find it difficult, and sometimes impossible, to refuse to carry out federal mandates. Among those mandates are requirements to establish a minimum drinking age of 21 or to end any discriminatory hiring practices by state agencies. Federal administrators, who may have no other means for imposing their will on other government jurisdictions, welcome such leverage.

From the perspective of state and local administrators, federal grant programs provide resources that may not otherwise be available for certain government functions. In some cases, federal funds supplement current expenditures, as when a city receives federal money to help make downtown streets and public buildings more accessible to the handicapped. In other instances, federal funding is the primary source of revenues. This was the case when states undertook the construction of the interstate highways system. The federal government paid as much as 95 percent of all costs for those highways. Finally, there are times when states and localities use federal funds to undertake programs and projects that they may not otherwise even consider. For example, the availability of funds for employment training and bilingual education often act as a stimulant for recipient governments to establish such programs.

Current trends indicate that vertical relationships are in the throes of change. For many years the percentage of state and local revenues coming from federal grant programs increased annually. In 1958, federal grants accounted for just over 11 percent of all state and local government expenditures. By 1973, that figure rose to nearly 24 percent, and to more than 26 percent five years later. As states and localities became more dependent on federal funds, they also became more susceptible to federal program requirements and mandates.

Since 1978, however, this dependence has declined. In 1983, only 21 percent of state and local outlays depended on federal funding. That figure was projected to drop to 17.1 percent as the 1980s ended. These changing vertical relationships are having an impact on officials at all levels of government. They have forced states and localities to rely more on their own revenue sources for funding and to reconsider many of their public programs.[24] Local governments are increasingly turning to state capitals for more funding, and the states have generally responded positively.[25] In short, the shift in vertical IGR has meant significant changes in American public administration at all levels.

Horizontal Relationships

Horizontal intergovernmental relations are typically less reliant on financial transactions, although their very existence is often linked to financial considerations. In a few instances, they take the form of formalized legal agreements. These include *interstate compacts* and other formal contractual agreements. Among the best-known interstate agreements are those dealing with the use of river basins such as the Colorado River and the Delaware River.[26] On the local level, some jurisdictions enter into formal contracts with other local governments to provide specific services. As discussed in Chapter 2, this was the approach taken by the city of Lakewood, California, in its formal agreements with Los Angeles County to supply more than forty public services.

Another form of horizontal IGR is the *council of governments* (COGs). Emerging on the American scene during the 1950s, there were nine major COGs in operation by 1965, including those in Detroit, Washington, Atlanta, Seattle, and San Francisco. These organizations provide a means through which local officials from a metropolitan area can meet to deal with common problems. Oftentimes the COGs are the foundation for coordinated program efforts. The number of COGs increased from only a handful to hundreds after 1965, when the federal government began to provide funding for their establishment and operation. Many of these COGs are still operating today.[27]

At a more political level, governments and government officials often belong to *public-sector interest groups*. These groups help members share information and common concerns while also providing them with representation before legislative bodies or in other political contexts (see Insight 7.2). Among the most prominent of these public-sector interest groups are the National Governors Association (NGA), the U.S. Conference of Mayors, the Council of State Governments (CSG), the National League of Cities (NLC), and the International City Management Association (ICMA).

At a programmatic and service delivery level, many local governments enter into *mutual assistance agreements* with neighboring jurisdictions. Many such agreements deal with services like fire protection, where neighboring governments agree to come to each other's assistance when needed.[28]

On a policy level, governments also pass *reciprocal legislation* in an effort to promote interaction and consistency among the laws and regulations of different jurisdictions. For example, neighboring states may pass laws allowing lawyers licensed in each other's jurisdictions to practice in both states. In a similar type of agreement, states may have reciprocal agreements about university tuition. For example, for many years Kansas agreed to allow students from Missouri to pay in-state tuition fees while attending Kansas University's medical school. In exchange, Missouri allowed the same tuition arrangements for citizens of Kansas who attended its dental school.

Overall Characteristics

Each governmental institution has a unique and varying impact on the work of American public administrators. Together they have a more widespread influence on administrative operations. This is due to three key characteristics of the constitutional and legal ecology: fragmentation of government authority, slowness to take action, and stability.

The governmental ecology is highly fragmented. The *fragmentation* of American government is a result of the dispersal of authority built into the constitutional system. Many of our key institutions were intentionally designed to disperse the authority of government among various actors and jurisdictions. This strategy was developed as a means for keeping any one group or coalition of groups from easily gaining control of too much governmental power. It was for this reason that the framers of the Constitution established a separation of powers and a system of checks and balances among the three branches of government. It is the reason behind our rather confusing electoral system with its staggered election cycles and overlapping constituencies. Under this system, the House of Representatives is elected every two years from districts made up of relatively equal numbers of people; the president is elected every four years; and members of the Senate (representing the states) serve staggered six-year terms. Finally, the dispersal of

INSIGHT 7.2

THE POLICE COME TO CONGRESS

While it may seem strange to think of government officials "lobbying" Congress just like private interest groups do, the efforts of public-sector interest groups has been impressive and often successful. Among the most successful public-sector lobbyists are those interest groups representing law-enforcement personnel around the country. There are few if any members of Congress who would turn down a visit from a local police chief seeking support for more federal funds to fight crime, or a representative from the Police Foundation seeking more money for criminal justice education and research.

As successful as law-enforcement lobbying has been, police groups knew they faced a mighty challenge when they organized to take on the powerful "gun lobby" in the ongoing battle over gun control. Led by the National Rifle Association (NRA), the gun lobby has been a powerful force in Congress in blocking major gun-control legislation and working to roll back tough gun-control laws that were already on the books. Prior to 1985, the pro-gun-control forces were weak and fragmented. In fact, there were surprisingly few instances when the police groups pooled their lobbying efforts despite agreements on many issues. Furthermore, various police groups found that the NRA was more often an ally than an enemy in efforts to get tougher criminal justice legislation passed in Congress.

This all changed in the fall of 1985, when eleven major police groups ranging from the Fraternal Order of Police (FOP) and the National Organization of Black Law Enforcement Executives (NOBLEE) to the International Association of Chiefs of Police (IACP) and the National Sheriffs Association (NSA) joined forces to attempt to block NRA-backed legislation that would significantly weaken the 1968 gun-control law. Although they failed to stop the gun lobby from winning that legislative battle, the police groups did obtain some concessions. More important, the groups agreed to continue their joint efforts.

What has eventually emerged is a formal coalition called the Law Enforcement Steering Committee, which has gained considerable strength. The group has been increasingly effective, getting a ban on "armor-piercing" (also called "cop killer") bullets in 1986 and generating support for other gun-control legislation.

Despite some difficulties in keeping the coalition together (the NSA withdrew in 1988 over a disputed tactical decision of the Steering Committee), the police group has gained momentum in Congress. While the coalition faces considerable obstacles, most observers consider it quite capable of success in its future battles with the NRA.

SOURCE: Based on information in Nadine Cohodas, "High Noon at the Capitol as the Police and the Gun Lobby Face Off," *Governing* 1 (July 1988): 19–23.

authority is manifest in the concept of federalism, which divides power between the state and national governments.

The design of America's governmental system encourages slow, deliberate government action, if there is to be any action at all. This *slowness to take action* is a result of the limits on authority that are structured into our governmental institutions. Many of our most cherished institutions limit government actions, or at least make government action slower and more deliberate. The idea behind this slowness is to assure that government only acts after adequate consideration of all sides of an issue. These mechanisms include the Bill of Rights, the many due-process safeguards provided in other parts of the Constitution, and the numerous administrative law procedures and protections.

Finally, American government institutions reflect an urge for *stability*. Formal methods for making changes in our national and state constitutions are extremely difficult and rarely successful. Change does take place, but usually in the form of innovations *within* the context of long-established institutional frameworks.

Much Ado about What?

Does the government institutional context of public administration really make that much difference, or is the discussion in this chapter much ado about nothing? One way to test the importance of the governmental ecology is to consider how the work of the American public administrator differs from that of a foreign government administrator doing a similar job in a country where the institutional conditions are opposite those in the United States. For example, consider how the job of administrators working for NASA differs from that of their peers working on the space program in the Soviet Union, prior to recent reforms. Or consider the differences in how law-enforcement officials operate in the United States and South Africa. Both examples will lead us to the same conclusion: Governmental institutions do make a difference for the work of public administrators. The constitutional and legal ecology provides limits on the activities of public administrators and defines the opportunities for government action.

The governmental ecology has an additional and more subtle influence on the work of public administrators. American governmental institutions have endured for over two centuries because they have adapted to changing public expectations about what government is and should be like. The American people may be critical of their elected officials and the growing reams of "bureaucratic red tape" that they perceive to be spewing forth from government. Nonetheless, they are clearly devoted to the American constitutional system as the best possible one. The resulting legitimacy of American government in the public's eyes can be maintained only if those who work for government attempt to live up to the people's expectations. Thus, the governmental ecology is more than just a stage on which public administrators perform; it is also the script that the system's expectations has written for them.

Summary

1. Governmental institutions have a major impact on the operations of public administration because they provide the stages on which government administrators and other policymakers play their roles.
2. For American public administrators, there are two types of relevant governmental institutions: *intra*governmental (within the same government jurisdiction) and *inter*governmental (those in other jurisdictions).
3. A key question for any public administration agency is how it fits into the government's constitutional arrangement of executive, legislative, and judicial authority.
4. Peer agencies and administrative management structures are becoming increasingly important parts of the public administration environment, especially as resources become tighter and programs more complicated.
5. The American federal system has created a situation in which intergovernmental institutions play a significant role in the functioning of American public administration. This is especially true with the emergence of the intergovernmental relations (IGR) system over the past fifty years, and the increasing use of horizontal relationships such as public-sector interest groups and mutual assistance agreements.
6. The overall characteristics of the American governmental ecology include the fragmentation of government authority, slowness to take action, and stability.

Study Questions

1. Assume that you are a budget analyst for the City of Dallas, Texas. As you look at your list of phone calls made and appointments kept, you realize that you've had a very long day. Among others you have spoken with the city manager, the fire chief, an aide to the governor, an official of the U.S. Department of Commerce, and a budget analyst who works for the neighboring Fort Worth, Texas. Which of these individuals are part of your intragovernmental environment? Which are part of your intergovernmental environment?
2. What type of city government does the town you reside in have? How

do the public administrators in the town fit into the overall design of the government?

3. How is your state government organized? How many executive officials are elected by the people and how many are appointed by the governor? Do you think the governor should have more or less power? Explain.

4. Who do you think should be in charge of federal agencies: Congress, which creates them, or the president, who oversees their operation?

5. There are a growing number of public-sector interest groups representing the wishes and interests of public agencies and employees. Should these groups be permitted to lobby Congress or the legislature? Why, or why not?

6. Most federal government programs are actually implemented through state and local governments. What role does the federal government play in each of the following agencies: your local library, school system, university, law-enforcement agency, and state highway department.

Notes

1. See the study of gubernatorial powers in Advisory Commission on Intergovernmental Relations, *The Question of State Government Capability* (Washington, DC: Government Printing Office, 1985), pp. 127–41.

2. Ibid., p. 129.

3. Edwin S. Corwin, *The President, Office and Powers, 1787–1957: History and Analysis of Practice and Opinion*, 4th ed. (New York: New York University Press, 1957), pp. 3–4; also see chaps. 3 and 4; also see Harvey C. Mansfield, Jr., *Taming the Prince: The Ambivalence of Modern Executive Power* (New York: The Free Press, 1989).

4. See Louis Fisher, *The Politics of Shared Power: Congress and the Executive*, 2d ed. (Washington, DC: CQ Press, 1987), chaps. 4 and 5.

5. Ibid., chap. 4.

6. Ibid., chap. 3.

7. On the creation of the EPA, see Alfred A. Marcus, *Promise and Performance: Choosing and Implementing an Environmental Policy* (Westport, CT: Greenwood Press, 1980), chap. 1. On Nixon's plans for reorganizing cabinet departments, see Richard P. Nathan, *The Administrative Presidency* (New York: John Wiley & Sons, 1983), chap. 4.

8. See Aaron Wildavsky, *The New Politics of the Budgetary Process* (Glenview, IL: Scott, Foresman, 1988).

9. See Ed Bean, "Small Rival Hospitals Struggle for Survival Under Medicare Setups," *Wall Street Journal*, 4 January 1988, p. 1.

10. In addition to Fisher, *The Politics of Shared Power*, see James L. Sundquist, "Congress as Public Administrator," in *A Centennial History of the American Administrative State*, ed. by Ralph Clark Chandler (New York: The Free Press, 1987), chap. 8.

11. David H. Rosenbloom, *Public Administration and Law: Bench v. Bureau in the United States* (New York: Marcel Dekker, 1983), pp. 33–34.

12. See *Myers* v. *United States*, 272 U.S. 52 (1926); and Humphrey's Executor v. U.S., 295 U.S. 602 (1935).

13. Robert E. Taylor, "Coal Firms Start to Cooperate with Small-Mine Cleanup Bid," *Wall Street Journal*, 30 December 1986, p. 17. Also see R. Shep Melnick, *Regulation and the Courts: The Case of the Clean Air Act* (Washington, DC: Brookings Institution, 1983).

14. Rosenbloom, *Public Administration and Law*, pp. 48–49.

15. See Kenneth F. Warren, *Administrative Law in the American Political System* (St. Paul, MN: West, 1982).

16. Rosenbloom, *Public Administration and Law*, pp. 192–193.

17. Ibid., pp. 185–200. Also see Warren, *Administrative Law in the American Political System*, chap. 10.

18. For an interesting case study of the relations among these military "peer institutions," see Frederic A. Bergerson, *The Army Gets an Air Force: Tactics of Insurgent Bureaucratic Politics* (Baltimore: Johns Hopkins University Press, 1980).

19. David A. Stockman, *The Triumph of Politics: How the Reagan Revolution Failed* (New York: Harper & Row, 1986), p. 101.

20. For a comparison of the functions of the OMB and the GAO, see Frederick C. Mosher, *A Tale of Two Agencies: A Comparative Analysis of the General Accounting Office and the Office of Management and Budget* (Baton Rouge: Louisiana State University Press, 1984).

21. Penelope Lemov, "Purchasing Officials Push New Techniques to Get More for Their Money," *Governing* 1 (August 1988): 40.

22. Deil S. Wright, "Managing the Intergovernmental Scene: The Changing Dramas of Federalism, Intergovernmental Relations, and Intergovernmental Management," in *Handbook of Organizational Management*, ed. by William B. Eddy (New York: Marcel Dekker, 1983), pp. 422–26.

23. Such a system has some potential for getting out of control, which is the case described in Martha Derthick, *Uncontrollable Spending for Social Service Grants* (Washington, DC: Brookings Institution, 1975).

24. See John Shannon, "The Return to Fend-for-Yourself Federalism: The Reagan Mark," *Intergovernmental Perspective* 13 (Summer/Fall 1987): 34–37 and Robert W. Burchell et al., *The New Reality of Municipal Finance: The Rise and Fall of the Intergovernmental City* (New Brunswick, NJ: Center for Urban Policy Research, 1984).

25. See Ann O'M. Bowman and Richard C. Kearney, *The Resurgence of the States* (Englewood Cliffs, NJ: Prentice-Hall, 1986), esp. chaps. 5–6.

26. See Martha Derthick, *Between State and Nation: Regional Organizations of the United States* (Washington, DC: Brookings Institution, 1974), chap. 3; and Philip L. Fradkin, *A River No More: The Colorado River and the West* (Tucson: University of Arizona Press, 1984).

27. John C. Bollens and Henry J. Schmandt, *The Metropolis: Its People, Politics, and Economic Life*, 4th ed. (New York: Harper & Row, 1982), pp. 303–309.

28. See the discussion of interlocal agreements in Bollens and Schmandt, *The Metropolis*, pp. 294–97.

THE POLICY-MAKING

ECOLOGY

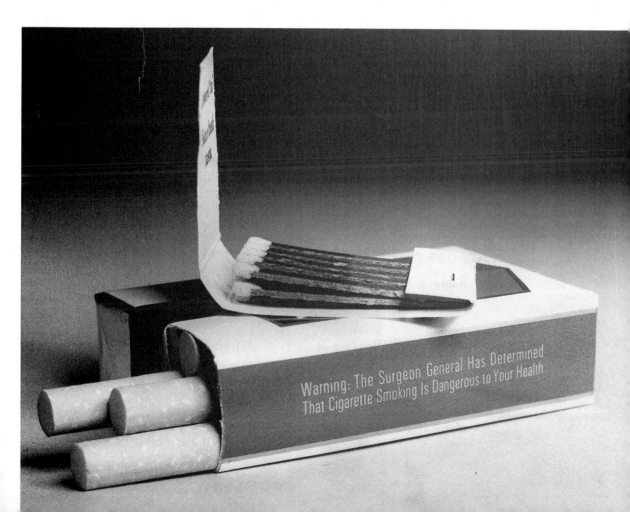

Warning: The Surgeon General Has Determined That Cigarette Smoking Is Dangerous to Your Health

Policy Making: The Dynamics of Government

In this chapter, our focus is on the *policy-making ecology* of public administration. Many things occur in government. Policy makers establish, change, and terminate programs. Public agency managers hire and fire employees. Public employees serve clients and enforce laws. At the heart of all these activities, however, are those government activities associated with public policy making.

The policy-making ecology can influence the work of public administrators in a variety of ways. However, there are four key characteristics of the policy-making environment that have the most significant impact on the work of American public administrators. First, public policy making takes place within different contexts or *policy arenas*. It is the organization of these arenas that has an influence on public administration. Second, each *stage in the policy-making process* poses distinctive challenges to America's public administrators, especially since public administrators do more than merely implement government programs. Third, the *type of policy action* involving the administrator is a potential source of influence. Finally, to understand how policy can shape the job of public administrators, we need to appreciate the extent to which *bureaucratic power* plays a major role in the policy-making process.

As in our earlier discussions of the other dimensions of the public administration ecology, we must keep in mind that there are two ways in which the policy-making ecology can influence the work of public administration. First, policy-making processes and those who work in the policy-making arena can have direct impacts on what a public-sector worker does. Second, and of equal importance, these factors can have an indirect impact through their effect on expectations.

The Arenas of Policy Making

Public policy making doesn't take place in a vacuum. Policies are developed, implemented, and evaluated in different contexts or *policy arenas*. As with other arenas, policy arenas provide the space within which policy actions take place. There is a policy arena for just about every major policy issue, such as education, social welfare, and environmental protection. In these arenas of action, those who are most directly concerned with the policy issues interact with one another. Among these actors are individuals and interest groups who have a stake in the outcomes of policy choices. Legislators and other policy makers who have a direct role or interest in specific policy choices also participate in these policy arenas. Oftentimes the media and the general public are active as well. Most important for our purposes, however, are the relevant members of public-sector agencies who play central roles in many policy arenas.

Policy arenas differ from each other in two important ways. First, they vary according to how those involved in the arena relate to one another. In this sense, we can discuss the *organization of the policy arena*. Second, policy arenas also differ from each other in their openness to change; that is, the *opportunities for policy changes* vary from arena to arena.

Policy Arena Organization

When we discuss the organization of policy arenas, we are focusing on how those involved in the arena relate to each other. Policy arenas are inhabited by a variety of political actors ranging from interest groups and elected officials to the mass media and public administrators. Political scientists describe three distinct patterns characterizing how these groups and individuals interact: iron triangles, subgovernments, and issue networks.

Iron Triangles. There are three principal sets of participants in iron-triangle policy arenas: interest groups, elected officials, and public administrators. Representatives of these groups who have large stakes in the policy-making process play an important role in these arenas. So do elected officials, whose constituents are directly concerned with policies in the issue area. Public administrators who specialize in dealing with the programs that implement these policies represent the third component of the iron triangle.

At the heart of iron-triangle policy arenas are the positive and supportive relationships among those involved. These relationships are built on basic agreements about policy objectives and program implementation. Iron-triangle participants usually resolve whatever differences exist among the various groups without difficulty. The relationship is a close and closed one, with little or no involvement by the media or general public. In fact, from the standpoint of the public, iron-triangle policy arenas are almost invisible.

Historically, perhaps the best-known examples of iron-triangle policy arenas are in the realm of American agricultural policy. Prior to 1964, for example, policies dealing with tobacco farming and tobacco products were formulated and carried out by a small group of individuals in Washington. The group included lobbyists, members of Congress, and public officials in the Department of Agriculture. The lobbyists represented the interests of tobacco farmers. Most of the members of Congress were from tobacco-growing states and served on congressional subcommittees that had jurisdiction over tobacco price supports and other programs dealing with tobacco farming. The officials within the Department of Agriculture were responsible for implementing tobacco farming programs. "As long as no one objected too loudly," observed one student of the tobacco policy arena, "the important and complex tobacco programs, like price supports and export promotion, were conducted without interference from those not included. . . ."[1]

Subgovernments. Subgovernment policy arenas most often involve the same major actors found in iron triangles, but the relationships among them are much looser and open to outside influence. Two factors contribute to the differences between a subgovernment and an iron triangle. First, while there may be some common agreement among the participants in a subgovernment relationship, it is typically limited. In short, there probably exists some differences of opinion among major members of the arena regarding either policy objectives or the means for achieving them. Second, members of subgovernment policy arenas usually have some concern about issues raised by those outside the subgovernment (e.g., the media, other members of the legislature, or the chief executive). Despite such differences and concerns, members of a subgovernment arena are likely to close ranks against any serious outside threats to the policy-making autonomy of their group. There is also a greater role for the media and general public in subgovernmental relationships, but their participation is usually episodic, temporary, and rarely significant.

In the case of tobacco policy, for example, the iron triangle that existed before 1964 is today a subgovernment. Although the coalition of tobacco interests, members of Congress from tobacco-growing states, and administrators of relevant tobacco farming programs remains intact, its decisions and actions are no longer invisible or lacking in controversy. Since 1964, when the Surgeon General issued a report linking cigarette smoking to lung cancer, other key policy-making actors have entered the arena. Until the late 1980s, the tobacco subgovernment fought with general success major efforts by anticancer groups, other federal agencies, and elected officials to reduce tobacco price supports, ban all cigarette advertising, and prohibit smoking in public places. Anticancer subgovernment actors include the American Cancer Society, the American Heart Association, the Federal Trade Commission, the Federal Communications Commission, and the U.S. Public Health Service. In addition, the subgovernment now includes more members of Congress than the iron triangle of the past, ranging from such antitobacco allies as liberal Senator Edward Kennedy to conservative former Senator Wallace Bennett of Utah. Members of the tobacco subgovernment now find themselves responding to criticisms and defending policies in the face of these powerful political forces. Tobacco price supports are constantly threatened, and in 1989 Congress enacted legislation banning smoking on all domestic airline flights.

Issue Networks. Issue-network arenas are much more open than either iron triangles or subgovernments. Participants involved in policy making vary from specific issue to specific issue and from time to time. Thus, the principal actors in an issue network are difficult to identify. This type of policy arena includes individuals and groups with different degrees of interest in and commitments to the policy questions raised within an arena. It is easy for anyone with some concern about a policy issue to become involved in an issue network. "The price of buying into one or another issue network," states Hugh Heclo, "is watching, reading, talking about, and trying to act on particular policy problems."[2]

In an issue network, there is no overall consensus built on agreements among the major actors. As a result, there are no stable relationships. What keeps these networks together is the knowledge and awareness the participants share about certain policy issues. The media and parts of the general public can have significant and long-term influence on these networks. Like other actors, they only need to pay the price of attentiveness to the policy concerns of the issue network.

The environmental regulation policy arena has many of the characteristics of an issue network. Actors within this network concern themselves with programs dealing with clean air, clean water, wilderness areas, the disposal of hazardous wastes, and the like. There are special interest groups concerned with environmental issues such as the Sierra Club. There are also members of Congress and administrators at the Environmental Protection Agency (EPA) and the Department of Interior who have a stake in these issues. Nevertheless, these participants are not able to establish an effective long-term alliance based on a consensus about environmental regulation policies. Instead, they form alliances from time to time to support or fight public-sector activities related to environmental issues. When the battle on that issue is over, the coalition dissolves while the network of contact among the various actors in the policy arena continues.

During the early years of the Reagan presidency, for example, the environmental regulation policy issue network found common cause to work together. Using the courts and the media, they fought the efforts of Interior Department Secretary James Watt and EPA Administrator Ann Gorsuch to dismantle many environmental and conservationist programs. By the end of 1983, both administrators were replaced by appointees more acceptable to members of the environmental policy network. Within a short time, the environmental regulation policy arena returned to its loose and open form.

Implications.   The picture we have drawn of the three major types of policy arenas is, of course, greatly simplified. Each arena also includes influences that represent a variety of participants. A great many public sector-programs, for instance, are intergovernmental in nature. Thus, many federal government policy arenas include relevant actors from state and local governments and vice versa. Since tobacco farming plays a key role in the economy of states like North Carolina and Kentucky, it is not surprising that state and local officials from those regions became involved in the tobacco policy arena to help support their local interests. Similarly, because many EPA programs have an impact on state and local governments, officials from those levels of the intergovernmental system are frequently involved in the policy debates over environmental regulation. Further, the national government does not stay out of the way when states are making certain decisions. Rather, it becomes involved in state and local issues ranging from the construction of local highways to the opening of a toxic-waste dump.

What are the implications for American public administrators of having to work in these different policy arenas? The role of public administrators varies according to which type of arena they participate in. In iron triangles, administrators typically identify closely with the concerns of special interests and certain elected officials. They usually work on behalf of those concerns to the point of representing and protecting them at all times. Administrators involved in an iron-triangle policy arena play a major role in policy-making as facilitators of the interests and demands of those involved in the arena relationship. They do not operate as independent authorities. Political scientists argue that such administrators and their agencies are essentially "captured" by the other actors in their policy arena.[3]

In subgovernment policy arenas, administrators are likely to favor the interests of the other major policy arena actors. In contrast to iron triangles, however, administrators in a subgovernment are more open to alternative points of view from outside the arena. They are typically more susceptible to public pressures or oversight by actors outside the arena. As the visibility of policy arena activities increases, administrative officials come under increasing scrutiny. Consequently, they are open to criticism should they seem to favor some special interest over the general public interest. Such was the case for Department of Agriculture employees involved in the tobacco policy arena after the Surgeon General reported a link between tobacco use and cancer.[4]

In issue networks, the public administrator usually takes either a detached or leadership role. Which role the administrator chooses depends on the specific controversy involved or other circumstances. Throughout most of the 1970s, for example, the EPA was a leading force in efforts to enhance government's regulatory powers for dealing with environmental issues. The agency often helped mobilize political coalitions among members of the environmental regulation policy issue network. However, after the Reagan administration took office and Ann Gorsuch became head of the agency, the EPA became less of a factor. It ceased to play a leadership role and instead resisted new policy initiatives. In some instances, the EPA opposed efforts by others in the environmental regulation policy issue network to pass new legislation or to improve the enforcement of controversial or costly regulations.

Policy Arena Opportunities

Policy arenas are also characterized by the opportunities they provide to those who seek policy changes. Some policy arenas are open to change; others are resistant to change. Some arenas facilitate long-term strategies for policy changes; others offer only short-lived opportunities for change.

The policy arena's structure of opportunities influences the work of public administrators.[5]

Some policy arenas are quite open to policy changes; that is, they offer a conducive environment in which major policy changes get serious consideration. In such an arena, policymakers are willing to consider proposals for policy change at any time. We find this situation in policy arenas where government activities have considerable support from political leaders or the general public. Such support makes the public administrator's job a relatively easy one. For example, city managers in small, homogeneous communities are likely to encounter a widely shared political consensus. Managers who enjoy the support of leaders in such communities are likely to find little opposition to their suggestions for reforms of government operations. Widespread political consensus can facilitate administration at the federal level as well. During the 1960s, administrators at NASA enjoyed considerable political and public support. Consequently, they were able to develop some extremely innovative organizational forms and management techniques. In both of our examples, the policy arena provided ample opportunities for—and little opposition to—change.[6]

Some policy arenas provide opportunities for change on only a temporary and limited basis. Often these policy arenas are characterized by a lack of confidence in government or a suspicion of public officials. The Occupational Safety and Health Administration (OSHA) operates in such an arena. From its inception in 1970, the OSHA has been criticized for its ineffectiveness, often the subject of news stories demonstrating the wastefulness and stupidity of some government regulations. Even efforts to reform the agency in the late 1970s did not make the work of OSHA's administrators any easier. Today the agency has only a limited set of opportunities to bring about the policy and program changes necessary for more effective regulation of worker health and safety.[7]

There are still other policy arenas in which frequent opportunities for change exist, but the changes are severely limited in size and nature. These policy arenas are usually characterized by the presence of a few political actors who tend to dominate government activities in the arena. Typically, the policies and programs in these arenas are responsive to the needs of the dominant actors. As a result, it is difficult to bring about any changes that might significantly change the direction of government policies in these arenas. For example, farmers do not want any radical changes in public programs that support prices for agricultural commodities, nor do veterans want a massive overhaul of the Department of Veterans Affair's benefits system. In both cases, the groups are likely to support small, incremental policy changes. Thus, administrators at the Departments of Agriculture and Veterans Affairs are unlikely to have many opportunities to seek major policy changes.[8]

In contrast, the record-breaking, 508-point drop in the Dow Jones Industrial Index on October 19, 1987, is an example of how dramatic events can enhance policy opportunities for public administrators. The sharp decline in the value of corporate stocks opened up a window of opportunity for the Securities and Exchange Commission (SEC) and the Federal Reserve Board. The fluctuation in the stock market caused the SEC to consider restricting the practice of program trading, which had been controversial even before the stock-market plunge. Similarly, the decline in stock-market values gave the Federal Reserve Board reason to consider reducing interest rates. In these two instances, the relevant federal agencies responded to unusual events that created opportunities for policy changes.

Stages in the Policy-making Process

Public policy making is a complex process. Models of the policy-making process vary. Nonetheless, it is helpful to view the policy-making process as involving ten major steps: problem identification, problem articulation, agenda setting, policy formulation, policy legitimation, program design and development, program implementation, program evaluation, policy reassessment, and program/policy continuation, change, or termination (see Figure 8.1). The particular stage in the policy-making process undoubtedly affects the role of the public administrator.

Program Implementation

The work of public administration is most often associated with program implementation. In fact, implementation is the reason most public-sector agencies exist; their intended primary function is the implementation of public policies. By *program implementation* we mean *those activities that occur when government agencies respond to the policy and program mandates of policy-making officials.*

What are the activities involved in program implementation? A first step in carrying out the mandates of policymakers is to *acquire the necessary resources.* Where financial resources are at stake, this means developing a budget and presenting it to the policymakers in charge of appropriating and allocating public funds. In the case of needed human resources, it means requesting authorization from the central personnel office to hire employees. When administrators need equipment or office space, it means making formal requests to the central purchasing office.[9]

Policy implementation also involves *interpreting the agency's mandate.* Mandates can come in a variety of forms, such as a legislative statute requiring the agency to regulate a sector of the economy or enforce a criminal law, or an executive order or directive. A mandate may involve carrying out orders issued by a court. Regardless of the source of the mandate, it is likely that public administrators must clarify just what they are being asked to do.

Some policy and program mandates are relatively clear in stating the

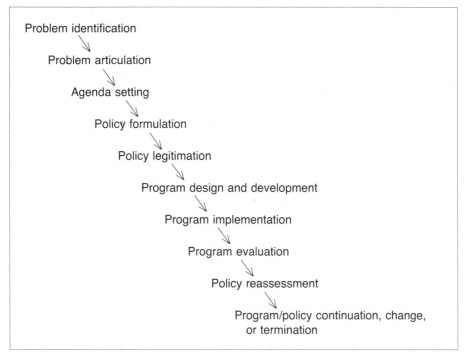

FIGURE 8.1   Stages in the policy-making process.

expectations for the administrator. The Clean Air Act of 1970, for example, explicitly states the pollution-emission goals that automobile manufacturers were required to meet by 1975.[10] Other aspects of these mandates may be vague and even confusing to the administrator. Under the same Clean Air Act, Congress left the EPA to determine the circumstances under which it might allow automobile manufacturers additional time to meet the antipollution goals. Similarly, mandates for state public utility commissions usually require the commissions to establish electric and gas rates that will guarantee utility companies a reasonable rate of return on their investments. In the case of a utility commission, it must determine what is considered reasonable. In either case, some interpretation is necessary.

The task of interpreting mandates oftentimes creates problems for administrators. In 1984, for example, Congress required that incinerated trash be disposed of under stringent hazardous-waste rules if the trash that was burned fell under the EPA's definition of toxic waste. The amendment also includes a clause that exempts wastes from incinerators that burn only household or nonhazardous commercial and industrial waste. The problem was that sometimes the burning of some household and nonhazardous commercial and industrial material creates hazardous wastes. In 1985, the EPA strictly interpreted the amendment when it decided that all hazardous wastes from incineration plants must be disposed of under the stricter rules, regardless of its origin or what was being burned. This interpretation drew criticism from local governments across the country, who were becoming increasingly dependent on incineration to handle their trash. In October 1987, the EPA reinterpreted the policy to exempt municipal incineration waste. This action, in turn, generated criticism from environmentalists and members of Congress, who regarded it as an unwarranted and dangerous change in policy.[11]

After interpreting what a mandate requires, a government agency must develop a *plan of action and an organizational setting* for implementing the program. Depending on the nature of the program, planning and organizing can be either simple or difficult tasks. For example, the program may involve merely extending current city services, such as police or fire protection, to a newly annexed neighborhood. Or the plans might call for building new facilities and hiring new personnel, or reassigning current personnel and changing shift patterns to cover the newly acquired area.

Sometimes even the best-made plans run into problems. In 1972, for example, Congress passed the Supplemental Security Income (SSI) program and charged the Social Security Administration (SSA) with the task of implementing the program. SSI represented a major reform of the American welfare system. Under the program, the national government took over the primary responsibility for helping to support the elderly, blind, or permanently disabled. Administrators at the SSA worked hard to implement SSI by the appointed deadline, January 1, 1974. The planning and organization of the program involved nearly sixty thousand federal workers and almost $120 million in overtime pay. The project ran smoothly until just two days before the scheduled day for mailing out the first checks, when an SSI project manager in California discovered that thousands of SSI checks were made out for the wrong amounts. In fact, an audit conducted several months later revealed that approximately 55 percent of the 540,000 SSI checks sent to Californians during the first six months of 1974 had errors. Overpayment during that period amounted to nearly $50 million. Similar errors were found at different locations throughout the United States. By 1976, administrative problems in the SSI program caused an estimated loss of $547 million.[12]

The media tends to emphasize such "horror stories" about program implementation. Nonetheless, there are thousands of other effectively planned and organized programs and projects that do not get much fanfare. Once these programs are put into operation, the public administrator's job is to make certain that the organization functions and to provide the program's benefits and services effectively. This is the heart of policy implementation.

Involvement in Other Stages

The traditional view of the role of public administration limits the administrator's activities to the program-implementation stage of public policy making. In recent years, however, this perception has changed. We have become increasingly aware of the important role that public administrators play in other stages of the policy-making process. It is now widely expected and accepted that administrators should have greater degrees of responsibility in the design, development, and evaluation of government policies and programs. In addition, administrative officials are increasingly engaged in those stages of the policy-making process that were previously in the exclusive domain of elected officials.

Government administrators today are as likely to *identify and articulate public problems* that require public-sector solutions as are elected officials. This is especially true at the local levels of American government, where public-sector employees are usually the first government officials called when a citizen has a problem. It is also increasingly the case at the state and federal levels of government. Administrators in the Department of Labor during the Nixon administration were the first to identify and articulate the problems of workplace safety and occupational health. Their efforts eventually led to the creation of the Occupational Safety and Health Administration (OSHA). Similarly, studies funded and published by the National Oceanic and Atmospheric Administration (NOAA) and other government agencies identified important issues requiring government responses, such as acid rain and the depletion of the earth's ozone layer. As we depend more on government agencies for information on current physical and social conditions, we can expect them to be a growing source of problem identification in the policy-making process.

Agenda setting and *policy formulation* are also areas of increasing administrative activity. Consider, for example, the important role played by foreign affairs agencies, such as the State Department or the Central Intelligence Agency (CIA), in setting the foreign policy agendas of the country. A government report about Soviet or Chinese military strength or an agency-leaked story about a possible foreign policy problem can certainly attract the attention of the media. In turn, such media coverage can generate pressure for America's policy-making institutions to take some action. In effect, agency actions can trigger a series of events that place some particular issue or problem on the agenda of the country's policymakers.

State and local officials also engage in agenda-setting activities. They are even more effective when they use their collective voices — that is, public-sector interest groups — to draw national attention to specific problems. For example, the decaying condition of America's highways, bridges, sewer systems, and other parts of the physical infrastructure became a prominent issue during the 1980s after the Council of State Planning Agencies published a widely read report titled *America in Ruins*. Their message was reinforced by several major accidents involving collapsed bridges and buildings that occurred since the 1981 publication of that report.[13]

Once the agenda is set, policymakers are likely to turn to the experts in various administrative agencies for formal policy proposals and other program evaluations (see Profile 8.1). Some government agencies even have

PROFILE 8.1
Politics and Administrative Policy Making

The growing role of public administrators in actually formulating public policies is, in part, a response to the increasing complexities of public problems and the need for greater expertise in government. Once engaged in policy formulation, however, public administrators cannot ignore the political implications of what they are doing. All policy formulation eventually involves politics.

The following interview demonstrates how politics and administration mix at the policy-formulation stage of the policy-making process. The interviewee, Thomas Downs, is currently commissioner of Transportation for the State of New Jersey. At the time of this interview, he was deputy mayor and chief administrative officer of the city of Washington, D.C. Downs has a background in local government, having served as city manager in Leavenworth, Kansas, and other small cities early in his career. In 1979–1980, however, he served as a White House fellow in the Carter administration and was given a variety of assignments that would use his expertise in local government. One of his tasks was to help the Department of Transportation develop a comprehensive surface transportation systems act. His comments show how policy decisions are sometimes driven more by political concerns than by concerns for the effective administration of government programs.

The proposal involved a reauthorization and reappropriations bill dealing with highways and mass transit and airport development. One of the issues the staff tried to come to grips with was how to broaden the constituency and congressional support for a federal public transit bill. Public transit is a medium-size city issue. Small rural communities or rural legislators had no perceived stake in public transportaion funding. In order to broaden the public transit constituency you had to rethink how you thought about public transporation.

One way to do that was to find some way of meeting a specific rural public transportation need. We did this by focusing on the elderly, the handicapped, and other "shut-ins" — people without any regular means of access to shopping. It was very difficult for rural communities to provide support for a transportation program that served the needs of these shut-ins. So we started with an initial proposal for a federal program to provide that kind of support to rural communities and counties. It would be a four-year program that would have to be big enough to get the attention of Congress and the support of members from rural areas. After it went through the internal process, the budget folks came up with a $75 million annual authorization for the program. They obviously didn't think much about it.

Then we bring the whole proposal to the Secretary [of Transportation]. The Secretary's conference room is one of those with a huge table in the middle, and Secretary [Brock] Adams is going around the table asking members of his staff about reactions to various components of the act. He gets to the rural transportation assistance portion of it, and he asks everybody what they thought. And they all say, yeah, this does this, and this does that, it builds this constituency, and it makes it easier for rural congressmen to vote on this issue, etc. Adams is impressed because he was once a member of Congress and I have the feeling it was partly his idea in the first place.

He goes all the way around the table and finally gets to me and says, "Tom, what do you think of it?" And I say, to paraphrase Cactus Jack Nance Garner, "I don't think it's worth a bucket of warm spit." Brock was from Harvard, and that comment kind of gagged him a little. I said it's not going to do what you want it to do. He said, "Why not?" I told him that there are three to four thousand counties in the United States. The states and counties will take money off the top to cover their administrative costs and when you distribute what is left over you maybe have enough money for one bus per

county every other day. And he asked what I thought would do the job, and I said "double it" — $150 million rather than $75 million per year. Instead of a four-year authorization for $300 million, I suggested a package totaling $600 million for four years. It went to Congress that way and it passed.

That was $300 million worth of decision-making in a context where the only thing we were talking about at first was the political value of money and not how much money it would take to do the job. The money wasn't important for what it would pay for out in rural America. What was important was getting the attention of Congress. When the program was first being discussed, there was more concern about buying support for the legislation than about what it would take to deliver the transit services to rural area shut-ins.

SOURCE: Quotes and information from a personal interview with Thomas Downs, October 26, 1987.

---

administrative subunits that are directly responsible for the design and analysis of agency policies and programs. The Defense Department, for example, has an assistant secretary who heads a staff of systems analysts and operations researchers. Similarly, the Department of Transportation has an office devoted to planning and program review, and the Department of Labor has an office of policy evaluation and research.[14]

And so it is with almost every stage in the policy-making process: Public administrators are playing an ever-expanding role. The one major exception may be in the policy-legitimation stage, in which a constitution requires that elected officials pass the laws of the land. Nevertheless, even here there is an increasing tendency to make some administrators at least indirectly responsible for policy legitimation. The President of the United States, for example, has the authority to impose import quotas or raise tariffs on certain imported goods if the International Trade Commission and its staff recommends such actions. The president, in other words, can establish policy, but only on the recommendation of an agency that, in turn, relies on the findings of its staff.

How does all this affect the work of American public administrators? As public administrators become more involved in more stages of the policy-making process, their power and influence are bound to increase. With this comes expanded expectations and responsibilities that can prove extremely burdensome. The actual scope and extent of the administrator's involvement at different policy-making stages varies from policy arena to arena. Furthermore, there are significant differences in the policy-making roles played by public administrators in different jurisdictions. While state welfare agencies may play a critical role in the policy making of Pennsylvania or Massachusetts, their peers in Arkansas or Oklahoma may have little or no impact on state policies. Hence, it is difficult to generalize about how the policy-making process affects American public administration as a whole.

Types of Policy Actions

Clearly, public administrators perform a variety of tasks and functions in the policy-making system. But how does the *type of policy action* involved influence the activities of public administrators? There are four major types of policy actions to consider:

1. *Microdecisions:* Policy actions that involve the specific or routine application of policy with reference to some individual or group (e.g., giving a speeding citation).
2. *Distributive:* Policy actions that deal with the processing of claims or entitlements for some specific segment of society (e.g., issuing general revenue sharing or formula grant funds to local governments that apply for them).
3. *Regulative:* Policy actions that involve selecting winners and losers in the allocation of some social good or highly valued scarce resource (e.g., deciding who gets a particular frequency ban in a local television or radio market).
4. *Redistributive:* Policy actions that involve expropriating some highly valued resource from one group and appropriating it to another (e.g., the Social Security System).

Microdecisions

Microdecisions are policy actions involving some specific or routine application of a public policy. The role of the administrator is central in microdecisions. Under this type of policy action, civil servants make any specific policy choices that are necessary. In enforcing speed limits, for example, state troopers and local patrol officers have considerable discretion regarding where, when, and how they will take actions. Knowing that it is often difficult to maintain a speed of 55 mph, a trooper may establish a higher speed (e.g., 60 mph) as a basis for stopping a driver. Having stopped the driver going 60 mph, the officer has the option of giving either a speeding ticket or a warning. Seeing an open beer can in the vehicle, the trooper can elect to ignore it. If he or she chooses to respond to the open beer can, the trooper can ask the driver to step out of the car and test whether he or she was driving under the influence of alcohol. In microdecisions, all these choices are in the hands of the specific administrator.[15]

Distributive Policy Actions

Distributive policy actions differ from microdecisions in two respects: (1) distributive actions involve dealing with a segment of the population as opposed to single individuals, and (2) they typically involve the noncontroversial processing of claims or entitlements.[16] In this instance, the public administrator is more like a clerk who processes forms and claims. This is not to imply that distributive policies are unimportant; millions of Americans depend on the efficient operation of distributive agencies. The Social Security Administration (SSA) and state unemployment insurance agencies, for example, issue literally millions of checks each month to eligible recipients who depend on those drafts arriving on time.

In most instances, the role of the public administrator in distributive policy situations is not a critical or powerful one. If an individual meets the criteria for receiving a Social Security or unemployment check, then the civil servant's job is to issue it in the appropriate amount at the appropriate time. If, however, the criteria for eligibility are vague or the situation calls for administrative judgment, then the public administrator plays an important and crucial role.

This was the case for SSA administrators in charge of the Social Security Disability Insurance (SSDI) program during the early 1980s. Starting in the late 1970s, there was growing concern that the criteria for granting disability claims under SSDI were not being stringently enforced. The number of SSDI program recipients had more than doubled over a ten-year period. As a result, Congress called for tighter review procedures by the SSA. When the Reagan administration came to office in 1981, it ordered an increase in investigations of new disability claims and a detailed review of previous claims. SSDI case reviews increased fourfold from 1980 to 1982. As a result of these reviews, many disability claims were rejected or terminated and program costs were cut by 10 percent. The public reaction to this tightening of enforcement was quite negative, however. Each day the media reported another instance of a worthy recipient of disability benefits being turned away by the SSA. By 1984, Congress was calling for the reinstatement of many individuals who had lost their SSDI benefits.[17]

Regulative Policy Actions

Regulative policy actions involve selecting winners and losers in the allocation of some public good or highly valued and sought-after resource. The role of a public administrator in this type of policy action is usually indirect. Typically, elected or appointed political officials are responsible for making the final choice between winners and losers. Ultimately, the decision of whether to impose import quotas on Japanese goods is up to the president, and a decision about granting or renewing a VHF-TV frequency broadcast license is up to appointed members of the Federal Communications Commission (FCC). In such cases, however, the public administrator often plays a significant role as advisor to the actual decision maker. This is the case when the FCC allocates a broadcast band to one of several applicants or when a state public utility commission grants a private gas company the right to serve a certain area of the state. The appointed political officials on these commissions make the determination, but they do so after getting a staff report on the pros and cons of awarding the license to each applicant. Frequently, these reports include specific staff recommendations that commissioners often follow.

Redistributive Policy Actions

Redistributive policy actions involve taking away some valued resource from one party and giving it to another. Public administrators are likely to play only a limited role in such situations, usually acting as program implementors and policy enforcers. Consider, for example, the role of the Internal Revenue Service (IRS) as an implementor of the federal tax code. The IRS leaves the making of general tax policy to elected officials and attempts to concentrate instead on enforcement activities. However, there may be occasions when IRS agents are in a position to make a judgment call about the deductibility of a certain item on a taxpayer's return (a microdecision). Faced with such a situation, the agents base their judgments on interpretations of highly technical rules and numerous tax court decisions. Furthermore, IRS agents must follow detailed rules of due process when making such judgment calls.

How do these different types of policy actions influence the work of public administrators? In addition to shaping the role that public administrators play in regard to each policy, each type of policy action generates expectations about administrative behavior. For example, we expect IRS agents to carry out the specifics of the Internal Revenue Code without imposing their personal views on who should pay and how much. We expect the state troopers to use sound judgment and understanding in deciding whether to stop a vehicle or issue a summons. Similarly, we expect administrative staffers to offer sound advice to the political appointees responsible for deciding who will and will not receive licenses. These are just some examples of the sources of expectations that affect the world of America's public administrators.

Bureaucratic Power

The concept of power is important to any study of government and politics. It is important whether we are discussing the power of the people, the president, Congress, or the courts. When we speak of the *power* of these individuals and institutions, we typically think of their constitutional authority to make decisions or influence events. When we apply the term to bureaucracies, however, its tone and meaning often have negative connotations. *Bureaucratic power* is popularly regarded as a threat to constitutional authority, an abuse of public office, and a characteristic of modern government that must be strictly controlled if not eliminated.

Contrary to the conventional view of bureaucratic power, informed students of public administration realize that it is an essential ingredient in the conduct of public affairs. Without power, those whose job it is to carry out the policies and programs of government would be facing an impossible task. In the words of one writer, power is the "lifeblood" of public administration;[18] without it, the value of government bureaucracies would be extremely low.

Exactly what is bureaucratic power?[19] *Power is the ability to influence or determine the behavior of others through the control or manipulation of resources.* When located in the hands of public administrators, we call it *bureaucratic power*.

The exercise of power can take many forms. *Coercive power* rests on the application or threat of force. Most American public administrators do not rely on force or threats of violent action. Those with the authority to do so (e.g., police officers) must follow fairly strict rules. It is more common for public administrators to rely on *remunerative power*—that is, the use of material rewards or punishments to gain the cooperation of others. Government policies to reduce unemployment sometimes involve providing a special subsidy or tax break to private companies willing to train and hire the hard-core unemployed. Similarly, imposing hefty fines on speeders is one way of encouraging drivers to obey speed limits in school zones.

Public administrators also can rely on their power of persuasion or their ability to manipulate symbols to convince others to act in appropriate ways of their own volition. When people behave a certain way because they have been convinced it is the right thing to do, they are responding to *normative power*. For example, Lt. Colonel Oliver North used normative power when he testified in 1987 before the Senate about his activities as National Security Council staffer involved in the Iran-*contra* affair. His televised testimony included comments that were intended to persuade members of Congress and the viewing audience of the correctness of his behavior. In addition, by appearing in his full-dress military uniform, North was tapping into the normative power of patriotism. Such a manipulation of important symbols, such as the American flag and service uniforms, together with a careful use of the media, enables administrators to tap normative power.

Like other forms of power, bureaucratic power relies on the resources available to those who exercise it. There can be no bureaucratic power unless the public administrator possesses the appropriate resources. All of us have some resource we can use to exercise power. Some Americans rely on their wealth to get power. In the United States, money (usually in the form of campaign contributions) can at least get you access to many policymakers.[20] For others, a charismatic personality or exuding confidence can prove to be an effective power resource. For still others, information, social standing, and a variety of other resources can be used to obtain power.[21]

Public administrators also possess a variety of potential power resources. Max Weber, a noted student of bureaucracy, held that *rationality* and *expertise* were the principal sources of bureaucratic power. What makes bureaucrats necessary—that is, their control over knowledge and their ability to take rational actions—is what makes them powerful.[22] Today many public administrators rely on their expertise as a basis for power. The weapons expert at the Defense Department or the Middle East expert in the State Department both have the potential for exercising considerable influence in their respective agencies. Likewise, city attorneys often have considerable power to influence municipal practices because of their expertise. Increasingly, senior members of the public service can claim expertise in the management of government organization.

There are other power resources relevant to the work of the modern public administrator. For example, the *external support* that public agencies receive from those they serve can be an important power resource. The Department of Agriculture, for example, often counts on the support of farmers, just as the Department of Education frequently depends on the support of teachers and their unions.

The *espirit de corps* within a public agency is also an important source of power. The commitment of peace corps volunteers to the Peace Corps' program has always been high, just as many agents of the Federal Bureau of Investigation are extremely loyal to their organization. In both instances, there exists a sense of pride and commitment that is at the root of this power resource.

In addition, the quality of *agency leadership* can be an important factor in determining bureaucratic power. A relatively weak or unpopular leader who lacks executive skills can weaken the influence of a public agency. This was the case when Ann Gorsuch headed the EPA during the early years of the Reagan administration. The influence of the EPA steadily declined during Gorsuch's tenure in office. But when William Ruckelshaus, the agency's first administrator when it was formed in 1970, returned to head the EPA in 1983, his leadership reinvigorated the agency and enhanced its political position in the policy-making arena.[23]

Perhaps the most effective source of bureaucratic power is the amount of discretion the public administrator has in any policy-making situation.

INSIGHT 8.1
LIVING WITH EXPERTISE

Although expertise is often a major source of power for public administrators, it is not always an easy resource to live with. Expert ecologists at the National Park Service, for example, came under severe criticism from politicians and the press in 1988 for what became known as the "let-burn policy." Based on ecological studies, this policy called for the Park Service to allow naturally set fires to burn themselves out as long as they didn't threaten human habitats. The policy was fully supported by conservationists and environmental groups that understood the ecological benefits of natural fires. Outside the community of experts, however, the policy was viewed suspiciously by the media and others.

When several lightning-caused fires started in Yellowstone National Park (which is located in an area covering parts of Wyoming, Montana, and Idaho) during the summer of 1988, Park Service personnel allowed the conflagrations to burn while monitoring their movement. They brought in fire-fighting crews during July but ordered them to avoid aggressive actions against the fire. In the meantime, local businesses and public officials began to express concern that the fires were keeping tourists away from the usually busy Yellowstone area. There was also growing concern about the potential danger of the fire's spreading because of worsening drought conditions in the region. Bending to these pressures, the Park Service began an effort to contain some of the fires in mid-July. Most of the fires had been contained by mid-August, when high winds blew into the park area and quickly spread the blazes. A major effort to put out these fires followed, and by the end of September only a few fires remained active.

The media's reports on the Yellowstone fires greatly exaggerated the actual damage, and political leaders added to the complaints by calling the fire a "disaster" and the Park Service's let-burn policy "absurd." Park Service personnel noted that the fires caused severe damage to only a small portion (1 percent, according to the Park's superintendent) of the Yellowstone area. There were major costs associated with fire-fighting efforts and lost tourist trade, but Park Service experts and their supporters tried to point out the positive ecological benefits of the 1988 fires.

Despite efforts to defend their expert decisions, Park Service personnel feared that public criticisms and investigations would result in an unwise change in the let-burn policy. In this situation, their expertise was of no help.

SOURCE: Based on information in Peter Matthiessen, "Our National Parks: The Case for Burning," *New York Times Magazine,* 11 Dec. 1988, pp. 38–41, 121–123, 128–129.

Discretion is the "ability of an administrator to choose among alternatives" related to government decisions.[24] Agencies and administrators who have little discretion in carrying out their jobs also have little potential power for influencing decisions. In contrast, an agency or administrator whose job affords considerable discretion has a good deal more potential power to exercise. For example, there are times when administrators receive orders that are reasonably clear regarding when they should act and what steps they should take. Most of the agents who process tax returns for the IRS have little discretion in determining what happens to a tax form and tax payment when it reaches their desks. Yet there are some IRS employees such as auditors who have a degree of flexibility in determining whether to allow or disallow a questionable deduction on a tax return.

The degree of discretion a public administrator possesses depends on several factors. Among these is the policy arena in which the administrator operates. Administrators working in policy arenas where there are many opportunities for change are more likely to have greater discretion to choose among policy alternatives. Given their expertise in management, these administrators are more likely to have discretion in the policy-implementation stage of public policy making. In addition, they are likely to have greater discretion when engaged in microdecision activities than in the other levels of policy actions.

Generally, the discretion of public administrators has increased over the past several decades. More and more policy-making authority has passed into the hands of America's public servants. For some observers, this has been a necessary and highly beneficial development. "Given the needs of modern government for economic regulation, specialization, continuity, and speed in the dispatch of business," argues Peter Woll, " . . . it is the bureaucracy that has stepped in to fill the gap created by the inability of the other branches to fulfill all of these requirements."[25] In contrast, Theodore J. Lowi and others believe that too much bureaucratic discretion is destroying the foundations of our constitutional system. Lowi argues for government reforms that would help minimize the discretion of America's bureaucrats and place responsibility for policy making back into the hands of Congress.[26] Between those two extremes are analysts like Kenneth Davis, who see a need for greater administrative discretion as well as a need to control for the potential abuse of bureaucratic power.[27]

Clearly, bureaucratic power is always present but it is not always seen in a positive light. Here again, expectations play a role. Some people see bureaucratic power as a necessary ingredient to the work of public administrators. Others—perhaps far too many—look at bureaucratic power in a negative light. They see a high potential for the abuse of power, too many opportunities for corruption, and a general reduction in democratic government. These perceptions and feelings have a definite impact on the millions of Americans who work in the public service.

The Policy-making Role

The policy-making ecology is a major force in shaping the work of America's public administrators. It emerges from the organization of the policy arena, the stage in the policy-making process, the type of policy action, and the degree of bureaucratic power. Thus, the question is not whether public administrators engage in public policy making but what role they play in policy making.

Under certain conditions, the public administrator can play a dominant role in the policy-making process. Typically, this occurs in policy arenas where there exist many opportunities for administrative action and where other policy makers rely on the expertise and knowledge of the administrator and the amount of bureaucratic discretion tends to be high. In other instances, the public administrator plays a minor or peripheral role in policy making. When Congress and the White House debate the future of Social Security, the administrators involved in that program usually will sit on the sidelines awaiting the outcome.[28] In a great many instances, the administrator works side-by-side with other actors in the policy-making system to solve public problems—sometimes successfully and sometimes not.[29]

A key determinant of what role administrators play in public policy making is what role they are *expected* to play by those who have an interest in what government is doing. It may be rational for us to let some public administrators make decisions for us. After all, we hire many public-sector workers because of their expertise. Shouldn't we let them decide where to locate hazardous-waste dump sites or which books to use in the classroom? Yet what is rational is not always acceptable to many segments of the American public who wish to retain the ultimate authority to make such decisions. Such is the power of expectations in the American policy-making system.

Summary

1. Public administrators are deeply involved in the policy-making process, and their involvement has an impact on the expectations that shape the work of government employees.
2. This influence depends, in part, on the type of policy arena within which the policy making occurs. Administrative roles differ among the iron triangle, subgovernment, and issue network arenas.
3. The stage in the policy-making process also makes a difference. Although public administrators work primarily in the policy-implementation stage, they are becoming increasingly involved in other phases of the process.
4. Public administrative roles vary according to the kinds of policy actions

undertaken. These range from microdecisions, in which the role of administrators is considerable, to redistributive actions, in which their role is much more limited.

5. Bureaucratic power plays an important role in shaping the work of public administration. There are a variety of resources that administrators and agencies can mobilize to generate bureaucratic power.

Study Questions

1. Select a public policy issue that has received attention in the news lately. Based on the facts available to you, which kind of policy arena is involved in this issue — an iron triangle, subgovernment, or issue network? Explain your choice.
2. Spend a day in a government office observing the work of one employee. Keep a log of the policy issues with which that employee deals. Then categorize the administrator's involvement in terms of where it fits within the policy-making process.
3. Review the major stories in today's newspaper. Identify those stories that make reference to some government policy and characterize the types of policy actions involved. Consider what roles public administrators are playing in those policy actions.

Notes

1. A. Lee Fritschler, *Smoking and Politics: Policymaking and the Federal Bureaucracy*, 3d ed. (Englewood Cliffs, NJ: Prentice-Hall, 1983), pp. 6–7.
2. The concept of issue networks is presented in Hugh Heclo, "Issue Networks and the Executive Establishment," in *The New American Political System*, ed. Anthony King (Washington, DC: American Enterprise Institute for Public Policy Research, 1978), pp. 87–124.
3. On the idea of agency "capture," see Marver Bernstein, *Regulating Business Through Independent Commissions* (Princeton, NJ: Princeton University Press, 1955).
4. See Peter Navarro, *The Policy Game: How Special Interests and Ideologues Are Stealing America* (New York: John Wiley & Sons, 1984).
5. See Richard J. Stillman, II, *The American Bureaucracy* (Chicago: Nelson-Hall, 1987), pp. 191–200; and John W. Kingdon, *Agendas, Alternatives, and Public Policies* (Boston: Little, Brown, 1984), pp. 174–80.
6. Stillman, *The American Bureaucracy*, pp. 194–95.
7. Kenneth J. Meier, *Regulation: Politics, Bureaucracy, and Economics* (New York: St. Martin's Press, 1985), chap. 8.
8. Stillman, *The American Bureaucracy*, pp. 195–96.

9. See Charles O. Jones, *An Introduction to the Study of Public Policy*, 2d ed. (North Scituate, MA: Duxbury Press, 1977), chap. 7; Randall B. Ripley and Grace A. Franklin, *Bureaucracy and Policy Implementation* (Homewood, IL: Dorsey Press, 1982), pp. 4–8; and Daniel A. Mazmanian and Paul A. Sabatier, *Implementation and Public Policy* (Glenview, IL: Scott, Foresman, 1983).

10. Alfred A. Marcus, *Promise and Performance: Choosing and Implementing an Environmental Policy* (Westport, CT: Greenwood Press, 1980).

11. Robert E. Taylor, "EPA Weighs Exempting Incinerator Ash from Rules Covering Hazardous Wastes," *Wall Street Journal*, 13 October 1987, p. 12.

12. See John J. Fialka, "Ailing Computers Give Social Security System Another Big Problem," *Wall Street Journal*, 5 October 1981 pp. 1 and 12.

13. See Pat Choate and Susan Walter, *America in Ruins: Beyond the Public Works Pork Barrel* (Washington, DC: Council of State Planning Agencies, 1981); and Jonathan D. Salant, "America's Aging Bridges," *Governing* 1 (May 1988): 52–57.

14. Arnold J. Meltsner, *Policy Analysts in the Bureaucracy* (Berkeley: University of California Press, 1976).

15. On the concept of microdecisions, see Emmette S. Redford's discussion of micropolitics in *Democracy in the Administrative State* (New York: Oxford University Press, 1969), chap. 4.

16. The following distinction between distributive, regulative, and redistributive policy actions is based on a well-known typology developed by Theodore J. Lowi. For a summary and relevant applications of the typology, see Randall B. Ripley and Grace A. Franklin, *Congress, the Bureaucracy, and Public Policy*, 3d ed. (Homewood, IL: Dorsey Press, 1984).

17. D. Lee Bawden and John L. Palmer, "Social Policy: Challenging the Welfare State," in *The Reagan Record: An Assessment of America's Changing Domestic Priorities*, ed. by John L. Palmer and Isabel V. Sawhill (Cambridge, MA: Ballinger, 1984), p. 190.

18. Norton E. Long, "Power and Administration," *Public Administration Review*, 9 (Autumn 1949): 257–64.

19. There are many definitions of *power*; see, for example, David V. J. Bell, *Power, Influence, and Authority: An Essay in Political Linguistics* (New York: Oxford University Press, 1975); and Dennis H. Wrong, *Power: Its Forms, Bases, and Uses* (New York: Harper Colophon Books, 1979). On the typology of power provided in this discussion, see Amitai Etzioni, *A Comparative Analysis of Complex Organizations*, rev. ed. (New York: Free Press, 1975).

20. See Larry J. Sabato, *PAC Power: Inside the World of Political Action Committees* (New York: Norton, 1985).

21. See the discussion of political influence in Robert A. Dahl, *Modern Political Analysis*, 4th ed. (Englewood Cliffs, NJ: Prentice-Hall, 1984), chaps. 3–4.

22. See Wrong, *Power*, p. 58.

23. For an excellent discussion on bureaucratic power, see Francis E. Rourke, *Bureaucracy, Politics, and Public Policy*, 3d ed. (Boston: Little, Brown, 1984).

24. Ibid., pp. 35–44.

25. Peter Woll, *American Bureaucracy*, 2d ed. (New York: W. W. Norton, 1977), p. 248.

26. Theodore J. Lowi, *The End of Liberalism: The Second Republic of the United States*, 2d ed. (New York: W. W. Norton, 1979).

27. See Kenneth Culp Davis, *Discretionary Justice* (Baton Rouge: Louisiana State University Press, 1969).
28. See Paul Light, *Artful Work: The Politics of Social Security Reform* (New York: Random House, 1985).
29. See Eric Redman, *The Dance of Legislation* (New York: Simon & Schuster, 1973).

CHAPTER 9

THE PERSONAL

DIMENSION

Public Employees and the Human Factor

We now know that environmental factors ranging from physical surroundings to the policy-making system can influence the jobs and expectations facing public administrators. However, we must also recognize that human factors can influence the dynamics and outcomes of public administration. By *human factors*, we mean *the various emotional, psychological, and physical needs that public employees bring with them to the workplace.*

Individual employees are the final arbiters in the public administration arena. They are on the receiving end of most of the environmental expectations and are the final mediators of those expectations. Thus, we must consider the influence of the public employees themselves and the unique dynamics they bring to the administrative arena.

The Filtering Process

Individual employees often act as filters through which must pass all of the various expectations and dynamics discussed in earlier chapters. They interpret the various expectations generated by ecological forces. Individual administrators decide which expectations are legitimate and whether to respond to them. How they filter those expectations depends in part on their particular needs and circumstances.

Influence of the Ecology on Individuals

As we know, the environment directly affects the job challenges of public administrators and indirectly affects the expectations we have for them. In addition, the environment affects the attitudes and behaviors of public employees.

One example is technology, which can have tremendous impacts on the expectations public employees have about their participation in the work force. The widespread availability of relatively safe and reliable birth control was a technological breakthrough in medicine in the 1960s. Prior to this time, women often had to leave the work force when they had children. The inability to reliably control fertility made it difficult for women to sustain careers outside the home. Birth-control technology made it possible for women in their childbearing years to enter the work force and sustain their careers.

Similarly, new social technologies have also had an impact on women and their career opportunities. In the past, women who chose to have children usually faced social pressures to stay home to raise them. The creation of commercial and organized child day-care centers has eased those pressures somewhat, thus making a career in the public or private sector more feasible.

Technology can also affect working conditions. The introduction of the high-speed computer, for example, has revolutionized the twentieth-century world of work. Technological advances during the 1980s made mini- and microcomputers a fact of life for many workers. The ready availability of these computers has increased management's ability to monitor some employees' work habits every moment of the day. For example, the computers can be used to monitor employees whose jobs include word processing, record keeping, calculating, and even telephone solicitation. Such computers can monitor how many errors employees make in a day, how long it takes them to complete a transaction, or how long they spend on the phone with clients. This situation has led some employee unions and others opposed to computerization of the workplace to resist these developments. They argue that computer monitoring is psychologically intimidating for workers because they feel that their every action—even how long they are away from their desks for restroom breaks—is being watched. At the same time, computerization has provided employees with greater control over their jobs. In some cases, it has brought about major changes in responsibilities. With word processors at their desks, many managers are becoming less dependent on secretarial help to translate verbalized ideas to the written word. The same word-processing technologies have freed secretaries from much of the drudgery of typing and dictation. Thus, they can devote more time and energy to other less mundane and oftentimes more challenging tasks.

Demographic factors and trends can have profound effects on the wants and needs of individuals. The different attitudes of people born during the baby boom (1946–1964) and those born during the baby bust (mid-1960s to the early 1980s) illustrate this aspect of the environment's impact on individuals. The baby boomers have had to contend with crowded schools and a competitive work force. In contrast, those born during the baby bust attended less crowded schools and as they now enter the work force, they are finding many more job opportunities.

The cultural ecology affects individuals' values and aspirations as well as the social norms that define acceptable behavior. For example, American society has a sufficiently strong work ethic that individuals often define their identities in terms of the jobs they hold. At social gatherings the first question usually asked of a stranger after initial introductions is "What do you do for a living?" or "Where do you work?" The roughly equivalent question for the college set is "What's your major?" We ask these questions because they give us some insight into the status, abilities, and ambitions of the individual we are meeting for the first time.

The most subtle influence of the cultural environment on individuals is on their expectations about their own lives and work experiences.[1] Culture affects how adults evolve over their total life span. It shapes their personalities, the definition of what is important to them, and the values they pursue. For example, in the United States most everyone has some immigrant ancestors who came here in search of a better life. Consequently, the notion of upward social and economic mobility is a basic expectation for most Americans. Today's young people expect to be better off than their parents were in terms of economics, education, and status.

Changes in cultural expectations can occur over time. During the past twenty years, for instance, there have been changes in how individuals define themselves. The work ethic led many Americans to identify themselves and their self-worth primarily in terms of work. Today's social norms provide more support for individuals who recognize the importance of spending time with families and on personal hobbies or interests.[2] We see this recent moderation in the work ethic more and more frequently in both the public sector and private industry. Successful and ambitious employees sometimes turn down job transfers because they believe the cost to their families is too high.[3] These choices are not made easily. Turning down a transfer often amounts to a self-imposed limitation on an employee's career progress. Organizations often hesitate to offer a second promotion opportunity to an individual who places family ahead of work.

Culture also influences the definition of *family* and the basic norms surrounding the family. For instance, during the post-World War II baby boom, the norm was for husbands to work outside the home and for wives to stay at home. Married women, and especially mothers, only worked outside the home when there was extreme economic necessity. In the 1980s, however, the number of women entering the work force with the expectation of lifelong careers rose dramatically. Although economic necessity is a large part of today's two-career family, the expectation that women can and should pursue their own careers outside the home is another socially defined factor.

In addition to these basic social and cultural norms, many individuals are affected by professional standards of behavior. The number of public-sector employees with professional training is increasing. Professional education influences the attitudes and values of members of a profession.[4] Further, as individuals associate with other professionals, they reinforce each other's sense of appropriate behavior and standards for their profession. Professional standards usually are specified in the criteria for certification as a professional engineer, accountant, attorney, or physician. Professional associations periodically review these standards to keep them current with the growth of knowledge in their particular fields. The standards serve as reference points for individuals who seek to determine what is appropriate behavior under given circumstances. As such, professional standards can be a potent source of influence on the values, attitudes, and behavior of public employees.

Economic forces in the task environment can influence what individuals see as important characteristics in jobs. For example, the expectations of many individuals during the 1930s were profoundly influenced by the Great Depression. Workers and their children came to value job security very highly. Their aspirations for work were influenced by the economic uncertainties of the depression—what they wanted was the security of a regular paycheck. The epitome of this mind set is the "organization man" described by William F. Whyte—someone who is more than just a person working for a company or agency; he also *belonged* to it, heart and soul. "They are the ones of our middle class who have left home, spiritually as well as physically, to take the vows of organizational life. . . ." [5]

The economic conditions facing individuals who entered the work force during the 1980s was reflected in their unique economic experiences. People reaching adulthood during this time had grown up in an era of relatively high inflation, both in the United States and worldwide. This inflation cycle spanned the period from the mid-1960s through the 1970s, reaching double-digit levels in the late 1970s. Children of this period saw the value of their parents' earnings diminish with inflation. This experience led people entering the work force today to emphasize earning potential in their choice of occupation. A corresponding high demand for college courses in business and economics reflects students' interest in preparing themselves for the intense work force competition while pursuing their notion of economic security. It is not that there are fewer jobs; rather, it is harder to get a job that can allow the individual to keep ahead of inflation and feel financially secure.

The governmental and policy-making environments can also affect the willingness of certain groups of individuals to pursue jobs in particular government agencies. During World War II, for example, Americans considered it patriotic to work for government, and especially for agencies directly associated with the war effort at home (e.g., the Office of Price Administration, which set prices for consumer goods). Similarly, during the early 1960s, there was a tremendous upsurge in the value of public service, both within Washington D.C. and in unique foreign policy programs such as the Peace Corps. This political condition allowed government service to recruit many bright, ambitious, and hard-working people to government service. [6]

The popularity of certain political policies can cause fluctuations in the attractiveness of employment in certain agencies. During the Vietnam War, for instance, many college-age males who normally would not have considered attending college did so. Many went to college to take advantage of the student draft deferment to delay or avoid military service. Thus, those individuals who ordinarily would not have wanted to teach high school or join military reserve units chose to do so as a way to avoid active service in Vietnam. In other words, people pursued options they would not have otherwise followed to avoid active-duty military service.

Political events and policies can influence the pool of individuals interested in certain careers and willing to join certain organizations. Although not the only presidents to do so, Jimmy Carter and Ronald Reagan helped set a negative tone for public-sector employment. Both blamed government bureaucracies and their employees for the failures of the political system.

The antigovernment rhetoric and employment policies of both administrations contributed to substantial erosion in the attractiveness of public-sector employment.[7]

The Needs of Public Employees

Philosophers and theologians have debated the nature of human beings throughout most of our history. The issue of human nature is important in public administration because people are the fundamental units of government organizations. People have needs and drives that affect their feelings about work as well as their behavior on the job. Government employees bring with them to their public agencies their personal needs and values. However carefully agencies may attempt to structure employees' job responsibilities and work environments to minimize the impact of individual idiosyncrasies, their efforts cannot succeed completely.

Human Needs

Psychologists recognize that human beings have a variety of needs that they seek to fulfill. Some of these needs derive from biology, others are learned culturally, and still others are determined situationally. A *need* is an internal state that causes an individual to pursue particular outcomes or things. For example, a need for survival may cause an individual to pursue food or shelter. Similarly, a need for public recognition may cause an individual to pursue a highly visible career as a professional athlete or politician. While different people may have different needs, all people have many needs that are likely to change over time.

Maslow's Hierarchy of Needs.   Of the various competing theories about human needs, the best known is Abraham Maslow's. His theory arranges human needs in a hierarchy, with unmet needs being a source of individual motivation (see Figure 9.1). The most basic needs in Maslow's hierarchy are *physiological* needs for food, water, and sex. In a sense, these are the minimal needs for human survival.

The next highest needs are related to *safety* or a personal sense of security. These needs are manifested in desires for job security, "nest egg" savings accounts, health insurance, and so on. Next in Maslow's hierarchy are *love* and *affiliation*, which are manifested in the need to develop emotional ties, friendships, and a sense of belonging to a group. These are followed by *esteem*, such as personal esteem, self-respect, and a sense of achievement and integrity. Esteem needs can also show up as a need for recognition and respect from one's co-workers, friends, and family. The highest level of Maslow's hierarchy is *self-actualization*. At this level, individuals are motivated to live up to their potential as human beings. Its most common manifestations

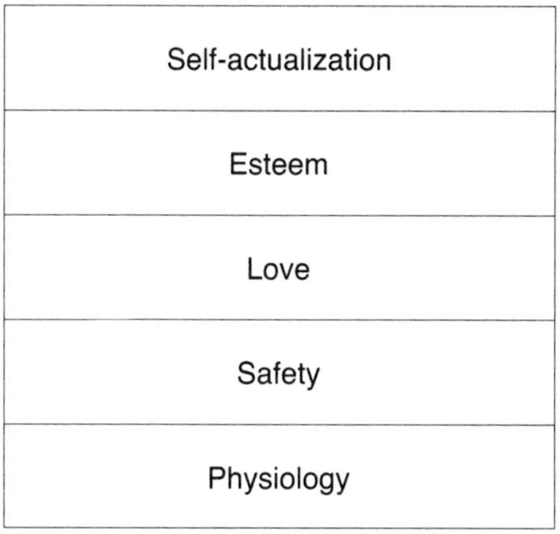

| Self-actualization |
| Esteem |
| Love |
| Safety |
| Physiology |

FIGURE 9.1 Maslow's hierarchy of human needs. (Source: "Hierarchy of Needs" from *Motivation and Personality* by A. H. Maslow. Copyright 1954 by Harper & Row, Publishers, Inc. Copyright © 1970 by Abraham H. Maslow. Reprinted by permission of the publisher.

are in an individual's striving for personal growth and trying new, personally satisfying endeavors.[8]

According to Maslow, needs at the lowest level of the hierarchy (i.e., physiological and survival) are the most important; they dominate the motivation of human behavior until the needs at this level are relatively well met. When met, those needs cease to be a source of motivation. Instead, the next highest level in the hierarchy of needs becomes the dominant motivator. This pattern repeats itself on up the hierarchy until the individual reaches the top level, self-actualization. For example, in the early stages of an individual's work life, he or she may be concerned about finances. Perhaps the individual has several thousand dollars of college loans to repay or a mortgage that consumes a large portion of his or her disposable income. This person is likely to have a need for job security and income, corresponding to Maslow's safety needs. After a few years, the individual may have paid back those college loans and built up equity in a home. Maybe the person has also received a few raises in pay and made some modest financial investments that provide a degree of financial security. In this case, the individual is no longer motivated by safety needs because those needs have been met. Instead, the need for love and friendship is now likely to be the most important source of motivation. Such an individual would be motivated to develop friendships or a romantic relationship to fill the need for love.

Maslow's theory holds that the highest level of human need — self-actualization — is unlike the other levels of the hierarchy in one important respect: its complete fulfillment is unlikely. The more successful an individual is at self-actualizing, the greater the need for self-actualization. Thus, an individual is continually being motivated at this highest level. However, if conditions change so that the ongoing fulfillment of lower-order needs is threatened, then the individual will shift focus down to that lower-level need, which then becomes the dominant motivator. For example, the sudden threat of losing a job or falling victim to a serious illness may jolt an individual from a higher-level need down to the security level. If so, a person motivated by self-esteem or self-actualization may suddenly feel a need for security or physiological needs.

Alderfer's Theory of Needs. Another theorist, Clayton P. Alderfer, categorizes basic human needs in a different way. According to Alderfer, human needs fall into three categories: existence, relatedness, and growth. Unlike Maslow, he argues that more than one need may be motivating an individual at one time.

Existence needs are those required to sustain human existence, such as food and shelter. This category also encompasses the safety and security needs as specified by Maslow. *Relatedness needs* include social needs, the need to feel a part of some group greater than oneself, and interpersonal safety (e.g., nonthreatening interactions with other people). Relatedness needs show up as the desire of individuals for friends they can trust, with whom they can share their joys and sorrows. Another common manifestation is the urge to feel accepted by one's co-workers and social acquaintances—to be part of the group. *Growth needs* include self-esteem, recognition, and self-actualization needs. These are manifested in individual efforts to try new skills, have new experiences, and, in the process, expand the limits of one's abilities. Individuals who care about what they accomplish and whether others recognize those accomplishments are manifesting growth needs.[9]

Herzberg's Workplace Motives. While the human needs theories of Maslow and Alderfer apply to life in general, that of theorist Frederick Herzberg applies to the work setting specifically. Herzberg argues that there are only two types of human needs that can result in dissatisfaction or satisfaction at work—hygienes and motivators.

According to Herzberg, certain working conditions or *hygiene factors* are important to employees only if they are absent. For example, low salary, low levels of job security, poor supervision, and unsafe or unsanitary working conditions can make employees dissatisfied at work. However, the presence of high salary, high levels of job security, good supervision, and safe working conditions does little to satisfy employees. If hygiene factors are present, the best results we can hope for are employees who are neutral or not dissatisfied at work.

At first glance, Herzberg's observations about hygienes may be a bit puzzling. If the absence of a certain working condition causes dissatisfaction, then why doesn't the presence of that same condition contribute to satisfaction? The answer, according to Herzberg, is that dissatisfaction and satisfaction are not opposite ends of the same continuum. Those factors that cause dissatisfaction at work are not the same ones that yield satisfaction at work.

If we take a moment to contemplate the label Herzberg has given to these factors—hygienes—we can get a sense of his intent. The use of the term *hygiene* captures the idea that people take these factors for granted when they are present and notice them only when they are absent. Think of how we feel about personal hygiene. It's important to have opportunities to bathe regularly and brush our teeth, but we don't think much about these factors of personal hygiene unless we are denied opportunities to have them. Although we may feel better after brushing our teeth because we do not like to have an aftertaste of our last meal, few people would say that having clean teeth is a rewarding experience in and of itself. Thus, for satisfaction to be present, employees must have working conditions that Herzberg calls *motivators*. These include opportunities for growth and achievement in job skills, recognition for one's contributions to the job, and responsibility on the job. If such factors are absent, Herzberg says, employees are not likely to be satisfied.[10]

McClelland's Basic Needs. Other theorists have posited additional frameworks for codifying human needs. One frequently cited approach derives from David McClelland's work on power, affiliation, and achievement.[11] McClelland argues that power, affiliation, and achievement are the three basic needs that motivate individuals.

A need for *power* is manifested in an individual's desire to have an impact, to be strong and influential. Power-oriented people like to make things happen, preferably their way. *Affiliation* is the need to interact with and relate to other human beings in a friendly and supportive manner. Affiliation needs are manifested when people seek out interaction with others just for the sake of being around other people. Affiliation-oriented people like to work with other people rather than with objects, and they enjoy being with people. In contrast, *achievement*-oriented individuals are motivated to do things better than they have been done before. They are always trying to improve their performance, oftentimes without reference to whether others have done the same thing better. Many joggers manifest this achievement orientation in quests to lower their "personal best" times for running particular distances. Achievement-oriented runners do not always care about winning the race; they just want to do better than they have in the past.

Comparing the Human Needs Theorists. There are similarities among the various categories that the human needs theorists have posited to help us understand the nature of human beings. Table 9.1 compares the four approaches to human needs and highlights the similarities. While each

TABLE 9.1   A Comparison of the Human Needs Theorists

Maslow	Alderfer	Herzberg	McClelland
Physiological	Existence	Hygienes	
Safety			Power
Affiliation	Relatedness		Affiliation
Esteem		Motivators	
Self-actualization	Growth		Achievement

SOURCE   Adapted from Edgar Schein, *Organizational Psychology*, 3d ed. (Englewood Cliffs, NJ: Prentice-Hall, 1980), p. 86.

theorist provides us with a picture that is partially useful to understanding individual needs, no one theory adequately captures the complexity of the topic.[12] However, two important generalizations can help us understand the human ecology of public administration.

First, different people have many different needs. Each theorist argues that individuals are motivated by a variety of human needs. Different people may feel a need for different experiences, objects, or outcomes. The diversity of needs among individuals is such that we cannot expect all people to be motivated by the same needs at the same time.

Second, the needs of any one individual may change as circumstances change. This is especially true over time as an individual moves through the stages of the adult life cycle.[13]

We try to understand human needs because they influence individuals' behavior within an organization. The needs that people bring with them into the organization motivate them to pursue certain courses of action that they expect will lead to desirable outcomes or rewards. These needs sometimes act as a filter through which individuals interpret the various expectations they face as public administrators.

Work-related Needs

The most basic work-related need of public employees is for the demands of their work obligations to be compatible with their needs as human beings. In this regard, public-sector employees are no different from their private-sector counterparts. All employees want the hours that they spend at work to provide some opportunities for fulfilling their needs as human beings. This general principle of compatibility translates into specific concerns that employees have about the quality of their work life and their ability to balance their work and personal lives.

Quality of Work Life.   People want jobs that offer them opportunities to fulfill their needs as human beings while they are at work. Because different people have different needs (e.g., in terms of friendship, esteem, achievement, power, and growth), it is difficult to capture the diversity of human needs in one all-encompassing concept. One concept that captures this notion of the "fit" between employee needs as human beings and their work environments is *quality of work life*.[14]

The quality of work life relates to how well the employee is able to fulfill his or her needs as a human being while at work. Employees have a high-quality work life if their jobs offer them opportunities to meet their personal needs as human beings while simultaneously fulfilling their responsibilities at work. A high-quality work life does not require employees to "check their humanity at the door" when they come to work. Instead, employees are able to fulfill their needs as human beings while also meeting the agency's expectations. In contrast, a low-quality work life does not allow an employee to meet important personal needs while at work.

Included in this concept of a high-quality work life are the notions of stability and individual rights. Employees want a *stable work experience*. This does not mean that employees want the same job forever. Rather, it means that employees want a career in which they feel they have at least some control over their futures and in which there exists some pattern of predictability and continuity. A stable work experience can extend across several organizations and involve changes in jobs over time. Employees who have a stable work experience do not feel trapped in their jobs or threatened by external forces like market fluctuations or changes in organizational leadership.

This notion of a stable work experience means something much different today than it did in the 1950s. The model of work stability in the 1950s stressed that an individual should pursue one career with one organization. A successful employee could expect to start out at a low level in an organization and work his or her way up the hierarchy over several decades until retirement age. Today, however, an employee expects to change jobs several times within one organization and is likely to work for several different organizations.[15] The important difference is that these changes are usually the result of the employee's initiative. The contemporary employee often seeks out a work situation that is of a higher quality, as the individual defines it. While today's employees contribute much to the development of their careers, agencies contribute as well by creating viable career-development options.

Also included in the notion of quality of work life is the idea that employees should be treated with dignity and that they have individual rights that must be respected by the agency.[16] By *individual rights* in the workplace we mean the right of employees to fair treatment under the terms of due process. *Due process*, in this sense, refers to the following of proper procedure. An employee may be concerned about receiving notice of job openings so he or she has a chance to apply for positions that represent interesting opportunities for transfer, training, or promotion. Similarly, an employee whose performance is below the acceptable level has a right to be notified of such and to be given an opportunity to improve his or her performance level before being fired.

Balancing Work and Personal Lives. Another work-related need of public employees is the ability to balance their work and personal lives. Some psychologists suggest that an overemphasis on either work or one's personal life is unhealthy. The need to sustain a life away from work gives rise to employees' interest in having jobs that allow them to balance their work and personal lives. Employees want job responsibilities that do not obstruct their ability to fulfill their personal goals away from work. In other words, individual employees want work experiences that allow them to pursue their personal lives as they choose.

Ideally, jobs should not demand so much of employees' psychic energy and time that they do not have the capacity to develop relationships and hobbies away from work. In concrete terms, the job should not be so stressful or involve so much overtime that the employee goes home each night too tired to interact with family or friends.[17] A job that is so demanding that it precludes these nonwork interests is likely to be stressful in the long run.

Employees tend to follow one of three basic patterns as they try to accommodate the various expectations for their work and personal lives: spillover, compensation, and segregation.[18] A *spillover* pattern of accommodation occurs when the attitudes and behaviors in the work arena spill over into the personal arena. For example, if someone has a job that requires frequent interaction with the public, that association with lots of people may spill over into the employee's personal life. Under such circumstances, the employee may seek out a lot of social interaction after work hours. This may be manifested in social entertaining, joining clubs, participating in amateur team athletics, and so on. In contrast, a negative spillover may occur when someone has a bad day at the office and brings that bad mood home. Spillover patterns of accommodation, whether positive or negative experiences, are most likely to occur among white-collar employees.[19]

A *compensation* pattern of accommodation occurs when a person makes up in one arena for excesses or shortcomings in the other arena. For example, an employee who works alone, say as an archivist in the tax assessor's office, may compensate for that isolation by seeking out social interaction after work. Alternatively, an employee who has extensive interaction with the public at work may compensate by spending evenings alone at home. Blue-collar employees are more likely to follow a compensation pattern of accommodation.[20]

A *segregation* pattern of accommodation occurs when an employee makes a concerted effort to keep work and personal life separate. Such an employee would discourage personal calls at work and refuse to take work home in the evenings. While segregation between work and personal life is possible in terms of time, it is relatively unlikely to occur in terms of psychological attachment. This is because most people cannot turn off their feelings when they leave home or leave the office. If there is something bothering someone at work, it is very hard for that person to avoid thinking about it at home. Similarly, if an employee has a sick family member or encounters difficulty in a personal relationship, he or she is likely to have a difficult time not thinking about it at work.

Public employees bring these general and work-related needs to their workplace. These needs affect the attitudes of public administrators, their reactions to their jobs, and the multitude of expectations they face. If the fulfillment of their needs is compatible with the expectations public administrators face, then the human dimension of public administration can be a positive force in the administrative process.[21] The human drive to fulfill personal needs complements the expectations emanating from various sectors of a public agency's environment. However, if these human needs are not compatible with the expectations for public administration, then the human dimension can work against fulfillment of the expectations emanating from the environment.

Strategies for Fulfilling Work-related Needs

Individual public administrators not only have different expectations of the agencies for which they work, but they also have different ways of communicating those expectations. The strategies available to employees for trying to fulfill their personal needs while at work include *exit, voice,* and *loyalty.*[22]

The Exit Option. The exit option is the choice employees have to leave an organization and find work elsewhere if their work experience does not allow them to fulfill their personal needs.

Exit options are not always available. Other job opportunities may be scarce when economic conditions are particularly unfavorable. The exit option may be further restricted for public employees because there may not be other organizations that offer similar job opportunities. For example, someone who wants to be a diplomat or work as a foreign service officer has few options outside the federal government because it has a near monopoly on these occupations. A diplomat who did not like his or her treatment at the State Department would have few other opportunities for employment as a diplomat. It is unlikely that the employee could transfer to the Spanish diplomatic corps. Similarly, an employee unhappy with the career opportunities available in the Public Health Service would find few other government organizations that offer opportunities to deal with the medical and public policy implications of epidemics.

In contrast to popular belief, a substantial proportion of public employees choose to exercise this exit option. In 1987, more than half a million federal civilian employees left government service—a turnover rate of more than 19 percent for that year alone. Of that number, approximately 206,100 left their positions voluntarily, either through resignations or by refusing to take new assignments.[23] These turnover and resignation figures tend to be higher during periods of transition between presidents, even if the new president is of the same party as the outgoing one. Between October 1988 and January

1989, for example, the annual turnover rate increased to 28 percent, with more than half those coming through resignations.[24] Transitions are a time when people are more likely to take the "exit" option.

The Voice Option.   The voice option refers to employee opportunities to influence working conditions so that people are able to meet their general needs as human beings. The tactics available for exercising the voice option include collective bargaining, using grievance procedures, participation in quality circles, and whistle-blowing. Each of these voice options provides for employees speaking out about working conditions and informing supervisors of desirable changes. Such changes may make it easier for employees to accommodate their work and personal obligations, improve the quality of their work life, or contribute to a more stable employment experience.

For example, employees might collectively bargain for the elimination of mandatory overtime, thereby easing the "squeeze" on their time with their families. Or an employee might take the opportunity afforded by a quality circle meeting to suggest adjustment in the working relationships that ease intragroup tensions. If an individual feels his or her employment rights have been infringed, filing a grievance may be in order. Each of these tactics allows the employee to communicate to the employer about the effect of working conditions on the individual.

The most controversial manifestation of the voice option is whistle-blowing. This occurs when an employee goes outside the usual reporting channels to reveal some policy or practice that is contrary to the agency's official authorization. In most instances, whistle-blowing occurs after an employee finds evidence of illegal or unethical behavior. A well-known whistle-blower is Frank Serpico of the New York City police force. After Serpico informed his superiors of widespread corruption in the police force and they failed to take action, he turned to the media. His story is particularly well known because it was the basis for a popular movie. Oftentimes, the whistle-blower goes to an elected official or the news media with evidence of wrongdoing.

Whistle-blowers are special people in public administration (see Profile 9.1). Usually, they are employees with a strong sense of honesty and integrity. They "blow the whistle" out of a sense of commitment to their agency, the public service, or their profession. Occasionally, they are merely troublemakers or disgruntled employees interested in self-aggrandizement or in making life miserable for their supervisors. Notwithstanding these few who falsely blow the whistle, whistle-blowing is an important source of information about practices in the public sector. The Civil Service Reform Act of 1978 mandated special protections for whistle-blowers against retaliation by their supervisors (see Insight 9.1). After the explosion of the space shuttle *Challenger* in early 1986, some observers speculated that the tragedy was avoidable had potential whistle-blowers at NASA come forward. As a result, NASA established a special toll-free phone number that any employee of the agency or its contractors can call if they want to draw attention to some problem.

PROFILE 9.1

A Whistle-blower's Experience

Whistle-blowers in public administration find themselves caught between two crosscurrents. While the general public may applaud whistle-blowers for their efforts to expose mismanagement, the personal experiences of whistle-blowers once they do "blow the whistle" is often distressing, ranging from social ostracism at the workplace to retaliation in the form of undesirable transfers or firings.

Such was the experience of Bertrand G. Berube, a former buildings supervisor for the U.S. General Services Administration (GSA). Berube, who was fired from the agency in 1983, had repeatedly charged that top GSA officials were claiming savings in agency management that came at the cost of neglecting the condition of many major buildings. Congressional investigations subsequently corroborated many of Berube's complaints.

Berube charged that his dismissal from the GSA was in retaliation for his complaints. He claimed that he was fired because he had "angered the agency's political appointees with his repeated charges that they were allowing federal buildings to deteriorate

into hazardous conditions." The Merit Systems Protection Board agreed with Berube's claim, ruling in July 1988 that the GSA had failed to prove it had a valid basis for firing Berube and ordering that he be reinstated into his former job with the GSA.

Following the board's ruling, the GSA told Berube that his former position as head of the agency's National Capital Region was filled. The agency offered him a deputy regional administrator's job in Philadelphia, which Berube declined because he felt the job was not meaningful and did not want to leave the Washington area where he has lived for twenty-five years. The agency then offered Berube a financial settlement based on accumulated back pay, leave, legal fees, and interest. He decided to accept this offer. According to a September 1988 newspaper account, Berube was working with the Government Accountability Project, a nonprofit organization that provides advice and support to government whistle-blowers.

SOURCE: Based on information in Bill McAllister, "Whistle-Blower, GSA Settle," *The Washington Post*, 3 September 1988, p. A-2.

The Loyalty Option. The loyalty option refers to employees doing their best to understand and accept agency working conditions as they are and to work for the long-term success of the agency. The loyalty option occurs when the employee feels a sense of shared values with the organization. Doing what is good for the agency makes the employee feel good as well. This sharing of values is possible when employees' personal values and those important to the survival and effectiveness of the agency are the same.

Essentially, the sharing of values reflects a psychological attachment or

INSIGHT 9.1

GUIDELINES FOR WHISTLE-BLOWERS

Whistle-blowers have often been treated as social outcasts within an organizational setting. Even though the Civil Service Reform Act of 1978 makes it illegal to retaliate against individuals who disclose government corruption, progress on changing the negative experiences that whistle-blowers encounter has been slow.

Today there are a number of institutional mechanisms in place to make the price of whistle-blowing less devastating to those who do so. For example, there are hotlines in government offices to encourage disclosure of waste, fraud, or abuse. There is also free legal counsel available from the Government Accountability Project and psychological and sometimes financial help from the Whistleblower Assistance Fund. According to Louis Clark, executive director of the Government Accountability Project, whistle-blowers are "no longer being identified as tattletales and finks and the like, but as people who are standing up for their principles."

The Whistleblower Assistance Fund was founded by psychotherapist Donald R. Soeken, who was also a whistle-blower. Soeken conducted a survey of nearly one hundred whistle-blowers that suggests they are not the misfits they are commonly thought to be. The prototypical whistle-blower is "a family person, 47 years old, employed by the government or private business for seven years before exposing a wrong."

The survey also indicates that the personal costs of whistle-blowing are high. Out of the one hundred whistle-blowers surveyed, "10 percent had attempted suicide, 17 percent had lost their homes and 15 percent were divorced. One out of five lost their jobs and more than half reported that they had been harassed by their peers at work."

SOURCE: Quotes and information from Clyde H. Farnsworth, "In Defense of the Government's Whistle Blowers, *New York Times*, 26 July 1988, p. 10.

organizational involvement among employees of an organization. Organizationally involved employees share the values of their agencies. For example, some employees of the Civil Rights Commission have a personal commitment to the protection of civil rights. Many employees of the Department of Defense and the Central Intelligence Agency share their agencies' commitment to national security programs. Similarly, employees who work for a bank and value honesty share this important value with their work organization.

The notion of psychological attachment is somewhat abstract and requires explanation. In everyday life, we often talk about such ties as commitments or emotional attachments. Love is a kind of psychological attachment, but it differs from organizational involvement in that it is directed toward other people rather than toward an organization. Nevertheless, both are psychological attachments. An important aspect of psychological attachments is that they often reflect a continuum of attachment, from very positive to very negative (e.g., the love-hate continuum). Like most psychological attachments, organizational involvement ranges from positive to negative.

Positive organizational involvement is manifested in feelings of commitment on the part of employees, a sense of identification with the goals and values of the organization, and approval from one's family and friends for that commitment.[25] Negative involvement shows up as employee alienation. Committed employees are more likely to go above and beyond the limits of their official job responsibilities because they share the goals of the organization. They want to do the little bit extra needed to get the job done because they accept the organization's goals and values as their own. When doing their jobs for the good of the organization, they are pursuing their own values as well. When the agency needs extra effort, committed employees do not ask "What's in it for me?" They already have the answer to that question—a sense of personal satisfaction from successfully pursuing the organization's goals. Committed employees are also less likely to be absent from work and less likely to leave the organization for another place of work.[26]

Some observers note the damaging effects of too much psychological attachment.[27] Employees who are too strongly committed to their organization may equate proposals for change and innovation as thinly veiled criticism of the organization's operations. The potential for highly committed employees to view such proposals as disloyalty can be troublesome if it stifles creativity in organizational policy-making.

Alternatively, excessively committed employees may exceed legal bounds in their efforts to promote their organization's programs. A good example of excessive commitment emerged in the 1987 Iran-*contra* congressional hearings. During that widely publicized investigation, Marine Lt. Colonel Oliver North, a former member of President Reagan's national security staff, testified about his role in the sale of arms to Iran. Although he knew his actions were illegal, North said he did so in the belief that his orders came from the president. In defense of his role in the affair, North dramatically stated that "This lieutenant colonel would stand on his head in a corner" if ordered to do so by his commander-in-chief, the president of the United States. North's argument was criticized by other military officers as being contrary to the military code of conduct.

The opposite of employee commitment—alienation—can also be a problem in public administration. Alienated employees feel that what they do in the organization is of no importance to themselves or the organization. They do not share the organization's values; in fact, they usually feel that the goals and values of the agency are inconsistent with their own values. Furthermore, people who feel alienated from work are likely to have friends or family members who disapprove of where they work. Employees who have job responsibilities that require them to carry out tasks that violate their conscience are likely to feel alienated toward their work place. Similarly, employees of a state Department of Social Welfare who do not feel that helping the poor through government aid is an important goal are likely to feel alienated from their agency.

When called on to exert extra effort, alienated employees are more likely to ask, "What's in it for me?" Alienated employees are also more likely to find excuses not to exert any more effort than absolutely necessary to get by on the job. A sense of alienation on the part of employees can be seriously detrimental to their efforts to meet their needs as human beings. For example, alienated employees have a hard time fulfilling any needs for group membership or for self-esteem based on their association with the organization. They are also detrimental to the organization because they are more likely to be absent from work or to leave the organization altogether. Alienated employees are likely to exercise the exit option.

The Human Factor

This chapter on public employees highlights two important facets of public administration. First, that forces in the external environment directly affect the experiences of public administrators by influencing their attitudes and behaviors. Technology, demographic trends, and social values affect what public employees expect from their work experiences. Second, just as ecological factors affect individual public administrators, so too, can individuals affect public administration. Because public employees are human beings they bring a variety of needs to the workplace and they try to accommodate those needs in several ways. This is what we mean by the *human factor*.

The human factor directly affects public administration by influencing what public administrators seek from their jobs. The human factor has indirect effects by influencing how public employees react to their jobs and how they ultimately interpret (or filter) the expectations they face on the job. The complexity of why and how public employees filter the expectations they confront as public administrators presents a difficult challenge for us as we try to understand the dynamics of public administration.

In chapters 4 through 9 we have outlined the various dimensions of the context within which public administration operates. Each of the ecological factors we discussed influences the major tasks of public-sector management. Public administrators must deal with the problems and dilemmas created by a diverse set of challenges and expectations. We see the results of their efforts to manage these challenges and expectations in how our public organizations are structured and managed — our focus in Part III of this text.

Summary

1. Individual public employees act as filters through which other environmental/ecological factors influence public administration expectations.
2. The needs and values of individual employees have an important influence on the expectations facing public administrators. Among other things, these include basic human needs, work-related needs, and the need to balance work and personal lives.
3. Individual employee efforts to fulfill personal needs can be either a positive or negative factor in public administration, depending on how those needs relate to expectations.
4. Employees can use the exit, voice, or loyalty strategy for dealing with their personal expectations.

Study Questions

1. Apply the various human needs theories to your role as a student or employee. Which of the theories best reflects your personal needs as a student or employee?
2. Apply Herzberg's concepts of hygiene and motivator factors to your classroom or workplace environment. What are the hygiene factors of interest to you as a student or employee? What are the motivator factors?
3. Profile your own expectations regarding the quality of your student "work life." How would you describe your life as a student in terms of the following dimensions: dignity, stability, and the balance between your personal life and your responsibilities as a student?
4. Using a scale of 1 to 10, where 10 represents high involvement and 1 reflects alienation or negative involvement, estimate your level of organizational involvement in your school, family life, workplace, and social clubs.

Notes

1. For a detailed discussion of American culture, see Robert N. Bellah, William M. Sullivan, Ann Swidler, and Steven M. Tipton, *Habits of the Heart: Individualism and Commitment in American Life* (New York: Harper & Row, 1985).
2. For a discussion of these trends by a noted pollster on the American scene, see Daniel Yankelovich, *New Rules: Searching for Self-Fulfillment in a World Turned Upside Down* (New York: Random House, 1981).

3. See Abraham K. Korman and Rhoda W. Korman, *Career Success/Personal Failure* (Englewood Cliffs, NJ: Prentice-Hall, 1980).

4. See Frederick Mosher, *Democracy and the Public Service* (New York: Oxford University Press, 1982), chap. 2; Robert Denhardt and John Nalbandian, "Teaching Public Administration as a Vocation: A Calling for Theorists," *Southern Review of Public Administration* 6 (Summer 1982): 151–62; and John Nalbandian and Terry Edwards, "The Values of Public Administrators: A Comparison with Lawyers, Social Welfare and Business Administrators," *Review of Public Personnel Administration* 4 (Fall 1983): 114–28.

5. William F. Whyte, Jr., *The Organization Man* (Garden City, NY: Doubleday–Anchor Books, 1956), p. 3.

6. See David Halberstam, *The Best and the Brightest* (New York: Random House, 1969).

7. See Edie N. Goldberg, "The Permanent Government in an Era of Retrenchment and Redirection," in *The Reagan Presidency and the Governing of America*, ed. Lester M. Salamon and Michael S. Lund (Washington, DC: Urban Institute, 1985), pp. 381–404; Charles H. Levine, "The Federal Government in the Year 2000: Administrative Legacies of the Reagan Years," *Public Administration Review*, 46 (May/June 1986): 195–206; and Bernard Rosen, "Crises in the U.S. Civil Service," *Public Administration Review* 46 (May/June 1986): 207–14.

8. Abraham Maslow, *Motivation and Personality*, 2d ed. (New York: Harper & Row, 1970).

9. Clayton P. Alderfer, *Existence, Relatedness and Growth: Human Needs in Organizational Settings* (New York: The Free Press, 1972).

10. Frederick Herzberg, *Work and the Nature of Man* (Cleveland, OH: World Publishing, 1966).

11. David McClelland, *The Achieving Society* (Princeton, NJ: Van Nostrand Reinhold, 1961).

12. For an excellent summary of the research to date on these theories of human motivation, see John Miner, *Theories of Organizational Behavior* (Hinsdale, IL: The Dryden Press, 1980), chaps. 2–4. While part of the problem of corroborating these theories lies in the limitations of research in the social sciences, it is also difficult to generalize about all human beings in all situations.

13. For a popular account of such changes in individual life stages, see Gayle Sheehey, *Passages: Predictable Crises of Adult Life* (New York: Bantam Books, 1977). For more scholarly treatments, see Donald Levinson, *The Seasons of a Man's Life* (New York: Ballantine, 1978); and George Vaillant, *Adaptation to Life: How the Best and Brightest Came of Age* (Boston: Little, Brown, 1977). For yet another perspective, see Carol Gilligan, *In a Different Voice: Psychological Theory and Women's Development* (Cambridge, MA: Harvard University Press, 1982).

14. See Louis E. Davis and Albert B. Cherns, eds., *The Quality of Working Life*, Vols. 1 and 2 (New York: The Free Press, 1975).

15. See Mark L. Goldstein, "Loyalty's Death Litters Career Paths," *Industry Week*, 7 September 1987, pp. 82–85.

16. See Donald Klingner and John Nalbandian, *Public Personnel Management*, 2d ed. (Englewood Cliffs, NJ: Prentice-Hall, 1985); and Richard E. Walton, "Criteria

for Quality of Working Life," in Davis and Cherns, eds., *The Quality of Working Life: Problems, Prospects and the State of the Art*, vol. 1, chap. 5.

17. See James S. House, *Work Stress and Social Support* (Reading, MA: Addison-Wesley, 1981).

18. See William A. Faunce and Robert Dubin, "Individual Investment in Working and Living," in Davis and Cherns, eds., *Quality of Working Life*, vol. 1, pp. 299–316; Barbara S. Romzek, "Work and Nonwork Psychological Involvements: The Search for Linkage," *Administration and Society* 17 (November 1985): 257–81; and Gerald Staines, "Spillover versus Compensation: A Review of the Literature on the Relationship between Work and Nonwork," *Human Relations* 33 (February 1980): 111–29.

19. Staines, "Spillover versus Competition," 111–129.

20. *Ibid.*

21. Barbara S. Romzek, "The Human Factor in the Federal Workforce: Work Experiences, Self-Esteem and Organizational Involvement among Public Employees," *Review of Public Personnel Administration* 5 (Fall 1984): pp. 43–56.

22. See Albert O. Hirschman, *Exit, Voice, and Loyalty: Responses to Decline in Firms, Organizations, and States* (Cambridge, MA: Harvard University Press, 1970).

23. Bureau of the Census, *Statistical Abstracts of the United States, 1989* (Washington, DC: Government Printing Office, 1989), table 516; also see Richard Stillman, II, *The American Bureaucracy* (Chicago: Nelson-Hall, 1987).

24. U.S. Office of Personnel Management, *Employment and Trends as of January 1989* (Washington, DC: OPM, 1989), Table 22.

25. See Barbara S. Romzek and J. Stephen Hendricks, "Organizational Involvement and Representative Bureaucracy: Can We Have It Both Ways?" *American Political Science Review* 76 (March 1982): 75–82.

26. See Richard T. Mowday, Lyman W. Porter, and Richard M. Steers, *Employee-Organization Linkages: The Psychology of Commitment, Absenteeism, and Turnover* (New York: Academic Press, 1982), chap. 2.

27. See Gerald R. Salancik, "Commitment and the Control of Organizational Behavior and Belief," in *New Directions in Organizational Behavior*, ed. by B. M. Staw and G. R. Salancik (Chicago: St. Clair Press, 1977), pp. 1–54.

PART **III**

THE MANAGEMENT
OF
EXPECTATIONS

In Part III, our focus is on how American public agencies and their administrators attempt to manage the wide-ranging expectations they face.

Public agencies are not passive objects in the American political arena; rather, they are busy and often highly visible governmental actors. Much of their activity involves dealing with the many expectations of public administration—their responsibilities, obligations, and standards of conduct. One way to cope with these expectations is through organizational structures. In Chapter 10, we examine how public agencies are structured to manage most effectively the forces and expectations emanating from the external environment. To do this, we must understand what makes public agencies bureaucracies.

Those who administer government programs must cope not only with external factors but also with forces from within the organization. In Chapter 11, we examine the internal dynamics of public agencies—how they manage the processes and expectations that emerge from within the organization. The ways in which public agencies cope with the challenges of acquiring, maintaining, and improving the quality of their personnel is discussed in Chapter 12. Chapter 13 then explores how public agencies use the politics and processes of budgeting to manage questions of resource allocation. Finally, in Chapter 14, we reflect on what we have learned and what it tells us about the future of American public administration.

CHAPTER **10**

PUBLIC

ORGANIZATIONS

AND EXTERNAL

EXPECTATIONS

Types of Public Organizations

The Complexities of Public Agency Forms

If you have ever had to register a complaint about a product purchased in a local store, you probably had a relatively easy time finding out whom to complain to and how to go about getting a refund or exchange or service on that product. You may have been sent to a customer service area, where you were given a refund or allowed to exchange the product for one that fit better or was more appropriate to your needs. If the store couldn't handle your complaint, it may have told you to contact the manufacturer. If so, you probably found that the manufacturer has a customer relations office designated to handle complaints or other product-related problems. If your problems were not resolved to your satisfaction, you may have contacted a supervisor or someone at the next level of the company. Eventually, someone probably resolved your difficulty, even if you had to contact the highest authority at the company — the chief executive officer.

Trying to figure out whom to contact when you want to express concern about some public problem or obtain some help from a public agency is not as easy. The public-sector "customer" — and that includes all of us — has a number of hurdles to overcome. For example if you wanted to complain about some public problem such as air pollution, first you would have to figure out which agency to contact. This could be some city authority, a county health department, a state agency, or even the regional office of the U.S. Environmental Protection Agency. Once you determined which agency or agencies to contact, you would then need to find out which office or division to contact. If you are seeking some action as opposed to information, you would need to determine which division of the local, state, or federal agency you should deal with. Should you speak with the inspections division or the enforcement office? Should you describe your problem to whoever answers the phone, or should you write directly to the head of the agency or to one of its divisions? Or, realizing that an elected official is likely to get speedier results, should you instead contact your local council member, legislative representative, or member of Congress? The complexities of dealing with public-sector agencies, even when seeking what you believe is a simple public service can be overwhelming to the average citizen (see Insight 10.1).

One of the primary reasons for this complexity is that public organizations take a variety of shapes and forms far beyond those typically found in the private sector. To a large degree, each public agency is unique. Each pursues its own goals and agendas and each tends to develop a distinct organizational approach to accomplishing its objectives. Some are organized to regulate citizen behavior, as is the case with many law enforcement agencies. Others, such as the Bureau of Labor Statistics in the Department of Labor and the

INSIGHT 10.1

THE "DEAD DOG" CAPER

A Sad (but Somewhat True) Story of Life in a Small American City

Just how complicated life can be for the person who confronts the complexities of public organizations is illustrated by the story of a family who had to find a quick solution to a rather sticky problem. One of the youngsters in the family took on the responsibility of "dog-sitting" for a neighborhood family that was going on a two-week vacation. The task involved daily feedings of two dogs, one a small and perky young mongrel and the other a rather old and lethargic mutt.

After a few days, the young dog-sitter noticed that the older dog was becoming even less active than usual. The summer days were hot, but despite plenty of water, food, and shade in the fenced-in yard, the old dog just sat under a locked car in the neighbor's open garage and gave no sign of life except for short, quick-breathing patterns. On the sixth day, the youngster found the dog lying completely still. Other family members were called to the scene, and a local veterinarian was consulted. Sadly and reluctantly it was determined that the dog had died of old age.

It was 3:00 on a Friday afternoon, and the problem facing the youngster's family was how to deal with the corpse now lying under the neighbor's car. Given the 100-degree temperature and the long weekend ahead, there was little doubt that the animal's remains had to be taken care of as soon as possible. Under such conditions, animal carcasses tend to generate a rather strong, distinctive, and

unpleasant odor. The veterinarian's recommendation was to call the local humane society.

Most local humane societies are quasi-public agencies; that is, while officially private, not-for-profit organizations, they do receive public funds to help support their activities. The person at the local humane society told the family that although the society does have facilities to dispose of the animal's carcass, it is not able to come out to pick up the remains. The society suggested that the family call the local sanitation department to see if it could send someone out. A phone call to that city office revealed that it cannot pick up an animal's remains unless a public health threat exists and then only if the county health department or a local police officer makes the request. In addition, the sanitation crews were leaving by 5:00 P.M, so they would not be able to make the pick-up until Monday unless the request was put in immediately. It was now 3:30 P.M.

The telephone at the county health department rang for several minutes before being answered. The family was told that there was no one on duty at the time who could authorize the request for a pick-up.

When local police were contacted, they said they would call the city animal control officer (also known as the local "dog catcher") to the scene. Several minutes later, the uniformed animal control officer pulled into the neighbor's driveway,

INSIGHT 10.1 *continued*

asked several questions, and decided to issue the necessary request for a pick-up by the sanitation department. The appropriate calls were made. It was now 4:05 P.M.

When the sanitation truck arrived on the scene 15 minutes later, the driver asked whether the owner of the home was present. It seems that city workers are prohibited by law from entering private property unless they have the owner's expressed permission. Since the neighbors were away and there was no way of contacting them, it was not possible to obtain their permission. It was now 4:30 P.M. and the sanitation crew was eager to return to city facilities where

they would check out for their weekend break.

It was then that the animal control officer remembered an exception to the rule. Police officers and firefighters are authorized to enter private property when the owner is not present in cases of emergency.

A call to the police station brought a patrol car to the area within minutes. The situation was quickly assessed and it was decided that the police, the sanitation workers, and the animal control officer would remove the dog's body. It was 4:55 P.M. The crisis was resolved, and everyone left a bit wiser about the workings of local government organizations.

Census Bureau in the Department of Commerce, organize their activities around collecting data on economic and social conditions. Still others, such as public schools and municipal-owned utilities, are organized to provide services and goods to local residents.

Most important, however, is that each public agency must contend with multiple expectations that come from a wide range of sources. Relatively speaking, the number and significance of the expectations that private-sector organizations face are far less than those with which the public agency must contend. The result is a greater diversity and complexity in the organizational forms of public-sector agencies.

Agency Types

The diversity and complexity of public organizational forms is most evident in the federal government, where there are dozens of distinct types of agency structures. The most visible type is the *cabinet-level department*, which includes the Departments of State, Treasury, Commerce, Labor, Transportation, Veterans Affairs, Education, Health and Human Services, and so on. According to official federal government documents, the status of "department" is reserved for "those agencies which administer a wide range of programs directed toward a common purpose of national importance" and that require "frequent and positive Presidential direction and representation at the highest levels of government."[1]

Another organization type at the federal level is the *independent agency*, which comes in many shapes and sizes. Even though independent agencies are not cabinet departments, most are politically sensitive enough that they report directly to the president. The most sensitive of these agencies are the Central Intelligence Agency (CIA) and the National Security Agency (NSA). Other independent agencies carry out many of the housekeeping duties of government, such as the General Services Administration (GSA) and the Office of Personnel Management (OPM), while still others have special purposes, such as the EPA.

Another distinct type of agency at the federal level is the *regulatory commission*. The president appoints a designated number of commissioners, usually between three and seven, to head these agencies. These commissioners and their agency staffs focus on the chores of establishing and enforcing rules and regulations over some sector of the U.S. economy. For example, the Interstate Commerce Commission (ICC) regulates interstate trucking, rail, water, and bus transportation; the Federal Communications Commission (FCC) regulates the commercial use of the airwaves; and the Securities and Exchange Commission (SEC) oversees the operations of various stock and securities markets. These and other regulatory commissions are unique because they operate as much as rule-making (legislative) and rule-adjudication (judicial) bodies as they do as rule-enforcement (executive) agencies. Because of their special functions, they are relatively free of presidential control.

Other types of federal government organizations include *foundations* (e.g., the National Science Foundation), *endowments* (e.g., National Endowment for the Humanities), *institutes* (e.g., the Smithsonian Institution and the National Institutes of Health), and *government corporations* (e.g., the U.S. Postal Service, the Tennessee Valley Authority, the Federal Deposit Insurance Corporation, and the Corporation for Public Broadcasting).[2]

Even at the state and local levels there are departments, boards, commissions, and other organizational types that make the task of understanding government organization quite complicated. Amid this organizational diversity, however, are some common patterns characteristic of most public agencies.

Public Agencies as Bureaucracies

Although public agencies serve distinct purposes, perform different functions, and come in a variety of shapes, sizes, and forms, for the most part they are bureaucratic organizations.

An *organization* is a *group of people linked together for some common purpose or goal*. Members of an organization are interdependent, meaning that they must coordinate their efforts if they hope to accomplish their common purpose. There are many different kinds of organizations. One type is the nuclear family, in which members share a common purpose in the maintenance, growth, and nurturing of family members. Another form of organization is the commune, in which many people work toward common goals with carefully delineated divisions of labor and rules. *Bureaucratic organizations* represent a form of organizational interdependence that is distinctively modern.

The German scholar Max Weber is credited with developing the concept of bureaucracy.[3] His views were not well known in the United States until after World War II, when his major works were translated into English. According to Weber, bureaucracy is the ultimate form of modern organization in both the public and private spheres. The primary force shaping modern government or the corporate organization is the pursuit of efficiency and rationality in goal achievement. For Weber, an ideally functioning bureaucratic organization is the most efficient means for solving large-scale problems. While personally concerned about the impact of bureaucracies on social and political life,[4] Weber was careful to provide an objective description of their basic characteristics.

Bureaucratic Hierarchies.   According to Weber, one of the cornerstones of a bureaucratic organization is the system of delegating different degrees of authority, commonly called a *hierarchy of authority*. All organizations need to deal with the issue of how to allocate authority among their members. One of the major contributors to the development of organization theory, French industrialist Henri Fayol, defines authority as the "right to give orders and the power to extract obedience."[5]

There are two major components in organizational authority. The first component reflects the formal distribution of power in an organization; that is, those who possess authority have the right to issue orders and demand obedience. The second component in organizational authority is closely linked with responsibility for what the agency does or accomplishes. According to Fayol, "Responsibility is a corollary of authority, it is its natural consequence and essential counterpart, and wheresoever authority is exercised responsibility arises."[6] Thus, positions in any formal organization that have authority over certain functions are also likely to have responsibility for those same functions.

In bureaucracies, ultimate authority is at the top of the organization. Each echelon lower in the hierarchy typically represents a lower level of formal authority and responsibility. We see these hierarchical arrangements at all levels of government (see Figures 10.1, 10.2, and 10.3). In addition, the hierarchical approach to organizational design permeates most of the literature on government reform. For example, in 1949, the Commission on the Reorganization of the Executive Branch of the Government (also known as the First Hoover Commission) stressed the need for department heads under the president to

> hold full responsibility for the conduct of the departments. There must be a clear line of authority reaching down through every step of the organization and no subordinate should have authority independent from that of his superior.[7]

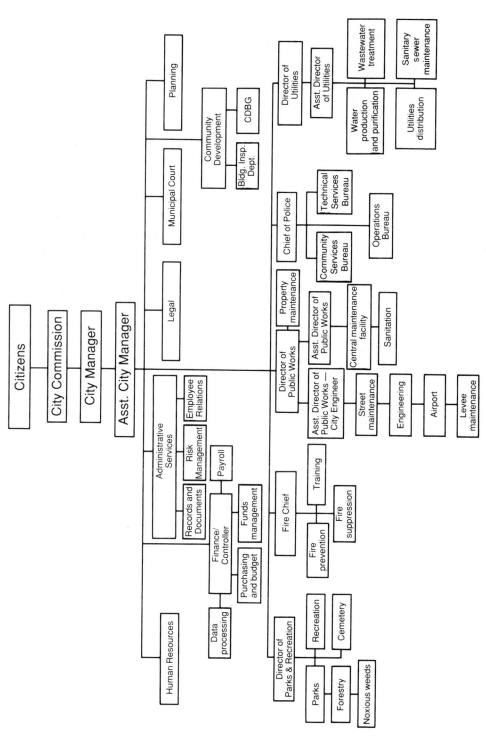

FIGURE 10.1 City government hierarchy: Lawrence, Kansas. (Source: City of Lawrence, Kansas.)

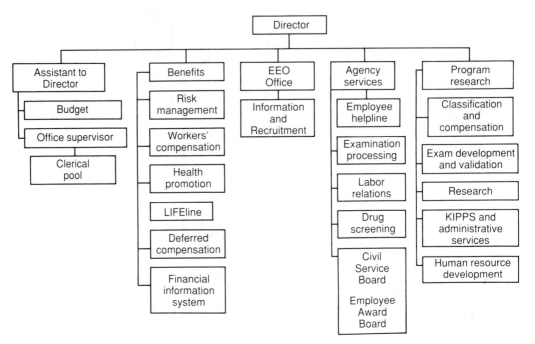

FIGURE 10.2   State agency hierarchy: Kansas Division of Personnel Services. (Source: State of Kansas, Department of Administration.)

The use of hierarchies in public administration is often justified on the grounds of efficiency or accountability. Those who seek greater efficiency in government administration regard hierarchies as a means for reducing operating costs through the centralization and coordination of effort. In 1984, President Reagan's Private Sector Survey on Cost Control (also called the Grace Commission) criticized the lack of a single agency "responsible for overall Executive Branch administrative direction and policy setting." The commission called for the establishment of an Office of Federal Management, which, it argued, would save the American public over $12 billion.[8]

Hierarchical arrangements are also seen as a means for making public bureaucracies more accountable by giving ultimate authority to the political appointees who head many agencies. According to political scientist Emmette Redford, a public organization with a strong hierarchy will promote the exertion of democratic controls by allowing elected officials to enforce their policy positions on those who administer public programs.[9] Whatever the justification, the hierarchical form is the primary structural approach used in America's public-sector organizations.[10]

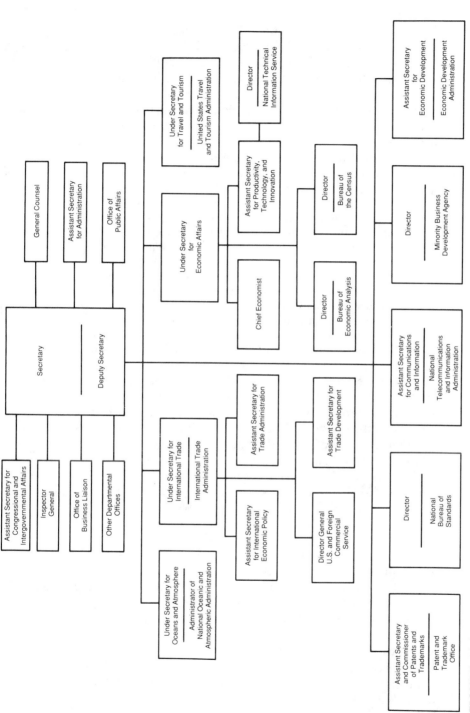

FIGURE 10.3 Federal agency hierarchy: the Department of Commerce. (Source: *The United States Government Manual, 1989* [Washington, DC: Government Printing Office, 1989], p. 144.)

Bureaucratic Specialization. Bureaucracies are also characterized by *specialization* or a *division of labor*, wherein different people have responsibility for accomplishing particular parts of the overall task. Under a division of labor, individuals intentionally specialize and concentrate their attention on their assigned tasks and ignore other tasks.

Students of organizations have long recognized the importance of the division of labor in any large-scale human endeavor. Adam Smith, the founder of capitalist economic theory, wrote in 1776 of the revolutionary impact a well-designed division of work had on industrial production. Where once a lone pin-maker would work all day to produce only a few pins, the division of labor radically changed that situation.

> One man draws out the wire, another straights it, a third cuts it, a fourth points it, a fifth grinds it at the top for receiving the head; to make the head requires two or three distinct operations; to put it on, is a peculiar business, to whiten the pins is another; it is even a trade by itself to put them into the paper; and the important business of making a pin is, in this manner, divided into about eighteen distinct operations, which, in some manufactories, are all performed by distinct hands. . . . I have seen a small manufactory of this kind where ten men only were employed, and where some of them consequently performed two or three distinct operations. . . . Those ten persons . . . could make among them upwards of forty-eight thousand pins in a day.[11]

Early in the twentieth century, another observer of modern organizations, Frederick Winslow Taylor, also took note of the importance of the division of labor. According to his *scientific management* approach to organizations, it is not only the division of labor into specific tasks that is important but also the design of those tasks. Taylor's argument is based on his belief in the ability of trained managers to divide and organize work so that productivity can be maximized. The basic element in his approach is the "task idea," in which the "work of every workman is fully planned out by the management." Further, "each man receives in most cases complete written instructions, describing in detail the task which he is to accomplish, as well as the means to be used in doing the work."[12] Taylor also advocated time and motion studies for each job, a pay plan based on worker productivity, the standardization of tools, and other specific means for improving organizational efficiency. He labeled these various suggestions the "mechanisms of management."

The basis of the division of labor in any given bureaucratic organization varies but it is usually based on one of the following:

1. Process
2. Line/staff
3. Purpose
4. Geographic location
5. Clientele
6. Project

Many times organizational work is divided according to the specialized parts in the production or service delivery *process*. This is the logic behind the division of labor in Adam Smith's pin-making factory, which divided the production process into eighteen specialized tasks. One can find similar approaches taken in the Internal Revenue Service and other agencies whose primary responsibility involves processing forms or claims.

One of the traditional divisions found in many organizations is between line and staff tasks. *Line* positions are those in which the job holders actually deliver public services. The sanitation worker who picks up the trash, the driver of the city bus, and the FBI agent investigating a crime are all performing line tasks. *Staff* jobs, in contrast, provide support for line operations. Staff positions involve individuals engaging in a wide range of activities from giving advice to agency chiefs to issuing payroll checks for agency employees. The Social Security Administration (SSA), for example, has district offices throughout the country carrying out the day-to-day work and public contacts (line tasks) of the agency. Back at its headquarters in Baltimore are staff units such as the Office of Public Affairs and the Office of Research and Statistics.

The *purposes* an organization serves can also be the basis for a division of labor. City governments often divide tasks according to distinct municipal functions, such as public works, sanitation, public safety, and building-code enforcement. Organizations responsible for providing services over a large area often divide tasks on the basis of *geographic location*. The Forest Service, for example, is divided into ten districts covering the entire country. In the Department of State, there are five regional bureaus, each of which focuses on American interests in a specific area of the world: African Affairs, European Affairs, East Asian and Pacific Affairs, Inter-American Affairs, and Near Eastern and South Asian Affairs.

The *clientele* being served provide still another means for dividing the tasks of an organization. The Department of Agriculture, for example, organizes the administration of price-support programs according to producer groups (e.g., wheat farmers, dairy farmers, and so on). Some organizations divide work according to the *projects* undertaken by the agency. During the 1960s, for instance, NASA organized its work force according to the several specific projects underway at the agency at the time. Thus, while some NASA employees were working to complete the *Mercury* Project, which initially put Americans into space, others were involved in the *Apollo* Project, which put an American on the moon in 1969.

These approaches to dividing and arranging an organization's work are far from exhaustive. Innovative ways of dividing organizational tasks are constantly being developed in both private and public organizations. Furthermore, many organizations use two or more approaches simultaneously, depending on their specific needs. Within each district office of the Forest Service or the SSA, for example, are divisions based on the distinction between line and staff positions. Students of public administration realize that the design of any government organization is based on the particular needs and situations faced by the agency.[13] They also know that whatever the initial design of organizational tasks might have been, the actual operation of the organization is likely to lead to adjustments and reorganizations in the structure of tasks.

Bureaucratic Standardization. Weber observed that bureaucratic organizations are characterized by a set of operating *standards* or *rules*. More formal or older bureaucracies codify these rules in thick operation manuals that specify the standard procedures the agency and its members should use in their daily operations. Bureaucracies create rules for at least two reasons.

First, bureaucratic rules reduce the need for close and direct supervision of personnel. Under close supervision, one individual directs and oversees every activity of his or her subordinates to make certain their jobs are being done right. Modern organizations rarely use such close supervision. In most cases, close supervision is impractical or impossible to maintain over time. It is difficult to have one individual constantly overseeing the work of several others. In addition, close supervision is likely to produce negative reactions from workers, especially in a society such as ours that values equality so highly. Thus, close supervision may make it more difficult to coordinate organizational operations. It is much easier to rely on standard bureaucratic rules.[14]

Second, bureaucratic rules are the foundation for standardized behavior. Many bureaucratic organizations tend to rely on standardization. Frederick Taylor was one of the first to articulate the benefits of standardization. In describing his principles of scientific management, Taylor noted what he accomplished at one steel mill where workers were provided with shovels designed for specific tasks and instructions on their proper use for particular jobs. Through the standardization of tools and work procedures, he was able to achieve a significant increase in worker productivity.[15]

The standardization of procedures and tools is common in public organizations where the work is repetitive, as in the processing of tax returns by the Internal Revenue Service (IRS). The tools in such work include the common forms used for filing taxes and step-by-step instructions for processing them at regional IRS offices. The U.S. Postal Service uses similar standardization. Workers sort and handle each piece of mail according to standard, often mechanized, procedures based on ZIP codes.

Bureaucratic Impersonality. Another aspect common among bureaucracies is their reliance on *impersonal relations*. While impersonality is often a complaint of people trying to get some service from a bureaucracy, it is also an important component of the way many public agencies operate.

The impersonality of relations that characterizes bureaucracies requires people to interact with any individual who occupies the appropriate position within the organization, regardless of their personal feelings toward the individual and even if it is not the same person they dealt with previously. This emphasis on position rather than on people (impersonality) allows organizations to continue functioning and serving clients even with tremendous employee turnover.

For example, when you go to renew your driver's license, you must deal with whoever is handling that function that day. Quite likely it is not the same person who was there when you got your last license four years earlier. It may not even be the same person who worked in that position last week. Perhaps last week's occupant is sick or on vacation. Nonetheless, the driver's license renewed by this week's employee at the state license bureau is valid because the employee occupies the appropriate position.

Bureaucratic Careers.   Another common characteristic of bureaucracies is their reliance on *career employees* who occupy full-time positions. For a bureaucracy to function effectively in the long run, it needs to have full-time employees who are dependent on the organization for their livelihood. When people need their jobs to support themselves, they are much more likely to be willing to follow directions and comply with organizational mandates. Also, full-time employees are more likely than part-time workers to develop some allegiance to their organizations. Bureaucracies function best when most of their members have their primary work allegiance (and attention) focused on the organizations. To understand the importance of this characteristic of bureaucracies, think back to some part-time job you've worked in and how you felt about that experience. By definition something else— whether school, family, or maybe another full-time job—was your first priority.

Modern Bureaucracies.   While public agencies differ in many respects, they also share some structural characteristics because they are bureaucratic organizations. We have used Weber's model of bureaucracy to highlight some of those organizational characteristics, including the roles that hierarchy, specialization, rules and standardization, impersonality, and career employment play in the modern bureaucracy.

Despite the similarities among government bureaucracies, however, there are important differences. These differences are in part a reflection of the distinctive conditions and circumstances surrounding each public agency. As we learned in Part II of this book, the pressures on public administration emerge from a variety of sources. Over time, any given organization must adapt to its unique surroundings by developing appropriate organizational characteristics.[16] Thus, the differences among public organizations are largely the result of the differences that exist in their surroundings and in the expectations they face. These differences most often arise in the goals, values, and strategies of public agencies.

Organization Goals

Goals and Organizational Form

In many respects goals are the key to understanding why public agencies exist. Public agencies often are created in response to demands for government actions and services from "politically mobilized segments of society. . . ."[17] In other words, government policymakers have decided to meet some goal or objective on behalf of their constituents by creating a government agency.

At times, agency goals reflect constituent demands for material goods or services, such as the demand for roads and highways or police protection. At other times, public agencies have goals related to the control of some social or economic activity. Thus, we have agencies like the Federal Communications Commission to regulate the operation of the broadcast industry and the Environmental Protection Agency to help prevent or control the deterioration of our physical ecology. At still other times, agencies emerge to satisfy the demand for participation, such as the citizen advisory boards that operate at every level of American government.[18]

Yet goals not only stimulate the birth of public agencies; they also influence the shape and operations of those organizations throughout their histories. Some agencies have clearly defined and widely accepted goals, while others have goals that are ambiguous or controversial. For example, the clearly defined objectives of the local fire department are rarely if ever questioned— it exists to prevent and fight fires within its jurisdiction. Thus, it is not surprising that fire departments throughout the United States are structurally and operationally quite similar. Whatever changes do occur in these organizations usually represent innovations that build on existing arrangements rather than radical changes in structure and operation. In contrast, the employees of a state prison are more likely to debate what objectives their agency serves. Some may believe the agency's job is to rehabilitate the prison's inmates, whereas others may believe that prisons exist to punish criminals. Still others may see prisons as merely preventing interaction between society and its convicted felons. Such uncertainty and debate over agency goals has an impact on the structure and operations of state and federal prisons throughout the United States. Each time a new warden or agency head comes to office, there exists the possibility of a major and disturbing organizational overhaul.

Some public agencies even face the prospect of achieving their goals or finding that their objectives are no longer relevant, either of which can lead to the termination of an agency. Presidential study commissions, for example, often have a limited life span that ends when they issue their final reports. In other cases, however, agencies adopt new goals and continue to survive. In the late 1970s, for instance, a Colorado board responsible for licensing morticians and funeral directors was threatened with elimination when a legislative study indicated that the agency served no useful purpose. The board was originally constituted to protect the public from the health hazards associated with cadavers. A legislative study determined that such hazards were insignificant, and that the board really served as a means for funeral directors to minimize competition among morticians in the state. At first, legislative action called for the termination of the mortician's board. Eventually, though, the board was reconstituted to serve different purposes through legislation that modified the board's objectives from protection of the public health to protection of consumer interests. Thus was the Colorado Morticians Board resurrected as a consumer protection agency.

Policymaker Goals

All organizations exist to achieve some specific goals established by those who set overall policy for them. In private corporations, stockholders or, more often, the board of directors and top-management personnel set these *policymaker goals*. In the public sector, elected officials usually perform this function. Most often legislative bodies (e.g., Congress, the state legislature, or the city council) determine policy in cooperation with elected executives (e.g., the president, governor, or mayor). Sometimes even the voters may have a more direct role in developing such policies, through initiatives and referenda elections. Whatever their origin, the goals often become a top priority of the organization.

The organizational goals set by policymakers can take at least two forms. At times they are *mission goals*—the explicitly and publicly stated objectives of the organization. For example, the U.S. Army has traditionally regarded its mission as being prepared to control the battlefield in times of conflict. Similarly, the U.S. Air Force's mission focuses on its preparedness to control the air under conditions of war, and the navy to control the seas.[19]

There are times when policymakers establish multiple missions for an organization. The Federal Emergency Management Agency (FEMA) has a wide range of missions, including maintaining civil defense (especially against nuclear attack), preventing and controlling fires, providing disaster relief, offering flood and crime insurance, preparing for national and local emergencies, stockpiling strategic materials, coordinating responses to environmental catastrophes, and planning for economic recovery after military attack.[20] (See Insight 10.2.) At other times policymakers define organizational objectives as the actual provision of the goods and services produced and distributed by the organization. These *output goals* may take the form of some quantitative aim or qualitative objective. In recent years, output goals have been linked to efforts to improve public-sector productivity.[21] The search for increased productivity has resulted in many government agency reorganizations and the introduction of new management techniques at all levels of government. The federal government, for example, has introduced such changes in the postal delivery, the operation of health-care facilities, and defense procurement.

INSIGHT 10.2

THE FEMA's "CIVIL (DEFENSE) WAR"

This is a story about an agency that is having problems living up to its mission statement. The agency is the Federal Emergency Management Agency (FEMA) (see Chapter 5), the "latest incarnation" of what was once the Office of Civil Defense (OCD).

In 1978, President Jimmy Carter issued an executive order creating the FEMA by consolidating the OCD with other governmental agencies that performed tasks related to disaster planning and emergency preparedness. Thus, FEMA's overall mission is much more inclusive than was the OCD's; it calls for preparing the civilian population for hazardous waste and natural disasters as well as nuclear war. Nevertheless, most of the agency's budget is still appropriated under provisions of the 1950 Civil Defense Act, which designates that money be spent on protecting the civilian population in the event of a nuclear attack.

Two other facts are relevant to this story. First, the FEMA's leadership and its funding base have their roots in the old OCD. The OCD was nominally a civilian agency, but its management was drawn primarily from the Pentagon, especially from both active and reserve military personnel. The FEMA retains these close ties with the military. Its director in 1988 was Army General Julius W. Becton, Jr., and many of its key staff at all levels of the organization have positions in the armed forces reserve units. Second, the FEMA is one of those federal agencies that relies on the coopera-

tion of local and state officials to implement their programs. A great many of its programs — especially in the area of emergency preparedness — require the cooperation of nonfederal government officials.

Given its broadened mission, the FEMA has developed an emergency preparedness plan that includes having communities throughout the country conduct exercises on dealing with various disasters. The exercises are accomplished on a three-year cycle, with one year devoted to hazardous-waste emergencies, another to prepare for natural disasters such as tornadoes and floods, and a still another in anticipation of a nuclear attack. While state and local officials are more than willing to cooperate with the FEMA in preparing for hazardous waste and natural disasters, some often fail to see any reason for spending the time and money to prepare for a nuclear attack.

The problem reached a crisis in 1987, when a nuclear attack exercise was planned for the northwestern United States. "Alaska and Idaho conducted the exercise as planned," reports Elder Witt. "Washington and Oregon refused, objecting to the scenario as unrealistic and unwise." In Oregon, the opposition came primarily from local communities who gained the support of the governor; in Washington, state officials led the "rebellion" against the exercise. The FEMA responded by threatening to withhold more that $1 million in agency-controlled grants from each state that failed to cooperate. The governors of both Oregon and Washington responded by asking the House Armed Services Committee (which is responsible for the FEMA's program authorizations in that chamber) to consider their complaints. They received a sympathetic hearing.

Ironically, the FEMA's insistence on the nuclear attack exercises was out of character for that agency. Despite its OCD background and continued links to the military, the FEMA typically took a rather loose attitude toward how states prepared for emergencies. In fact, the agency often looked the other way when states and localities used civil defense funds for fire engines and other items not directly linked to a nuclear attack. In 1987, the FEMA was criticized by a General Accounting Office (GAO) study (ordered by the same House Armed Services Committee) for being too lax in its insistence that states use those funds for preparing for a nuclear attack. Thus, when faced with the challenge by Oregon and Washington, the FEMA took a tough stand.

In the end, Oregon and Washington conducted modified versions of the nuclear attack exercise. But their point had been made; in December 1987, Congress took away the FEMA's capacity to withhold emergency preparedness funding from the states. Nevertheless, under pressure from the White House, the Pentagon, and the GAO, the FEMA continues to stress the requirement that states and localities use their funds for nuclear attack as well as other possible emergencies.

> State officials respond that politics and practicality prevent them from emphasizing planning for a nuclear attack to the detriment of preparing for more likely threats. "The state and local mission is the protection of people and property against disasters of all kinds," says [a Washington state official]. "In a time of limited resources we are going to devote our resources to preparing for floods, another eruption like Mount St. Helens, or an accident involving radioactive defense materials. Our preparation for those kinds of eventualities is paramount."

And so the FEMA's "civil (defense) war" goes on.

SOURCE: Quotes and information from Elder Witt, "The Civil (Defense) War between the States and the Federal Government," *Governing* 1 (June 1988): 19–22.

Systemic Goals

In addition to the goals set by the organization's policymakers, an enterprise is attentive to its own needs as well. As a functioning system of relationships, an organization can have two *systemic goals*.

First, public and private organizations have goals for their *survival and maintenance*. These focus on protecting the entity from threats to its existence and providing resources for its continued operations. The federal government's Tennessee Valley Authority (TVA), for instance, has often been threatened with legislation that would either sell off its assets to private power companies or impose restrictions on its operations.[22] In response, the

TVA has established programs that generate support from local communities and a financing system that insulates the agency from the whims of congressional and presidential politics. This is the strategy of co-optation that we discussed in Chapter 4. Studies by organizational analysts indicate that similar survival dynamics are at work in many government agencies.[23]

The second type of systemic goals relates to the *growth and expansion* of an organization. The U.S. Army Corps of Engineers, for example, has often been criticized for operating in a way that promotes projects it can work on. Under this expansionist mode of operation, the Corps might point out some problem to the leaders of a local community. In turn, those community leaders would suggest that their representative in Congress formally inquire about the feasibility of some flood-control or power-generation project. This inquiry, conducted by the Corps, results in a study that includes assessments of the project's costs and a recommendation. If that recommendation is positive (as it frequently is), the member of Congress would sponsor legislation to authorize the project. Thus, in this way, the Corps has been able to help itself grow into a major public works agency in the federal government.[24]

Organization Values

Organizations, like other human endeavors, are reflections of the values they adopt. In the public sector, those values frequently take the form of ethical standards of behavior (see Chapter 3) for the work of public organizations. Among the many values applied by public agencies, two stand out as significant contributions to the way agencies organize and operate: efficiency and responsiveness.

Efficiency

The value of efficiency is important to Americans inside and outside of government. Many of the criticisms aimed at government today focus on the inefficiency of public-sector organizations. The conclusions reached by one recent presidential study commission are typical:

> It is abundantly clear to anyone who reads through [these] reports . . . that the Federal Government is suffering from a case of inefficient and ineffective management, evidenced particularly by the hemorrhaging of billions of tax dollars and mounting deficits. For decades the Federal Government has not managed its programs with the same eye to innovation, productivity, and economy that is dictated by private sector . . . balance sheets.[25]

Many public organizations place a high value on efficiency. This concern first emerged in the late 1800s, when the American public began equating "good" government with "efficient" government. By the 1910s, the goal of administrative efficiency had become a full-fledged political movement.[26]

It was an ardent concern for efficiency that led many public administrators to turn to the work of Frederick Taylor and other scientific management specialists for ideas on how to structure and manage public agencies. For Taylor, the primary objective of scientific management is not merely to maximize productivity or profits, but also to maximize the "efficiency and prosperity" of each individual in the organization. For the employer, the objective is the "development of every branch of business to its highest state of excellence." For the employee, it means "the development of each man to his state of maximum efficiency, so that he might be able to do . . . the highest grade of work for which his natural abilities fit him. . . ."[27] In short, Taylor ties human needs — the needs of both the employer and employee — to the efficient operation of an organization.

Among students of American public administration, this striving for efficiency has been a primary motivation for undertaking organizational and managerial reforms over the past several decades. Efficiency was at the heart of the work of President Franklin Roosevelt's Committee on Administrative Management (also known as the Brownlow Committee), which issued its report in 1937. A series of studies developed for the Brownlow Committee by its staff (published as *Papers on the Science of Administration*, edited by Luther Gulick and Lyndall Urwick) argue the need for governmental reforms based on principles of administration that would maximize efficiency. "In the science of administration," contends Gulick, "the basic 'good' is efficiency."[28] This "good" could be achieved through (among other things) increasing specialization, developing a clear hierarchy of authority, and limiting the span of control at any point in that hierarchy.

By the early 1940s, the work of Gulick and Urwick — especially their preoccupation with efficiency — had become the key reference for many public-sector managers. After the war, however, Herbert A. Simon began to challenge what he considered the simplistic approach that Gulick, Urwick, and others were taking to efficiency. Simon, who later won a Nobel Prize in economics for his work on administrative behavior, pointed out that the term *efficiency* has many meanings. To some, efficient behavior means appropriate or good behavior; to others, it means the reduction of agency expenditures; while to still others, it is synonymous with rationality. Simon also pointed out the problems that can arise when efficiency is overemphasized, such as a mechanical and de-humanized approach to management or a preoccupation with the means and a neglect of agency ends. Simon argued for a more focused and limited view of efficiency, asserting that "the fundamental criterion of administrative decisions must be *efficiency*. . . . [That is,] to maximize social values *relative* to limited resources."[29]

Organizational responses to the value of efficiency varied. In some instances, the call for efficiency results in ongoing efforts to reorganize an agency. The State Department, for example, is constantly involved in organizational changes intended to improve the efficiency of our foreign policy bureaucracy.[30] Other agencies like the Department of Defense have made efforts to merge their budgeting and management systems to improve organizational efficiency through increasing organizational rationality.[31] Still others have hired policy analysts and program evaluators as a means for achieving greater efficiency.[32] Regardless of the problems and failures of many of these efforts, the "search for government efficiency" remains a high priority both within and outside of public-sector agencies.[33]

Responsiveness

At the turn of the twentieth century, most students of modern organizations were preoccupied—some would say obsessed—with the need for greater efficiency. Those who studied and worked with private-sector organizations followed the lead of Frederick Taylor's scientific management in this regard. Similarly, students of government administration mounted influential (and often successful) reform movements throughout the country.[34] Their efforts to improve government efficiency, however, only temporarily diverted attention to another powerful value in American public life: responsiveness.

All organizations have to be responsive. After all, we form an organization not only to solve some problems, but also to benefit some sectors or groups in the population. In fact, most organizations can be classified according to the special interests they seek to serve.[35] Some organizations operate to serve the interests of their owners. In the private sphere, *economic organizations* seek to make their shareholders better off, usually by generating a surplus or profit that the owners divide among themselves. In principle, many government corporations (e.g., the U.S. Postal Service and the TVA) are structured to act as economic organizations, although there are few mechanisms for directly distributing their "profits" to the citizenry that "owns" the agency.

More common among public agencies are entities that operate for the benefit of their clients or customers. These *service organizations* include government agencies involved in everything from social services to prisons. Many states have agencies that specialize in economic development or commerce to service the interests of private industry. At the national level, the Department of Veterans Affairs serves the needs of those who have served the country during times of war and hostile action. Also at the cabinet level, the Department of Agriculture serves farmers, the Department of Commerce serves business, and the Department of Labor promotes the interests of workers.[36]

Another type of organization serves the interests of its members. *Mutual benefit organizations* operate throughout the private sector and they include labor unions, trade associations, and even mutual savings associations. In government, perhaps the most important mutual benefit organization is the Federal Reserve System. While chartered by the federal government, the "Fed" membership includes several thousand banks who receive a variety of services from the agency. In exchange for adhering to certain rules and regulations (e.g., maintaining a minimum cash reserve), member banks receive check-clearing services and access to loan funds from the "Fed." Local governments rely on benefit districts (comprised of property owners in the affected area) to fund the construction of such things as sewers and sidewalks.

Finally, there are organizations designed to serve what they perceive to be the interests of the general population: *commonwealth organizations*. In the public sector, these agencies include regulatory bodies such as the Federal Communications Commission (FCC) or public health agencies such as the Centers for Disease Control (CDC) and the Surgeon General's office.

In the United States, responsiveness has a special meaning for public-sector organizations. American society aspires to be democratic. According to Dwight Waldo, this commitment to democracy is "our form of patriotism"; it is

> our form of spiritual imperialism. The "mission of America" . . . has been conceived as witnessing Democracy before mankind, bearing democracy's ideals of freedom and equality, and its material blessing, to the nations of the world.

None of this, of course, escapes the notice of those who administer government programs. According to Waldo,

> American students of administration have not loved democracy the less, but the more, because of their critical attention to its institutions and their desire to extend its services. They have not loved it the less dearly when they have insisted that it be worthy of its mission abroad by being noble at home. . . . [37]

In view of our strong commitment to democracy, it is not surprising that responsiveness is highly valued among American public administrators. In fact, democracy has taken on the characteristics of a moral obligation that no public-sector agency can ignore. In 1952, Paul H. Appleby wrote about what living up to this obligation entails: Administrative actions must conform to the procedures developed to protect political freedom and at the same time remain open to modification or reversal. Further, the individuals responsible for those actions must be made clearly identifiable, for their administrative decisions and actions reflect "popularly felt needs, and not merely responses to the private or personal needs of leaders."[38]

Living up to the moral obligation of democracy has not been an easy task for American public administrators. Among the most difficult problems facing them is deciding which particular institution in American government best represents "popularly felt needs." That is, if they are to fulfill their democratic calling, to whom or to what should they be responsive? Many people believe public administrators are fulfilling their democratic responsibilities when they follow the wishes and agenda of the president. After all, the president is the only elected official whose constituency includes all of the American people. Others believe that administrative agencies should be responsive to the demands and priorities of Congress because it is more closely linked to the American electorate. Still others call for a greater commitment to constitutional standards and democratically determined laws as a basis for administrative actions.[39] While no firm consensus exists (see Chapter 7), a number of organizational mechanisms and policies have emerged to help meet the challenge of responsiveness in public administration. Reflected in these mechanisms are four complementary approaches.

The first approach, *agency openness*, includes policies that promote or require public access to agency personnel or records. Many states, for instance, have passed what is called "sunshine" legislation, requiring that meetings of government boards be open to the public. The federal government and many states have passed freedom-of-information legislation, which makes most government records open to public scrutiny. The underlying idea behind this approach is that an open government leads to an informed public, which, in turn, leads to greater input and pressures to respond to those inputs.

A second approach to increasing responsiveness involves expanding *agency representativeness*. The underlying idea of this approach is that an agency composed of individuals who reflect the population they are serving is more responsive to that population.[40] The specific means for accomplishing these objectives are discussed in greater detail in Chapter 12. For now, it should be noted that there is no conclusive evidence indicating that more representative organizations are more or less responsive to public needs and wishes.[41]

In a third approach, agencies seek greater responsiveness through the *collection and assessment of clientele preferences*. Some agencies attempt to accomplish this by forming advisory committees composed of individuals who reflect the interests of agency clientele groups. The Department of Agriculture, for example, has established state advisory councils as part of its cooperative extension service programs. The Department of Education requires states to create citizen advisory boards in a variety of program areas for which federal grants are provided. Other agencies actually conduct or sponsor surveys and opinion studies to assess clientele needs and opinions about their operations. Many cities rely on such surveys to ascertain their citizens' perceptions and attitudes toward municipal services. Others use them to obtain the public's views and feedback on specific programs or projects. For example, in 1986, Wichita, Kansas, commissioned a study of its program to reduce drunk driving that included a survey of changes in public attitudes toward drunk driving. Wichita officials sought to determine whether their programs were having any effect. Similarly, in 1987, Lawrence, Kansas, surveyed its citizens' attitudes about locating a major retail shopping development in the community. Lawrence city officials sought to obtain citizen input before any decision was made.[42]

Finally, an increasing number of public organizations use mechanisms that promote *direct citizen participation* in their decision-making processes. At the federal level, the first major program to require citizen participation was the Federal Housing Act of 1954. The most famous mandate for citizen participation in a federal program, however, is the requirement of "maximum feasible participation" by local residents in community action programs funded under the 1964 Economic Opportunity Act.[43] Some state and federal regulatory commissions have established offices of consumer advocacy to represent actively the interests of the public at commission hearings. In addition, many states are requiring citizen participation in other regulatory areas like land-use planning.[44] While the form and nature of these efforts vary from agency to agency, together they reflect the high value that many American public administrators place on responsiveness.

Other Values

Although efficiency and responsiveness play the most significant roles in the development and operation of public-sector organizations, they are not the only values that influence public administration. Depending on the era and special tasks involved, other organizational values have been important as well.

During the early 1950s, for example, the federal government went through the period of McCarthyism, named after Joseph McCarthy, a Republican senator from Wisconsin who, along with other members of the Senate and House, conducted investigations into the loyalty of officials in the foreign and defense policy fields (see discussion in Chapter 4). Claims that some government administrators were Soviet spies or Communist sympathizers were widespread. The fear that such sympathizers were intentionally subverting U.S. policies led to an internal upheaval at the Department of State and elsewhere. *Loyalty* became a highly valued characteristic within the foreign policy establishment, and public servants were under increasing pressure to assert and demonstrate their loyalty. Although both McCarthy and McCarthyism eventually passed from the public arena, they left a legacy in the State Department and elsewhere that is still felt today.[45]

Another highly regarded organizational value is *rationality*. Closely associated with efficiency, rationality calls for the application of systematic methods and techniques in agency decision making.[46] Because of its relationship to efficiency, rationality has been a concern of government administrators at all levels throughout the twentieth century. At times, rationality has even taken center stage in public administration, such as when President John F. Kennedy appointed Robert S. McNamara as secretary of defense in 1961. A former president of the Ford Motor Company, McNamara was an advocate of program planning, systems management, and other analytic techniques that apply the rationality of economics to the operations of large-scale organizations. Then, in March 1967, President Lyndon B. Johnson enthusiastically endorsed the Defense Department's Planning-Programming-Budgeting (PPB) approach for all federal departments. Thus, the technical rationality approach used within one department soon spread throughout the federal bureaucracy as well as into state and local governments.[47]

Equity is another value often highly regarded by American public administrators. As discussed in Chapter 3, it is a widespread ethical standard of administrative behavior. By *equity*, we mean the fair treatment of individuals. Sometimes this fairness takes the form of making certain that everyone receives equal treatment. At other times, it means providing public goods or services according to need or in light of what the recipient had earned. Just as rationality is related to efficiency, so equity is often associated with responsiveness.[48]

At times, equity values have been the central focus of administrative concerns. During the late 1960s and early 1970s, for example, many public administration scholars engaged in discussions about their commitment to social equity. According to H. George Frederickson, social equity includes those "activities designed to enhance the political power and economic well-being of . . . minorities."[49] Frederickson and other members of what they called the "New Public Administration" movement advocated a more activist role for public administrators in achieving social equity values.

The list of relevant organizational values does not end here. Among the other major social values that organizations adopt are justice, freedom, reliability, and stability.[50] Whatever specific values an organization adopts, they are bound to have an impact on the organization's arrangements. While a desire for efficiency usually leads to changes in the organization of agency decision making, the desire for responsiveness usually results in greater attention to mechanisms for increasing citizen participation. Similarly, insuring worker loyalty calls for the development of security clearance procedures, and the urge to improve rationality can radically alter the way some agencies manage their budgets. In short, the organizational impact of agency values can be significant.

Organization Strategies

Strategy Defined

Just as organizations differ in their goals and values, so they develop different strategies for managing the diversity of expectations that emanates from their external environments. In organization theory, a *strategy* is the *"adoption of courses of action and the allocation of resources necessary for carrying out"* the *basic long-term goals and objectives of an agency* (emphasis added).[51]

Both public and private organizations typically use two major strategic approaches. The first attempts to anticipate changes in the environment in order to protect the organization from the uncertainty of environmental turbulence; we call this the *buffering* approach. The second attempts to develop a means for interacting with the environment that will promote the growth and survival of the organization within its surroundings; we call this the *bridging* approach.[52] Through these strategies public organizations attempt to *control* their environments by contending with the environmental forces that seek to control them.

Buffering Strategies

When relying on buffering strategies, an organization attempts to reduce its exposure to external forces. There are various ways to accomplish this in terms of organization. Some agencies use *forecasting*, in which they attempt to gather information about current and future changes in the external environment and adjust their future behavior accordingly. School districts, for example, monitor census data on their communities to determine how many classrooms will be needed two, four, or six years from now. Similarly, state colleges and universities track high school enrollments to determine their future resource needs.

Forecasting has its limits, however. In some program areas, for instance, it is not possible to gather the necessary data. Consider how difficult it is for Department of Agriculture analysts to estimate accurately the crop production in wheat or corn over the next ten years. Or, when dealing with people, consider how fickle human behavior can be. When colleges and universities projected a downturn in the number of students who would enroll in higher education in the late 1980s, the downturn was not as great as expected, and many major state universities even recorded steadily increasing enrollment totals each year.

Another buffering strategy involves *stockpiling* those resources that may be critically important in the future. For example, highway departments in northern climates stockpile tons of salt and gravel during the summer and fall in anticipation of winter blizzards. But material needs aren't the only type of resource that can be stockpiled. Agencies can also try to accumulate the necessary kinds of experience their employees might need in the future, such as through the simulated disaster drills discussed in Chapter 5. Stockpiling is usually part of a general strategic plan to help buffer the agency from future environmental shocks.

Still another buffering strategy involves actions taken to make the environment conform with the organization's needs. One such approach is *leveling*, through which an organization seeks to reduce the variations or fluctuations within the environment that make its work difficult or uncertain. Thus, by issuing the now-familiar social security number to every American, the SSA effectively reduces the potential problem of having to contend with millions of individual clients whose names differ in length, form, and spelling. As far as the SSA, IRS, banks, schools, and hundreds of other institutions that use the nine-digit Social Security code, are concerned, we *are* those numbers.[53]

A related approach is *coding*. Under a coding scheme, the elements of the environment with which an agency must deal are classified according to some relevant set of criteria. For instance, those who file for disability insurance through Social Security are categorized according to age, the nature of their disability (e.g. blindness), the severity of their disability, and the like. The Selective Service System (SSS) had developed one of the most famous examples of coding, which it used for the military draft from the late 1940s through the mid-1970s. The draft system required each male resident of the United States to register with the Selective Service at age 18; this is still the current policy. However, the earlier SSS system assigned each registrant to one of fourteen categories, ranging from Class I–A ("Available for military service") to IV–F ("Physically, mentally, or morally unfit") to V–A ("Over the age of liability for military service").[54]

Finally, some organizations deal with their surroundings through *adjustments in scale of operations*. During the post-World War II baby boom, many school districts addressed the anticipated expansion in enrollments through consolidation with other districts and sizable increases in staff and facilities. They met the expected challenges of environmental change through a strategy of growth and expansion. During the 1970s, however, school districts and other units of government faced reductions in demands for their services or sharp cutbacks in fiscal resources. Many of these governmental units engaged in cutback management techniques, such as the elimination of services, reductions in the work force, user charges for services (see Chapter 13), and related tactics.[55]

Bridging Strategies

In contrast to buffering strategies, through which an organization attempts merely to *adjust* its surroundings, bridging strategies rely on an organization's willingness and ability to *influence* its surroundings. Agencies using bridging strategies carry on planned interactions with other organizations in their environment. Thus, *power* is a key ingredient in any bridging strategy. As noted in Chapter 8, power is the ability to influence or determine the behavior of others through the control or manipulation of resources. Our discussion at that time focused on bureaucratic power and the importance of administrative discretion in shaping the role of public administrators in America's policy-making system. Here, however, our focus turns to the strategic uses of power by public organizations.

Some organizations use their power to pursue a *competitive* relationship with other organizations. Explicit forms of direct competition are rare in the public sector, although less direct forms are commonplace. Public colleges and universities, for example, often compete with private institutions and among themselves for students and faculty. Some competitiveness also exists in the budgetary process, such as when several agencies compete for limited resources.

Some agencies engage in *bargaining* when they must relate to other organizations. According to James Q. Wilson, bargaining is a "process by which two or more parties seek to attain incompatible ends through the exchange of compensation."[56] Bargaining techniques involve the agency in negotiations with others in the environment who either pose a threat to the agency or can develop into an effective ally. A prime example of bargaining occurs in the area of antitrust policy enforcement, in which two federal agencies — the Federal Trade Commission and the Antitrust Division of the Department of Justice — have similar jurisdictions and overlapping functions. Despite the potential for interagency conflict, these agencies have avoided any serious disputes through a long-standing process of consultation and negotiation. In 1948, the two agencies entered into an agreement establishing a formal liaison system, in which representatives from both agencies meet regularly to discuss the initiation and disposition of cases and complaints. This process "has prevented a wasteful duplication of effort. There have been no instances in recent memory," reports one source, "of both agencies committing resources to the same investigation."[57]

Many of the alternative service-delivery mechanisms discussed in Chapter 2 are also actually bridging strategies. *Contracting*, for example, allows an agency to accomplish tasks it is incapable or unwilling to undertake (see Profile 10.1). The federal government has carried out experiments in welfare reform through contracts, just as many state social service agencies use contractors to operate local counseling and job-training centers.[58] More importantly, an agency can use contracting to impose constraints and guidelines on contractor firms, thus providing itself with additional control over its environment. In addition, public agencies can get involved in *joint ventures* or agreements, such as the 911 emergency telephone number arrangement found in most metropolitan areas.

There are also other bridging strategies that we discussed earlier in different contexts. For instance, we noted in Chapter 4 how the TVA used *co-optation* as a means for generating support for its massive redevelopment projects in the Tennessee Valley. Similar bridging techniques were used in many community action and welfare programs of the 1960s.[59] We also discussed the increasing use of *associations* among public agencies and government officials, particularly at the local and state levels. At the local level, councils of government (COGs) have formed throughout the country to help coordinate solutions to common problems among municipal and county entities. Other associations take the form of public-sector interest groups that endeavor to increase the political effectiveness of government agencies at higher levels of American government. Thus, the National League of Cities is an effective lobby for local governments in Washington, just as the Council of State Planning Agencies works to achieve improvements in the federal public works program.[60]

Of course, this is far from an exhaustive list of the bridging strategies used by public organizations. Bridging and buffering strategies together constitute a significant arsenal of organizational approaches to the problems posed by external environmental forces. With each strategic approach, a

PROFILE 10.1

Managing L.A., "Inc."

Richard B. Dixon's resumé lists "work" as his number one interest. "Work may be my only interest," he told a reporter in 1988. "I cannot think of a single morning I woke up that I would rather do anything other than go to work. . . ." What Dixon does when he goes to work is manage the County of Los Angeles, California. What is most interesting about Dixon is how he is going about his job. The 51-year-old administrator assumed his current position as Los Angeles county executive in 1986. He began working for the government as a court aide during the late 1950s, at a salary of $303 a month. Today he receives $123,000 a year to run a government operation that serves 8.4 million residents, employs 79,000 workers, and spends nearly $7.6 billion annually.

"If it were an independent nation," notes one observer, the county's "gross national product would make it the sixteenth richest country in the world." Despite its affluence, Los Angeles County government has not been affluent, and in the 1980s it was actually running up deficits that Dixon had to deal with as county executive. He met the challenge, in part, through innovative financing. But he also accomplished his tasks by streamlining county government operations—that is, by making it operate more like a competitive corporation. "We are molding ourselves very consciously in a corporate image," Dixon says. "I believe the County of Los Angeles is a corporation. It ought to

walk, waddle and quack like one."

Central to Dixon's approach is a basic principle: "Do things you are good at, hire people to do things you are not good at. . . ." Following that rule, Dixon turned over a number of public services to private contractors—a move that saves the county an average $50 million a year in operating and associated costs. Furthermore, those services that the county continues to provide are operated at such high efficiency and effectiveness that many municipalities in the area contract with county officials to provide them.

Within the county government organization, Dixon has a reputation for making decisions and carrying them out aggressively. "Management is not a popularity contest." He says he is "not subtle, not indirect, not always nice. If a loud bark and a pretty nice bite are necessary, I'll deliver it." Dixon takes pride in this approach. "People may not always like the decisions I make, but most people who know me know I will make decisions in a timely way. You always know where you stand with me."

One of Dixon's employees described him as an "energetic" and "often impatient" man who does not expect people to do more than he does. But "he does so much it's difficult for people to keep up with him. He has high expectations."

SOURCE: Quotes and information from Ellen Perlman, "Meeting the Corporate Challenge," *City & State*, 29 August 1988, pp. 22–23.

unique set of organizational arrangements emerges, whether it is an office of contract compliance, a citizen's advisory board, or a liaison office. Strategies, like goals and values, have implications for the design of many public organizations.

Public Agencies as Dynamic Actors

In this chapter, we examined public agencies as actors in the public administration arena. Public agencies are not passive in their relationships with their ecology. Rather, they actively seek to pursue their own interests and promote their own values without losing sight of the reality of those external expectations that are so much a part of their ecology. That is to say, public organizations seek to manage the direct and indirect forces that are part of their external environments.

We also explored how public agencies use organizational arrangements to cope with the constant challenge of external expectations. We considered the structure of the modern bureaucracy, which contains the organizational elements that most public agencies share, as well as how differences in organizational goals, values, and strategies provide each agency with a distinctive look as it attempts to adapt to its unique situation.

Of course, public-sector agencies are rarely completely successful at managing their relationships with their external environments. The external environment is dynamic and expectations are constantly changing. The strategies that worked last year or last week may not work in the future. Agencies can accomplish their ultimate goals only if they are adaptable and flexible to changes in their external environments.

Our discussion in this chapter has focused on the characteristics, goals, values, and strategies of public agencies as they try to manage externally derived expectations. In the following three chapters, our focus turns to how organizations cope with the challenges generated by their internal environments.

Summary

1. Government organizations take a variety of structural forms. At the national level, they range from the well-known forms of cabinet departments and independent agencies to the less common foundations and endowments.
2. Despite differences in structure, government agencies share the characteristics of modern bureaucratic organizations.
3. Public organizations differ in terms of the goals and purposes they pursue. Some goals mirror the objectives of the policymakers who created or

fund the agency; other goals are more systemic and serve the survival and growth needs of the organization.

4. Public agencies also differ in terms of the organizational values under which they operate. Two of the most important values are efficiency and responsiveness, although there are many others that require attention, such as loyalty and equity.

5. Public organizations rely on a variety of buffering and bridging strategies to deal with their environments.

Study Questions

1. Select an organization in which you have worked or one that operates in your college town. Profile the organization using the dimensions discussed in this chapter: What type of organization is it? How "bureaucratic" is it? What are the organization's goals? Its key values? Its strategies? Gather information for the profile by interviewing key individuals in the organization. As you describe the central characteristics of the organization, be sure to cite evidence to support your analysis.

2. Select a public-sector agency and conduct an analysis similar to the one you did for question 1.

3. Focusing on the college you attend, describe the activities undertaken by the faculty, administrators, and staff that can be classified as buffering or bridging strategies.

Notes

1. Quoted in Harold Seidman, "A Typology of Government," in *Federal Reorganization: What Have We Learned?* ed. by Peter Szanton (Chatham, NJ: Chatham House, 1981), p.36

2. See ibid., chap. 3; and Harold Seidman and Robert Gilmour, *Politics, Position, and Power: From the Positive to the Regulatory State*, 4th ed. (New York: Oxford University Press, 1986), chap. 11

3. The widespread pejorative connotation that people usually attach to the term *bureaucracy* is not the image we intend to convey. What makes bureaucratic forms of organization different from nonbureaucratic forms is exactly what makes bureaucracy the most efficient way to organize the large-scale activities of a lot of people: hierarchy of authority, division of labor, rules, and impersonality. In other words, public agencies tend to be bureaucratically organized because that is the most effective way to try to accomplish the administrative tasks they are charged with carrying out.

4. See Reinhard Bendix, *Max Weber: An Intellectual Portrait* (Garden City, NY: Anchor-Doubleday, 1962), esp. chaps. 8 and 14.

5. Henri Fayol, "General Principles of Management," in *Classics of Organization Theory*, 2d ed., ed. by Jay M. Shafritz and J. Steven Ott (Chicago: The Dorsey Press, 1987), p. 52.
6. Ibid., p. 52.
7. Quoted in Victor A. Thompson, *Bureaucracy and the Modern World* (Morristown, NJ: General Learning Press, 1976), p. 40.
8. The Grace Commission [The President's Private Sector Survey on Cost Control], *War On Waste* (New York: Macmillan, 1984), pp. 25–36.
9. Emmette S. Redford, *Democracy in the Administrative State* (New York: Oxford University Press, 1969), p. 195.
10. For critical assessments of the use of hierarchies in public organizations, see Vincent Ostrom, *The Intellectual Crisis in American Public Administration*, rev. ed. (University, AL: University of Alabama Press, 1974); Robert B. Denhardt, *Theories of Public Organization* (Monterey, CA: Brooks/Cole, 1984); and Judith E. Gruber, *Controlling Bureaucracies: Dilemmas in Democratic Governance* (Berkeley: University of California Press, 1986).
11. Adam Smith, *An Inquiry into the Nature and Causes of the Wealth of Nations*, Cannan ed. (New York: The Modern Library, 1937), pp. 4–5.
12. Frederick Taylor, *The Principles of Scientific Management* (New York: W. W. Norton, 1967), p. 39.
13. Harvey Sherman, *It All Depends: A Pragmatic Approach to Organization* (University, AL: University of Alabama Press, 1966). Also see Barry Bozeman, *Public Management and Policy Analysis* (New York: St. Martin's Press, 1979), chap. 5.
14. See Alvin W. Gouldner, *Patterns of Industrial Bureaucracy* (New York: The Free Press, 1954), pp. 159–62.
15. Taylor, *The Principles of Scientific Management*, pp. 63–69.
16. See Howard E. Aldrich, *Organizations and Environments* (Englewood Cliffs, NJ: Prentice-Hall, 1979).
17. Herbert Kaufman, *Are Government Organizations Immortal?* (Washington, DC: Brookings Institution, 1976), p. 66.
18. See James Q. Wilson, *Political Organizations* (New York: Basic Books, 1973), chaps. 2 and 3. Goals are not the only factor in the creation of organizations; for a summary of the literature on the creation of organizations, see W. Richard Scott, *Organizations: Rational, Natural, and Open Systems* (Englewood Cliffs, NJ: Prentice-Hall, 1981), chap. 7.
19. For a study of how important organizational missions can be, see Frederic A. Bergerson, *The Army Gets an Air Force: Tactics of Insurgent Bureaucratic Politics* (Baltimore: Johns Hopkins University Press, 1980).
20. See Peter J. May and Walter Williams, *Disaster Policy Implementation: Managing Programs under Shared Governance* (New York: Plenum Press, 1986), esp. chap. 3.
21. See Ralph C. Bledsoe, "Effectiveness and Productivity in Public Organizations," in *Handbook of Organizational Management*, ed. by William B. Eddy (New York: Marcel Dekker 1983), chap. 9.
22. On the emergence and initial survival of the TVA, see Philip Selznick, *TVA and the Grass Roots: A Study of Politics and Organization* (Berkeley: University of California Press, 1949). For a critical assessment, see William U. Chandler, *The Myth Of TVA: Conservation and Development in the Tennessee Valley, 1933–*

1983 (Cambridge, MA: Ballinger, 1984). Also see Annmarie Hauck Walsh, *The Public's Business: The Politics and Practices of Government Corporations* (Cambridge, MA: MIT Press, 1978).

23. For an excellent assessment of how this urge for survival works in the U.S. Coast Guard and in the public's interest, see Louis K. Bragaw, *Managing a Federal Agency: The Hidden Stimulus* (Baltimore: Johns Hopkins University Press, 1980).

24. The Corps has actually changed its ways in recent years; see Daniel A. Mazmanian and Jeanne Nienaber, *Can Organizations Change? Environmental Protection, Citizen Participation, and the Corps of Engineers* (Washington, DC: Brookings Institution, 1979).

25. Grace Commission, *War on Waste*, p. 3.

26. On the intellectual history of the criterion of efficiency, see Dwight Waldo, *The Administrative State*, 2d ed. (New York: Holmes and Meier, 1984), chap. 10.

27. Taylor, *The Principles of Scientific Management*, pp. 9, 128–44.

28. See Luther Gulick and L. Urwick, eds., *Papers on the Science of Administration* (New York: Institute for Public Administration, 1937); p. 192.

29. Herbert A. Simon, *Administrative Behavior: A Study of Decision-Making Processes in Administrative Organization*, 3d ed. (New York: The Free Press, 1976), chap. 9; quote is from p. 213. Also see his discussion of efficiency in Herbert A. Simon, Donald W. Smithburg, and Victor A. Thompson, *Public Administration* (New York: Alfred A. Knopf, 1950), chap. 23.

30. See Donald P. Warwick, *A Theory of Public Bureaucracy: Politics, Personality, and Organization in the State Department* (Cambridge, MA: Harvard University Press, 1975).

31. See Ida R. Hoos, *Systems Analysis in Public Policy: A Critique*, rev. ed. (Berkeley: University of California Press, 1983).

32. See Arnold J. Meltsner, *Policy Analysts in the Bureaucracy* (Berkeley: University of California Press, 1976).

33. George W. Downs and Patrick D. Larkey, *The Search for Government Efficiency: From Hubris to Helplessness* (New York: Random House, 1986).

34. See Martin J. Schiesl, *The Politics of Efficiency: Municipal Administration and Reform in America, 1880–1920* (Berkeley: University of California Press, 1977).

35. See Peter Blau and W. Richard Scott, *Formal Organizations* (San Francisco: Chandler Publishing, 1962).

36. For critical historical assessments of these "clientele" agencies, see Grant McConnell, *Private Power and American Democracy* (New York: Alfred A. Knopf, 1966); and Theodore J. Lowi, *The End of Liberalism: The Second Republic of the United States*, 2d ed. (New York: W. W. Norton, 1979).

37. Waldo, *The Administrative State*, p. 15.

38. Paul H. Appleby, *Morality and Administration in Democratic Government* (Baton Rouge: Louisiana State University Press, 1952), p. 36.

39. See Emmette S. Redford, *Democracy in the Administrative State* (New York: Oxford University Press, 1969); John A. Rohr, *To Run a Constitution: The Legitimacy of the Administrative State* (Lawrence: University Press of Kansas, 1986); and Lowi, *The End of Liberalism*.

40. See Samuel Krislov, *Representative Bureaucracy* (Englewood Cliffs, NJ: Prentice-Hall, 1974).

41. See Samuel Krislov and David H. Rosenbloom, *Representative Bureaucracy and the American Political System* (New York: Praeger, 1981).

42. See Advisory Commission on Intergovernmental Relations, *Citizen Participation in the American Federal System* (Washington, DC: Government Printing Office, 1980), p. 276; William F. Heiss, "Listening to the City: Citizen Surveys," *Urban Affairs Papers* 2 (Summer 1980): 1–9; Steven Maynard-Moody and Dennis Palumbo, *Final Report for the Wichita Comprehensive Program to Reduce Driving While Intoxicated* (Lawrence: Institute for Public Policy and Business Research, University of Kansas, 1986); and Steven Maynard-Moody and Paul Schumaker, *Downtown Redevelopment and Public Opinion: A Survey of Citizen Attitudes for the Downtown Improvement Committee* (Lawrence: Institute for Public Policy and Business Research, University of Kansas, 1987).

43. See Daniel P. Moynihan, *Maximum Feasible Misunderstanding: Community Action in the War on Poverty* (New York: The Free Press, 1970); Paul E. Peterson, "Forms of Representation: Participation of the Poor in the Community Action Program," *American Political Science Review* 64 (June 1970): 491–507; and Elaine B. Sharp, *Citizen Demand-making in the Urban Context* (University, AL: University of Alabama Press, 1986).

44. See William T. Gormley, Jr., *The Politics of Public Utility Regulation* (Pittsburgh: University of Pittsburgh Press, 1983), chap. 2; and Nelson M. Rosenbaum, *Citizen Involvement in Land Use Governance: Issues and Methods* (Washington, DC: Urban Institute, 1976).

45. For an overview of the political atmosphere during the McCarthy era, see Fred I. Greenstein, *The Hidden-hand Presidency: Eisenhower as Leader* (New York: Basic Books, 1982), chap. 5.

46. See Simon, *Administrative Behavior*, pp. 75–77.

47. See Hoos, *Systems Analysis in Public Policy*, chap. 3.

48. Redford notes that one central component of "democratic morality" is adherence to the belief that all people have "worth deserving social recognition." This is closely related to the concept of social equity advanced by the "New Public Administration." See Redford, *Democracy in the Administrative State*, p. 6.

49. H. George Frederickson, "Toward a New Public Administration," in *Toward a New Public Administration: The Minnowbrook Perspective*, ed. by Frank Marini (Scranton, PA: Chandler , 1971), p. 311.

50. For a critical discussion of the role of values in modern organizations, see Ralph P. Hummel, *The Bureaucratic Experience*, 3d ed. (New York: St. Martin's Press, 1987), chap. 2.

51. Alfred D. Chandler, Jr., *Strategy and Structure: Chapters in the History of the American Industrial Enterprise* (Cambridge, MA: MIT Press, 1962), p. 13.

52. The following discussion relies heavily on Scott, *Organizations*, pp. 188–203. Also see James D. Thompson, *Organizations in Action: The Social Science Bases of Adminsitrative Theory* (New York: Harper & Row, 1967), pp. 20–23.

53. For a critical view of this development, see Hummel, *The Bureaucratic Experience*.

54. On the categorization of disabled persons, see Jerry L. Mashaw, *Bureaucratic Justice: Managing Social Security Disability Claims* (New Haven, CT: Yale University Press, 1983), pp. 86–87; on the Selective Service, see Clyde E. Jacobs and John F. Gallagher, *The Selective Service Act: A Case Study of the Governmental Process* (New York: Dodd, Mead, 1967), pp. 119–23.

55. See Charles H. Levine, ed., *Managing Fiscal Stress: The Crisis in the Public Sector* (Chatham, NJ: Chatham House, 1980), esp. pp. 19–25.

56. Wilson, *Political Organizations*, p. 282.

57. Robert A. Katzmann, *Regulatory Bureaucracy: The Federal Trade Commission and Antitrust Policy* (Cambridge, MA: MIT Press, 1980), pp. 193–94. Also see William G. Shepherd and Clair Wilcox, *Public Policies toward Business*, 6th ed. (Homewood, IL: Richard D. Irwin, 1979), pp. 114–15.

58. See Ira Sharkansky, *Wither the State? Politics and Public Enterprise in Three Countries* (Chatham, NJ: Chatham House, 1979), pp. 124–28.

59. See Selznick, *TVA and the Grass Roots;* and Moynihan, *Maximum Feasible Misunderstanding*.

60. See Donald H. Haider, *When Governments Come to Washington: Governors, Mayors, and Intergovernmental Lobbying* (New York: The Free Press, 1974).

CHAPTER 11

MANAGING

BEHAVIOR

IN PUBLIC

ORGANIZATIONS

The Puzzle of Employee Behavior

We have seen how public agencies try to cope with external expectations through organizational structures. But how do they contend with the pressures and expectations emerging from *within* the organization? What happens when the human factor (discussed in Chapter 9) meets the organizational factor (discussed in Chapter 10)?

Here we explore the strategies available to the public agency for dealing with the problems generated by its internal enviroment. Our focus is on individual behavior and the challenges it poses to public agency management. For example, what kinds of behaviors and expectations do public agencies want from their members? How do they attempt to achieve them? Which organizational and human factors affect employee reactions to these efforts to control? What linkages develop between organizations and individuals as a result of these interactions?

The Hawthorne Effect

There are many theories about why people act the way they do in organizations. Some of the earliest research in this area was conducted in the 1920s at Western Electric's Hawthorne Plant in Chicago. These well-known experiments studied the human relations aspect of employee behavior.[1] The researchers began by studying the effect of changing physical working conditions on the productivity of workers. They were surprised to find that productivity increased even when negative changes (such as reduced space and poor lighting) were introduced into the working environment. The study concluded that the workers had responded to the attention they received as part of the special study group. Today we call this type of employee reaction the *Hawthorne effect*.

The other major discovery of the Hawthorne experiments is that social relations—that is, the way workers interact with their co-workers and officials—affect employee behaviors at work. In other words, employees are affected by the human interactions in their work surroundings. Years later, Chester Barnard, a former executive at New Jersey Bell Telephone Company, argued that organizations are primarily social entities and that individual workers are the basic component of organizations.[2]

As knowledge of why people act the way they do has increased, the early theories have become less useful. Social scientists have yet to arrive at a grand theory that explains all human behavior under all circumstances, and students of public organizations have yet to develop a viable theory specific to human behavior in all government agencies. However, we do have general theories of human behavior that help us understand organizational life under certain circumstances. These studies of what goes on within organizations reveal a great deal about many aspects of the dynamics of human activity in organizations.

Our situation is analogous to working with pieces of a difficult jigsaw puzzle. We begin such a puzzle by assembling the individual pieces into groups or clusters, and then trying to fit the clusters together to form a larger picture. Students of organizational life have succeeded in assembling small groups of pieces of the puzzle of human behavior, but they are not sure how those groups fit together to form the larger picture. As is often the case with challenging jigsaw puzzles, it is entirely possible that the pieces already assembled into groups do not belong together. From our observations, we have discerned some limited patterns of employee behavior that have led to limited explanations for that activity. However, if we rearranged the pieces of our puzzle, we might draw entirely different conclusions.

Working with the Pieces

It is important to understand the limits of our knowledge of organizational life as well as to resist the temptation of looking for simple answers to complex questions of human behavior in public agencies. It is equally important to recognize the knowledge and understanding that we do have—as limited as it is—about people in organizations. It is the best that students of organizational life have to offer so far.

Theories that attempt to explain specific behavior under specific circumstances are called *contingency theories*. The warning associated with contingency theories is "it all depends." That is, human behavior in organizations depends on the circumstances faced by the individual as well as the needs and personality of that individual. We know enough to say that under certain conditions we can expect certain behaviors.[3]

Our understanding of the complexities involved in managing human behavior in organizations is daigramed in Figure 11.1. At its simplest level, the basic problem facing all organizations is how to exercise *control* over employee behavior through managerial means. This simple approach is complicated by two ever-present barriers: employee reactions to those efforts and the numerous organizational and human factors that come into play in organizational life. We cannot understand the dilemmas of public agency management until we understand these barriers.

Control and the Manager's Tasks

Organizations recognize that they need people to function; indeed, they cannot exist without members. Nonetheless, many organizations tend to view the diversity of individual behavior as a bothersome but unavoidable challenge to their functioning and control. The organizational challenge is to harness the self-interested or cooperative tendencies of individuals and groups within the agency for organizational purposes and to minimize the counterproductive impacts of employee behaviors.

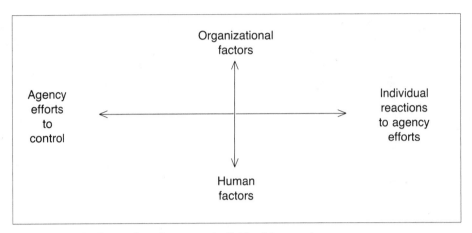

FIGURE 11.1   Dynamics of agency–individual interactions.

On the one hand, public organizations need employees to do their assigned tasks when they are supposed to be accomplished. On the other hand, there are situations when the agency needs its employees to be flexible enough to go beyond their specified roles and do what is necessary to get the job done. Thus, agencies sometimes require their employees to go beyond their job limits, or to perform "beyond the call of duty." They need employees to do what they are supposed to do (according to their job assignments) but not to be so rigid that they refuse to go beyond their job descriptions when necessary. Toward these ends, agencies seek to integrate, influence, coordinate, and (ultimately) control employee behavior. Agencies concern themselves with integrating their employees into work teams and influencing the behavior of team members. They also try to coordinate the activities of their various teams, so that the collective agency effort contributes to organizational adaptability and survival. And, when called for, organizations attempt to exercise control over the behavior of individual workers in order to generate compliance.

There are several methods that organizations use to elicit desired employee behaviors, three of which are most common. In the first approach, agency managers attempt to *structure* the responsibilities and relationships of individuals. The second management approach uses a *distribution of power* within the organizations to get compliance from members. In the third type, agency managers attempt to cultivate among members a *feeling of psychological attachment* to and involvement in the organization. Through these and other techniques agency managers seek to take the multitude of isolated individuals the agency has hired and form them into a cohesive and integrated group. If these attempts are successful, the collective efforts of an agency's members often foster the best interests of the organization. Without such links between individuals and the organization, however, the agency runs the risk of having employees who decide for themselves what to do at work. The danger in this is obvious: If left to their own choices, people may not always choose to engage in tasks that are in the best interests of the organization.

Managing through Structure

One of the primary means for managing employee behavior is through the structural design of organizations. Historically, both Frederick Taylor's scientific management approach and Max Weber's vision of the modern bureaucracy reflect this approach to management (see Chapter 10). Included among the many structural management mechanisms are systems of specific job assignments and division of labor, a hierarchy of authority, standard operating procedures, and communication networks. Each of these structural mechanisms attempts to influence employee behavior by channeling it toward agency goals.

Job Assignments. An employee's job assignment serves to direct the individual's attention to specific tasks and to limit his or her responsibilities to a particular set of expectations, duties, and responsibilities. With job assignments, the agency says to the employee, "We want you to concentrate on these tasks and no others."

While helpful in maintaining some control over employee behavior, specific job assignments also have their drawbacks. For example, they can be annoying to citizens seeking public services. When a citizen has a specific problem that needs quick resolution (see Insight 10.1 in Chapter 10), he or she may have to contact several different public offices before reaching the person responsibile for dealing with the problem. The drawbacks of job assignments are most obvious to citizens when they encounter that time-worn response, "I'd like to help you, but that's not my job."

Another limitation of job assignments as a means for control is their ambiguity. Job descriptions are usually general and incomplete. As a result, situations often occur that require employee actions not specified in their job descriptions. This lack of clarity can prove troublesome when employees are too literal in their interpretation of written job assignments. Under such conditions, it is unlikely that workers will exert extra efforts to solve a special problem. Thus, job assignments must be as effective in providing flexibility as they are in establishing control over the organization's workforce. If employers fail to provide accurate job assignments, and employees are too literal in their interpretations of their job assignments, employees may be unlikely to exert effort beyond the call of duty, or to engage in any important facilitative behaviors.

Hierarchical Authority. Through a hierarchy of authority, an agency designates which individuals will act as supervisors responsible for holding their subordinates accountable for acceptable role behavior. In turn, supervisors have their behavior monitored by individuals at the next highest level in the agency, and so on up the organization to the highest level of supervision, the chief executive officer. Such a hierarchy increases the chances that the employee's role behaviors will be appropriate and consistent with organizational standards and expectations.

Hierarchy seems to come more naturally to government agencies than to private-sector organizations. Inherent in the operations of American government is the norm that the elected official is ultimately responsible for what occurs as a result of public-sector actions. It is assumed that the politician—whether serving as president, governor, mayor, sheriff, or in some other executive capacity—is able to exercise some control over those who work under his or her authority. To achieve this accountability, the politician appoints department or agency heads who carry out his or her orders. In turn, these top officials make managerial appointments within the agency to assure that the same relationship holds throughout the government organization. Thus, the hierarchy seems almost a natural response to a system that requires those who head a governmental unit to be responsible for the actions taken by that part of the public sector.

However, hierarchical authority does not guarantee that direct supervision will be applied. In many instances, a hierarchy operates through established rules or as a formal line of communication, rather than as a means for the direct exercise of control. In part, this is because the constant application of direct control is costly and often ineffective. When too stridently used to control employee behavior, hierarchical authority can weaken initiative within the agency or create a stultifying working climate.

We are more likely to see hierarchical authority invoked in situations involving investigations of who was responsible for some accident or error. For example, after several unrelated fatal accidents occurred aboard U.S. Navy vessels in October 1989, the chief of Naval Operations, Admiral Carlisle A.H. Trost, called for an investigation. Nearly two months later he issued a letter to navy commanders strongly criticizing them for "inadequate supervision, lax safety procedures and complacency. . . ."[4] Investigations such as this are carried out, blame (if any) is assessed, and sanctions are imposed (if warranted).

Standard Operating Procedures.   Standard operating procedures (SOPs) are rules of operation established by an organization that specify how to handle routine matters within the agency. SOPs help the organization control employees' behavior by limiting the need for individuals to exercise discretion. They reflect the results of the agency's efforts to anticipate likely circumstances and to specify authorized employee responses. Hence, SOPs minimize the need for employees to make decisions each time a routine issue arises.

The widespread existence of SOPs in the public sector is a tribute to both the complexity and large-scale operations of modern American government. Highly technical and complex tasks must often be carried out "according to the book" in order to ensure that they are correctly accomplished and to minimize the potential for favoritism. Each day workers at local sewage-treatment plants must follow a specified procedure for testing and treating city water. Failure to do so can lead to significant health and environmental problems for local or regional residents. SOPs are also common in the large-scale operations of the Social Security Administration, where handling the accounts of every U.S. resident would be impossible without some standardization of procedures.

One cost associated with excessive reliance on standard operating procedures is a stifling of innovation. When there are set ways to do things, newer, more efficient, or more creative ways of accomplishing the same tasks are often stifled. Since the agency already has approved procedures for certain tasks, there is little incentive to try new procedures. In addition, situations arise when employees need to ignore some of the rules (or "cut through the red tape") so that the organization can continue to run smoothly. Furthermore, supervisors are not always available for consultation when employees face nonroutine decisions.

Communication Networks.   Organizations may establish communication networks to direct the transmission of information throughout the agency. Communication networks can influence agency behavior by determining who shall have access to information and who shall be denied that same access.

Such networks serve several purposes. They insure that the individuals who need to know certain information receive it. Communication networks also keep employees from being overloaded or distracted by information irrelevant to their jobs. In addition, they serve to maintain secrecy within an organization. If someone is not part of an official communication network, then the agency does not consider the information transmitted along that network to be essential to that person's job. Although communication networks are used in both the private and public sectors, military and national security agencies are the most notable examples of organizations that operate on a "need-to-know" basis. These organizations have several classification levels of information.

Communication is a multidirectional process in all organizations. Formal communication networks usually make use of the agency's hierarchy by providing for the downward transmission of orders and policy initiatives and the upward transmission of information about performance. This combination of hierarchy and communication does have limitations. An excessive reliance on hierarchically defined formal communication networks tends to restrict input from employees lower in the organization. Oftentimes, employees at the heart of the organizational process (e.g., those who operate machinery or deal directly with clients) have valuable ideas about how to solve organizational problems as a result of their firsthand experiences. Yet, with a strict hierarchy and exclusive reliance on formal communication networks, the input of these employees is rarely solicited.

The transmission of information in public organizations is often lateral. Because information is the main currency of an organization, groups of individuals often develop informal communication networks—referred to as "the grapevines"—that supplement the more formal network. The grapevine is an instance of informal interpersonal dynamics (gossip along the grapevine), which can affect agency functioning for better or worse. Sometimes an informal grapevine serves to transmit information more broadly than a formal communication network. For example, when a state welfare agency considers revising the documentation requirements that welfare recipients must fulfill to qualify for aid, the grapevine can provide an opportunity for informal feedback on the feasibility of the proposed requirements. This process is known in bureaucratic jargon as "running it up the flag pole." At other times, however, the use of a grapevine can subvert agency functioning.

Managing through Power

Agencies can also use power within their organizations to gain compliance from members. As we noted in our discussion of bureaucratic power in Chapter 8, there are three different types of power: coercive, remunerative, and normative.[5] In our earlier discussion, we learned how agencies can use power to deal with external expectations. Here we focus on how agencies can use power to manage internal expectations. Each kind of power can be used to elicit predictable and desirable behavior from agency members.

Organizations using *coercive power* try to get people to behave in acceptable ways by relying on fear. Workers fear, for example, what would happen if they behaved unacceptably: they might lose their jobs. If an employee believes that no other job prospects outside the agency exist, then the threat of being fired can have the effect of coercion. Because of the demise of the supportive extended family and the limited scope of the American social welfare system, most people need their jobs to survive. Those who see little chance of getting another job are most susceptible to coercion. Many working women who come forward with complaints of sexual harassment report that they held off complaining because they feared losing their jobs.

While the threat of coercion is a possibility for most employees, steps have been taken in the public sector to reduce the abusive use of coercion in certain jobs. For example, professors and others who teach at state universities can gain job protection through tenure. After serving in a university for several years, professors are awarded tenure status, which protects them from being fired for arbitrary or political reasons (e.g., because of the views they publicly espouse or express). Without the threat of coercion, tenured instructors are less inhibited in promoting ideas that might not sit well with politicians or other powerful groups in the state or nation. As we will see in the following chapter, however, the protection of tenure is not limited to those in higher education. It is also a fundamental part of civil-service protections at every level of government. As we saw in Chapter 9, for example, special protections exist for whistle-blowers, who might not otherwise come forward with their evidence of illegal or unethical behavior (see Profile 9.1).

Another basis of power is the ability to reward people, referred to as *remunerative power*. This kind of power taps the calculations individuals make about the rewards they will receive for acceptable behavior. Under this system of power, employees may behave in acceptable ways because of the salary and fringe benefits they will receive. As we will see in Chapter 12, remuneration for public employees usually depends on what specific personnel system they belong to. While rarely a lucrative career, work in the public service is not entirely unrewarding relative to other careers. In fact, public servants' salaries are often based on studies that examine the salaries of private-sector employees in comparable positions.

The third basis of power in organizations is *normative*; that is, the influence derived from individuals' sense that they ought to behave in certain ways. Under this form of power, individuals choose to behave in acceptable ways because they want to further the values of the organization. Normative power works best when employees' personal values are consistent with those most important to the agency. For example, individuals who value a clean and healthy environment and work for the EPA could be relied upon to do their jobs because of the normative power of the shared values. Normative power is also extremely important in the military and in law-enforcement agencies, where danger and a strong sense of mission help to create the right kind of atmosphere for normative power.

The use of any type of power to gain employee compliance with agency needs has its limitations. Coercive power based on fear is not likely to work in many modern organizations, especially in the public sector where many employees are under civil-service protection (see Chapter 12). Even in those organizations where coercion is possible—such as in the military—supervisors are more likely to stimulate hostility rather than efficiency by using fear or force to get things done. Remunerative power is more likely to generate cooperation, but the costs involved can be quite high. The possibility of tapping normative power among public employees depends on the agency's values and the extent to which its members value serving the public by working in a government organization. Moreover, it may be difficult to establish normative power in an agency made up of employees who are ill-informed about the organization's mission or objectives.

Managing through Psychology

Given the inherent shortcomings of managing through structures and power, agencies often cultivate psychological attachments to supplement their efforts to elicit appropriate employee behavior. If successful, the agency is able to harness effectively the employee's conscience to work on behalf of the agency's interests. Through psychological ties, the organization hopes to increase the chances that individuals will exercise their administrative discretion in ways that are in the agency's best interests.

Organizational Socialization. Socialization is the process of inculcating the prevailing norms and values of a society or social group to its members. The most common arenas for the transmission of values are social institutions, such as the family, schools, churches, and organizations like the Boy Scouts or Campfire Girls. The transmission of the values of a public agency to its members is an example of the socialization process, one which is ongoing and focuses on adults. The way in which agencies attempt to cultivate the sharing of values is called *organizational socialization.*

Agencies engage in this socialization process through formal and informal means.[6] The formal process usually begins with an employee-orientation program, wherein key representatives explain the goals and policies of the agency. The socialization process continues at a much more informal level as new employees are introduced to their jobs and interact with their supervisors and co-workers. This is the first chance given new employees to observe and evaluate the values and operating norms of the agency.

Supervisors communicate the norms and values of the organization when they give directions about the standards for performance and expectations for observance of work rules. These expectations are reinforced through agency structure and power relationships. For example, a casual comment like "We all take long coffee breaks around here; what matters is that you get the job done, not how long you sit at your desk" may indicate to the new employee that this particular office does not worry about close accounting for time. Similarly, when a co-worker casually comments that agency accounting procedures dictate a strict accounting of expenses, then the new employee knows that fiscal integrity is one of the norms of the agency.

Employees are free to ignore the norms of the agency, but they do so at their own risk. In some instances, they risk only mild rebuke from their supervisors. In other instances, however, they may risk termination. The seriousness of the sanction depends on how central the value is to the organization's ideology.

Organizational Values. Although organizations hope that employees will share all their values, some values are much more important than others.[7] It is most important that employees share those values essential to the long-term survival of an agency—called *pivotal* values. Sharing nonessential or *peripheral* values is desirable but not mandatory for the successful functioning of the organization.

A pivotal value is essential to the long-term survival of an organization. In a tax-collection agency, for example, honesty is a pivotal value. If this agency's employees consistently violated this value, the agency would quickly lose the public's trust and may even undermine the legitimacy of the governing body itself. In a public safety organization, such as a police or fire department, discipline is a pivotal value. These organizations require their members to be willing to risk their lives. Hence, each member has to be able to rely on other members to act in a consistent manner and to obey orders.

Since pivotal values are essential to survival, agencies who find their employees not living up to pivotal values must take action. For example, a state auditor's office must insist on accuracy in order to survive and accomplish its mission (i.e., auditing the work of other state agencies). Employees not willing or able to live up to this pivotal value would have to leave the auditor's office.

An agency also holds peripheral values, which are not essential to its survival but are nonetheless widely shared within the agency. Some typical peripheral values include norms about employee socializing beyond the workplace and dress codes. Some agencies encourage employees to socialize after work by sponsoring softball teams and other social events. Other agencies have explicit policies discouraging such activities.

Organizational Involvement. When an agency socialization process is successful, its employees share at least the pivotal values of the agency. This sharing of values is called *organizational involvement*, or identification with the organization.[8] When employees feel psychologically involved in the organization, they accept the agency's pivotal values as part of their own value systems. For example, if employees of a city planning department accept the city's values regarding growth and development as part of their own value systems, then the city can rely on its employees to use those values when making decisions about zoning compliance.[9] The net result is that any discretionary decisions that planning department employees make are likely to be consistent with the interests of the city. Although employees who share the city's values may make errors in their decisions, those errors will be in reasoning rather than intentional violations of the intent of the zoning policies.

There are dangers associated with this tendency for employees to identify with their agencies. One danger takes the form of excessive rigidity of belief on the part of employees (see Profile 11.1)—referred to as the zealot or true believer phenomenon.[10] Zealous employees are generally unwilling or unable to see any faults in the operation of the agency or the need for change. Agencies with zealous employees are often severely constrained in their ability to adapt to changes in operations or programs.

PROFILE 11.1

Zoning Zealot

Zealots are people who have lost a sense of proportion in their work. Their extremely strong sense of identification with their work organization can blind them to the practical implications of implementing certain organizational policies. Because of this blindness, zealots go overboard in their enforcement of established rules and regulations and are usually resistant to change. They fail to see that such rigid enforcement of the rules may not be consistent with the original intentions of the requirements.

The approach of Michael Filippon, the building director for Garden City, New York, toward his job of enforcing zoning-code violations illustrates a zealot in action. Garden City has a zoning code that probihits "accessory structures" in the front half of lots. The penalty for violating this regulation (zoning law 200–52) is a fine of $250 a day. In June 1988, several residents of Garden City were notified that they were in violation of this regulation. It seems that the poles on which they installed basketball hoops are covered under this zoning law prohibition.

According to newspaper acounts, in 1988, city officials received scattered complaints about basketball hoops in driveways that might violate that regulation. Of course, most driveways and basketball poles are located in the front half of lots; hence, they violate the regulation. The building department conducted its own survey and found seventy-five illegal hoops.

One young, dedicated basketball player, Mike Epter, decided to do some research of his own after receiving notice that his hoop was in violation of the code. Epter studied the zoning book. He scouted the area and found that flagpoles and light posts in front yards were also in violation of the code. When asked about these inconsistencies, Filippon replied, "Look, I'll admit to you right now there are dozens and dozens of violations in this village. We don't have the manpower. . . . We're now in what I'd call Phase One."

Faced with pro-hoop residents, the [city] trustees are now reviewing the policy. Mr. Filippon worries that if hoops are allowed, everyone will want exceptions. He fears the slippery slope. Lately he has noticed small decorative walls popping up at the foot of driveways. "A violation," he said. "I don't know, maybe we'll have to make a survey of those walls."

SOURCE: Quotes and information from Michael Winerip, "Hoopsters and Village Poles Apart," *New York Times*, 26 July 1988, p. 12.

Need for Multiple Tactics

When trying to understand why an agency attempts to influence its members' behavior, we must recognize that the agency has to coordinate the activities of its employees or risk being ineffective. In seeking to elicit appropriate, predictable, and flexible employee behaviors, organizations use structural, power, and psychological tactics. In general, each of these tactics is only partially successful. Effective management of employee behavior requires the use of *multiple tactics*.

All of the best-executed plans to control employee behavior are susceptible to reinforcement and failure — people may react to organizational tactics by either cooperating or resisting agency efforts.

Factors Influencing Employee Reactions and Behavior

Public employees bring their human needs with them to work. They pursue these needs within the work setting, making them subject to the influence of the internal agency environment. Various internal factors can affect employees' expectations as well as their reactions to the agency's efforts (through structure, power, and psychology) to shape their behavior.

General Organizational Factors

Four aspects of the internal agency environment have the most dramatic impact on human behavior: *culture, climate, managerial philosophy*, and *resource availability*. Each of these aspects of organizational life can encourage or discourage certain kinds of employee behaviors and create or discourage employee expectations. The impact depends on employees' needs and the effects of the culture, climate, and managerial philosophy on employees' efforts to fulfill those needs.

Agency Culture.   An agency's culture reflects the most basic shared beliefs and assumptions by which individuals operate within the organization. The content of an agency's culture can have a dramatic effect on its members as well as on its ability to survive.[11] Cultural assumptions arise out of the agency's successful coping with its basic survival and adaptation to changes in its external and internal environments. The strategies and tactics that worked successfully in the past become widely accepted as the proper way to operate in the future. These beliefs and assumptions are so deep in the consciousness of organizational members and so taken for granted that members often are unaware of these beliefs.

Agency culture affects employee behavior by defining the thinkable and acceptable strategies for coping with changes in the agency's environment.

By logical extension, agency culture also defines the unthinkable strategies (i.e., strategies are unthinkable when they conflict with the culture's most basic assumptions).

Cultural assumptions are so fundamental and widely shared that agency members usually cannot even conceive of pursuing strategies inconsistent with them. For example, in the U.S. Postal Service (USPS), the concept of free delivery to all homes, whether urban or rural, is a basic assumption. Although the USPS needs to cut its costs as much as possible, eliminating rural free delivery is not seen as an acceptable way to do so. Similarly, in a wealthy city like Glencoe, Illinois, residents as well as city workers take for granted backdoor trash pick-up despite its rarity nationwide.

Although the content of an agency's cultural assumptions is not always accurate, this does not necessarily keep people from clinging to faulty basic assumptions. For example, the Flat Earth Society is an organization founded on the basic assumption that the earth is flat. Although today we have ample physical evidence that the earth is not flat, some people still cling to the old assumption. Likewise, some argue that the assumptions made by some government agencies are equally off-target. In the domestic policy arena, for example, there are ongoing debates over the appropriate assumptions to be used for designing and operating our welfare system. Should it be organized on the assumption that those who are on welfare are willing to work but unable to find work? Or should we assume that they are merely lazy individuals who enjoy living "on the dole" and therefore must be forced to find employment? In regards to U.S. foreign policy, consider the potential differences in how we might organize our international efforts. The emphasis in our foreign-aid programs and diplomatic efforts could be developed on the assumption that the Soviet Union is an "evil empire" bent on the destruction of the Western world, or on the assumption that the Soviets are "folks like us"—a world power trying to maintain its position in the world arena without having to resort to war or other forms of physical intervention. Dramatic changes in the governance of the Soviet Union and eastern Europe in the late 1980s brought the "evil empire" assumptions under sharp scrutiny. The opening of the Berlin Wall in 1989 was just one of the more significant events that symbolized the need for Americans to reconsider the assumptions of the cold war era.

Agency Climate.   As agency culture represents the shared assumptions of an organization's members, agency climate reflects the shared perceptions of employees about the quality of the work environment. An agency's climate covers a variety of dimensions, including the degree of trust, norms for handling conflict and openness of communication, degree of emphasis on reward versus punishment, degree of risk or caution encouraged in decision-making, degree of flexibility or rigidity concerning following rules, and expectations for employee commitment to the organization.

Each agency develops a distinctive character that reflects the prevailing norms and values by which it operates. Sometimes subunits of the same agency have different climates. This is possible because the perceptions that make up the climate are subjective. In other words, those perceptions may or may not be accurate assessments of organizational functioning, and different people may perceive the same behavior differently. The important point is that the perceptions become a reality to employees and can affect their expectations and behavior accordingly.

Research has shown that organizational climate can have significant effects on employee motivation and job performance.[12] Employees who perceive the agency's climate as hostile or suspicious are less likely to take advantage of opportunities to go beyond the call of duty in their job performance. Similarly, individuals who work in a climate that discourages risk taking are less likely to take risks in the performance of their jobs. For example, an agency climate characterized by rigid rule enforcement is likely to stifle employee innovation. Further, employees are likely to feel threatened by punishment if they fail to follow the agency's rules. Their perceptions may or may not be accurate, but what is important is that they believe punishment is likely. As a result, these employees are not likely to try doing things in new ways, even if those new ways might prove more efficient or effective.

In contrast, an agency climate that encourages openness of communication is likely to have employees who perceive the transmission of information—both good news and bad news—as acceptable. In an organization that discourages openness of communication, however, employees are more likely to view the transmission of complete information as working against them. In this agency, an individual may withhold information from others because he or she does not perceive that such information is valued. Or, a division of the agency may perceive that withholding information will give it an advantage in organizational decision making.

Managerial Philosophy. The managerial philosophy of an organization also affects its internal environment. Managerial philosophy affects behavior in the most basic way: People react to the treatment they receive. When treated with dignity, people usually respond with dignity. When treated with suspicion, people often respond with suspicion, thus setting up a cycle of defensive behaviors.

The most popular managerial philosophies are summarized by Douglas McGregor as Theory X and Theory Y. Recent elaborations of the concept of managerial philosophy have given rise to yet a third theory, called theory Z.[13] Each of these theories reflects some basic notions about human nature and how people are likely to behave in an organizational setting.

In the world of work, *Theory X* is the most common managerial philosophy. It presumes that most people are basically unreliable, lazy, and untrustworthy. Under this philosophy, management relies heavily on controlling employee behaviors through external forces — such as rules, tight supervision, the promise of monetary rewards, and threats of punishments. Recent patterns of elected officials (including Presidents Carter and Reagan) using harsh rhetoric to criticize public employees are examples of this managerial philosophy.

Theory Y is in sharp contrast to Theory X. Theory Y assumes that people are basically hard working, self-disciplined, responsible, trustworthy, and interested in having meaningful jobs. This theory stresses encouraging employee input into organizational problem solving and designing work settings that are challenging. Reward systems under Theory Y emphasize higher-order needs such as recognition, autonomy, opportunities for growth, and increasing responsibilities.

Theory Z assumes that people are basically social beings who are most highly motivated when they feel a sense of belonging and participation. Management under Theory Z tries to provide work conditions that encourage worker participation and foster organizational loyalty.

Given the diversity, complexity, and changeable nature of human needs, there is a danger in the wholesale adoption of any one managerial philosophy to the exclusion of the others. Each managerial philosophy makes assumptions that are not likely to be true of all individuals within an organization. Thus, each managerial philosophy is useful for only a portion of the agency's work force. The remaining employees — those motivated by needs other than those incorporated into the managerial philosophy — will find their needs in conflict with their manager's philosophy. While Theory X is likely to elicit appropriate behavior from people with physiological or safety needs, it is of little help with employees who have higher levels of needs. Similarly, Theory Y is likely to motivate employees with esteem and self-actualization needs, and Theory Z is most useful in motivating employees with needs of affiliation and belonging. Thus we see why agency efforts to shape employee behavior can never be completely successful.

Managerial philosophies are also of little value in identifying employees whose needs have changed recently or are likely to change in the near future. For instance, a city clerk who once responded well under Theory X techniques may have fulfilled his or her lower-order needs sufficiently. The clerk may now be motivated by the need for recognition, and hence would be better managed by the Theory Y philosophy.

Agency Resources and Constraints. The availability of agency resources and the existence of agency obstacles can affect employee behaviors and expectations. Resources enhance the likelihood of successful and desirable behaviors, whereas constraints hinder successful and desirable behaviors. Such factors include the design of the task itself (e.g., job design), resources made available to employees (such as support services or important raw materials), and the reward structure within the agency.

A job's design can be a resource or a constraint, depending on whether it facilitates accomplishment of the task or if it is not coordinated with other necessary jobs. The availability of resources can affect performance and expectations in obvious ways. For example, an employee needs the necessary raw materials to accomplish his or her job. These may include such simple things as a reliable photocopying machine or paper clips. Resources also can take the form of more subtle working conditions, such as the availability of a quiet, conducive work setting or cooperative co-workers. If the necessary raw materials and support services are available when the employee needs them, then the chances of success are better than if the individual must operate with shortages of raw materials or support services.

The organizational reward structure can be a resource or a constraint as well. If the reward structure is tied to performance, then employees are more likely to perceive links between their performance and outcomes. If, however, the reward structure relies on some other nonperformance measure, such as seniority or supervisory favoritism, then employees are not likely to perceive links between their performance and outcomes. Another way the reward structure can be an organizational constraint is if it is underfunded to such an extent that only insignificant rewards are available. This is a common circumstance in the public sector.

Coordinating Critical Factors. Agency culture, climate, managerial philosophy, and availability of agency resources and constraints can have significant and dramatic effects on employee expectations, motivation, performance, and job satisfaction. These organizational factors, in turn, can be critical in determining the success or failure of agency efforts to manage employee behavior.

It is important to have an agency culture that is consistent with the demands of the external environment and the needs for internal integration of employee activities. Agencies also need a climate that fosters the cooperation and coordination among employees essential to smooth organizational functioning. To do this the organizational climate must be at least minimally compatible with the needs of employees as human beings. Furthermore, the managerial philosophy affects employee behavior by setting a tone for the interaction between supervisor and subordinate. We must remember that agencies can organize themselves in ways that enhance or detract from employees' willingness and ability to perform in ways that benefit the organization.

Sometimes an organization does a poor job of coordinating these various internal factors, giving rise to an internal environment that sends contradictory messages to its members. For example, an organization that at once holds the basic cultural assumption that most of its employees are dispensable and yet professes to subscribe to a Theory Z managerial philosophy would be a confusing place for employees to work. This situation might occur even when agency managers sincerely convey to workers how indispensable they are. Despite attempted adherence to Theory Z, those same managers might rely more on Theory X approaches during times of crisis or challenge. Air-traffic controllers, for example, were constantly told that they were a vital and critical part of the national aviation system. They thus regarded themselves as part of a professional team, and in the late 1970s, they organized into the Professional Air Traffic Controllers Organization (PATCO), which lobbied hard for better wages and working conditions for its members. However, when PATCO members went on strike in 1981 and were then fired by President Reagan for doing so, they soon learned that being "vital" is not the same as being irreplaceable.

While the PATCO episode is an extreme case, there are numerous situations in which the basic operating assumptions of an agency contradict or clash with the managerial philosophy of those running the agency. Such situations are likely to create cynical, confused, or alienated employees. Similar problems arise when the organizational climate is inconsistent with the agency culture, or when the agency does not provide enough resources to enable its employees to accomplish their assignments.

Human Factors

In addition to general organizational factors, human factors such as leadership, group dynamics, and individual reactions to organizational and managerial efforts at control can influence employee behavior.

Leadership.   The nature and quality of leadership can affect the behavior of people in organizations. One authority defines *leadership* as a "process (act) of influencing the activities of an organized group in its efforts toward goal setting and goal achievement."[14] It is important to understand that leadership is a social relationship; there must be a follower before there can be a leader. Equally important, leadership is not the same as management.[15] Leadership is a factor that affects employees' behavior when nonroutine circumstances prevail. The application of administrative principles and rules of operation to routine organizational matters usually serves to direct behaviors in approved channels. But with extraordinary challenges, administration alone is not enough. This is when leadership becomes an important factor in organizational behavior. In nonroutine circumstances, a leader serves to stimulate the group (the followers) facing a challenge to go beyond their routine role behaviors, so that they may deal effectively with the challenge of new events. Leadership, then, serves to encourage employees to do more than they might otherwise do.

We see leadership working in this way in the Environmental Protection Agency (EPA) under William Ruckelshaus, who served as the first administrator of the agency during the Nixon administration (1970). Ruckelshaus helped to reinvigorate a severely demoralized EPA when he reassumed its

INSIGHT 11.1
MR. MEESE IN WONDERLAND

The Reagan administration provides us with another example of the effects of weak leadership on a public agency. The long-running ethics controversies surrounding the president's good friend, Attorney General Edwin Meese, had so demoralized key subordinates at the Department of Justice in the spring of 1988 that several resigned in protest.

In testimony before Congress in July 1988, former Deputy Attorney General Arnold I. Burns and William F. Weld, former head of the criminal division, charged that Meese's conduct in office made him unfit to head the Justice Department. Burns and Weld testified that they "had been brought to Washington by Mr. Meese, that they had once been loyal deputies to the Attorney General and that they had now come forward to accuse Mr. Meese of having disgraced his office." They charged that

> Mr. Meese had lost touch with reality, that he seemed oblivious to the fact [that] the work of the Justice Department was being impeded by a deep malaise that was setting in by virtue of Mr. Meese's problems and the public outcry for his resignation. You get a flavor of what life was like in the Department of Justice. It was a world of Alice in Wonderland — a world of illusion and allusion: a world in which up was down and down was up, in was out and out was in, happy was sad and sad was happy.

SOURCE: Quotes and information from Philip Shenon, "Two Former Top Aides Assail Meese Leadership," *New York Times*, 27 July 1988, p. 1, 8.

leadership in 1983, after its disastrous experience under the direction of Ann Gorsuch. (See Insight 11.1.) Another example of leadership in operation is the experience of the Chrysler Corporation under Lee Iacocca. The 1950s and 1960s were a time of relative prosperity and stability for the American automobile industry, and the Chrysler Corporation was able to get by on routine management decision making. When oil embargoes and foreign competition threatened Chrysler's survival in the 1970s, extraordinary decision making and motivation of the automobile manufacturer's work force were essential. Leadership was needed to accomplish several unprecedented changes in Chrysler's corporate operations, including obtaining federal loan guarantees and appointing a United Auto Workers union representative to the Chrysler Board of Directors. It took the dynamic leadership of Lee Iacocca (who had been recently dismissed as president of the Ford Motor Company) to negotiate the Chrysler Corporation through these troubled years.[16]

Few public-sector managers would enjoy the visibility or prestige of Iacocca, and so their stories are not well known. Among the twentieth-century American presidents, Franklin Roosevelt is best known for his ability to generate ideas and action from federal employees. He had what one historian calls a "competitive approach" to leadership. Using this approach, he tested his subordinates by putting them in situations where they would compete with each other for his attention and agreement. In short, Roosevelt led by letting his subordinates "fight it out."[17]

Among public servants, examples of leadership often focus on controversial agency heads whose motivations have been brought into question. However, three well-known effective agency leaders are Hyman Rickover, the Navy admiral credited with almost single-handedly creating the "nuclear Navy"; J. Edgar Hoover, who took the obscure Federal Bureau of Investigation (FBI) and made it into a central law-enforcement agency; and Robert Moses, who held numerous administrative positions in New York state and New York City and who is credited (even by his critics) with shaping the modern American city.[18]

Like other forms of organization behavior, what we know about leadership today dramatically contradicts what was once the conventional wisdom. It was once believed that leadership qualities were something one was born with and that all leaders shared certain inherent personality traits. Then the notion that leaders could be trained gained popularity. Now the contingency theory of leadership has widespread acceptance.[19]

The contingency approach to leadership suggests that different circumstances require different leadership behavior. Furthermore, individuals who exhibit leadership qualities under some circumstances are not necessarily equally effective under different circumstances. Although certain individuals may be born with leadership potential, that potential must be cultivated by systematic exposure to personal and career development opportunities.[20]

Among theorists there is general agreement that leadership consists of two separate orientations: task and relationship.[21] A leader with a *task orientation* emphasizes the accomplishment of the assignment, such as the availability of resources, the necessary skill levels, the time frame for completion of the assignment, and so on. A *relationship-oriented* leader emphasizes the people who are to carry out the assignment and how they feel about handling the assignment in the belief that task accomplishment grows out of good working relationships. Researchers have found that the more successful managers maintain a balance between these two orientations. These managers emphasize task *or* relationship, depending on the situation, rather than relying exclusively on one or the other.[22]

Thus, leadership is the process of getting people to go beyond their routine organizational behaviors when events call for them to do so. Leadership gets everyone to exert their extra effort in a concerted direction rather than having everyone going off in uncoordinated directions. As such, it can be a potent tool for influencing employee expectations and managing their behavior. Effective leadership can be either task or relationship oriented, depending on the circumstances and individuals involved.

Group Dynamics.   Individuals are also susceptible to influence from the dynamics of the groups they work in. The formation of groups is unavoidable in an organizational setting. For the most part, they are welcomed by employees as an important source of fulfilling personal needs, such as friendship and recognition. Further, most of the work in organizations is done in groups or requires a coordinated group effort. Thus, group interaction is more than just a social need of individuals.

Agencies can take advantage of the presence of groups. The interaction and friendships that arise in groups can enhance job performance. Friendships can enhance the communication processes and employees' willingness to engage in facilitative behaviors, especially if the behavior is for the sake of a friend in another part of the organization.

Formal groups within an agency are comprised of individuals who interact because the structure of the organization and their work roles make such interaction unavoidable. For example, the employees who work in payroll or the motor pool constitute the payroll and motor-pool groups. *Informal groups* can also arise from the structure of work roles; the important difference is that the interaction is voluntary. Informal groups reflect casual and voluntary patterns of interaction among members, such as employees who take their coffee breaks together or play on the agency softball team. Both formal and informal groups can affect individuals' attitudes toward their jobs, the overall organization, and other groups within the agency.

Like all social groups, formal and informal groups develop norms of behavior for their members. Groups can facilitate or obstruct organizational functioning by the norms they set, the communication patterns they support, and the rewards they provide members. Sometimes the group norms are compatible with the agency's goals and priorities. At other times, however, group norms are in conflict with the agency's norms and expectations for behavior. For example, when a particular group within an organization sets for itself a goal of being the most productive group, then the group's norms enhance the overall functioning of the agency. Similarly, groups that encourage open communication and cooperation across group lines are likely to enhance organizational functioning more than groups that foster closed communication, secrecy, or competition with other groups.

A classic example of group norms conflicting with organizational goals occurs when groups set informal norms for productivity. For example, in the U.S. Postal Service (USPS) there are norms for the amount of time it should take to sort and deliver mail. Most agencies have general norms regarding the minimum productivity expected of employees. Individuals who produce above or below the acceptable range often face pressure from group members, either through ridicule or, in extreme cases, ostracism.[23]

Groups also have their own dynamics that can enhance or hinder their effectiveness on the job. One problem to which groups are susceptible is *groupthink* — a phenomenon that occurs when a group strives so hard for cohesion and agreement that critical and independent thinking among its members is discouraged if not completely sacrificed.[24] Psychological experiments have shown how difficult it is for an individual to express an opinion contrary to the collective opinion of the group, even when the individual strongly supports the contrary opinion. The pressures of groupthink that operate in experimental settings (in which the subject is not personally acquainted with the other members of the group) can have a substantial impact on individual behavior. The pressures are likely to be even stronger when the individual is a long-standing member of the group and values continued membership. Pressures to conform to the group's opinions contribute to a tendency on the part of individual members to change their opinions to coincide with that of the other group members. They also foster a tendency to try to change the opinions of others as well as to redraw the group boundaries to exclude individuals who disagree with the consensus.[25]

Individual Factors.   Another set of factors entering into the management picture relates to the actions and reactions of employees who are trying to meet their own personal needs. The agency environment provides a context within which employees try to do this—a situation that agency managers can take advantage of.

Chester Barnard and Herbert Simon formulated a theory of the motivation underlying the *inducements and contributions* that individuals make as a result of their organizational membership.[26] Inducements are desired by employees; contributions are those individual behaviors that positively relate to the functioning of the agency. Inducements can include a sense of personal fulfillment—as would be the case for employees of the Civil Rights Commission who strongly value the cause of civil rights—as well as more mundane factors like salary. Contributions can range from hours of labor to being available to respond to emergencies at any hour of the day. According to Barnard and Simon, employees are motivated to maximize, or at least increase, their inducements while keeping their contributions in balance with their inducements. In other words, individuals hope to get as much out of their employment in the agency as they give back. The experiences of individuals within the agency can affect how they calculate these inducements and contributions.

Many other factors influence employees' decisions about how to behave at work that go beyond a motivation to satisfy their personal needs. These factors include the employees' expectations of the likely results of their efforts, the nature of agency resources and constraints relevant to their job tasks, and employees' skills and abilities. The term we apply to the theory that helps us understand the effects of these factors is *expectancy theory*.[27] Expectancy theory explains the links between effort and performance and between performance and work outcomes. At the same time, expectancy theory recognizes the influence of the idiosyncratic force of employee perceptions.

According to expectancy theory, people make conscious decisions about their behavior. They base their decisions on calculations of the subjective probabilities (the chances or odds) that, if they try a particular task, they will be successful in their efforts. Another factor in their calculations is their estimation of the probability that, if they are successful, certain anticipated outcomes will occur. A final consideration is the degree to which an individual values the outcomes that are likely to be forthcoming. In other words, people will put forth the effort if they think they can do the task successfully *and* if they think their performance will result in outcomes they desire. If the outcomes are undesirable or unlikely to be forthcoming, then employees are not likely to expend the effort. Figure 11.2 highlights the influence of employees' perceptions and calculations (of probabilities or expectations) on their behaviors. Employees calculate the amount of effort required to do a particular task and the likelihood that their efforts will result in success. They also calculate the chances of that success resulting in an outcome that they value. If employees decide that the task will take an inordinate amount of effort or that the probability of success is too low, they may decide not to exert the effort. If they decide that the task will take a reasonable amount of effort, they may decide to give it a try. If they decide that their efforts have a low probability of success no matter how much effort they put forth, then they may decide not to exert the effort. Alternatively, if they think that they can accomplish the task with a reasonable amount of effort *but* they do not think there will be any reward (or punishment if they fail) forthcoming, then they may decide not to exert the effort.

Employee perceptions and expectations of success are necessarily subjective and hence are susceptible to errors of judgment. In fact, people often are mistaken in their calculations of the probabilities for success or of forthcoming rewards. For example, an employee may grossly overestimate his or her ability relevant to the task at hand. Similarly, an individual may underestimate his or her ability to accomplish the task at hand and decide not to pursue the project at all, for fear of failure. Each of us probably can name at least a few people who consistently over- or underestimate their abilities. Organizations (through their cultures, climates, managerial philosophies, and use of resources) can influence an individual's calculation of these subjective probabilities.

Employees also may make errors in judgment as to the likelihood that

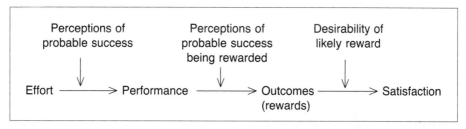

FIGURE 11.2 Expectancy theory. (Source: Adapted from David A. Nadler, J. Richard Hackman, and Edward E. Lawler, III, *Managing Organizational Behavior* [Boston: Little, Brown, 1979, Figures 2.2 and 2.3.])

their supervisors will recognize their success and reward them. Similarly, employees may misjudge the extent to which they will value a reward once it is forthcoming. In other words, they may be successful and appropriately rewarded, but the reward may not yield the satisfaction that they had anticipated.

Besides this potential for errors in judgment, there is another important caution about expectancy theory as the sole explanation for employee behaviors: It is based on the questionable assumption that people always act on the basis of conscious decisions.

Employee skills and abilities are yet other factors that can affect expectations and behavior in obvious ways. Individuals who lack the skills or abilities necessary to accomplish their assigned tasks are not likely to be successful at accomplishing them, no matter how hard they try. Another problem in performance occurs when an employee has skills or abilities that far exceed those needed for the job. Someone who is highly overqualified for a job may quickly become bored with work and fail to put forth the effort needed.

Beyond Motivation

Human factors—including leadership, group dynamics, and individual factors—together yield a complicated picture of what influences the behavior of employees in organizations. Figure 11.3 diagrams these relationships and summarizes the major point of our discussion: Not all performance successes or problems are a result of employee motivation. Other factors, including employee perceptions, organizational resources and constraints, and individual skills and abilities, can also influence behaviors. Consequently, when there is a problem with employee performance, improvement may necessitate something more than just figuring out the motivation of employees.

Behavior is not exclusively a matter of employees' attitudes about work;

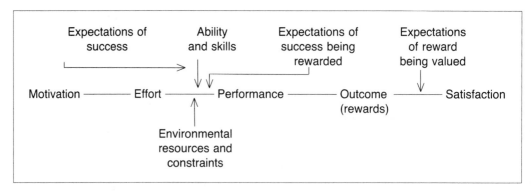

FIGURE 11.3 The basic motivation–behavior sequence. (Source: Adapted from David A. Nadler, J. Richard Hackman, and Edward E. Lawler, III, *Managing Organizational Behavior* [Boston: Little, Brown, 1979], p. 37.)

other factors are also important. No matter how much they want to behave in an appropriate manner, employees may not be able to do so. Employees need to have the requisite skills and abilities and organizational resources to do their jobs successfully.

Linkages between Individuals and Organizations

For a successful working relationship to develop between agency and employee, the agency must reconcile its expectations and needs with those of its employees. If the agency's efforts to manage employee behavior are compatible with employees' efforts to fulfill their personal needs, then a successful relationship is likely to be forged. A successful relationship occurs when what the agency needs from its employees corresponds with what employees want to give the organization. When either agencies or employees cannot meet their needs, then less than desirable outcomes are likely. When agency efforts at control result in employee reactions that are in the desired direction, then a successful organization–employee linkage is formed.

There are several processes by which agencies and individuals try to reconcile their separate interests and forge an effective link between them. There are also several possible linkages that result from efforts to reconcile individual and organizational needs and expectations. *Explicit linkages* are forged in direct discussions of responsibilities and privileges of membership. *Implicit linkages* occur at the psychological level. Both kinds of linkages result when organizational and individual needs and expectations are reconciled. When the reconciliation is inadequate, a weak linkage between the individual and the organization is likely. Weak or faulty linkages can have a detrimental effect on the chances for a successful long-term relationship between the agency and employee.

Explicit Linkages: Employment Contracts

When individuals join an agency, both the organization and the employees explicitly agree to abide by certain terms of membership. Those terms of membership, which specify the responsibilities and privileges of belonging to the organization, reflect the needs and expectations of both the agency and its employees. For example, because an organization such as a private club needs financial support from its members, it is likely to require a membership fee. Similarly, individuals expect to avail themselves of the various privileges of membership, such as access to organizational facilities, benefits, and opportunities.

For employees, the terms of membership are outlined explicitly in the employment contract. The *employment contract* specifies the terms of the work relationship by which both the agency and its employees agree to abide. If the individual does the assigned job, then the agency will provide certain rewards. The employment contract defines job duties, working conditions, degree of responsibility, regular and overtime rates of pay, hours of work, vacation and sick leave, retirement benefits, and so on. For example, a typical employment contract provides that, if the individual shows up on time for work and does the job satisfactorily, then the agency will provide the individual with the agreed-upon amount of wages, vacation and sick leave, and retirement benefits.

The general public usually associates the notion of an employment contract with unions. Union-negotiated contracts specify the terms of employment for all individuals included in the agreement, covering such areas as wages, seniority rights, and grievance procedures. Organizations without unionized employees also have explicit employment agreements with their employees that cover the basic terms of pay, job assignment, and vacation/sick-leave accrual rates. For public-sector employees, civil service rules and guidelines established by legislation specify the terms of their employment contracts.

Nonunion employment agreements are not usually the result of lengthy negotiations. In fact, in the public sector, most of the terms are preset in legislation. Nonetheless, these employment contracts represent explicit understandings between individual and employer regarding what the individual will give to the organization in exchange for benefits the employer agrees to provide. These agreements are usually concluded at the time an individual is hired, although they may be modified when an employee is transferred or promoted. When an employee leaves the organization, the employment contract is terminated.

We usually know when the explicit linkage between the organization and one of its employees has gone awry. Typically, there is some observable event that indicates a failure of the employment contract. For instance, an employee who fails to perform adequately is likely to face some form of sanction, such as suspension, leave without pay, or termination. Public employees who are negligent or irresponsible in the discharge of their job duties may also face legal liability. The Supreme Court holds that a government employee is liable for damages "if he knew or reasonably should have known that the action he took within his sphere of responsibility would violate" a citizen's constitutional rights.[28]

When employees believe the organization has failed to live up to its part of the employment agreement, they are likely to behave in predictable ways. For example, employees who feel they did not receive the rewards due them may file grievances, quit, find excuses to use sick leave, goof off on the job, or (at the most extreme) sue their employer. In short, noncompliance with the terms of the employment contract is likely to lead to a lowering of employee performance levels in some form or other.

Because of its explicit nature, an employment contract is usually enforceable in a court of law. For example, if your employer agrees to pay you $8.50 an hour for a certain job and you perform that job satisfactorily, the employer must pay you the agreed rate. The organization cannot decide unilaterally that the job you did was worth only $5.75 an hour. If it did so, it would set itself up for a lawsuit for breach of contract. The areas in which managers have more discretion, such as merit pay and promotion decisions, are those more likely to generate lawsuits.

Implicit Linkages

In contrast to explicit linkages like the employment contract, implicit linkages between individuals and organizations are somewhat amorphous. Implicit expectations focus on the costs and benefits of membership for each party to the relationship. They are important to the success of the employee–organization relationship.

Implicit linkages are the often unarticulated hopes and feelings about what each party is expected to contribute and accomplish in the employee–organization relationship. These notions rarely are discussed directly. When such issues are raised, it is usually because the implicit linkage is weak or faulty.

Implicit linkages between individuals and organizations develop around three separate bases. The first involves a *psychological contract* between the organization and the individual. The second is a sense of *commitment*, a linkage which forms when the personal values of the employee are compatible with the pivotal values of the organization. The third is a sense of employee *investment* in the organization.

Psychological Contracts. A psychological contract is an unwritten set of expectations that both the individual and the organization bring to their relationship.[29] These expectations are labeled "psychological" because they reflect unarticulated hopes and feelings rather than concrete demands. They focus on more subtle aspects of the work relationship than those covered in explicit employment contracts. These expectations constitute a contract because both parties consider their expectations to be part of the bargain they struck when they mutually agreed to form a relationship.

Some individuals may expect a certain kind of treatment from supervisors or have hopes for opportunities for promotion or for meeting interesting people. For example, an employee may have expectations of being treated with dignity by supervisors or of opportunities for early promotion. Another common expectation is that valuable experience will be gained toward advancing a career. Employees also have expectations about how much effort they will need to exert to be a member of the organization. For example, individuals may accept some routine jobs on the basis that the agency will require little effort from them and no overtime. Under other circumstances, employees may accept jobs thinking that they will have to work extra hours just to do their assigned tasks. Employees of a state's budget office, for instance, can expect to put in many additional hours during critical periods in the budgetary process.

On the agency's side, there are implicit expectations about employees' effort, quality of performance, loyalty, and retention. These are unstated assumptions that the agency makes about its employees. It hopes, for instance, that its employees will be willing to exert effort above and beyond the call of duty when emergencies arise, and it expects its employees to be loyal to the organization. Occasionally, an implicit expectation is indirectly manifested. Sometimes agencies make benefits available to their employees in the hopes that such benefits will be advantageous to the organization. For example, an agency that makes a college tuition-reimbursement plan available to its employees does so with the implicit expectation that employees who take advantage of the program will not leave the agency soon after graduating from college. In some cases, if they do leave, they must repay the cost of the tuition.

When both parties to a psychological contract feel the other side has lived up to the terms of the agreement, then the implicit linkage between individual and agency is likely to be strong. Under such circumstances, both the employees' needs as human beings and the agency's needs for productive, loyal, and flexible employees are fulfilled. But like the employment contract, the terms of the psychological contract also change over time. As agency environments and personal circumstances change, the implicit needs and expectations of organizations and employees change as well. An agency that at one time sought creative input from its employees may experience changes in its environment that necessitate changes in the kind of behavior needed from employees. An agency that is trying to implement a new program may need employees who are able to work with minimal direction simply because the agency is entering into a new area of management. Later, the organization may need employees who are more willing to comply with established routines. Similar changes can occur for individuals. People who once found jobs acceptable because of the opportunities for promotion may later feel a need for better treatment from their supervisors or the need to work in a more stimulating environment.

As needs and expectations change, there is a need for a renegotiation of the psychological contract. If the adjustment is not mutual, then there may be a feeling of betrayal similar to that of a breach of contract. In other words, if the agency's expectations for its employees change but the employees do not adjust their expectations of their necessary contributions accordingly, then the psychological contract is strained. Either the agency feels let down when its employees do not adjust accordingly or the employees feel that the organization has changed the rules unfairly, expecting behaviors from them that they never agreed to contribute.

Such renegotiations of the psychological contract are most likely to occur during times of change. For instance, when an agency is threatened by some external force, employees may be willing to work harder or longer hours than before in the interests of helping the agency cope with the threat. Changes in an employee's personal situation, such as divorce or a lengthy illness of a family member, may also initiate renegotiations of the psychological contract for the affected individual. Under the stress of such changes in their personal lives, people may not be willing or able to bring the same level of intensity or effort to their work. A newly divorced parent, for instance, may reorient his or her priorities away from work because of increased family responsibilities.

Commitment. Another way individuals and agencies can form an implicit linkage is through commitment to the organization. This situation occurs when the values important to the survival and effectiveness of the agency are the same as those held by its employees. This connection has an implicit character because the sharing of values rarely is advocated openly.

Essentially, employee commitment reflects a psychological attachment, or organizational involvement, that develops between the individual and the agency. We see the importance of employee commitment in management's efforts to recruit people who "fit in"—that is, who already hold key organizational values as their own personal values. Agency socialization processes that transmit organizational values to members are specifically geared to communicating the important, pivotal agency values to individuals—in the hope that, if employees do not already share important values, they will accept them as their own in time.

Research has found that agencies differ in the levels of value sharing they are able to elicit from their employees.[30] Some agencies apparently are better than others in forging commitment among employees. Employees whose expectations are met in the workplace are likely to have higher levels of commitment than those with unmet expectations.[31] Employees who feel committed to the organization are more likely to be willing to exert effort above and beyond the limits of their official job responsibilities. Committed employees want to do the little bit extra needed to get the job done because they accept the organization's goals and values as their own.

Investments. Employees can develop ties to the organization based on investments they have made in the workplace or on important values they share with the organization. Feelings of investment in the organization result when employees feel they have more to gain from staying with the organization than from leaving it. The nature of the tie depends on what the employee wants out of work and what the organization has to offer its employees. Individuals who feel they have invested a great deal of time and energy in an organization often decide to stay with the organization because of what they have already contributed (e.g., the time and money they have invested toward retirement, seniority, promotion opportunities, and the like).[32]

Getting employees to feel they have a valuable investment in the organization is not complicated, although investment ties are oftentimes expensive to develop and maintain. To foster these ties, the agency has to offer opportunities and working conditions that are competitive with other prospective employers. Once employees have accrued investments in an organization, the agency need only remain competitive with other organizations in terms of the opportunities it offers its employees.

Without a competitive stance on investment opportunities, the agency runs the risk of losing employees who may have more to gain by changing employers than by staying where they are. Investment-oriented employees can be lured away by competitors who offer them higher salaries, better retirement plans, greater promotion opportunities, more office perks, and so on. To the extent that an agency emphasizes investments as a tie for its employees, it is subject to the vagaries of the marketplace. As such, its ability to attract and retain qualified employees may be influenced by what its competitors are offering their employees. In this way, an organization's recruitment and retention patterns can be influenced by circumstances beyond its control.

Weak Linkages

The opportunities for linkages between the employee and the organization have positive and negative aspects. As we have seen, positive consequences result when the organization's efforts at control adjust effectively to the organizational and human factors that determine employee behavior (see Figure 11.1). But what happens when no such effective adjustment occurs? What if the organization's efforts at control generate negative responses from employees? And what if managerial controls cannot overcome the barriers imposed by organizational constraints? The results are weak linkages between agencies and their employees.

The existence of or potential for weak linkages is important in understanding organizational behavior because it represents distorted employee expectations and diminished employee performance. Weak linkages have negative consequences and obviously detract from the agency's ability to manage its internal environment. Sometimes the consequences are the result of an inappropriate application of a rule or managerial philosophy (see Insight 11.2).

What are the options facing an organization plagued with weak linkages? One option is for the organization to continue to operate with no adjustments—that is, to "muddle through" its day-to-day activities despite the problems and inefficiencies of weak linkages. A second option is for either the agency or the employee to terminate the relationship. An individual's decision to resign from an agency or an agency's decision to fire an employee is not taken lightly in the public sector, particularly when either party has

INSIGHT 11.2
MISMANAGEMENT IN THE MAIL ROOM

The U.S. Postal Service (USPS) has been the subject of much criticism and humor in recent years. Ever since it was reorganized from a cabinet-level department to an independent government corporation in 1971, the USPS has had its problems. While postal rates have increased (first-class rates for a 1-ounce letter went from 8 cents in 1971 to 25 cents in 1988), service levels and productivity in the post office have steadily declined. Some attribute these contradictory trends to the agency's "impossible missions," which mandate that the USPS break even financially while providing unique services at rates that guarantee it will always come out "in the red."

Another plausible argument states that the problems with the USPS are due as much to mismanagement as they are to conflicting expectations. Supporting this perspective is evidence of management policies that fail to generate the kind of behavior that enhance worker productivity. One such policy prohibits letter carriers and those who process letters in postal facilities from dealing with improperly addressed mail. For example, if a letter carrier or sorter comes across an envelope with an incorrect ZIP code, he or she is required to return the envelope to the central mail facility rather than make the necessary (and helpful) correc-

tion. While the rationale behind this policy may warrant its existence, the policy's impact on postal workers has not been positive. This and similar regulations governing the work of postal workers fill a dictionary-size volume that, according to one observer, is usually enforced with "a turn-of-the-century factory-floor discipline that may actually reduce efficiency."

Perhaps the most dramatic example of mismanagement in the USPS occurred in Indianapolis in 1988, where a glass cage was installed in the middle of a postal mail room. "Postal workers injured on the job were required to spend the day in the cage, rather than at home, and were not allowed even to read. The effect on employees was to discourage productivity," for if employees worked hard they might be injured and find themselves the subject of this punishment through public humiliation. Although complaints made through the union led to the removal of the cage within a few months, the management approach that created the "glass cage" tactic is still largely at work in the USPS.

SOURCE: Quotes and information from John B. Judis, "Mission Impossible," *New York Times Magazine*, 25 Sept. 1988, pp. 30–33, 50–51, 54.

a significant investment in the other. A third option is for either or both parties to take some action that will strengthen the relationship in the future. The agency might adjust to the needs of its employees or vice versa. Contracts—explicit and implicit—can be renegotiated and modified. Weak linkages do not have to be permanent.

Coming up Short

We have explored the need for agencies to manage employee behavior and the various tactics used toward that end. We have discussed the potential positive and negative outcomes when agency efforts at control meet individual efforts to fulfill their human needs in the workplace. Human behavior in organizations is a function of the relationship that develops between individuals and the agency. This relationship is affected by forces in the external and internal environments. Some relationships are mutually beneficial. Others are tilted in favor of one party or the other. Still other relationships are mutually dissatisfactory. This last kind of relationship does not tend to last for long; generally, one or both parties seek to end a mutually dissatisfactory relationship.

All agency plans and efforts at controlling individual behaviors are destined to come up short. They prove to be ineffective to some degree. While structure, power, and psychological strategies for influencing employee behaviors can be partially effective, the human idiosyncrasies people bring with them to the workplace make complete control impossible. But this inability to dictate completely employee behaviors is healthy for organizations. It is healthy because the human factor is the only factor that can deal with unforeseen events in creative ways. Human creativity and adaptability enable the agency to accommodate changes in its environment and therefore enhance its chances of survival.

Agency efforts to manage employee behaviors are affected by the expectations that employees bring to work and their reactions to their experiences and treatment at work. Agency managers who take their employees for granted, who try to administer without regard to the concerns of the employees, are destined to find their management efforts yielding undesirable employee behavior. They are likely to find themselves in a situation similar to that which President Harry Truman predicted incoming President Dwight Eisenhower would encounter as chief executive: "He'll sit here and he'll say, 'Do this! Do that!' *And nothing will happen.* Poor Ike—it won't be a bit like the Army. He'll find it very frustrating."[33] And Eisenhower did have this experience. If the president of the United States can be shocked and dismayed because his orders as chief executive are not carried out, then lower-level public administrators (who have so much less power) can expect the same factors to affect their experiences.

Summary

1. One of the basic tasks facing all public-agency managers is dealing with the tensions and opportunities arising from what their organizations demand from employees and the human needs and personal requirements of agency workers.
2. The Hawthorne experiments of the 1920s highlight the importance of human and social relations in all organizations. Since that time, students of management have been trying to understand how organizations deal with human behavior. The result has been the development of contingency theories of organizational behavior.
3. The manager's task is to harness the self-interested or cooperative tendencies of individuals and groups within the agency for organizational purposes, while minimizing the counterproductive impacts of employee behaviors. Managers attempt to do this through structural arrangements, the distribution of power, and developing psychological attachments between the organization and its employees.
4. Agencies must contend with a variety of organizational and human factors that both support and constrain their efforts. These include agency culture, agency climate, managerial philosophy, agency resources, leadership, group dyanamics, and individual responses to managerial efforts.
5. Management efforts ultimately result in the formation of linkages between the employee and the organization. These linkages can be explicit or implicit, strong or weak. However, the manager can never be completely successful in controlling employee behavior.

Study Questions

1. List the pivotal and peripheral values of some group of which you are a member (e.g., the university, a student group, church).
2. Briefly outline your classroom or social encounters that illustrate the different managerial philosophies of Theories X, Y, and Z.
3. Outline the provisions of the explicit contract between the students and the instructor in this class. How would the students respond if the provisions of this contract were not met by the instructor? How would the instructor respond if the students failed to live up to the contract?
4. Outline the content of the implicit psychological contract between yourself and the instructor in this class. What do you expect to give to and get from this class? What do you think the instructor expects to give to and get from you?
5. If you have a part-time or full-time job, repeat the tasks described in questions 1–4 for your place of employment.

Notes

1. F. J. Roethlisberger and P. Dickson, *Management and the Worker* (Cambridge, MA: Harvard University Press, 1939).

2. Chester I. Barnard, *The Functions of the Executive* (Cambridge, MA: Harvard University Press, 1938/1968).

3. The notion of a contingency theory is generally derived from Fred Fiedler's work on leader–member relationships. See, for example, F. E. Fiedler, "A Contingency Model of Leadership Effectiveness," in *Advances in Experimental Social Psychology*, vol. 1, ed. by Leonard Berkowitz (New York: Academic Press, 1964), pp. 149–90. The state of knowledge about human behavior in organizations is characterized by this same limited ability to generalize beyond narrowly proscribed boundaries. Hence, the term *contingency theory* as used here is meant to have a broader application than that proposed by Fiedler.

4. Michael R. Gordon, "Navy Chief Says Lapses in Safety Led to Series of Deadly Accidents," *New York Times*, 20 Dec. 1989, p. A20.

5. See Amitai Etzioni, *A Comparative Analysis of Complex Organizations: On Power, Involvement, and Their Correlates*, rev. ed. (New York: The Free Press, 1975). For an alternative conceptualization of the social bases of power, see John French, Jr. and Bertram Raven, "The Bases of Social Power," in *Group Dynamics: Research and Theory*, ed. by Dorwin Cartwright and A. F. Zander (New York: Harper & Row, 1960), pp. 607–23.

6. See John Van Maanen "Breaking In: Socialization to Work," in *Handbook of Work, Organization, and Society*, ed. by Robert Dubin (Chicago: Rand McNally, 1976), chap. 3.

7. This discussion draws on the work of Edgar H. Schein, *Organizational Psychology*, 3d ed. (Englewood Cliffs, NJ: Prentice-Hall, 1980).

8. See Barbara S. Romzek and J. Stephen Hendricks, "Organizational Involvement and Representative Bureaucracy: Can We Have It Both Ways?" *American Political Science Review* 76 (March 1982): 75–82.

9. For a thorough discussion of the impact of identification on decision making, see Herbert Simon, *Administrative Behavior: A Study of Decision-Making Processes in Administrative Organizations*, 3d ed. (New York: The Free Press, 1976), esp. chap. 10.

10. On the benefits and drawbacks of zealots in organizations, see Anthony Downs, *Inside Bureaucracy* (Boston: Little, Brown, 1967), esp. pp. 109–10.

11. For a more extensive discussion of organizational culture, see Edgar H. Schein, *Organizational Culture and Leadership* (New York: Jossey-Bass, 1985).

12. See George H. Litwin, "Climate and Motivation: An Experimental Study," in *Organizational Psychology: A Book of Readings*, 3d ed., ed. by David A. Kolb, Irwin M. Rubin, and James M. McIntyre (Englewood Cliffs, NJ: Prentice-Hall, 1979), pp. 147–60; and John S. Kimberly and Warren R. Nielsen, "Organization Development and Change in Organizational Performance," *Administrative Science Quarterly* 20 (September 1975): 196–201.

13. See Douglas McGregor, *The Human Side of Enterprise* (New York: McGraw-Hill, 1960); and William G. Ouchi, *Theory Z: How American Business Can Meet the Japanese Challenge* (Reading, MA: Addison-Wesley, 1981).

14. See Ralph M. Stogdill, *Handbook of Leadership: A Survey of Theory and Research* (New York: The Free Press, 1974).

15. Abraham Zaleznik, "Managers and Leaders: Are They Different?" *Harvard Business Review* 55 (May–June 1977): 67–78.

16. Lee Iacocca, with William Novak, *Iacocca: An Autobiography* (New York: Bantam Books, 1984).

17. See Arthur M. Schlesinger, Jr., *The Coming of the New Deal* (Boston: Houghton Mifflin, 1959), pp. 535–36.

18. Eugene Lewis, *Public Entrepreneurship: Toward a Theory of Bureaucratic Power; The Organizational Lives of Hyman Rickover, J. Edgar Hoover and Robert Moses* (Bloomington: Indiana University Press, 1980).

19. See Fred E. Fielder, *A Theory of Leadership Effectiveness* (New York: McGraw-Hill, 1967); and Fred E. Fiedler, "The Leadership Game: Matching the Man to the Situation," *Organizational Dynamics* 4 (Winter 1976): 6–16.

20. See W. Warner Burke, "Leaders: Their Behavior and Development," in *Managing Organizations: Readings and Cases*, ed. by David Nadler, Michael Tushman, and Nina Hatvany (Boston: Little, Brown, 1982), chap. 18.

21. See Robert R. Blake and Jane S. Mouton, *The Managerial Grid* (Houston: Gulf Publishing, 1964); and R. F. Bales, *Interaction Process Analysis* (Reading, MA: Addison-Wesley, 1950).

22. See John Hall, "To Achieve or Not: The Manager's Choice," *California Management Review* 18 (Summer 1976): 5–18; and Janet T. Spence and Robert L. Helmreich, *Masculinity and Femininity: Their Psychological Dimensions, Correlates, and Antecedents* (Austin: University of Texas Press, 1978).

23. See William Foote Whyte, Jr., "Quota Restriction and Goldbricking," in *Perspectives on Behavior in Organizations*, ed. by J. Richard Hackman, Edward Lawler, III, and Lyman Porter (New York: McGraw-Hill, 1977), pp. 324–28.

24. See Irving L. Janis, *Victims of Groupthink* (Boston: Houghton Mifflin, 1972).

25. Dorwin Cartwright and Ronald Lippitt, "Group Dynamics and the Individual," in *Concepts And Controversy in Organizational Behavior*, 2d ed., ed. by Walter R. Nord (Santa Monica, CA: Goodyear Publishing, 1976), pp. 532–45.

26. See Barnard, *The Functions of the Executive*; also Simon, *Administrative Behavior*, p. 267.

27. See David A. Nadler, J. Richard Hackman, and Edward E. Lawler, III, *Managing Organizational Behavior* (Boston: Little, Brown, 1979).

28. See Wood v. Strickland, 420 U.S. 308, 321–22 (1975). For an extensive discussion of this issue, see David H. Rosenbloom, *Public Administration and the Law* (New York: Marcel Dekker, 1983), pp. 185–200.

29. See Schein, *Organizational Psychology*; and Chris Argyris, *Understanding Organizational Behavior* (Homewood, IL: Dorsey Press, 1960).

30. Barbara S. Romzek and J. Stephen Hendricks, "Organizational Involvement," pp. 75–82.

31. See Richard T. Mowday, Lyman W. Porter, and Richard M. Steers, *Employee–Organization Linkages: The Psychology of Commitment, Absenteeism, and Turnover* (New York: Academic Press, 1982).

32. See Gerald R. Salancik, "Commitment and the Control of Organization Behavior and Belief," in *New Directions in Organizational Behavior*, ed. by Barry M. Staw and Gerald R. Salancik (Chicago: St. Clair Press, 1977), pp. 1–54.

33. Richard Neustadt, *Presidential Power* (New York: John Wiley & Sons, 1964), p. 22.

CHAPTER 12

PUBLIC

PERSONNEL

MANAGEMENT

Coping with Human Resource Needs

How can public agencies and public-sector managers attempt to cope with the challenges of acquiring, retaining, and improving the quality of their most critical resource—their employees? *Human resource management*—also called *personnel management*—is not a simple task in the public arena. The kinds of jobs filled by public employees reflect the diversity of services provided by all levels of government in the United States. Although the rules and procedures of public personnel management are too numerous and complex to catalog here, we can gain insight from an overview of public-sector personnel administration that emphasizes the tensions caused by administrative efforts to accommodate the expectations of three key actors: political institutions, public agencies, and public employees. To understand American public personnel management, then, we must evaluate how government personnel administrators attempt to respond to the expectations of those three groups (see Figure 12.1).

Political Institutions

Various political institutions are responsible for articulating the interests of the general citizenry at their respective levels of government (see Chapter 7). These institutions play a central role in the personnel arena: They make the personnel rules that public agencies and public employees must follow. Among those who articulate the demands and standards of political institutions are Congress, the president, and the federal courts at the national level; governors, state legislatures, and state courts at the state level; and typically city councils and mayors at the local level. In addition to these governing bodies, there are numerous political appointees at all levels of government (e.g., department heads and city managers) whose purpose is to articulate the concerns of political institutions within public agencies.

It is difficult to specify all of the expectations that these political institutions have of public-sector human resource management. Collectively, they share a common expectation about the role of public employees in government; namely, that public employees be responsible and accountable for their actions. This means that those representing political institutions expect public

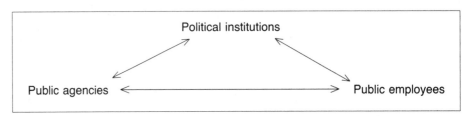

FIGURE 12.1   Key actors in the public personnel arena.

employees to do their jobs in a manner consistent with the intentions of the appropriate political institutions. Furthermore, public employees are held accountable for their actions in the event that they fail to implement the policies.

The strategies used by political institutions to articulate and promote their expectations regarding public personnel issues vary. Legislatures pass laws structuring the personnel policies of public agencies dealing with a variety of important subjects. For example, Congress passes legislation about federal employee retirement benefits; likewise, state legislatures and city councils annually decide on the appropriation of funds for employee pay raises. In addition, they oversee the personnel activities of public agencies through hearings and investigations.

Chief executives issue executive orders, which put the principles of personnel policies into effect. In some jurisdictions, the mayor or governor plays a central role in the hiring and firing of government personnel, while in other jurisdictions, civil-service systems or professional managers perform these tasks. The situation is more complicated at the federal level. Although the president can make some direct appointments (mostly with the advice and consent of the Senate), most positions are filled under provisions of federal civil-service laws that the president is obliged to enforce.

Courts issue judicial rulings that define the legal roles and responsibilities of public employees. State and federal courts are increasingly relied on to settle disputes over issues like affirmative-action programs and employment discrimination in the public sector.

Political appointees also make key personnel policy decisions, such as when a city manager issues a directive for affirmative-action practices in the police department or one requiring firefighters to live within city limits. These actions help give shape and direction to the management of the government personnel arena.

Public Agencies

Public agencies are a key group in shaping the expectations of public personnel administration. They are constantly working to cope with the pressures of the expectations generated from outside and within their boundaries (see Chapters 10 and 11). These organizations are directly responsible for implementing the personnel practices established by the political institutions. In addition, public-sector agencies depend on employees who perform in ways that contribute to their survival and the accomplishment of their official missions. They use personnel policies to increase the chances of recruiting the types of employees they need.

Public agencies perform four basic personnel-management functions: (1) recruiting suitable employees (*procurement*), (2) assigning them to proper jobs (*allocation*), (3) planning and training them for future job assignments (*development*), and (4) making sure that employees abide by the terms of the employment contract (*sanction*).[1] These functions are at the heart of public personnel administration, in that they help the agency to meet external expectations, increase the stability of its daily operations, and remain flexible enough to adapt to changes over time.

Procurement.   The procurement function involves several tasks. First, public agencies ascertain the skills needed to do the jobs required by their respective missions or objectives. Once these skills are identified, they become the basis for defining the various positions available in the agency and for recruiting candidates to fill those jobs through official notices and newspaper advertisments. The screening of job candidates involves an assessment of several factors, such as test scores, previous job experience, written work submitted for review, and interviews. Finally, the agency must select one person from among the candidates and offer that individual the position.

Allocation.   The allocation function often takes place simultaneously with parts of the procurement process. Prior to hiring qualified employees, the agency must figure out what to do with them. Under both the procurement and allocation functions, agencies concern themselves with defining individual positions and writing accurate job descriptions. To accomplish these tasks, they engage in a detailed process of analyzing jobs to identify their key characteristics. Once this process is completed, individuals can be hired who possess the necessary skills for the appropriate jobs.

While allocation and procurement may occur simultaneously during the hiring process, the tasks of allocation often continue beyond that time. As we have seen, organizations are constantly adjusting to their surroundings and to changing conditions within the agency. The legislature may expand the agency's jurisdiction, thus requiring the creation of new or different positions. Key personnel might be transferred or leave for other positions. These situations frequently lead to the redefinition of agency jobs or to the reassignment of agency personnel. It is in these situations that allocation tasks take on considerable importance. These tasks include defining new positions and redefining old ones, assigning individuals to appropriate jobs through transfers and promotions, orienting them to their new positions, and determining what compensation should be received for the new assignments.

Development.   Once an agency has employees on staff, assigned them to their specific jobs, and determined their appropriate compensation, it can then devote its attention to the longer-term goal of developing employees. The development function involves evaluations of employee job performance, training, and career development. The ultimate goals of development are to retain the best employees and to weed out the poor performers.

Employee development is important for all organizations, but especially so for public agencies. The rules of public personnel management typically stipulate that agencies hire employees for the jobs they can do today, not for their potential alone. Yet agencies want more than immediate performance from their employees. They also want employees to stay around long enough to move up in the organization and assume increasing job responsibilities. Hence, agencies need to develop among their employees both positive attitudes and useful job skills. To develop positive attitudes, such as organizational commitment and loyalty, agencies use various *socialization* programs. Similarly, agencies develop useful job skills for its employees through *training*, both on the job and in classroom settings. They monitor the results of these socialization and training efforts through *performance appraisals*. By evaluating the performance of employees in their current jobs, the agency can identify the employees who need coaching to bring their performance up to acceptable standards. Performance appraisals also identify employees who are doing well. It is important to the agency to identify both kinds of employees — those who need training to bring their performance up to par and those who are doing well and deserve a raise. However, these are the short-term concerns of the agency. The long-term benefit of evaluations for agencies lies in the identification of employees who have mastered their current jobs and would benefit from further training. Performance evaluations also can identify those employees who are capable of assuming greater job responsibilities through transfer or promotion.

Sanction.   The term *sanction* implies punishment or some other negative reaction to employee misbehavior. In public personnel management, however, the sanction function relates to the enforcement of the employment contract that exists between the agency and its employees. Organizations use sanctions, for instance, to make certain employees are doing their jobs.

The sanction function involves more than merely disciplining employees. It also concerns the establishment of the terms of employment set at the time an employee is hired. If employees are represented by a union, many of the terms of employment are likely to be subject to negotiation between the union and the agency.

The sanction function may also involve creating mechanisms and procedures that determine if a violation of agency standards has occurred. Many police departments, for example, implement a set procedure each time a law-enforcement officer fires his or her weapon. Oftentimes this involves the employee being temporarily reassigned, the submission of a detailed report by the employee and all others concerned, an investigation by an agency team, and a formal hearing on the incident.

Once it is determined that an employee violated the terms of the employment contract, the individual is subject to sanctions that can range from the mild to the extreme. A typical stage in the sanction process involves an interview, during which the supervisor informs the employee of the perceived violation. Depending on the severity of the violation, the negative tone of this interview may be considered sufficient, or it may be followed by a letter of reprimand that remains in the employee's personnel file. Extremely serious violations may even result in suspension without pay or in termination.

One way in which employees can fail to live up to the employment contract is by not performing their jobs according to acceptable standards. In 1986, for instance, four building inspectors in Kansas City, Kansas, were suspended for approving building plans that violated established construction codes. As punishment for their failure to perform their jobs, the inspectors were placed on temporary suspension without pay.

The sanction function also involves protecting employee rights. This means providing the working conditions that employees have a right to expect, whether based on law, agency rules, or collective-bargaining agreements. Most working conditions are taken for granted and are rarely the subject of complaint, such as the accrual of retirement and sick-leave benefits or the payment of overtime to employees in nonsalaried positions. One common complaint in the area of working conditions is an equity complaint, in which it is charged that one employee has been treated differently than another employee in a similar circumstance.

There are other working conditions that are much more amorphous, such as the right to due process in personnel actions and to be free from discrimination, sexual harassment, or reprisals due to whistle-blowing. Because these rights are not as tangible as wages and sick-leave benefits, there is much more room for judgment about whether they are being provided to all employees equally. Consequently, these rights are much more likely to be the focus of disagreements.

Instances of the employer failing to live up to its side of the contract may occur in such areas as working conditions, due process in personnel actions, discrimination, sexual harassment, political interference, and retaliation against whistle-blowers. When the agency has not been living up to its end of the employment contract, employees have the option of filing a grievance through the agency's grievance process. If the breach of employment contract is severe enough, employees also have the option of filing a civil lawsuit against the agency to seek a court order for enforcement of the terms of the contract.

Interconnectedness. The personnel functions of procurement, allocation, development, and sanction are indispensable to agencies trying to transform human energy into organizational resources. Through these functions the agency articulates its own expectations about the kinds of employees it needs, the kinds of behaviors it desires, and the kinds of performances it will reward. Further, an agency cannot consider these functions as independent of each other—they are interconnected. An agency will not be successful in getting and retaining high-quality employees without engaging in all four functions.

The quality of the employees that an agency recruits affects its flexibility in assigning, transferring, and promoting those employees in the future. Similarly, the quality of the agency's allocation and development processes affects the performance and long-term career prospects of its employees. Without adequate enforcement of the employment contract, the agency runs the risk of having employees who are not doing their jobs. It also runs the risk of a serious breach of the employment contract, which can result in the voluntary exit of the better employees (who have job prospects elsewhere).

Public Employees

Public employees have expectations about agency management. They hope that the demands of their work obligations will be compatible with their needs as human beings. This general principle of compatibility translates into specific expectations that employees have about work: that they have a high-quality work life and be able to balance their work and personal lives. The specific form of these expectations depends on the particular situation facing each employee. Many of these expectations revolve around employee needs for security, power, self-fulfillment, and a variety of other personal objectives.

In many respects, agencies meet these employee expectations through the structure and operation of their personnel systems. For example, an agency's personnel system should address employee expectations in regards to reasonable wages and the local standard of living. Although a government employee in Mississippi may be satisified with a $10-per-hour wage, an employee holding an identical position in New York City might expect $25 an hour because of the higher cost of living in that area. What if an employee's expectations for the personnel system are based on the opportunity for advancement rather than on wages? If the New York City personnel system did not provide for the possibility for advancement and the Mississippi system did, the New Yorker might want to transfer to the South, accepting lower wages to fulfill his or her career expectations.

In short, when public personnel managers design their systems, they must take into account the expectations of present and potential employees. It isn't sufficient to respond to the demands of political institutions or to address the specific needs of the agency. Public-sector employees have several options at their disposal to deal with problems arising in their work situations. As discussed in Chapter 9, they can respond through exit, voice, or loyalty.[2]

The use of the exit option by employees depends on a variety of factors. Obviously, it depends on the degree of employee dissatisfaction with current working conditions. Employees who find their jobs physically, psychologically, or morally unbearable are more likely to consider the exit option. Yet there are other factors to consider as well. For example, employees are more likely to leave an organization if there is a strong market for their particular skills. An accountant who works for the Internal Revenue Service, for example, may easily find job alternatives if he or she becomes dissatisfied with working conditions in the agency. A local firefighter with close ties to the community, however, is not likely to have as many viable employment alternatives. Thus, the personnel manager who seeks to retain valuable employees must respond to the pressures from both within and outside of the agency.

Employee reliance on the voice option also depends on a variety of internal and external forces. Organizational leadership and culture (see Chapter 11) can either facilitate or suppress employee efforts to produce change. The inclination of employees to participate in organizational change also reflects the social backgrounds of individuals recruited by the agency, as well as the political environment within which the agency operates. Public employees with professional credentials—such as physicians and scientists—can be expected to voice their opinions about agency policies and programs more readily than other employees. Similarly, an agency facing a new environmental challenge may welcome suggestions from its employees regarding relevant organizational changes. Again, the personnel manager can do a great deal to influence the extent to which employees express their opinions through the voice strategy.

Cultivating employee reliance on the loyalty option is a major challenge to all personnel managers. As we discussed in Chapter 9, loyalty emerges from matching individual workers' values with those of the organization. The agency can accomplish this by either recruiting people who are inclined to adopt its values or by using socialization methods to instill agency values in employees.

Accommodating All Three Groups

The interdependence that exists among political institutions, public agencies, and individual employees requires public personnel administration to be attentive to and possibly incorporate and accommodate the expectations of each group. Ignoring the concerns of one of the key groups is analogous to trying to ride a tricycle with one flat tire. With only two good tires, the tricycle would not be an efficient mode of transportation and the ride would be bumpy. You could struggle along with the flat tire by peddling hard and riding on the rim of the flattened tire. Doing so would take a tremendous amount of effort and your progress would be much slower than if you had three good tires. And, if you continue to ride with that flat tire, the damage to the flat increases and the other two tires wear out more quickly.

The same is true of personnel policies that fail to consider the needs of all three groups. Without the support of any one of the key groups, a personnel policy is likely to be ineffective or ignored. If government officials ignore the expectations of any one of these groups or give those specific expectations short shrift in a personnel policy, then the full cooperation of that group may be in doubt. A lack of cooperation from the "ignored" group is the mildest form of negative impact possible under such circumstances. Serious repercussions result from failures to accommodate the expectations of a key group. For example, personnel practices that meet the expectations of agencies and employees but ignore the concerns of the relevant political institutions can be troublesome. Elected officials displeased with personnel practices adopted by agencies or employees have the option of cutting funding to the agency, its programs, or employees. Agencies tend to manifest their lack of cooperation by short-circuiting the legislative intent of practices that they do not support or by pursuing the policies without enthusiasm. Employee resistance often takes the form of job actions that may or may not be illegal, such as widespread absences among police officers to protest some unacceptable personnel policy. This kind of job action is known as the "blue flu."

It is not all that uncommon for the needs of one of the key groups to be overlooked when personnel policies and practices are under consideration. In fact, most controversial personnel policies are controversial because they fail to cope with the expectations of one or more of the three groups. For example, collective-bargaining agreements between public agencies and employees (e.g., police officers, firefighters, and teachers) are often controversial. While such agreements often suit the needs of the employing agencies and individual employees, they can be troublesome for the relevant political institutions and the citizens they represent. The needs of agencies and employees can be served in a collective-bargaining setting because such agreements often increase the predictability and order of the behavior of both agencies and employees for the period of time covered under the contracts. Thus, the agreement might cover salaries for the next five years or specific workplace rules that can increase productivity. While such agreements help the agency in performing its budgeting and management functions, they severely constrict political institutions' control over agency funding and administrative decisions.

A good example of a policy that failed to consider the needs of all three groups emerged as a result of a major reform of the federal civil-service system in the late 1970s. In 1978, Congress passed legislation (the Civil Service Reform Act) that included a provision for special bonuses for federal employees not to exceed 50 percent of the federal work force. The intent of these bonuses was to provide incentives to the best and most innovative federal employees. In 1981, the Office of Personnel Management (OPM) approved bonuses up to the maximum allowed by law, for 50 percent of federal employees. Congress objected to the OPM's authorization of so many bonuses. Although the percentage was specified in its own legislation, Congress viewed the bonuses as evidence of irresponsible management. The OPM quickly reacted by setting the administrative guideline for bonus eligibility at 20 percent of all employees. While this practice accommodated the need of the political institution for administrative responsibility and the need of the agency to be politically accountable to Congress, it had a detrimental effect on employee and agency morale throughout the federal bureaucracy. Since such bonuses had been specified in law as available for 50 percent of federal employees, many employees felt their explicit employment contract had been violated.

Successful public personnel administration is a process of accommodating the expectations and interests of several groups. The history of American public personnel administration reflects this accommodation process.

A History of Public Personnel Policies

The accommodation of public personnel policies to political institutions, public agencies, and public employees has evolved through three major historical stages.[3] At each stage, the emphasis was on one of those three groups. The first stage focused on meeting the needs of political institutions through patronage policies. During the second phase, merit systems were developed that stressed agency needs in light of demands for greater governmental efficiency and effectiveness. In the most recent phase, the needs of public employees have drawn more attention, although the concerns of political institutions and agencies remain extremely important.

The Era of Patronage

From the earliest days of the republic up to the late 1800s, personnel policies in the United States tended to emphasize the needs of political institutions and elected officials. At the heart of this system were personnel policies based on *patronage*—who you were or who you knew, rather than what you knew, was the most important factor in obtaining a patronage appointment.[4]

Even prior to the American Revolution, patronage played a major role in the administration of government. The British rulers of colonial America regarded appointment to public office as a special privilege of the aristocracy. This was a patronage system rooted in social status rather than in politics. After the Revolution, many former colonies and townships reacted to this class-based system by turning many of their appointed administrative offices into elected positions. And where an office wasn't elected, obtaining the position depended on who you knew. Political patronage, then, has deep roots in colonial and revolutionary America.

At the national level, the pattern was just a bit different. At first, Americans retained much of the old British social patronage approach under the assumption that the appointment of "good people" would produce "good government." In the earliest days of the Republic, the majority of federal public employees were drawn from the ranks of the wealthy and educated.

Officials expected to meet the needs of political institutions, such as responsibility and accountability, by drawing public employees from among the social elite. Those appointed to government jobs did not necessarily have any particular expertise in managing government's business, nor did they necessarily have to demonstrate or maintain political loyalty. Rather, their wealth and good breeding were viewed as indicators of sound moral character. Having achieved the status of "gentleman" was evidence enough of one's probable responsibility and accountability as a guardian of the public trust.

The inauguration of President Andrew Jackson in 1829 signaled the onset of a new era in federal public service, an era when political patronage replaced the social patronage system. Under Jackson, a growing number of government jobs in Washington were filled by people who were not part of the social elite. Instead, Jackson and his successors relied on people who were more closely associated with the emerging frontier culture of the time. In Jackson's era, the idea was that elected officials who won victories at the polls were deserving of the spoils of victory. Under this *spoils system*, those who scored electoral victories were able to pass out government jobs to their loyal supporters. This era reflected continuing emphasis on political institutions' concern for responsibility and accountability from public employees. The only difference was that employees were expected to be responsible because they owed their jobs to elected officials rather than because they had good character.

The philosophy of the spoils era was that anyone with common sense could handle the responsibilities of government jobs. Good breeding and wealth were not necessary to be a good government employee. Instead, all a person needed were the right political connections and loyalty. It was possible to recruit government employees from outside the nation's social elite because government jobs were not seen as complicated.[5] It was more desirable for government employees to have the right political connections, because they could be counted on to act responsibly and be accountable to the elected officials who got them their jobs.

The Influence of Reform

During the late 1800s, American governments began to shift away from this exclusive reliance on political patronage.[6] A civil-service reform movement emerged that focused attention on the need for government agencies to have employees with the appropriate skills and knowledge to carry out the public's business effectively and efficiently. These reformers stressed the needs of public agencies rather than those of political officials.

The changes began in Massachusetts and New York, where public-spirited reformers pushed for major changes in personnel policies. Their first major victory, however, came at the federal level with the passage of the Pendleton Act of 1883. The reformers lobbied for the removal of politics from government employment because they felt that political responsiveness had been carried too far under the personnel systems of the spoils era. Toward this end, the reformers proposed a system in which job candidates would be screened and employees hired based on their abilities to do the jobs in question.

The Pendleton Act emphasized hiring federal employees based on merit or job skills. The system of employment using this standard for making personnel decisions was known as a *merit system*. Over the next half-century, merit systems spread across the nation. By the outbreak of World War I, civil-service reforms had been adopted in Wisconsin, Illinois, Colorado, New Jersey, Ohio, California, and Connecticut. By 1935, most of the remaining states had initiated some type of merit-based personnel systems. These changes received a considerable boost in the late 1930s and early 1940s, as the federal government began to require that states establish merit personnel systems for those agencies and programs receiving federal grants-in-aid. Many cities also went through similar reforms, such as the adoption of the council-manager and city commission government structures.

Under civil-service reforms, the emphases in filling government jobs were on job skills, competence, and political neutrality of government employees. Capable public employees were expected to implement public programs in an efficient and effective manner while withholding their personal political judgments. To minimize political meddling in administrative practices, the merit systems also included job-security provisions for public employees. The idea behind these provisions was to allow public employees to resist political pressure without the fear that they would lose their jobs due to retaliation from elected officials. As such, the merit system succeeded in insulating public employees from political interference by giving them job security (see Profile 12.1).

Another effort to insulate public employees from political pressure came with the passage of the Hatch Act of 1939. This legislation prohibits federal employees from engaging in specific political activities, such as organizing political campaigns or running for partisan office. It also protects them from being solicited for campaign contributions at their work site. Many states passed similar legislation (commonly known as "little Hatch acts") restricting the political activities of their public employees. While protecting public employees from the pressures of partisan politics, the federal Hatch Act also restricts the political activities of those same public employees. Whether the Hatch Act provisions enhance or detract from the working lives of public employees is still a subject of controversy. Many argue that the political liberties of public employees are unduly restricted by the legislation.

The personnel policies of the early twentieth century were also influenced by the emergence of the scientific management movement, which is based on the principles of efficiency in job design put forward by Frederick Taylor. The approach emphasized efficiency in organizational operations. In public personnel administration, efficiency means a concern for defining job tasks

PROFILE 12.1

The Pathological Gadfly

To some people, Ward B. Stone is a hero. To others, including his boss, he's a gadfly who is causing chaos in New York State government.

Stone is an associate wildlife pathologist for the Department of Environmental Conservation in New York. He and his staff of five at the state's wildlife pathology laboratory are responsible for conducting animal autopsies at the request of department officials. The head of his department, Thomas C. Jorling, prefers that Stone limit himself to those activities. Jorling, a political appointee of Governor Mario Cuomo, thinks that Stone does more than he's asked to do and, as a result, disrupts the operations of the department.

It seems that Stone, who has been with the department for twenty years, takes a broader view of his job than does Jorling. Stone believes it is his responsibility to conduct investigations of environmental contamination wherever and whenever it may be uncovered, regardless of whether those investigations are requested by the department. In 1982, for example, Stone sent a team from his lab to investigate complaints about skin rashes and miscarriages among residents around the Adirondack Park area. That area is near the site of Caputo Pit, a toxic waste dump that had been cleaned up and capped earlier by state officials and declared safe. Stone's tests, however, showed that significant levels of PCB contamination remained, and he released his findings to local reporters.

While claiming that Stone's investigation had little to do with its decision, the Department of Environmental Conservation conducted more tests in the Caputo Pit area and eventually undertook additional clean-up operations. According to department officials, by releasing preliminary data and not cooperating with other members of the department, Stone interfered with ongoing investigations and made the agency's job more difficult.

Thus, it is not surprising that Jorling objected to Stone's request for a larger budget to hire more staff and upgrade his lab's equipment. Jorling wanted Stone to provide him with a detailed plan of how that money would be spent, but Stone refused. He believed such a commitment would limit his ability to respond "to urgent investigations." However, Stone's supporters in the New York state legislature voted to increase his appropriation to $443,000 in fiscal year 1990—more than double what the lab received in 1989. At Jorling's request, Governor Cuomo vetoed that increase and sent a clear message to Stone: You must work with other members of the department and be more responsive to your superiors.

The story of Ward Stone is an interesting one, for it demonstrates both sides of the many protections provided to today's civil servants. On the one hand, Stone's status as a civil servant protects him from being arbitrarily dismissed by some political appointee who disagrees with his methods. On the

---

PROFILE 12.1   *continued*

other hand, the same protection may allow some well-meaning but overzealous individuals to disrupt the operations of an agency. "Ward Stone seems to think he's a savior," says Jorling. "But if I had 4,000 people, all of whom thought they were the saviors of the

environment, we'd get nothing done at all. There would be chaos."

SOURCE: Quotes and information from Sam Howe Verhovek, "State Environmental Gadfly Nettles New York Officials," *New York Times*, 9 May 1989, pp. B1, B4.

---

precisely and carefully screening applicants according to their abilities to do those precise tasks.

However, this period was not completely devoid of policy changes reflecting a growing concern for the needs of public employees. The concerns of federal government employees were addressed in the Lloyd–LaFollette Act of 1912, which provides them with several important job features enhancing the quality of their working lives. This legislation requires supervisors who want to fire federal employees to give those employees the reasons for the firing and an opportunity to counter the charges if they disagree. Federal employees are also given the right to join unions and other associations and to lobby Congress to improve their working conditions. Prior to this legislation, federal law prohibited federal employees from lobbying Congress about their work conditions.

There was also a concern for the needs of political institutions, especially during the 1930s and particularly among supporters of a greater role for the White House in running the federal bureaucracy. President Franklin Roosevelt felt he needed government employees who were in sympathy with his programs and who would be responsive to his directives. At the same time, he believed it was necessary to keep federal workers insulated from congressional political pressures. Thus, the number and size of federal agencies expanded under Roosevelt, and he placed sympathetic appointees in the new positions. In addition, Roosevelt (and his successor, Harry S. Truman) sought to extend civil-service status and protection to more federal employees.

A major component of this effort was the passage of the Classification Act of 1949. This legislation mandates the decentralization of most personnel functions to the separate agencies, including position classification, recruitment, performance evaluation, and promotion. It provides agencies with significant control over the composition of their work force by allowing them to determine the types of positions required and the skills needed to perform those positions. Thus, when Republican Dwight Eisenhower became president in 1953, he faced a federal work force appointed primarily under

Democratic administrations that might not be responsive enough to Republican policies. Eisenhower believed that the accumulation of twenty years of Democratic hiring decisions in the executive branch left his administration with a staff of somewhat unsympathetic public employees. This trend was so stark that Eisenhower proposed establishing an exempt category of public employees, which the White House could appoint based on standards of political loyalty and other relevant credentials. Eisenhower's proposal recognized that the insulation of public employees from elected officials had gone too far away from the political system's concerns for responsiveness and accountability. The exempt category of public-sector workers, known as *Schedule C*, usually includes the top three or four levels of federal agency jobs. By making appointments under Schedule C, Eisenhower hoped to gain high-level public employees who were in sympathy with Republican administrative priorities. This is not to say that all of Eisenhower's political appointees were in absolute agreement with his priorities; rather, they were more likely to be sympathetic than those appointed by earlier presidents.

Focusing on Public Employees

While the concerns of political institutions and public agencies remain strong today, recent developments in public personnel management have been more attentive to the concerns of public employees than in previous eras. The legacies of the patronage and merit personnel systems provide a framework within which much of today's public personnel management takes place. Nevertheless, both systems have been significantly modified in light of three major developments that relate to the individual public employee: public employee rights, professionalization, and concerns over special populations within the work force.

Public Employee Rights.   Beginning in the 1960s, there have been several developments in the area of employee rights. Employee rights have been influenced in part by the increasing role of the courts in public administration, particularly in public personnel issues.[7] Many of these issues are currently being debated in the court system.

One important issue regarding employee rights is whether public employees have a "right" to their jobs. The Supreme Court has adopted the "public service model" of employment, in which it assumes that public employees do not sacrifice the constitutional rights that all citizens enjoy unless there is a broad public interest that must be balanced against these rights.[8] The Court will consider reviewing personnel practices when the constitutional rights of public employees are at issue. Beyond these constitutional issues, the Court appears willing to defer to normal administrative practices.

Today's public employees face challenges to their right to privacy in ways that are relatively new. Questions of office searches, polygraph interviews, and drug testing are all part of the public employment arena. Office searches usually relate to investigations of wrongdoing and questions of reasonable search and seizure. What are the reasonable levels of monitoring and scrutiny to which we can subject public employees as part of their normal working conditions? How much privacy does a public employee have in his or her office? Can it be searched? Under what conditions?

In *O'Connor v. Ortega* (1987), investigators conducted a search of an employee's office while looking into charges of sexual harassment and malfeasance. The Court said that the government must apply a standard of reasonableness when it searches offices; in the *O'Connor* case, it found that government officials acted reasonably in conducting the search.[9] In some instances, lower federal courts have upheld other limitations on privacy, such as the use of polygraph tests for preemployment screening.[10]

Drug testing of public employees gained prominence in American public administration during the 1980s. The American military has been conducting drug tests since 1981. In 1985, San Francisco passed an ordinance that covers testing of both public- and private-sector employees. The law specifies that there must be "'reasonable grounds' for believing an employee was impaired on the job or [the agency must] demonstrate that an employee represents a 'clear and present danger' to other workers or to the general public."[11] In 1986, President Reagan issued an executive order that mandates random drug testing of federal employees in sensitive positions. It also authorizes federal agencies to test employees who appear to be impaired on the job or who are involved in accidents in the workplace. Similarly, recent railroad accidents involving operator drug use, such as a train wreck in Chase, Maryland, in 1987, have caused states to consider drug testing for public employees. For example, in 1988, the state of Kansas implemented a drug-screening program for individuals employed in "safety sensitive" positions and for applicants for such positions.[12] Current employees in those positions were required to submit to a drug test if there was reasonable suspicion (such as deteriorated performance or a medical emergency on the job) that they were using drugs. And applicants for those and similar positions were required to pass the same drug test before they could be appointed. The program affected nineteen state agencies and more than 2,300 positions.

In 1989, the Supreme Court ruled on the constitutionality of federally mandated drug testing for certain individuals in *Skinner v. Railway Labor Executives*.[13] In that case, the Court held that government regulations requiring drug and alcohol testing of railway crew members involved in serious accidents are constitutional. The Court said that such tests are a reasonable and effective way to serve the government's interest in promoting the public safety.

In a related case dealing strictly with federal employees, the Supreme Court voted 5 to 4 to uphold the constitutionality of drug testing of U.S. Customs employees who work in drug interception, are required to carry firearms, or deal with classified material.[14] In this case, the Court decided that the federal government's compelling interest in safeguarding our borders and the public outweigh workers' privacy rights. The Customs Department program allows the agency to require such employees to submit to a urine test with five days' notice.

Another employee right relates to the right to work in an environment that is free of discrimination. As more women have entered the work force, the issue of *sexual harassment* has become a concern of employees and agencies. The 1972 Equal Employment Opportunity Act extended the right to a nondiscriminatory workplace at all levels of government and authorized the Equal Employment Opportunity Commission to hear and resolve complaints of sexual harassment for state and local governments. The Merit Systems Protection Board handles the complaints made by federal employees. One problem with this issue is how to determine what constitutes sexual harassment. One person's flattery may be another's harassment.[15] The Office of Personnel Management (OPM) defines sexual harassment as "deliberate or repeated unsolicited verbal comments, gestures or physical contact of a sexual nature which are unwelcome."[16] The OPM equates sexual harassment with sexual discrimination because it involves differential treatment based on gender. In 1988, a federal court ruled that harassment can occur whether or not submission to sexual advances is made a condition of continued employment. That is, a work environment that exposes individuals to unwanted sexual comments or behaviors can constitute sexual harassment.[17]

Collective bargaining and unionization are also important areas of employee rights.[18] For nearly a century, public employees at all levels have increasingly turned to employee *associations* and *unions* as a means for representing their interests. Governments did not adjust quickly to these early developments; it took several decades before unions were integrated into public personnel policies. At the federal level, postal workers were the first to unionize. Congress recognized these developments in the Lloyd–LaFollette Act of 1912, which allows federal employees to join organizations that represent their interests. Some public agencies, such as the Tennessee Valley Authority, developed model collective-bargaining arrangements during the 1930s and 1940s. However, it was Executive Order 10988, issued by President John F. Kennedy in 1962, that strongly promoted the idea of employee participation in the shaping of personnel policies. Kennedy authorized collective bargaining in most federal agencies while retaining most management prerogatives over salaries and agency mission. By 1964, federal agencies had signed more than two hundred agreements with employee organizations representing over 600,000 federal workers. By the early 1980s, over two thirds of all federal employees were under such agreements. The Civil Service Reform Act of 1978 brought federal labor relations under one comprehensive act. It created an independent Federal Labor Relations Authority responsible for supervising elections, deciding appeals, and resolving complaints about unfair labor practices.

At the local government level, unionization has existed in some jurisdictions since the 1930s. In 1939, Philadelphia adopted ground rules for bargaining with employee groups, and Cincinnati, Milwaukee, and New York City soon followed. Statewide legislation setting standards for local level collective-bargaining agreements began to emerge during the late 1950s. In the 1960s, many state governments began to recognize and bargain with unions representing their employees. By the late 1970s, all but twelve states had some form of legislation dealing with public employee unions and only two (North Carolina and Virginia) formally prohibited government worker unionization.[19] For a substantial part of the public sector, public employee unionism and collective bargaining are now accepted ways of operating in the personnel arena.

Professionalization.   Professionalism is on the rise in American society, as more and more people perceive themselves as professionals. Where once the label *professional* applied only to physicians, lawyers, and a few other occupations, it is now used to describe a wide variety of careers. Liberally defined, a *profession* is a "reasonably clear-cut occupational field," requiring completion of at least a specialized bachelor's degree, "which offers a lifetime career to its members."[20]

The public sector has felt the impact of this trend toward professionalization. A growing number of public-sector occupations — from city management, teaching, and law enforcement to social welfare and diplomacy — have adopted the standards of professionalism. The increasing professionalization of the civil service has its roots in the efforts of reformers to bring more knowledgeable employees and expertise into the public sector.[21] While the urge to make government more efficient and businesslike led to the recruitment of individuals who aspire to professionalism, the pressures for personnel policies to adapt to the demands and needs of professionals became most evident during the post–World War II era.

The postwar period was influenced by a scientific and technological revolution of historic proportions and the cold war.[22] The scientific revolution was stimulated by discoveries in physics and biology made prior to and during World War II. Efforts to translate the fruits of recent scientific research, as well as to continue to promote further research, were often left to government. Much of the responsibility for converting the force of atomic weaponry into peaceful uses, for promoting the development of chemicals that would increase food production, and for furthering the advances made in aviation fell to government agencies. This meant developing policies that would attract and retain scientific professionals on government payrolls. It also meant paying greater attention to the unique needs of professionals.

The early cold war period of the late 1940s and 1950s further promoted the push toward professionalization. The United States became increasingly concerned with its ability to compete with the Soviet Union. The intense competitiveness of this period had tremendous implications for public service. After the Soviets launched the first satellite, *Sputnik*, in 1957, there was a dramatic upsurge in the amount of federal money spent on science and education. More money was invested in research, especially in areas associated with defense. More scientists, engineers, and teachers were recruited to government service. The result was an emerging shift in the pattern of employee credentials in the federal government. By tapping the knowledge explosion of the post-*Sputnik* era, there was a sharp rise in the proportion of public employees who brought with them into government service professional credentials. For such employees, a professional orientation toward their jobs involved the application of specialized bodies of knowledge and expertise to government problems.

Today, a growing number of federal government employees are professionals of some sort. These employees pose new demands and challenges to the federal personnel system and a number of changes have resulted. A growing number of government jobs now require professional credentials — a license to provide psychological counseling, certification to be an elementary or secondary school teacher, a degree in forestry to be a forest ranger, and so on. Within agencies, professional standards set by outside organizations play a greater role in shaping personnel policies as well as agency operations in general. What may result from this continuing trend is the emergence of what Frederick C. Mosher calls "the professional state."[23]

Efforts to support the development of a corps of public management professionals is a special manifestation of professionalization. An increasing number of middle- and upper-management positions at all governmental levels now require a master's degree in public administration or some equivalent graduate-level education. Many government agencies also implement special programs to enhance the professional training of those who wish to improve their management education. For example, the Federal Executive Institute was established in the late 1960s to provide a residential training center for the highest-level federal executives in order to upgrade the abilities of those employees already on staff. Similarly, the passage of the Intergovernmental Personnel Act (IPA) in 1970 was a step toward improving state and local government management practices through the sharing of personnel. Essentially, this program provided for the exchange of personnel for fixed periods of time among levels of government. Although the idea was for state and local governments to tap specialized pools of expertise that might exist in agencies at different levels of government or in universities, the IPA was a source of new ideas for federal public service as well.

The adjustment of personnel policies toward the demands of professionalism has not been without its costs (see Profile 12.2). Many elected political officials perceive the growth of professionalism as a challenge to their authority. This situation characterized the Nixon administration. Administrative responsiveness — or a lack of it — was an especially important

---

PROFILE 12.2
The Censored Expert

Dr. James T. Hansen is one of the most respected scientists in his field. As director of NASA's Goddard Institute for Space Studies, Hansen's expertise is a valuable asset in government and his views are widely sought and read throughout the world. Thus, a great many people listen carefully when Hansen issues a report or statement about the earth's climate.

But what happens when the expert opinions of a federal employee like Hansen conflict with the policy objectives of the White House? That question came up in 1989, when a report issued by Hansen was censored by the staff of the Office of Management and Budget (OMB). Reflecting his examination of scientific studies, Hansen's report concluded that human-generated pollution is creating a global-warming trend that may lead to radical changes in the earth's climate. His conclusion did not sit well with OMB officials. The official government stand on the issue is that more study is needed before conclusions can be drawn and policies made. Asserting that position, a staff member at the OMB modified the report in a manner which suggested that Hansen questioned the reliability of the available scientific data.

Testifying before a Senate subcom-

mittee, Hansen expressed his dismay about the changes made to the report. "I don't think the science should be altered," he told one senator. "As a government employee, I can and certainly do support government policy. . . . My only objection is changing the science."

Hansen was not the only government scientist to be pressured by the White House to alter his views. Dr. Jerry D. Mahlman, director of the Geophysical Dynamics Laboratory at the National Oceanic and Atmospheric Administration, testified that he had recently faced similar censorship from the White House but was able to reject the changes. The proposed changes, he argued, would be "objectionable and unscientific."

These instances of policy censorship reflect the dilemma facing government policymakers who increasingly rely on the expertise of their employees. Whatever political loyalties they might expect from those who work for government must be weighed against the demands of professional integrity that those experts bring to their positions.

SOURCE: Quotes and information from Philip Shabecoff, "White House Admits Censoring Testimony," *New York Times*, 9 May 1989, pp. C1, C4.

---

preoccupation of President Nixon. His deep-seated distrust of federal government employees was manifested in his efforts to have his own politically loyal individuals appointed to key merit-system positions. Working within the rules of the merit system, the Nixon White House used position reclassifications, transfers, and a variety of other techniques to accomplish administration objectives. Needless to say, this effort was geared toward maximizing political responsiveness over the concerns of agencies or individual employees.[24]

Similar concerns for increasing administrative responsiveness led to passage of the Civil Service Reform Act (CSRA) in 1978, which generated substantial changes within the federal civil service. Like Nixon, President Jimmy Carter felt that the professional administrators were not sufficiently responsive to changes in policy directions that came about when administrations changed. The CSRA was an effort by elected officials to assert their control over the administrative machinery of the federal government through legislative actions. The act established the _Senior Executive Service_ (SES). The idea behind the SES was not new; it had emerged in various guises since the early 1950s. The purpose behind the SES was to develop an elite corps of high-level generalist public administrators who could be transferred by the current political leadership to higher-priority programs. In other words, the SES was intended to help elected officials impose greater responsibility and accountability on public employees by allowing those officials greater latitude in the assignment of top-level federal employees and greater freedom to use the managerial expertise of senior administrators.

When the SES provisions went into effect, 95 percent of those civil servants eligible to join the SES opted to do so. However, the overwhelming number of employees who chose to join should not be viewed as evidence of overwhelming support for the SES program. Most employees opted to join the SES because they feared not doing so would jeopardize their long-term careers as federal employees.

The reforms instituted under the CSRA affected the quality of the working lives of federal employees in other ways as well. The reorganization of the agencies charged with personnel responsibilities separated the management functions from the watchdog functions. Managerial responsibilities for the reorganized personnel system were assigned to the federal Office of Personnel Management. The Merit Systems Protection Board was to monitor the administration of personnel policies to insure against abuses of the merit system. And the Federal Labor Relations Authority was to mediate any labor disputes between public-sector unions and agency management. Since the implementation of the CSRA, federal agencies have witnessed a tremendous turnover in their senior civil-service positions. This is due in part to low morale and dissatisfaction with the SES system and the limited availability of bonuses. In addition, there were increased political pressures during the Reagan administration, which made effective use of the SES and other provisions of the CSRA to enhance the political responsiveness of federal bureaucracies.[25]

Despite these setbacks at the federal level, professionalization remains a strong force in shaping today's public personnel policies. One example is the creation of the National Commission on the Public Service, widely referred to as the Volcker Commission after its chair, former Federal Reserve

System head Paul A. Volcker, Jr. Formed in 1987, the commission had as its mission to

> build public awareness of the essentiality of the career service to carry out the national agenda, promote measures for strengthening morale and efficiency of government employees at all levels, encourage the pursuit of excellence by government workers themselves, and make government a more attractive and accessible career choice for young people.[26]

Speaking for the commission, Volcker expressed concern that recent patterns of antigovernment rhetoric indicate that "our best and brightest in undergraduate and graduate schools have not exactly been excited by the challenge of public service and especially the federal service."[27] The recommendations of the commission focused on revitalizing the leadership, talent, and performance of federal employees, with the intention of cultivating a "renewed sense of commitment by all Americans to the highest traditions of the public service."[28]

Special Populations.   Within the general population of public employees, there are special groups whose status or actions generate changes in American public personnel policies. Of special concern are those groups that are underrepresented or that had been discriminated against under past policies. Under the traditional merit systems, minority groups and women had been underrepresented, especially at the higher levels of public-sector administration. A 1969 report by the Civil Rights Commission found institutionalized discrimination in many state and local civil-service systems and even cited examples where discriminatory actions were consciously perpetuated.[29]

Many of the actions taken at the federal level to alleviate these problems were directly and indirectly associated with the civil rights movement of the 1960s. For example, the Equal Pay Act of 1963 prohibited pay differentials based on sex for employees who held similar jobs under similar working conditions in both the public and private sectors. However, the issue of equal pay for equal work was not resolved by that legislation. Today, the issue takes the form of debates over calls for *comparable-worth* legislation. Proponents of comparable-worth policies argue that agencies should compensate jobs of roughly equivalent worth at roughly equivalent salary or wage levels: "If two groups of workers hold different jobs, but those jobs require 'comparable' levels of education, skill, experience and responsibility, the entry level pay for those two groups of workers should be the same."[30] For example, clerks who process tax receipts (and are predominantly female) should be paid roughly the same as clerks who sort mail (who are predominantly male). Underlying the issue of comparable worth is the fact that some jobs are traditionally male dominated (e.g., truck driving) while others are traditionally female dominated (e.g., nursing). Many studies have shown that male dominated jobs tend to pay better (see Insight 12.1).[31]

INSIGHT 12.1
THE STATUS OF COMPARABLE WORTH

In the 1980s, several state and local governments investigated the need for comparable-worth assessments to uncover pay inequities based on gender. In this area, the states took the lead over the federal government. In 1983, District Judge Jack E. Tanner ruled that the state of Washington had illegally discriminated against thousands of women by paying them 20 percent less than men doing jobs of comparable worth. In 1985, a Circuit Court of Appeals overturned Judge Tanner's decision on the grounds that the plaintiff had not proved a discriminatory impact from the state's pay schedule and had not proved the state's intent to discriminate. Then-Judge Anthony Kennedy (now a Supreme Court justice) wrote the opinion in the appeal. In 1986, the state of Washington reached an out-of-court settlement with its public employee union on the issue of comparable worth. Based on the state's finding that jobs staffed predominantly by women had been subjected to systematic pay discrimination in the past, the state agreed to a long-term plan for pay adjustments for employees in those job categories. The state agreed to pay $41 million initially, without back pay, plus an additional $10 million a year for five years.

Given the defeat in the courts and Justice Kennedy's current position on the Supreme Court, the prospects are dim that comparable worth will survive a court test under existing legislation. As a result, the action has moved to the political arena, where interested groups are now working with state legislatures to fund studies to document whether comparable-worth adjustments are necessary and to pass legislation where appropriate. According to the National Committee on Pay Equity, in 1988 forty-six states were considering pay equity, and twenty states are beginning to adjust their payrolls to correct for bias. In addition, cities, counties, or school districts in twenty-four states and the District of Columbia had taken some steps to correct inequities in their pay systems. Included among those cities that made pay-equity adjustments for female- or minority-dominated job categories are Chicago; Seattle; Colorado Springs; Green Bay, Wisconsin; Virginia Beach; and Burlington, Vermont.

SOURCE: Based on information in Kathleen Sylvester, "'Comparable Worth' Revisited: Whatever Happened after Washington State?" *Governing* (June 1988): 42.

Title VII of the Civil Rights Act of 1964 banned discrimination in personnel functions based on race, color, religion, sex, or national origin for all public and private employers with over fifteen employees. In 1965, President Lyndon Johnson issued an executive order that prohibits discrimination in employment practices by any federal government contractors. Similarly, the Age Discrimination Employment Act of 1967 bans discrimination in employment based on age for people who are between 40 and 70 years of age and prohibits mandatory retirement prior to age 70 unless there are strong occupational reasons for doing so.

During the early 1970s, Congress went even further. Its Equal Employment Opportunity Act of 1972 (EEOA) prohibits any employment discrimination by state and local governments or by federal contractors. In addition, the EEOA and other congressional acts mandate that government agencies at all levels take positive steps to remedy any past patterns of discrimination. We refer to these positive steps as *affirmative action*. Because affirmative action introduces a criterion other than the traditional notion of job performance into public personnel administration, it has faced much controversy. Despite the Reagan administration's lack of sympathy for the concept, the Supreme Court upheld affirmative action for public employers. In *United States v. Paradise* (1987), the Court upheld a U.S. District Court–ordered affirmative-action plan for the Alabama Department of Public Safety to remedy intentional race discrimination.[32] The *Paradise* case dated back to 1972, when a District Court found that the Alabama State Patrol had not hired a minority trooper in its thirty-seven-year history; that court ordered remedial action. When it was challenged in the Supreme Court by nonminority troopers, the Court upheld the promotional quota system that requires the Alabama Department of Public Safety to make half of all its promotions from among qualified minorities.[33]

Similarly, in *Johnson v. Transportation Agency* (1987), the Court upheld Santa Clara County's (California) voluntary affirmative-action program to overcome gender imbalances in "traditionally segregated job categories."[34] Santa Clara County had not been found guilty of sex discrimination; rather, it had voluntarily acted to try to increase the number of women in traditionally male-dominated jobs. In this case, the county chose Diane Joyce for promotion to road dispatcher even though she had not received the highest score on the oral interview. Paul Johnson, who scored two points higher than Joyce on that same interview, filed a discrimination complaint with the Court.[35]

The picture regarding affirmative action nevertheless remains unclear. In 1989, the Supreme Court ruled in *Martin v. Wilks* that nonminorities can challenge voluntary consent decrees to which they were not a party. In this case, white firefighters in Birmingham, Alabama, challenged a decree issued as a result of a discrimination case filed in 1974. That decree contained extensive remedial relief for minorities in the fire department in hiring and promotion actions. The 1989 decision allowed white firefighters to challenge that decree.[36]

Other concerns of special public employee groups have been addressed in other ways as well. The Veterans Preference Act of 1944, for example, was designed to be responsive to veterans' needs for jobs after they returned from World War II. This legislation requires that public employers give veterans special consideration in government jobs. Like the Hatch Act, however, it has both positive and negative effects. The positive contribution to the quality of the working lives of public employees comes from the provision that requires a special review of the reasons management gives for removal of veterans from public service. Later, these protections accorded veterans were extended to nonveterans by President Kennedy. The negative side of this legislation derives from criticisms that it disadvantages individuals who have not served in the military in competition for jobs and promotions.

Evolutionary Development of Personnel Policies

This brief history reflects the evolution of public personnel policies in the United States from an era emphasizing the needs of political institutions to a period when agency efficiency and effectiveness took center stage to today's recognition of the needs of individual public employees. As with other forms of evolutionary progress, the lessons and pressures of previous developmental stages have not disappeared. While there is greater concern for public employees' needs today, there is no less awareness of the need to accommodate political and agency pressures. The juggling act of public personnel policymakers and managers continues.

The Structure of Government Personnel Systems

The modern-day structure and practices of the various public personnel policies reflect this history of American public personnel administration. Structurally, public personnel policies in this country abide by two traditional operational principles: patronage and merit. However, these operating principles are no longer implemented in isolation of each other. Nor can we describe them without acknowledging the recent stress on the needs of individual public employees. Public personnel management today represents the intersection of efforts to deal with the complicated situation emerging from this combination of evolving expectations and traditional personnel administration standards.

Political Appointees

Patronage remains an important part of American public personnel systems. In part, the federal personnel system is still based on patronage. For example, each new administration faces the task of appointing several thousand federal employees.[37] Although the president rarely knows all of these individuals personally, these patronage appointees usually share the administration's political perspective. The general pattern is for the president to appoint people to top positions on the recommendation of key advisors. In turn, these top appointees typically select their own immediate subordinates.

The generic label applied to this dimension of federal personnel admin-istration is the *political appointee system*. Political appointees range from cabinet-level secretaries of departments, whom the president often recruits and appoints personally, to lower-level deputy assistant secretaries, who usu-ally receive their appointments through the recommendation of the top political appointees they will work for. The practice of using political loyalty as the basis for making appointments is most prevalent at the upper levels of government agencies. Nonetheless, when confidentiality is important, such appointments also may extend to key support staff such as executive secretaries.

The appointing officials usually screen many political appointees for their partisan sympathies, and perhaps the majority of appointments made by the White House are based on individuals' political loyalties to presidential programs. Such appointees do not have any protection against getting fired. They can be fired if they do not carry out policies as expected. As a result, these top bureaucrats are likely to be responsive to the wishes of the president.

There may be instances, however, when a president or other political official might make a patronage appointment for other than partisan reasons. In 1961, for example, President Kennedy appointed Robert S. McNamara, then president of Ford Motor Company and a registered Republican, as secretary of defense. Instead of political loyalty, Kennedy relied on McNam-ara's reputation as an effective manager who could bring some semblance of rationality to the unwieldy cabinet department.

A similar pattern of using political criteria for appointments to the highest levels of public jobs goes on in state and local governments. In some state systems, these political appointees are appointed to "exempt" or "unclas-sified" positions—labels often used to indicate that such employees are not covered by the merit-system rules that apply to all classified employees. Governors appoint the top executive officers of state agencies with an eye to their loyalty and sympathies to the governor's programmatic goals. Sim-ilarly, in many local governments, the power of elected officials to make administrative appointments is limited by the municipal or town charter to the selection of the city manager or some similar chief administrator. Larger cities tend to have their department directors (e.g., personnel director or police chief) serve as political appointees as well. Many political appointments in local government reflect a nonpartisan approach. Individuals are often appointed because they are expected to carry out an elected official's agenda, not because of their partisan loyalties. In cities with strong mayoral forms of government, in which the mayor is the chief administrative officer of the city, the pattern of patronage appointments is common. County govern-ments, which as a group are only recently beginning to adopt professional standards of government, tend to rely heavily on patronage as well.

The most celebrated example of patronage appointments in local government occurred in Chicago under Mayor Richard J. Daley.[38] During Daley's tenure as mayor (1955–1976), it was said that no one ever got any city job, no matter how menial, unless the mayor had personally screened the candidate. In the Daley administration political loyalties were recognized as relevant job credentials for city jobs; the criteria used were related to party politics. Individuals who had been loyal and effective precinct captains, delivering votes and campaign workers to the Democratic party, were the ones awarded city jobs. Chicago mayors since Richard J. Daley have continued this practice. While not as widespread as under Daley's administration, patronage jobs remain the norm in Chicago today.

Under a pure patronage system, turnover in the office of chief executive is likely to result in the replacement of patronage appointees with individuals who share the political perspective of the incoming chief executive. In the past, when political parties were more cohesive organizations, the turnover from one chief executive to another of the same party did not usually result in high turnover among patronage jobs. A good Democrat working for the election of all Democrats could expect his or her reward. A good Republican working for the election of all Republicans could expect similar rewards.

Before the U.S. Post Office was reorganized into a public corporation in 1970 and renamed the U.S. Postal Service (USPS), postmasters fell into this category of political patronage appointees. Every time a new president came into office, there was the chance that local postmasters around the country would be replaced by individuals with political loyalties to the new administration. Of course, the president rarely made these appointments personally. Instead, the decisions were delegated to leading party members in each state. So, for example, if the turnover in administration was from the Democratic party to the Republican party, then the leading Republicans in the state would have the opportunity of nominating someone with strong ties to the party to serve as postmaster.

In the past twenty years or so, in conjunction with the erosion of political parties as effective national and state organizations, we increasingly have seen political leaders developing personal organizations. This change has affected the distribution of political patronage as well. Nowadays, many elected officials define political loyalty in terms of the individual candidate rather than the political party. Consequently, even when the turnover is from one chief executive to another of the same political party, a high proportion of the patronage appointees may still lose their jobs.

In short, elected officials expect such appointees to have a personal loyalty to the chief executive as well as programmatic loyalties. For example, when Ronald Reagan assumed the presidency in 1981, most of his key appointments to the White House staff went to people who had worked for him when he was governor of California. Because Reagan lacked long-standing ties to the Republican party, party identification was much less important than personal loyalty in his appointments. Likewise, when George Bush became president in 1989 he replaced many of Reagan's White House staffers and other appointees with people of his own choosing. Other Reagan appointees, realizing they were unlikely to be reappointed, resigned their positions. The Bush administration was slow to fill those slots. After one year in office, nearly half of the nearly three thousand political appointments available to the president remained vacant or were being filled temporarily.

In recent years, the courts have imposed some limits on the removal of lower-level patronage appointees. In some instances, patronage appointees are protected by the first and fourteenth amendments to the Constitution from being fired because of a change in the chief appointing official. In *Elrod v. Burns* (1976), the Supreme Court ruled that patronage public employees working in the Cook County, Illinois (Chicago), sheriff's office could not be fired because of the election of a new sheriff of another political party.[39] In this case, the newly elected Democrat sheriff, Elrod, dismissed all political appointees who were not acceptable to the Democratic party leadership. John Burns was one of those dismissed; he filed suit. The Court ruled that elected officials cannot dismiss patronage employees simply because they are affiliated with the political party that loses an election. The Court reaffirmed its position in *Branti v. Finkel* (1980). In this case, assistant public defenders who were patronage appointees in Rockland County, New York, had been dismissed. The Court ruled that the hiring authority must "demonstrate that party affiliation is an appropriate requirement for the effective performance of the public office involved."[40] The Court held that unless effective job performance depends on partisan affiliation and political loyalty, the use of partisanship for job removal of these public defenders is an unconstitutional violation of employees' rights.

Merit Systems

The federal government and most states and localities have some provision for a merit system of hiring public employees. Sometimes these systems are called *civil-service systems*; other times we label them *merit systems*. Whatever the label, these employment systems differ from patronage systems in one important way: they specify in advance the criteria and procedures to be followed in making personnel decisions. Merit systems use job descriptions and position classifications to specify the skills and tasks required for the various jobs.

Merit personnel systems require that employment decisions be based on specific job-related criteria. Under a merit system, the various personnel functions are performed with an emphasis on employees' job-related knowledge, skills, and abilities. Individuals are hired, fired, transferred, and evaluated based on their ability to perform the job in question. Although employment decisions in the private sector are based on these same criteria, students of government usually reserve the term *merit system* for public-sector employment.

At the heart of any merit system is the process of *position classification*. The integrity of a merit system is based on the ability to match qualified individuals with the appropriate jobs. Before this match can be made, the jobs in question must be analyzed to ascertain the knowledge, skills, and abilities necessary to do them. Following this job analysis, the positions are classified according to their varying degrees of responsibility, complexity, risk, and so on. This system of classification is fundamental to the operation of a government-wide personnel system based on merit and equity.

Position classification is an important feature of merit systems in this country. Most merit systems are organized according to jobs or positions rather than by the occupants of those positions. This system of position classification is the basis for determining the different levels of compensation appropriate for the various categories of jobs. The underlying principle for compensation is that positions requiring higher levels of expertise and responsibility should be compensated at higher levels than positions at lower levels of classification. Once jobs are classified in this way, they are then linked to a system of pay classification that assigns different levels of compensation based on the level in the classification scheme.

For most federal and state merit-system employees, rank is determined by the position they fill. Under this system of position classification, the usual way for an employee to get a promotion is to apply for a position with a higher classification. Sometimes the position that the individual holds is reclassified to a higher level. Because governments base their classifications on systemwide comparisons of job duties, the reclassification of an individual position is rare. Reclassification of an entire system of positions is even more rare. When undertaken, such reclassifications usually disrupt the morale and functioning of the employees who already occupy the classified jobs.[41]

The federal government uses several different merit systems, each of which has a distinctive classification scheme. The *general schedule* (GS) covers most federal white-collar employees. GS positions are classified into eighteen different grades that reflect increasing levels of complexity and responsibility (see Table 12.1). Within each grade, there are ten steps reflecting differences in time-in-grade and pay. There are also "Special Rates" for clerical employees with required typing proficiency. Many states base their merit systems on similar classifications of positions and graduated-pay scales.

Similar to the GS personnel system are the *specialized merit systems* developed for unique groups of public employees. This broad category covers groups of public employees who have certain unique characteristics that set them apart from the bulk of general civil-service employees. Like all merit-system

TABLE 12.1   Federal White-Collar Pay
Scales, 1989: General Schedule

Grade	Salary Range for 1990
1	$10,581–13,232
2	11,897–14,973
3	12,983–16,879
4	14,573–18,974
5	16,305–21,201
6	18,174–23,628
7	20,195–26,252
8	23,367–29,081
9	24,705–32,121
10	27,206–35,369
11	29,891–38,855
12	35,825–46,571
13	42,601–55,381
14	50,342–65,444
15	59,216–76,982
16	69,451–78,200 (86,251)[a]
17	76,990–78,200 (90,398)[a]
18	78,200 (93,484)[a]

[a]Officially, the top positions in the civil service (GS
16–18) can receive salaries above the max-
imum of $78,200 annually. Federal law, how-
ever, stipulates that these employees cannot earn
more than the amount paid to the lowest level
political appointee in a cabinet position (i.e.,
Level V Executive Schedule).

employers, agencies using these specialized merit systems base the hiring of
individuals on their abilities rather than on their politics. These systems
rank employees according to experience, training, and skills. Once classified
in a rank, an employee can be assigned to any job in the agency. These
employees retain their rank regardless of the specific job they hold.

The Senior Executive Service (SES) is one example of these specialized
personnel systems. As noted earlier, Congress established the SES under
provisions of the Civil Service Reform Act of 1978. Its membership includes
most positions that were levels 16 through 18 of the GS and levels IV and
V of the executive schedule. The SES classification system has six grades
(see Table 12.2). Those holding SES appointments receive pay based on
their rank within the system. They are also eligible for bonuses and have
less job security than GS employees. SES personnel are perceived as an elite
cadre of career civil servants. In fact, the SES was created to remove some
of the rules and protections from higher-level employees so that they can
be more readily reassigned to those programs or agencies that political

TABLE 12.2   SES Pay Scales

Grade	Salary Range for 1990
Senior Executive Service (SES)	
ES–1	$71,200
ES–2	74,400
ES–3	77,600
ES–4	79,200
ES–5	81,400
ES–6	83,600

SOURCE   "Executive Order 12698, Schedules 1–B and 4," U.S. Office of Personnel Management, 1990.

leaders deem high priority. Thus, SES employees can be reassigned, transferred, or reduced in grade much easier than can GS employees.

Other specialized merit systems include members of the armed services, the U.S. Foreign Service, state highway patrol forces, and some local cadres of employees such as police and firefighters. (See Profile 12.3.) Many of these *career systems* emphasize lifelong training and accumulated expertise as well as close identification with the agencies within which they operate. The most familiar examples of career systems are the various branches of the military. For example, colonels in the U.S. Army retain their rank regardless of their job assignments. The Forest Service is another example of a career system in which individuals can count on lifelong career opportunities and retain their rank regardless of their job assignment.[42] In state governments, career-system employees tend to work in specialized agencies such as the state highway patrol. Similar systems exist at the local level, especially among law-enforcement, firefighting, and other public-safety organizations.

Collective-Bargaining Systems

In a collective-bargaining system, employees form associations to represent their interests in negotiations with agency management. Most often these associations are called *unions* even though some of them choose not to use that term for political reasons. There is some overlap between the merit system and the collective-bargaining system in that some merit-system employees belong to employee associations.[43] Nevertheless, collective-bargaining systems comprise a distinct and important part of the American public service.

There is a long history of unionization among select groups of public employees. Letter carriers with the Post Office Department in New York established the earliest federal employee union in 1863; by 1892, postal workers formed a national union. State and local employees tend to unionize

PROFILE 12.3

Atlanta's Deputy Chief Harvard

Beverly J. Harvard joined the Atlanta police force in 1973. Like the other thirty-nine rookies in the Bureau of Police Services that year, the twenty-four-year-old Harvard expected to be assigned to a car patrol in some residential neighborhood after her graduation from the police academy. Instead, Officer Harvard found herself walking a beat in the high-crime area of Atlanta during the 6:00 P.M. to 2:00 A.M. shift.

The assignment was not quite what Harvard had wished for; nor was it what her husband expected, and he expressed his concern to his wife. His concern turned to anxiety the first few nights of Harvard's foot-patrol assignment. At about 10:00 each night he would get into the family car and begin his own patrol of the high-crime area, driving at an extremely slow speed several yards behind his walking wife. The embarrassment of a nervous spouse was bad enough, Harvard remembers; but the situation was made even worse by the traffic tie-ups he was causing in the process.

After a couple of weeks, Harvard was able to convince her husband that she could handle the job. Obviously, she was able to convince her supervisors of the same thing over the years, for by 1982, she had served in a variety of responsible positions. In that year, the bureau promoted her to the rank of Deputy Chief of Police, making Harvard the first woman in the nation to reach that rank in a police force.

Not surprisingly, her appointment drew considerable attention. Despite her wide range of experience on the force and her educational background (she holds a bachelor's degree in sociology and psychology and a master's degree in public administration), there were still some who doubted her ability. Within the bureau, the reaction to her promotion was "cool," as her associates wondered about the wisdom of her appointment. She was deluged with requests from the media for interviews, and call-in radio shows held informal polls among their listeners on whether the appointment of a young black woman to such a high rank was the correct move for the city of Atlanta.

By 1988, Deputy Chief Harvard was no longer so unique. Other women began to reach similar positions in other cities. Her own career advanced when she was given responsibility for the bureau's criminal investigations division. In that position, she commands 290 officers who serve in three units, each headed by a male officer. Harvard describes her management style as "hands on" and tries to get actively involved in the work of the criminal division. When asked to comment on the problems of being a woman in a male-dominated profession, Harvard speaks about the isolation and awkwardness she sometimes feels, especially at regional and national meetings with her peers. She also talks about the pressure of being a role model who must succeed.

Despite these and other problems, however, one doesn't get the impression that Harvard would have it any other way. Even if the pressures were ten times as great, she commented, she would still have accepted the job.

SOURCE: Based on information from an interview on October 22, 1988.

by separate occupations, such as police officers, firefighters, or teachers.[44] The International Association of Fire Fighters was established in the 1880s to serve mainly as social clubs and firefighter benefit societies. The American Federation of State, County, and Municipal Employees (AFSCME) was founded in 1936.[45]

By the mid-1980s, unionization among public-sector employees was fairly widespread, with over 40 percent of them covered by collective-bargaining agreements. The comparable figure for private-sector workers at that time was 14 percent.[46] Today's largest public-sector unions are the National Education Association; the American Federation of Teachers; the American Federation of State, County, and Municipal Employees; and the Service Employees International Union. City and township employees are the most likely to be organized; among these groups, police, firefighters, and teachers have the highest rates of union membership. State and county employees have the lowest levels of membership in employee associations or unions.[47]

Public employee unions can affect important aspects of employment systems through collective bargaining. For example, in 1892, the postal workers union was instrumental in gaining passage of the legislation for an eight-hour work day.[48] The wages and many of the working conditions of unionized employees typically are set through collective-bargaining agreements between agency management and the employee association. Employees covered by collective-bargaining agreements tend to have higher wages than those who are not covered by such agreements. The presence of collective-bargaining agreements also impacts on the public employee's job stability. Nonunion employees suffer more layoffs and job loss than employees covered by collective-bargaining agreements.[49]

Today, federal employees can negotiate over working conditions, technology, grievance procedures, and the like. They cannot bargain over salary and wages, fundamental management processes that affect substantive decisions concerning the agency's budget or programs, or internal security programs. And even though they can bargain collectively, federal employees cannot strike legally. In addition, public employee unions cannot require the employees they represent to join the union and pay union dues.

Until 1981, there was no record of a formal strike by federal employees, although nearly 200,000 postal employees did stage "wildcat" walkouts in March 1970 that effectively brought postal service operations to a halt. In 1981, however, the "no-strike" restriction was enforced when the Professional Air Traffic Controllers Organization (PATCO) authorized an illegal walkout against its employer, the Federal Aviation Administration (FAA). The Reagan administration suppressed the strike by replacing the strikers and successfully seeking to decertify PATCO through legal channels for conducting an illegal job action—the strike.

For the most part, state legislation is similar to federal law in this area. State and local employees operate under various labor relations laws. In 1959, Wisconsin was the first state to authorize collective bargaining for public employees.[50] By the early 1980s, most states had relatively well-developed labor relations policies for public employees. Some states only allow employee associations to meet and confer with management, while other states allow negotiations between employee associations and management. Some states allow strikes for some categories of public servants. In Alaska, for example, all public employees except teachers are permitted to strike. Ohio allows strikes by public employees in jurisdictions of five thousand or more, except for police, fire, and other safety-related employees.[51] Of course, not all bargaining leads to agreement.

Traditionally, governments discourage strikes among their workers. There are a variety of mechanisms available to the public sector for resolving labor–management disputes short of the strike. *Mediation*, a major means for settling disputes, involves bringing in a neutral third party who tries to reconcile the two parties by discussing the points of disagreement and suggesting how they might be overcome. Under mediation, the expectation is that the two parties reach the agreement; the mediator only facilitates discussion.

Fact-finding also uses a neutral third-party mediator to conduct a formal investigation of the issues in dispute and to report the "facts." Fact-finding is a more formal form of mediation, taking place in a quasi-judicial, adversarial atmosphere. The advantage of fact-finding is that disputes over facts are often the basis for impasses. Hence, having a neutral party determine the facts gives moral and political ammunition to the party whose position most closely matches the third party's findings.

Arbitration also occurs in a formal quasi-judicial setting, but it calls on a neutral third party to impose a settlement on the disputing parties. Sometimes states allow only advisory arbitration, wherein a third party recommends a solution; as such, it is similar to fact-finding. Compulsory arbitration tends to reduce the rate of strikes.[52] Agreements reached through arbitration tend to have less-costly financial packages than agreements negotiated between two parties.[53]

The most popular technique for resolving labor–management disputes is mediation. The Federal Mediation and Conciliation Service works with impasses between federal parties. Thirty-five states provide for mediation; thirty-two states provide for fact-finding, and twenty-seven include arbitration.[54]

Personnel and Diverse Expectations

The specialized arena of public personnel administration exemplifies the diverse, sometimes contradictory expectations that are typical of public administration. The structure of public employment at all levels of American government reflects the complicated situation of public administrators as they attempt to respond to the expectations of political institutions, public agencies, and public employees.

The need for public agencies to be responsive to political institutions is reflected in our retention of a patronage-based, political-appointee system. The concerns of agencies for capable and productive employees to help them accomplish their organizational tasks are manifested in employment systems that emphasize hiring decisions based on job-related skills. Calls for greater agency efficiency and effectiveness are the foundation on which governments base general and specialized merit systems. The effort to satisfy employee demands has led to an increased emphasis on employee rights and the creation of collective-bargaining systems and bargaining over working conditions. All of these aspects of public personnel systems are part of the complex pattern of expectations that public administrators must try to accommodate as they go about their business of getting and retaining employees. The reconciliation of these interests is not always easy and at times it is not even possible.

Summary

1. The major challenge facing public personnel management is how to reconcile the needs and expectations of the three key groups active in the arena: political institutions, public agencies, and public employees.
2. Political systems need and expect personnel policies and practices to yield accountable and responsible public employees. Public agencies need and expect personnel policies and practices to enable them to get and retain capable employees. Public employees need and expect personnel policies and practices that yield an acceptable level of quality in their work lives and that enable them to balance their work and personal lives.
3. Public personnel policies and practices that do not accommodate the needs and expectations of each of the three groups are likely to be controversial and difficult to implement.
4. The history of public personnel administration reflects shifting emphases on the needs and expectations of the different key groups.
5. Patronage systems, merit systems, and collective-bargaining systems offer public workers different terms of employment. In addition, the terms of employment can vary among state and local jurisdictions.

Study Questions

1. Choose three public personnel policies that are currently in the news (e.g., drug testing, affirmative action, or collective bargaining between firefighters and city hall). Analyze each policy for how well it accommodates the interests and needs of the three key groups active in the personnel arena.

2. Do some library research on public employment in your state. How many public employees in your state qualify as patronage appointees? Merit-system employees? How many are covered by collective-bargaining agreements? Then consider what the statistics suggest about the relative values given to the interests of political systems, agencies, and employees in your state.

3. Draw up a list of what you think the general public expects from public employees (e.g., honesty, hard work, courtesy). Then identify the personnel mechanisms (e.g., rules or policies at the federal, state, or local level of government) that increase the chances that those expectations will be met. Suggest other mechanisms that could further increase the chances. What are the obstacles to adopting your suggestions?

Notes

1. See Donald Klingner and John Nalbandian, *Public Personnel Management*, 2d ed. (Englewood Cliffs, NJ: Prentice-Hall, 1985); and Richard E. Walton, "Criteria for Quality of Working Life," in *The Quality of Working Life: Problems, Prospects and the State of the Art*, vol. 1, ed. by Louis E. Davis and Albert B. Cherns (New York: The Free Press, 1975), chap. 5.

2. See Albert O. Hirschman, *Exit, Voice, and Loyalty: Responses to Decline in Firms, Organizations, and States* (Cambridge, MA: Harvard University Press, 1970).

3. Compare with Herbert Kaufman, who argues that the history of public personnel management reflects shifting emphases on three basic values: representativeness, political neutrality, and executive leadership. See his "Administrative Decentralization and Political Power," *Public Administration Review* 24 (January/February 1969): 3–15.

4. Among the best historical sketches of American public personnel policies is Frederick C. Mosher, *Democracy and the Public Service*, 2d ed. (New York: Oxford University Press, 1982). See also Paul P. Van Riper, *The History of the U.S. Civil Service* (New York: Harper & Row, 1958).

5. In fact, considerable effort was made to redesign federal agencies and jobs to make them simpler and therefore more compatible with the spoils system philosophy. See Matthew A. Crenson, *The Federal Machine: Beginnings of Bureaucracy in Jacksonian America* (Baltimore: Johns Hopkins University Press, 1975).

6. See Dwight Waldo, *The Adminsitrative State: A Study of the Political Theory of American Public Administration*, 2d ed. (New York: Holmes and Meier, 1984), pp. 28–30.

7. See David H. Rosenbloom, *Public Administration and the Law* (New York: Marcel Dekker, 1983).

8. See Jay M. Shafritz, Albert Hyde, and David H. Rosenbloom, *Personnel Management in Government: Politics and Process*, 3d ed. (New York: Marcel Dekker, 1986), esp. chap. 8.

9. See International Personnel Management Association, "Supreme Court Approves Office Searches," *IPMA News* (May 1987): 1.

10. The U.S. Court of Appeals for the 3rd Circuit ruled in favor of preemployment polygraph screening by the police and prison departments in the city of Philadelphia. See *Anderson* v. *City of Philadelphia*, Docket no. 87–1546, 2 May 1988.

11. Tom Watson, "Drug Laws Are Catching On," *Governing* (June 1988), 162.

12. International Personnel Management Association, "Kansas Implements Drug Screening Program," *IPMA News* (February 1989): 3.

13. See Linda Greenhouse, "Court Backs Tests of Some Workers to Deter Drug Use," *New York Times*, 22 March 1989, pp. 1, 11.

14. Ibid.

15. See Dail Ann Neugarten and Monica Miller-Spellman, "Sexual Harassment in Public Employment," in *Public Personnel Administration: Problems and Prospects*, ed. by Steven W. Hays and Richard C. Kearney (Englewood Cliffs, NJ: Prentice-Hall, 1983), pp. 275–88.

16. Office of Personnel Management, *Memorandum to Heads of Departments and Independent Agencies, Subject: Policy Statement and Definition of Sexual Harassment* (Washington, DC): OPM, December 1979).

17. See *Broderick* v. *Ruder, Chairman, U.S. Securities and Exchange Commission*, Docket no. 86–1834, 13 May 1988; U.S. District Court for District of Columbia.

18. See Richard C. Kearney, *Labor Relations in the Public Sector* (New York: Marcel Dekker, 1984); Jay M. Shafritz, Albert Hyde, and David Rosenbloom, *Personnel Management in Government: Politics and Process*, 3d ed. (New York: Marcel Dekker, 1986); Felix A. Nigro and Lloyd G. Nigro, *The New Public Personnel Administration*, 2d ed. (Itasca, IL: F. E. Peacock, 1981); and Melvin Dubnick and Joel M. Douglas, "A Trashy Situation: Collective Bargaining in the Public Sector," in *Doing Public Administration: Exercises, Essays, and Cases*, ed. by Nicholas Henry (Dubuque, IA: W. C. Brown & Co., 1990). 3d ed., pp. 95–96.

19. Richard B. Freeman and Casey Ichniowski, "Collective Organization of Labor in the Public Sector," in *When Public Sector Workers Unionize*, ed. by Richard B. Freeman and Casey Ichniowski (Chicago: University of Chicago Press, 1988), pp. 404–405.

20. Mosher, *Democracy and the Public Service*, pp. 115–16.

21. See John Nalbandian, *Managing Cities Effectively* (San Francisco: Jossey-Bass, in press).

22. See Don K. Price, *The Scientific Estate* (Cambridge, MA: Belknap Press, 1965), esp. chap. 5.

23. Mosher, *Democracy and the Public Service*, chap. 5. On the general impact of professionalism, see Thomas L. Haskell, ed., *The Authority of Experts: Studies in History and Theory* (Bloomington: Indiana University Press, 1984).

24. See Richard Nathan, *The Administrative Presidency* (New York: John Wiley & Sons, 1983), pp. 39–40.

25. See ibid., pp. 77–78; and Edie Goldenberg, "The Permanent Government in an Era of Retrenchment and Redirection," in *The Reagan Presidency and the Governing of America*, ed. by Lester M. Salamon and Michael S. Lund (Washington, DC: The Urban Institute Press, 1985), pp. 381–404.

26. Elliot L. Richardson, "Civil Servants: Why Not the Best?" *Public Administration Times*, 25 December 1987, p. 1.

27. "Volcker Cites 'Quiet Crisis' in Government," *Public Administration Times*, 25 December 1987, p. 5.

28. National Commission on the Public Service, *Leadership for America: Rebuilding the Public Service* (Washington, DC: Government Printing Office, 1989), p. 1.

29. Nigro and Nigro, *The New Public Personnel Administration*, pp. 14–15.

30. Kathleen Sylvester, "'Comparable Worth' Revisited: Whatever Happened after Washington State?" *Governing*, 1 (June 1988): 41.

31. Ibid., p. 42. See also Henry J. Aaron and Cameran M. Lougy, *The Comparable Worth Controversy* (Washington, DC: Brookings Institution, 1986).

32. *United States* v. *Paradise*, 94 L Ed 2d 203 (1987).

33. International Personnel Management Association, "High Court Upholds Promotion Quotas," *IPMA News* (April 1987): 1, 3, 9.

34. *Johnson* v. *Transportation Agency*, 94 L Ed 2d 615 (1987).

35. International Personnel Management Association, "Voluntary Affirmative Action Plan Upheld," *IPMA News* (May 1987): 1, 9, 10.

36. Neil Reichenberg, "Legal Issues in the Public Sector," *IPMA News* (August 1989): 10.

37. See Patricia W. Ingraham, "Building Bridges or Burning Them? The President, the Appointees, and the Bureaucracy," *Public Administration Review*, 47, no.5 (September/October 1987): 425–35.

38. In 1989, Richard J. Daley's son, Richard M., was elected mayor of Chicago. On the patronage system in the elder Daley's Chicago, see Mike Royko, *Boss*.

39. *Elrod* v. *Burns*, 427 U.S. 347 (1976).

40. *Branti* v. *Finkel*, 445 U.S. 506 (1980).

41. See Steven D. Ealy, "Reform of the Georgia State Merit System," in *Public Personnel Administration: Problems and Prospects*, ed. by Steven W. Hays and Richard C. Kearney (Englewood Cliffs, NJ: Prentice-Hall, 1983), chap. 20.

42. See Mosher, *Democracy and the Public Service*, chap. 6.

43. Richard C. Kearny, *Labor Relations in the Public Sector* (New York: Marcel Dekker, 1984), p. 7

44. Ibid., p. 19.

45. N. Joseph Cayer, *Public Personnel Administration in the United States*, 2d ed. (New York: St. Martin's Press, 1986), p. 133.

46. Richard B. Freeman and Casey Ichniowski, "The Public Sector Look of American Unionism," in *When Public Sector Workers Unionize*, ed. by Richard B. Freeman and Casey Ichniowski (Chicago: University of Chicago Press, 1988), p. 1.

47. See Richard B. Freeman, Casey Ichniowski, and Jeffrey Zax, "Collective Organization of Labor in the Public Sector," in *When Public Sector Workers Unionize*, ed. by Richard B. Freeman and Casey Ichniowski (Chicago: University of Chicago Press, 1988), pp. 365–98; table on p. 379.

48. Mosher, *Democracy and the Public Service*, p. 191

49. Freeman and Ichniowski, "The Public Sector Look of American Unionism."

50. Cayer, *Public Personnel Administration*, p. 135.

51. Jay M. Shafritz, Albert Hyde, and David Rosenbloom, *Personnel Management in*

Government: Politics and Process, 3d ed. (New York: Marcel Dekker, 1986), pp. 322–23. See also Freeman and Ichniowski, "Collective Organization of Labor in the Public Sector."

52. Casey Ichniowski, "Arbitration and Police Bargaining: Prescriptions for the Blue Flu," *Industrial Relations* 21 (Spring 1982): 149–66.

53. Freeman and Ichniowski, "The Public Sector Look of American Unionism."

54. Kearney, *Labor Relations in the Public Sector*, pp. 246–47.

CHAPTER **13**

MANAGING

FINANCIAL

RESOURCES

Raising and Spending Money

In this chapter we focus on the role of public administrators in managing *financial* resources—that is, raising revenues, spending public dollars, and managing the public debt. We consider these financial management functions from the perspectives of the many public expectations influencing them. After reviewing some of the basic concepts of public finance, we discuss what some of those expectations are and how they vary over time and among places. Next, we focus on administrative processes to determine how agencies and administrators meet those expectations through day-to-day government operations. Finally, we consider several major issues and events that have shaped the way governments manage their finances.

Basic Concepts of Public Finance

Financial resource management covers a wide range of activities.[1] It deals with how governments raise the money (*revenues*) they need to pay for public services. It also focuses on how governments spend those revenues (*expenditures*), their plans for handling the public purse (*budgeting*), their management of public *assets* and *liabilities*, and a variety of other tasks.

Revenues. Government revenue collections come in a variety of forms, including taxes, user charges, and administrative fees. *User charges* are specific fees that governments require us to pay for certain services provided by public-sector agencies. For example, when you pay a city water bill or an admission charge to a municipal swimming pool, you are paying a user charge.

Administrative charges are the special fees we pay when the government processes some application or issues some legal document to us. When you renew your driver's license or obtain a title registration for your car, for example, you pay a special fee to help offset administrative costs. Often these fees are nominal, but they can be an important source of government revenues for many small public agencies.

Revenues take the form of *taxes* when the government requires a citizen to pay a certain amount based on a tax rate applied to a specified item or activity. Thus, a local government might require a local firm to pay a tax for every employee it has—this is called a *head tax*. *Property taxes* are levied on the value of specified possessions held by the taxpayer. Almost all homeowners pay a property tax, and a portion of the rent paid by most renters is used by the property owner to pay the property taxes assigned to the building. In some states, property taxes are also applied to personal possessions such as cars and boats. Several states even impose property taxes on business inventories.

When most of us think about taxes, however, we think of *income taxes*.

Income taxes are levied against the amount of money an employee earns or the amount of profit made by a company. Another common tax is the *sales tax*, which is assessed at the time of purchase in jurisdictions that have adopted this kind of revenue source. In some states and cities, sales taxes are levied on all purchases; in others, there are exemptions for such items as food and books. Related to the sales tax is the *consumption tax*, which is levied on the purchase of specific products, such as cigarettes, alcoholic beverages, and gasoline. In New York, for example, a consumption tax of more than 80 cents is paid each time someone purchases a six-pack of beer.

These various taxes are merely the tip of the taxation iceberg that supplies most governments with their operating revenues each year (see Insight 13.1).

Expenditures. Government expenditures usually take two forms: purchase expenditures and transfer payments. *Purchase expenditures* are those public funds spent to provide public goods and services. This money buys equipment, pays personnel, and purchases whatever other resources and services are necessary to get the job done.

In contrast, *transfer payments* involve government taking money from one source and giving it to another. For example, the Social Security Administration (SSA) collects payroll taxes from most U.S. citizens and redistributes those funds to individuals eligible for Social Security benefits. Similarly, the federal government collects fuel taxes from consumers and redistributes those funds back to the states, where they are used to help offset the costs of highway maintenance.

Budgeting. Every governmental unit develops projections and plans for how it will collect revenues and allocate expenditures. These activities are part of the *budgeting* process. Most governments have two major budgets: (1) the *operating* or *current budget*, which focuses on the revenues and expenditures needed to operate government services on a day-to-day basis; and (2) a *capital budget*, which concentrates on funding long-term, nonrecurring projects such as building highways or constructing schools.

Public Assets. Of course, governments do more than merely raise revenues and spend money. Often they accumulate funds temporarily or purchase public facilities needed to carry out their jobs. These are called *public assets*. For example, a certain percentage of every dollar you spend on gasoline for your car goes into a federal highway trust fund. This trust fund is used to pay for constructing or maintaining many of the nation's major roads. Government officials are responsible for managing that trust fund as a public asset.

Similarly, many government agencies need to purchase and maintain buildings and equipment in order to implement public programs. Local governments must have sewage-treatment plants, snow plows, courthouses,

INSIGHT 13.1

THE DEBATE OVER
THE SERVICE TAX

In their continuing search for more revenue sources, state governments have turned to a new form of the sales tax—the *service tax*. The problem is that states have faced fierce opposition to this new source of funds for the public purse.

The service tax is merely an extension of the sales tax—whereas the sales tax is levied on the purchase of goods, the service tax imposes a certain tax rate on the purchase of services. Thus, a car owner who previously paid a tax on only the parts used in an auto repair would also pay a service tax on the labor portion of that repair bill as well. Similarly, the service tax can apply to a wide range of other services, from those provided by plumbers and house builders to those of dentists and physicians. The specific services that are taxed depend on the way the state's law is drawn up.

Although there were only three states using some form of service tax in 1987, proposals for the tax showed up on the legislative agendas of Florida, Illinois, Washington, Texas, Oklahoma, Montana, and several other states. The service tax is especially inviting to states because it taxes the area of the American economy that has demonstrated the greatest growth in recent years. As the United States moves from an industrial-based to a service-based economic system, an increasing amount of money is being spent on services ranging from legal matters to day-care functions.

Of all the states considering the service tax in 1987, Florida's efforts drew the most attention. As the fastest-growing state in the nation, Florida was seeking new revenue sources to deal with its increasing financial needs and the service tax seemed to be the ideal source. After much debate and compromise (e.g., there was an exclusion for medical services), the Florida legislature adopted the service tax in April 1987. However, the state faced much opposition to the tax. One provision in particular was strongly opposed—a 5-percent tax on all commercial advertising in the state (no matter where it was produced). A lawsuit challenging Florida's service tax was filed in May 1987 by the Association of National Advertisers, which also threatened a boycott of the state's media. Eventually, the state's policymakers were forced to rescind the service tax.

Florida's attempt to adopt the service tax and its ultimate defeat had an impact on other state governments considering the tax. Governor James R. Thompson of Illinois, for instance, withdrew his recommendation for a 3-percent service tax to that state's legislature, and lobbyists in Montana, Washington, and Oklahoma had a hand in defeating similar measures in those states. In Oklahoma, the state medical society was a strong opponent. In the Oklahoma measure, even financial and insurance services were exempt. While those proposed adjustments ultimately resulted in the defeat of the tax proposal, the debate led to a compromise in which Oklahoma's general sales tax was increased from 3.25 percent to 4 percent.

The legislative battles over the service tax are not over. Most observers predict that the tax will be adopted by more states in the near future. For public finance managers and other administrative officials, service taxes will be both a source of financial relief and a source of administrative headaches.

SOURCE: Based on information in Georgina Fiordalisi, "Service Taxes under Attack," *City & State*, June 1987, pp. 1, 46.

jails, firefighting equipment, and the like to provide certain services. NASA has to build and operate launch sites, rocket boosters, and training centers for astronauts. Public administrators must manage, protect, and improve the value of these various public assets while they are under the control of the government.

Public Liabilities. With increasing frequency, governments must also manage the financial and other obligations of the public sector known as *public liabilities*. This is especially true today at the federal government level, where there exists a public debt (deficit) of billions of dollars. The management of this debt (e.g., arranging for loans by issuing government bonds and paying the interest on those loans) is also the responsibility of American public administration.

Managing the Public's Purse

Taken together, these areas of government activity—revenue raising, expenditure allocation, budgeting, and management of public assets and liabilities—constitute the area of *public financial management*. Some students of public administration regard these activities as highly technical tasks that are best left to accountants and other specialists trained to deal with financial matters. Yet it may be an area of public administration that is too important to leave to the actions of specialists. Much of the American public's expectations regarding the administration of government programs are closely linked to how public officials manage financial resources. Thus, while specialists may handle many of the details of public financial management, it is important that students and practitioners of public administration understand what is involved in carrying out these crucial governmental functions.

Expectations and Public Finance

The American public's expectations regarding how government handles its finances are not easily summarized. There is no single or overarching expectation that provides a clear and consistent challenge to public administrators. As in other areas of government work, managing the public purse is subject to many and often conflicting demands. For our purposes, however, these expectations can be summarized in terms of general objectives and standards of performance in public financial management.

General Objectives

At the most general level, there are several goals or objectives we expect of government financial administrators. These include (1) providing goods and services, (2) financial accountability, (3) achieving economic policy goals, and (4) achieving social policy goals.

Providing Goods and Services.   We expect government to raise enough funds to provide us with the goods and services required under programs established through our political system. In short, we want the government's financial resources to be spent on activities and purchases relevant to the implementation of duly authorized public policies. During the 1960s, for example, we expected administrators at NASA to use their budgeted money to purchase the equipment and pay for the personnel that would land an American on the moon by 1970. Similarly, when we pay local property taxes to the local school district, we expect school administrators to use those funds to provide the best educational opportunities possible for our children.

How government accomplishes these objectives depends on the delivery method selected by policymakers (see Chapter 2). Traditionally, governments provide many goods and services through *legal monopolies*, in which it is the sole provider. In many cities, for example, only a publicly owned or regulated utility company can sell electric power or offer trash-collection services to local residents. At other times, governments engage in *competition* with private-sector companies to provide certain services. The U.S. Postal Service (USPS) has an overnight package delivery service that competes directly with privately owned companies such as Federal Express and United Parcel Service (UPS). At still other times, the government enters into *joint ventures* with private-sector companies to provide a service to the public. In the 1960s, for instance, the federal government joined with American Telephone and Telegraph, RCA Corporation, and other corporations to form the COMSAT Corporation. COMSAT helped fund the development and launch of our first communications satellites into orbit around the earth.

Thus, there are a variety of ways in which American governments can accomplish this public finance objective. There is considerable pressure for government to provide goods and services in the least costly and most efficient manner. Nevertheless, it is clear that the very act of providing them is a basic response to the American public's general objectives.

Financial Accountability.   Another objective expected of government administrators is that they be held accountable for carrying out their financial management functions. The American public expects government agencies and administrators to keep careful records for every dollar of revenue raised and expenditure spent. Furthermore, many financial management procedures are designed to facilitate public input, legislative oversight, and other forms of accountability.

One important aspect of this accountability is open access to financial facts. For example, information about the salaries of managers in public agencies is part of the public record. In contrast, the salaries of managers in private corporations are rarely known by their co-workers or the general public. Similarly, the salaries of faculty and administrators at state universities are public information, whereas data about individual salaries at private colleges and universities are rarely released.

In responding to the objective of financial accountability, governments often establish special agencies to audit public-sector expenditures (see Chapter 7). At the federal level this task belongs to the General Accounting Office (GSA), which is an arm of Congress headed by the Comptroller General of the United States. Similar agencies operate at the state level and in most major city governments. Cities that are not large enough to justify separate audit departments rely on outside auditors to review annually their use of public funds.

Achieving Economic Policy Goals.   In addition to the provisions of goods and services and financial accountability, most Americans expect the design and management of public finances to complement or promote the economic objectives of government (see Chapter 6). For example, in many local and state governments, citizens expect taxes to be low enough to attract and retain business firms and employment to the area. At the same time, citizens expect government expenditures to be high enough to provide for the needs of those very same firms.

At the national level, we expect government taxation and expenditures to be managed in ways that help promote economic stability or growth. For example, under provisions of one federal law, the flow of federal money to the states can be speeded up or slowed down when conditions warrant it. The idea behind this legislation is that through management of grants to states, the federal government can help stimulate economic activity when necessary. For instance, when inflationary economic conditions exist, indicating a need for fiscal restraint by government, the president of the United States can order the temporary deferral of highway construction funds. When the opposite conditions exist and increased government spending is needed to stimulate economic activity, the White House can order the Department of Transportation to expedite or increase the flow of money to states for spending on new highway construction. Of course, presidential manipulation of federal funding depends on the cooperation of Congress, for the House and Senate can overturn presidential spending deferrals. This is what happened in the late 1970s, when Congress voted to order that $9 billion of presidentially deferred highway funding be released.[2]

Underlying this general objective is *Keynesian economic theory*. Named after the British economist John Maynard Keynes, this theory holds that government can use its expenditures and taxation—that is, *fiscal policies*—to adjust the U.S. economy. According to the Keynesian theory, when policymakers are facing an economy where unemployment is increasing and economic growth is on the decline, the government should step in to stimulate economic activity. Government can stimulate the economy by spending more money and thus increasing the demand for products, which, in turn, leads to increased demand for production and more jobs. Government can also stimulate the economy by decreasing taxes and thus placing more money in the hands of investors and consumers who, in turn, are more likely to invest or spend their money in ways that will generate new production and more jobs. Under the Keynesian approach, when the economy is growing too fast—that is, when price levels become inflationary and production begins to exceed the capacity of consumers to consume—government can reduce its spending and raise taxes to help arrest excessive economic activity.

The Keynesian approach was first adopted near the end of the New Deal period and became widely accepted among major policymakers after World War II. By the 1960s, many of the country's top economists and economic policymakers were convinced that the U.S. economy could be "fine-tuned" and operated at a prosperous level through the careful management of government expenditures and taxation policies.[3] In recent years, however, the Keynesian approach to the economy has come under criticism and challenge. These criticisms emerged during the late 1970s and early 1980s, when the U.S. economy was suffering simultaneously from both inflation and a growing unemployment rate. Called *stagflation*, the situation of the economy could not be easily explained or resolved by advocates of Keynesian economic policies.[4] As a result, two alternative economic policy perspectives gained popularity: monetarist policy and supply-side economics.

Monetary policy is advocated by policymakers and economists who believe that the government's control over the supply of money is the key to economic policy. Led by Nobel laureate Milton Friedman, these monetarists argue that too much government manipulation of the economy through expenditures and taxation actually causes more economic problems than it resolves. In contrast, advocates of *supply-side economics* favor reductions in government spending and taxes to stimulate greater investment and production by businesses rather than greater demand.

While all three approaches to managing the economy—Keynesian, monetarist, and supply-side economics—center on some government involvement in the economy, it is the Keynesian approach that most directly relies on government management of public finances. However, each perspective recognizes the role of government taxing and spending practices on the vitality of the U.S. economy.

Achieving Social Policy Goals.   Government also uses financial management practices to implement social policies. In most cases, such policies
involve providing financial benefits to the poor or needy either directly or
indirectly (see Insight 13.2). For example, governments wishing to aid the
poor may do so through direct cash subsidies such as welfare checks, which
are drawn on the general treasury of the government and sent to qualified
individuals or families. An alternative involves taking money from special
funds set aside for the poor. For example, unemployed Americans are eligible to receive weekly checks for up to twenty-six weeks from a special
trust fund financed through a tax imposed on employers.

Governments also use their tax systems to accomplish social policy objectives. For example, the poor may receive aid indirectly through a *progressive
income-tax* system. Under this system, the more a taxpayer earns, the higher
the tax rate that is applied to his or her income. Thus, most of the burden
of funding public services—many of which may involve helping the poor—
falls upon citizens at the upper-income levels. The federal income tax has
had a progressive rate structure for decades.

Still another tax-based approach involves a *negative income tax*. Under this
tax, the government makes up the difference between what a taxpayer
earned during a given period and a certain minimum amount of money
that policymakers determine to be sufficient for survival. While there is no
negative income tax program in effect today, the federal government has
experimented with the idea.[5]

Standards of Performance

When it comes to public finances, the American public expects quite a bit.
It expects the government to raise its money efficiently and to spend it
effectively. It wants public funds to be distributed equitably and without
favor. In short, most of the more important ethical standards of public
administration discussed in Chapter 3 (e.g., efficiency, effectiveness, and
equity) find direct expression in the standards of performance imposed on
public finance activities. In the area of public finance, however, those ethical
standards take on specific characteristics.

Efficiency.   In its most general form, efficiency focuses on taking actions
that maximize benefits and minimize costs. In somewhat narrower administrative terms, efficiency means getting the most out of every dollar spent
to implement a policy or program. In financial terms, the meaning of efficiency depends on the type of government fiscal activity. In government
spending, for example, efficiency calls for making expenditures in a manner
that generates the maximum amount of satisfaction from such spending. If
a city fire department has $50,000 to spend on a new fire truck, it wants
to purchase the best piece of firefighting equipment available at that price.

INSIGHT 13.2
BUDGET CHOICES
VERSUS PUBLIC HEALTH

This is the story of two local governments in California and the choices they had to make on spending public funds for public health services in 1987. It is the story of a city and a county, one a major metropolitan area and the other a rural community. It is the story of one community stretching its limited resources to meet its perceived social obligations and of another community cutting back under the constraints of budgetary realities.

The city is San Francisco, and the problem it faced in 1987 was how to fund its local fight against the epidemic of Acquired Immune Deficiency Syndrome—AIDS. San Francisco had long been known for its large and politically powerful gay community. Since the AIDS epidemic hit that community in the mid-1980s, the city had been responsive to the needs of those afflicted with the deadly disease. "The city has pieced together a network of services for AIDS patients," reported Rodd Zolkos, "setting aside more and more public hospital beds, establishing hospices, providing education and counseling, boosting medical staff and training, and providing outpatient care."

The costs of these efforts were not small and the commitment of city resources to them grew significantly. In 1983, San Francisco spent $184,447 on AIDS-related health care and services. By 1986, that figure had increased to $8.8 million, and in the fiscal year 1988, the city's budget called for $17.5 million to be spent on AIDS-related services. Those expenditures strained the city's resources and forced its mayor to call for more state and federal assistance. "We are fighting the public health crisis of the century with very limited municipal resources," the mayor said. According to reporter Rodd Zolkos,

Funding the AIDS programs has strained San Francisco's general fund budget, but city officials see no alternatives.

"After all, it is a public health problem," said Sally Osaki, an assistant to the mayor. "It's not something that local governments should have to finance by themselves."

While the San Francisco Board of Supervisors has readily approved the mayor's requests for more AIDS funding thus far, their cooperation is likely to be more strained as the city budget gets tighter.

Not far away, in rural Shasta County, California, the financial strain of health care was also taking its toll. In November 1987, despite a court order prohibiting it from doing so, Shasta County closed its seventy-three-bed inpatient health-care facilities at Shasta General Hospital. The largest health-care facility in this county of 150,000 residents, the hospital was well known for its high-quality medical care. Its closing was the latest in a series of steps taken by the county to deal with a $2.5 million deficit in its budget of $110 million. The first step was to close the county library system and then to order a 5-percent cut in spending for all county agencies. But when the Shasta General Hospital ran up a $250,000 deficit between July and November in 1987, the county's leaders felt they had no alternative but to close the inpatient facility.

Located in a rural area north of the state capital in Sacramento, Shasta County did not suffer firsthand from the onslaught of the AIDS epidemic. Rather, it felt the squeeze of lower tax revenues and higher service demands brought on by a combination of regional economic and state welfare policy conditions. Economically, the region was dependent on mining and timber, two industries that had their problems in recent years. Nevertheless, the area's low cost of living and, ironically, its reputation for providing high-quality health care attracted a growing number of indigent individuals and families to the county. Under state welfare policy rules, the people living in Shasta County received the same benefits as those living in areas like Los Angeles, where the cost of living is much higher. Thus, this made the county an inviting place for those who can make greater use of the local government's public health services. But it also made a poor fiscal situation even worse.

Like San Francisco, Shasta County turned to outside governments for assistance. Although the California State legislature provided some additional funds to Shasta and other poor rural counties, the problem had not been resolved. For the people of Shasta County and San Francisco it was more than a matter of money—it was a matter of the public's health.

SOURCE: Quotes and information from Rodd Zolkos, "San Francisco's Fight against AIDS Strains Budget," *City & State*, December 1987, p. 30; and William Fulton, "Rural California County Shuts down Services," *City & State*, December 1987, p. 48.

Similarly, a school administrator with an extra $36,000 to hire two new music teachers would search for the best teachers available within that salary range.

The greater the role of government in the economy, the more concern there is for economic efficiency in expenditures and taxation. Under this standard of performance, we evaluate each dollar that government spends or collects in terms of its impact on economic performance. Some critics of social welfare expenditures argue that every dollar given to welfare recipients is an inefficient use of government funds because it reduces the incentive for those individuals to look for a job and engage in productive work. They argue that the money should encourage economic activity rather than discourage it. Similarly, some analysts argue that the progressive income tax is economically inefficient because it reduces the incentive for high-income people to make more money through investments. That is, since the government taxes each additional dollar high-income earners make at a higher rate, the incentive to earn more money through investments is diminished.

Effectiveness.   Unlike efficiency standards, which measure each public expenditure or revenue-raising activity in terms of its costs, effectiveness considers the overall impact above all else. When assessing the Great Society programs of the 1960s and 1970s, for example, we are more likely to ask about how many fewer American families live below the poverty line than how much it cost to reduce the number of poor Americans. If we were to consider the effectiveness of antipoverty programs from 1965 through 1980, our assessment would be rather positive. While 18 percent of the U.S. families lived with incomes that fell below the poverty line in 1960, by 1970 that figure had dropped to 10 percent, and by 1974 to 8.8 percent. However, as we extend our assessment into the 1980s, the picture looks less positive, for by 1983 the number of American families living in poverty had climbed to over 10.4 percent and remained in the double digits for most of the decade (see Figure 13.1).[6]

Often program effectiveness is specific to the agency's tasks. The effectiveness of expenditures for law enforcement can take the form of reduced

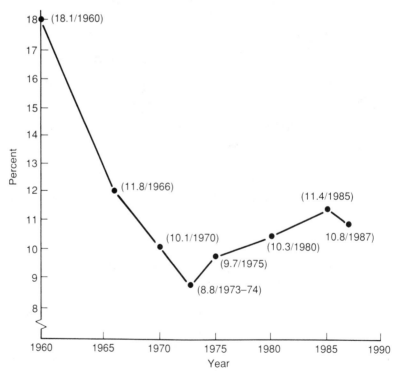

FIGURE 13.1 Families living below the poverty line, 1960–1987. (Source: Data from Bureau of the Census, *Statistical Abstract of the United States, 1989* [Washington, DC: Government Printing Office, 1989], table 739.)

crime rates or higher arrest rates. Similarly, the value of money spent on education may be assessed by considering how many students graduate from high school and how many of them go on to attend top-rated universities and colleges.

We can also evaluate tax collection in terms of its effectiveness. In public finance management, an effective tax is one that enables the government to collect as much revenue as possible from its efforts. The Internal Revenue Service (IRS), for example, is relatively effective in its collection of the personal income tax. Through a system that requires employers to report the wages they pay and taxpayers to report their earnings, the IRS is able to collect hundreds of billions of dollars each year from American taxpayers. Nevertheless, even the IRS has a long way to go. Although estimates vary widely, experts claimed in 1988 that approximately $100 billion of federal income taxes go uncollected each year.[7]

However, the IRS is not the only agency with revenue-collection problems. State and local governments depend on retail merchants to collect and report sales taxes, but some merchants fail to record all of their sales. To a degree, the fact that such behavior is illegal helps to generate merchant cooperation and therefore the effectiveness of sales-tax collections. It also helps that some states allow merchants to keep a small percentage of their sales-tax collections to help offset the administrative costs of complying with the tax law. Such incentives are bound to enhance the effectiveness of the sales tax.

Equity. Public finance managers also must concern themselves with the equity standard; that is, they must treat individuals fairly. What is considered "fair," however, depends on the particular standard being applied.[8]

In some cases, public finance managers are required to apply a *market equity* standard. Under market equity, the government gives you what you pay for. Public program resources are expended in accordance with the amount of money a citizen pays. The more one pays for the use of some public-sector service, the more one receives. This is the case with toll roads and turnpikes, where drivers pay for their use of the highway miles they have traveled.

Another form of equity standard for public expenditures is *equal opportunity*. Under this standard, the government spends an equal amount of program resources for each and every citizen. Several states, for example, have developed funding formulas for education, which guarantee that an equal amount of money is being spent on elementary and secondary education for each child throughout the state.

The equity standard can also focus on *equal results*, in which the government expends funds in a way that guarantees equal outcomes for every citizen. A city is expected to spend enough money on snow removal in hilly neighborhoods to make certain that streets in those areas are as accessible as those in flat areas. This may mean spending twice as much for the hilly areas, but the equal results standard requires such actions. A similar logic is often important when government spends money to promote social welfare. Many government welfare programs are structured so that families with greater need receive more support than those with lesser need. A single parent with three small children is likely to get more welfare benefits than a senior citizen who lives alone.

Equity concerns are particularly important in the area of taxation, where government often aims for both horizontal and vertical equity. *Horizontal equity* occurs when people with equal capacity to pay taxes actually pay the same amount in taxes. Thus, under an income tax that doesn't have any "loopholes," every person who earns $10,000 a year will pay an identical amount to the IRS. *Vertical equity* exists when those who have a greater capacity to pay do in fact pay more taxes. The idea behind a progressive income tax is vertical equity. A progressive tax accomplishes this by making the higher-income individual or family pay a higher tax rate. An individual earning $10,000 a year might pay a 10-percent tax on income, while a neighbor earning $20,000 might pay a 15-percent tax.

Of course, no tax currently used by American governments achieves perfect horizontal or vertical equity. Sometimes this is because the very structure of the tax works against true equity. Even with the major income-tax reforms passed by Congress in 1986, the federal income-tax code contains so many loopholes that horizontal and vertical inequities are impossible to eliminate.

There are other taxes, however, that are difficult to administer equitably. Property taxes paid by local homeowners, for example, are based on real estate assessments by local tax assessors. Studies of those assessments indicate that in almost every instance property is significantly undervalued. That is, the actual market value of a home is usually much higher than the tax-assessment value. More important, however, is the finding that equivalent properties are often assessed at different values. While one home worth $100,000 on the marketplace may be assessed at $25,000 for tax purposes, another home down the street with an identical market value might be assessed at $40,000 for tax purposes. Much of this discrepancy is due to the administration of property assessment by the local assessor's office. For example, oftentimes homes are not reassessed unless they are sold. Thus, someone who owns the same home for twenty-five years is probably paying taxes based on an outdated assessment value. However, someone who owns a home that has been sold four or five times in the past twenty-five years is probably paying taxes based on a more recent assessment value. Recently many state and local governments have attempted to reform the property-assessment process by providing clearer standards for assessment and by hiring more professionals to administer the property-valuation procedures.[9]

Many Masters to Satisfy

The task of the public finance manager is a complicated one. The raising of revenue and the spending of public funds are hefty responsibilities. These government functions are made even more complex by the diverse expectations of the American public—expectations covering almost every dimension of what public finance managers can do and how they do it (see Insight 13.3). These expectations are an everyday challenge for public finance managers as they deal with budgeting, tax collection, the expenditure of public funds, and debt management.

Getting the Job Done

Public finance management is not one job but many. For our purposes, there are three main components to this management task: (1) the development of a budget or plan for managing public finances, (2) the execution of the budget plan through tax collection and spending public funds, and (3) the management of public debts.

Budgeting

Each year, most governments throughout the United States go through a public ritual known as the budgetary process.[10] From the typical citizen's perspective, this process begins when the president, governor, mayor, or county or town executive presents budget recommendations to the legislative body for its consideration and approval. This is usually followed by weeks and sometimes months of legislative meetings and hearings, and ultimately passage of spending bills that detail the raising and spending of public funds over the next year (see Figure 13.2, page 363).

While this visible public process is important, it represents only a part of the entire budgetary process. Behind the scenes are usually hundreds of public-sector workers who devote many hours to putting together the information that ultimately appears in the budget document. These people also are responsible for implementing the budget decisions that eventually emerge from the legislature. It is the work of these public administrators that most concerns us here.

A budget is a unique government document. Because money is central to almost everything government agencies do, the budget represents a proposed plan of action for public-sector organizations. Specifically, a *budget* is a plan "for the accomplishment of programs related to [agency] objectives and goals within a definite time period. . . ."[11] It provides estimates for how much it will cost to achieve program objectives during that period, often including details about the source of funding for the programs and the distribution of products or services.

The budgetary process that develops this plan is an ongoing effort that takes place in annual budget cycles. A budgetary cycle typically involves several distinct tasks: (1) environmental analysis and policy planning, (2) expenditure estimates and the review of budget choices, (3) revenue estimates, (4) preparation of the budget document, and (5) legislative review and adoption.[12]

INSIGHT 13.3

THE HIGH COST
OF PROTECTING
THE PUBLIC'S PURSE

The politics of the budgeting process is a well-studied subject. In most cases, policymakers assume that agency heads will seek as much money for their organizations as they can. Yet there is just so much money to be distributed, and it is not unusual for the total amount requested by all agencies in a government to exceed the total amount of expected revenues. This is especially true in state and local governments, where there are constitutional and legal restraints on the amount of debt a jurisdiction can assume. In many instances, government officials cannot propose a budget calling for spending more money than they expect to collect through revenue sources. Thus, those who must evaluate agency requests and forward them to the legislative body often face the tasks of making difficult choices and cutting where necessary to fit within the recommended guidelines and revenue estimates.

Such choices are commonplace in the world of public financial management, but every now and then the consequences are dramatic and even tragic. Such was the case in Hackensack, New Jersey, where, on July 1, 1988, five firefighters lost their lives when the roof of a burning car dealership collapsed. An investigation into the deaths concluded that the firefighters had died needlessly. Communications flaws were a major contributing factor in the incident; for example, warnings ordering some firefighters to leave the area went unheeded, and pleas for

help by trapped firefighters were not heard in time. These were communications flaws resulting from a lack of sufficient communications equipment. Just a few months before, the fire department's request for upgraded radio equipment was rejected by the city manager's office. The investigation pinpointed that rejection for criticism.

On September 23, 1988, the city manager of Hackensack and his fire chief held a press conference to respond to the investigators' conclusions. "I believe there is a collective system failure that occurred," said City Manager Robert F. Casey. The system "did not provide to the department what was needed." While the fire department had requested funds for the new communications equipment and several additional firefighter positions, the requests were denied "because all city departments, including fire, police, and public works, had to trim proposed budgets by 10 percent to offset a $1.5 million increase in the city's garbage-disposal costs."

The city manager's explanation went beyond those points and focused on the fire chief who sat by him at the press conference. He spoke of how the "squeaky wheel" typically gets the most funding in local government finance and he noted that the fire chief—despite having formally protested the cuts in his agency's budget proposals—"was not forceful enough in making his depart-

ment's needs known to city officials."
Obviously, there was plenty of blame to
go around city hall.

SOURCE: Based on information in Robert Han-
ley, "City Manager Cites Failure of Government
in Fatal Jersey Fire," *New York Times*, 24 September 1988, p. 30.

Environmental Analysis and Policy Planning. During the environmental analysis and policy planning phase, agencies assess relevant environmental conditions, develop priorities for the coming year, and generate
information about the costs of maintaining and improving ongoing programs
or developing new ones. The analysis of relevant environmental conditions
can inform agency members if there is a greater or lesser need for their
services. School districts, for example, can analyze population trends or state
highway engineers can assess the increasing use of certain roads. Priorities
can be based on these assessments, as can general program cost estimates.

Expenditure Estimates and Budget Choices. Once there is some
semblance of agreement on overall program priorities, the budget cycle

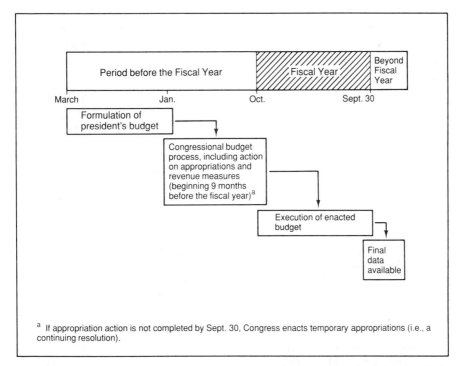

FIGURE 13.2   The budgetary process. (Source: *The United States Budget in Brief, FY
1989* [Washington, DC: Executive Office of the President, January 1988], p. 92.)

focuses on developing expenditure estimates. In this phase, agency personnel begin to detail the specific costs of implementing a program or carrying out a particular project. In some agencies, this phase merely involves listing personnel and material costs.

In recent years, however, governments have come under increasing pressure to increase the efficiency of their programs. Many agencies have responded by adopting more analytical approaches to estimating program expenditures—approaches that attempt to promote the most efficient use of public funds. These approaches include estimating the costs of a program or project relative to the benefits it generates. In the federal government, for example, the Army Corps of Engineers and other public works agencies have pioneered the use of cost-benefit analysis, which involves the application of basic economic principles to public decisions. Underlying this approach is the idea that governments must make the best choices among the various projects that it might fund.

When dealing with a request to provide flood control along a river, for instance, the Army Corps of Engineers may have several alternative means for achieving their objective. One option might be to construct an upstream dam to control the flow of water onto a flood plain. Another option might be to dig a deeper and wider channel for the river to contain excess water flows. Still a third option might be to do nothing and make local communities adapt to the prospect of flooding by not building near the river's banks. Through a cost-benefit analysis, the Army Corps examines what each of these options would cost and the benefits that each might yield.

Let us assume that building a dam for $5 million is likely to generate $10 million in benefits, in that it would stop floods and create a new recreational area around the reservoir located behind the dam. The estimate for digging out a bigger channel for the river is $5 million as well, but this option would generate only $7.5 million in benefits. Finally, let's say that doing nothing would impose a $2 million cost on local communities but would yield few benefits. Given this scenario, the analyst is likely to recommend the adoption of the dam option because it will provide the best cost-to-benefit ratio.[13]

The Department of Defense has also been at the forefront of developing highly sophisticated expenditure-estimating techniques. Using the techniques of operations research and systems analysis adopted from engineering, Pentagon analysts developed a means for estimating the potential costs of alternative administrative procedures. Called *planning-programming-budgeting*, this approach to budget analysis was widely adopted by federal, state, and local governments during the 1960s and 1970s (see Chapter 2).[14]

Ultimately, however, the agency's budget request involves political decisions as much as technical analyses. Armed with their analyses, plans, and estimates, agency members enter the next part of the budget cycle—a review of budget choices. As noted earlier, agencies are under constant political pressures, some of which come from clientele groups and from within the organization. Thus, the Army Corps of Engineers might recommend a less cost-effective alternative for flood control due to political pressures applied by local communities. Or the Pentagon might respond to pressures from the Joint Chiefs of Staff concerning the selection of a particular weapons system. Agencies can also be influenced by what they perceive to be the wishes of the chief executive or a member of the legislature. It is not uncommon for a mayor's or a city commissioner's pet project to show up as a budget recommendation. Thus, this review phase tempers much of the technical analyses that preceded it with a dose of political reality.

Revenue Estimates.   Of course, while calculating what it will cost to run agency programs, public finance managers must also consider how they will obtain the funds to pay for them. In many cases, special agencies whose primary function is the collection of taxes provide the revenue estimates. Thus, the Treasury Department handles revenue collection and estimates for almost all federal government agencies because most programs at that level are funded by general revenues. The same is true for many state and local agencies, which depend on a revenue department for estimates of available funds.

Over the past four decades, an important source of revenues for many state and local agencies has been *intergovernmental grants-in-aid*. These grants involve transfers of public funds from one level of government to another. Thus, many local school districts use money provided through the Department of Education to fund special education programs and other services for special student populations. Similarly, many state governments give those local school districts money to offset the costs of their day-to-day operations. The Federal Highway Trust Fund provides states with the money they need to build and maintain roads that are part of the U.S. interstate highway system. In a similar fashion, states allocate funds to county government officials who build and maintain county roads.

The intergovernmental grant system is not a new source of program funding. At the national level, it dates back to the Civil War, when Congress offered states funds and land to help establish land-grant colleges. In recent years, however, intergovernmental grants have become major factors in developing budget plans at all levels of government (see Chapter 7).

Grants designed for specific purposes are called *categorical grants*. The federal government, for example, offers local communities funds to help them build sewage-treatment facilities or senior citizen centers. Sometimes these are funded on a project-by-project basis. To obtain a federal *project grant*, a state or local government must provide the funding agency with a detailed proposal that meets agency specifications. At other times, distribution of intergovernmental funds is according to some set formula that might reflect the recipient government's needs. Factors that comprise these *formula grants* might include population size, per-capita income, population age, and the like. Until the 1970s, most categorical grants tended to be of the project type. Starting with the Nixon and Ford administrations, however, there has been a shift in grants for nonwelfare programs toward formula-based aid. This is part of an overall shift in intergovernmental relations that gives states and localities more control over the expenditure of funds they receive from Washington.[15]

The same intentions have led the federal government to rely more on *block grants* in recent years. Block grants first emerged during the Johnson administration, when a number of grant programs for health-related services were consolidated in a single comprehensive package. But it was the Nixon administration that made block grants a priority. Block grants usually involve the consolidation of a number of categorical grant programs. These grants, however, do not call for specific plans or projects on the part of recipient governments. Instead, they are distributed to recipient governments according to a set formula and with specifications that the money be spent on programs within a particular area (e.g., law enforcement or community development) and according to some general guidelines. This approach leaves recipient governments with considerable discretion about where and how to spend their grant money.[16]

In its most extreme form, this approach is known as *general revenue sharing*. Under general revenue sharing, governments provide funds to recipient agencies with minimal requirements or strings attached to the grants-in-aid. The Nixon administration initiated general revenue sharing on the federal level during the early 1970s. While never adding up to more than a small percentage of all federal aid to states and localities, these open-ended grants played a major role in the intergovernmental system of the 1970s by distributing federal funds to all general-purpose governments.[17] By the late 1980s, however, they had all but disappeared from the national scene. Similar programs are still in effect in some states where local governments receive open-ended grants from the states to spend as they please.

A major exception to this dependency on treasury and revenue departments involves agencies that have special revenue sources. The Federal Highway Trust Fund, for example, depends on revenues raised from taxes on gasoline sales. Other important exceptions are agencies that collect charges or fees directly from those who use its services. For example, the Triborough Bridge and Tunnel Authority in New York City gets its operating revenue from the tolls and fees it charges for the use of bridges and tunnels. State turnpike authorities use the funds they collect at their toll booths to maintain their roads. Cities often charge admission fees to zoos and swimming pools to cover the operating costs of these facilities.

In each case, the agency tries to develop a reasonable estimate of its revenues based on how much it expects people to use its facilities in the coming fiscal year. If its revenues fall short of operating expenses, then the agency must rely on additional sources of funding. State universities, for example, collect tuition and fees from students and use those funds to offset some of the costs of higher education. In most cases, however, the universities expect to receive funding from the state treasury to operate their campuses.

Preparing the Budget Document.   Once the separate agencies have prepared their estimates of expenditures and revenues, they submit these to the relevant central budgeting agency. At the federal level, this agency is the Office of Management and Budget (OMB). Similar control agencies exist at the state level and in many local governments. The budgeting agency pulls together budget information from throughout government and begins the preparation of the budget document. Typically, these central budget agencies prepare documents reflecting the overall priorities of the government's chief executive officer. For instance, at the federal level, the OMB draws up a budget document in accordance with the policies of the president of the United States.

Obviously, there are times when agency requests conflict with presidential, gubernatorial, or mayoral priorities. When this occurs, the job of the central budget agency is to adjust agency expenditure and revenue estimates to fit into the overall budget. For example, in the state of Kansas, the budget director is responsible for taking the state agency budget requests and reconciling them with the governor's programmatic priorities. Chief executives try to minimize this conflict at the outset of the budget cycle by specifying their spending guidelines in advance. Then they have their central budget agency send out policy instructions to agencies providing guidelines for their use in developing requests. For example, the governor may specify that no agency should anticipate a budget increase beyond 5 percent. This tells the agencies that any proposals for new programs or increases in program spending should fall within this 5-percent limit. Any proposal beyond this limit will not receive the governor's support.

Legislative Review and Adoption.   The chief executive forwards the comprehensive budget document to the relevant legislative bodies for their consideration (e.g., Congress, the state legislature, the city council, or a county commission). At the federal level and in many state and local governments, this takes place sometime in January each year. During this phase, the legislative body may consider two issues: (1) whether to *authorize* the expenditure of funds, and, if so, (2) how much money to *appropriate* to carry out that authorization.

Spending authorization is the legal basis for expending public funds. An agency can ask for an appropriation of $5 million to build a new bridge, but unless the county commission or state legislature provides legal authority to do so, the agency cannot spend that money. The same holds true for collecting revenues. No agency can charge user fees or tolls or tuition or collect taxes without authorization from the relevant legislative body.

Despite the fact that this phase involves legislative actions, administrative agencies may become engaged in the political maneuvering and debates that frequently characterize this part of the budget cycle.[18] Some agencies may work behind the scenes to obtain more authorization or appropriations than the central budget office document recommended. Others may work hard to ensure their allocations are not cut below the recommended level. In either case, public administrators play an important role in this critical phase of the budgetary process.

Executing the Budget Plan

Any public finance manager will testify that developing a plan for action and getting it adopted are not simple or easy tasks. Nor is the next major task: executing the budget. This phase involves implementing the taxing and spending decisions that the legislature approved.

Collecting Revenues.   The collection of taxes and other revenues can be a complicated administrative task, depending on the nature of the tax. Generally, tax administration involves several stages.[19] First, since every tax is a tax on something (called the *tax base*), tax collection involves the *process of discovering* the location of the tax base. For example, tax administrators must make certain that all income is being reported for an income tax and that all property owners are being billed for the property tax.

Having located the tax base, administrators must then *determine the value of the taxable items*. In the property tax, for example, tax collectors must assess the value of the property to determine how much tax property owners owe. In a sales tax, the state must ascertain the amount of sales on which to calculate the sales tax due.

The actual *collection* of the tax comes next, and in some cases this is no easy task. The IRS requires employers to withhold a portion of the wages they pay and to forward that money to the agency each quarter with the appropriate forms. State departments of revenue have elaborate procedures set up to collect state sales taxes, including paying merchants a small percentage of what they collect to help offset the costs of applying the tax to each purchase. When collection operations fail, tax agencies use *enforcement* procedures, which often include the power to place a lien on or seize taxpayer properties.

The administration of some taxes also includes conducting *audits*. Property assessments might be rechecked or the sales records of local merchants might be reviewed from time to time to make certain they are not circumventing the collection process or implementing it incorrectly. The IRS and state income-tax agencies regularly conduct audits of taxpayers' returns. Given the number of people involved, the IRS conducts a selective audit of tax returns. The selection criteria the agency uses for choosing which returns to audit are well-guarded secrets.

Tax administration also involves establishing *means for taxpayer protest and appeals*. If a property owner does not agree with the assessment of his or her holdings, or if an income taxpayer feels that the IRS should have allowed more deductions on his or her return, there are ways for each to appeal the decisions. Appeals often go through administrative channels. For example, a special local property assessment appeals board might review taxpayer complaints. Or there might be judicial channels for the taxpayer to follow. The IRS has taken a mixed approach. To challenge an IRS ruling on a tax return, a district tax court will hear the appeal. However, the tax court is really an administrative hearing that follows judicial-like procedures. If the taxpayer is not satisfied with the tax court's decision, he or she can take the case to the federal court of appeals.

Different administrative means exist for the collection of nontax revenues, such as federal grants or user fees. Many state and local governments have grants offices that monitor the availability of special funding and apply for them when appropriate. Agencies that collect revenues through fees or tolls must hire collection personnel and establish accounting systems.

Spending Public Funds. Implementing budgetary decisions is part of a larger process that begins when the legislative body authorizes the spending of public funds for a given purpose and formally appropriates the funds. While funds are appropriated for an entire year, the execution of the budget takes place on day-to-day, week-to-week, month-to-month, and quarter-to-quarter bases.[20] The process for distributing appropriated funds to agencies for actual spending is called *allocation*.

Agencies usually receive their allocations from the general treasury in periodic allotments, such as weekly, monthly, or quarterly. As outlined in Table 13.1, a local police department may be allotted only $1 million of its total $6 million annual appropriation on January 1. It receives only a portion of the total allocation because the city treasurer has projected that is all it will need to run the police department until March 1, when the department might receive a second allotment of $2 million. On July 1, a third allotment may be released for another $2 million, and October 1 may be the date for providing the final allotment of $1 million to the agency's managers.

TABLE 13.1   Allocation of Public Funds: An Example

The City Council Appropriates $6 Million to the Police Department		
City Treasurer Allocates	*Date Allocated*	*Cumulative Total*
$1 million	January 1	$1 million
$2 million	March 1	$3 million
$2 million	July 1	$5 million
$1 million	October 1	$6 million

There are several reasons for handling fund allocations this way. First, the process provides some control and oversight over agency expenditures. If the entire $6 million was allocated to the police department on January 1, it would be more difficult to monitor the operations of that agency than if the funds were allocated more slowly. Second, the city may have based its appropriations on projected revenues rather than money in hand. Thus, it may be necessary to allocate funds on a quarterly basis because the city is not capable of meeting its obligations to the police department "up front." Third, a quarterly allotment system provides the city with a financial safety valve. If an emergency arises that calls for a reduction in or reallocation of city funds, the allocation arrangement makes such changes easier to implement.

Another important part of the budget execution process involves the *auditing of government expenditures*. Audits are examinations of agency records and operations intended to gather information about how program funds are being used. They may be conducted by people within the agency (an internal audit) or by specialized auditing agencies such as the federal government's General Accounting Office (GAO). Most audits are merely efforts to verify that funds are being spent as they were intended and to uncover any problems that might exist.[21] Audits are also used to prevent or expose public-sector corruption. In each of these roles, auditors play a critical role in the management of public finances at all levels of government.

Managing the Public Debt

Americans have heard a great deal about public debts in recent years. On October 19, 1987, the Dow Jones Index of stocks on the New York Stock Exchange recorded its largest one-day drop in history—over five hundred points. Stock analysts and business leaders pointed to the growing federal government deficit as a primary cause of the stock market crash (see Figure 13.3). The deficit has also been blamed for more general economic woes, such as the high inflation rates of the late 1970s and the mounting international trade deficit.

The exact role of the federal deficit in any of these events has been fervently debated in Congress and the media. So has its cause. Some analysts argue that the federal debt has mounted due to increased government spending on military and domestic programs. Others blame the inability or unwillingness of Congress to raise taxes.

While the debate over the size and growth of the federal deficit continues, the fact remains that the federal government must carefully manage its debts. This is a task left to experts in the Treasury Department—public administrators who specialize in the financing of debt and its administration. In 1986, for instance, these managers of the public debt had to raise slightly

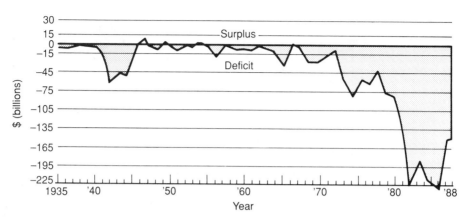

FIGURE 13.3   Federal budget surplus or deficit, 1935–1988. (Source: Bureau of the Census, *Statistical Abstract of the United States, 1989* [Washington, DC: Government Printing Office, 1989], p. 302.)

over $221 billion, representing the amount the federal government spent that year above its revenue income. Added to the deficits of previous years, Treasury Department officials in 1986 had to administer a cumulative federal debt of $2,130 billion.[22]

While its size makes the federal debt highly visible, state and local governments must also manage public debts. In 1986, state governments had $129.1 billion of long-term debts to administer while cities and other local governments carried over $367.8 billion of long-term debts. In addition, states and localities together had another $18.3 billion of short-term debts to pay in 1986.[23]

The job of debt management is a complicated one.[24] One complicating factor is that not all public debts are alike. Some public debts represent short-term loans, which must be repaid within a year or so. Nearly half of the federal debt comes to maturity (is due for payment) each year. Other public debts are long-term obligations, carrying pay-off dates years and oftentimes decades from the time they were incurred. Debts also differ in whether they represent loans that finance projects or cash transactions. Many governments incur public debts to fund specific projects. When a local community wants to build a new recreation facility or a county government wants to construct a new wing onto a local hospital, each typically arranges for a loan for the individual project. These *project loans* involve long-term indebtedness, usually ranging from ten to thirty years. *Nonproject debts* are usually short-term loans incurred to raise cash rather than to pay for a major project.

There is another important difference among debt obligations. Some public debts allow those lending the money to make claims on the general assets of the government issuing the debt. This is called a *full-faith and credit debt*, and it usually takes the form of a promise made by government officials to repay the debt through general tax revenues. Most of the federal debt is funded this way as the Treasury Department issues Savings Bonds and other general obligation debts that must be paid out of federal revenues.

Other public debts take the form of *limited-liability loans*, which give the lenders claims on particular sources of government revenue. This type of debt is common for project loans at the state and local levels. For example, a city might issue a revenue bond for $1 million to construct a new downtown parking garage. It may specify that the five-year loan will be repaid through a special assessment on downtown properties that will benefit from the structure. Similarly, a school district may ask local voters to approve a special property-tax assessment to finance a $1 million special revenue bond to build a new elementary school.

Governments use the limited-liability loan for a variety of purposes. In 1987, governments issued more than $20 billion in loans to support the construction of new public utility facilities to help generate electric power, treat city water supplies, and deal with local sewage. Governments incurred another $12 billion of limited-liability public debt in that year to finance public health-care facilities. Highways and other transportation programs generated nearly $7 billion in debt in 1987, while higher education institutions sought lenders for $4.3 billion in limited-liability loans they needed to fund dormitories and other campus facilities.[25]

The public administrators who manage government debts must engage in a number of important tasks. They must help develop an appropriate debt policy for their governments and design a debt structure for specific projects. *Debt policies* are general principles that governments and agencies follow regarding the type of borrowing they do. One common policy, for example, is not to issue a bond that has a longer life than the project it is financing. If money is borrowed to build roads that will have to be reconstructed within twenty years, it would be foolish to issue a bond that matures after twenty years.

Local governments face unique debt-management issues because they provide most basic public services, such as water and sewer lines. Growing communities often need a debt policy to deal with their growth. Real estate developers often ask the local government to provide roads, sidewalks, sewer lines, and other services to a currently undeveloped area. Their reasoning is that once the area is developed it would cost even more to put these basic city services in place. Most local governments have policies for financing such improvements. Some issue general obligation bonds (full-faith and credit loans) to pay for the improvements, whereas others have policies allowing them to impose special property taxes in the newly developed area that will pay for the necessary construction. This latter approach is known as managing debt through *special assessments*.

Still another debt policy is to mandate that governments minimize their reliance on loans and that large projects be paid for out of current revenues. This "pay-as-you-go" financing certainly reduces debt-management problems, but it often poses difficulties when applied to government projects that generate future rather than immediate benefits. Under a pay-as-you-go system, for instance, students would have to pay for the construction of a dormitory that, in all likelihood, they would not be around long enough to use. It makes more sense, then, to make those who are more likely to benefit from the new dormitory—future students of the university—pay for its construction.

These and other debt policies can prove extremely important to the operations of government. Just as important, however, is the *debt structure* designed for a particular project loan. Public debt managers must analyze each situation to determine what kind of debt is most appropriate under the circumstances. For example, is a full-faith and credit or a limited-liability loan more appropriate? What should be the maturity date for the loan? What interest rate is acceptable? What system of repayment should be used? Many of these decisions are shaped by the conditions of the economy. If interest rates are high, then the costs of borrowing will be high. If inflation is high, there is danger of underestimating the cost of a long-term project and therefore the amount of money needed.

Another factor influencing debt structure is the condition of the *municipal bond market*. The municipal bond market is that part of the American private financial market that deals with government loans. When a city or state agency wants to borrow money, it goes to private-sector bankers and securities brokers who specialize in finding lenders for the government bonds.[26] Sometimes these municipal markets are strong and governments find it relatively easy to finance their debts. At other times, however, the municipal bond market is weak and the loan may have to be restructured (e.g., by shortening the maturity date or raising the interest rate) to meet market demands.

A final important factor shaping debt structure is the perceived condition of the borrowing authority itself. Like every other organization trying to get a loan, each government and government agency with authorization to borrow money faces evaluation by lenders to determine how risky it is to lend them money. Several private-sector firms specialize in providing risk assessments of corporations and governments. Moody's Investor Service and Standard and Poor's are the best known of these firms, and each offers ratings of public-sector agencies to potential lenders (see Table 13.2). These ratings can make a significant difference in the costs of borrowing money. In 1980, for example, a "Aaa" rating from Moody's (its highest) meant a government agency could borrow funds at an interest rate of 9.44 percent. At the same time, an agency with a Moody rating of "Baa" would have paid a 10.64-percent interest rate for a similar loan. When dealing with loans

TABLE 13.2   Credit Rating Systems of Two Major Rating Services

Credit Risk	Moody's	Standard and Poor's
Prime	Aaa	AAA
Excellent	Aa	AA
Upper medium	A-1, A	A
Lower medium	Baa-1, Baa	BBB
Speculative	BA	BB
Very speculative	B, Caa	B, CCC, CC
Default	Ca, C	D

SOURCE: From *Fiscal Administration: Analysis and Applications* by J. L. Mikesell. Copyright © 1982 (second edition published in 1986) by The Dorsey Press. Reprinted by permission of Brooks/Cole Publishing Company, Pacific Grove, CA 93950, a division of Wadsworth, Inc.

worth millions of dollars, such minor differences in interest can add up to plenty of money. Thus, it is important for public debt managers to try to keep their agency's ratings as high as possible.

Public debt administration doesn't end here. The actual administration of loans — such as contending with the paperwork and paying mature debts on time — is part of the functions of public finance managers. As they manage the public debt, they are constantly aware of the responsibilities and obligations they have to those they serve. Like others who work in the public sector, they must try to reconcile the diverse expectations that relate to their jobs.

The Continuing Issues

We have surveyed public finance management and some of the most important activities involved in that job. We have considered some of the many expectations facing public finance managers and briefly described their involvement in developing government budgets, executing budget plans, and managing the public debt.

In each of these endeavors and the many other tasks associated with public finance management, the influence of expectations is obvious. As in other areas of the public sector, finance administrators must not only consider the constraints and opportunities provided by specific situations; they must also consider how those situations are influencing the expectations of policymakers, clientele and other special interest groups, the general public, and other potential sources of pressure. This is especially true in those areas where public-sector finance is most controversial. There are many issues surrounding the financing of government, ranging from the overall impact of government spending and taxation on the U.S. economy to the efficiency of local sales-tax collections. Almost all of these issues derive from the expectations others have about the work of public finance managers and their efforts to accommodate those expectations.

Consider the ongoing debate over the public debt. As noted earlier, debates in Congress and the media over the federal deficit focus on its size and growth in recent years. At the administrative level, there is growing controversy over the fact that a greater portion of the federal deficit is now owed to foreign lenders than in preceding years. In 1939, the U.S. government owed less than half of 1 percent of its $41.9 billion debt to foreign and international investors. In 1960, that figure climbed to 4.4 percent of the deficit. By 1980, however, the federal government owed nearly 15 percent of its debt to foreign lenders. As that figure continues to increase, so does the pressure to keep it to a minimum. Given the country's economic and other conditions, this is an expectation that federal debt managers cannot control.

At the state and local levels, public debt managers are under pressure to be more innovative and creative. During the 1970s, many local governments discovered they could use revenue bonds to help finance local economic development and building construction. Thus, debt management became a means for financing private economic activity (e.g., by financing the construction of a local K mart store or new housing) as well as public projects. Many of these creative uses of the public debt were eliminated during the mid-1980s as a result of changes in federal tax laws. Nevertheless, public officials—those who specialize in public finance and those whose work puts them in direct contact with budgeting issues—are constantly looking for new ways to use public debt financing to the advantage of their constituents.

In the area of taxation, voters around the country engaged in tax revolts during the late 1970s, posing new challenges to all government officials. Voters placed "caps" on property valuation and established elaborate procedures for instituting any new revenue-raising measures. At the same time, many state and local officials found themselves trapped by growing spending obligations as a result of high inflation and expanding public programs. The result was a period of fiscal stress that took a variety of forms. In some areas, it resulted in spending cuts; in others, it produced new forms of taxation that circumvented the tax-revolt restrictions. In a few instances, it led to defaults and bankruptcy. In 1975, for example, New York City was unable to meet its financial obligations. As a result, the state of New York established the Municipal Assistance Corporation (MAC) to help restructure its massive debts and an Emergency Financial Control Board (EFCB) to address longer-term issues. Within three years, the financial management of the MAC and EFCB had made progress in their efforts. In the process, however, the way New York City was governed was significantly changed.[27]

In these and many other instances, the public finance manager plays a crucial role despite being relatively invisible. So long as the costs of government and public services remain important issues on the American public-sector agenda, the job of managing the government's financial resources will remain a challenging one.

Summary

1. Public financial management covers a range of topics and activities, including revenue raising, expenditures, budgeting, and managing public assets and liabilities.
2. Public financial management is influenced by a variety of expectations, from the demand that government provide goods and services in an accountable fashion to the achievement of economic and social goals. In addition, public finance managers are subject to several standards of performance stressing the demands for efficiency, effectiveness, and equitable performance.
3. The primary tasks of public financial management are to develop budgets, execute budgets, and manage public debts. Each of these tasks requires the public administrator to engage in technical analyses as well as political judgments regarding the management of government finances.

Study Questions

1. Assume that you are working for your state government and that it is necessary to raise taxes next year to help fund higher education. If the governor asked you for a recommendation, which type of tax increase would you recommend—a raise in property, income, or sales taxes? Explain your choice.
2. Attend a local city council budget hearing and make a log of the intensity of discussions on different issues.
3. Obtain copies of the federal, state, and city or county budgets at your local library. Determine how much each budget proposes to spend for law enforcement, environmental protection, and education. Are each of these expenditure categories found in all three budgets?

Notes

1. For an excellent overview of public finance, see Richard A. Musgrave and Peggy B. Musgrave, *Public Finance in Theory and Practice*, 4th ed. (New York: McGraw-Hill, 1984).
2. See the discussion on impoundment and deferrals in Allen Schick, *Congress and Money: Budgeting, Spending, Taxing* (Washington, DC: Urban Institute, 1980), pp. 401–11.
3. On the rise of the Keynesian economic policy approach, see Herbert Stein, *The Fiscal Revolution in America* (Chicago: University of Chicago Press, 1969); for a follow-up history on its use through the 1980s, see Herbert Stein, *Presidential*

Economics: The Making of Economic Policy from Roosevelt to Reagan and Beyond, rev. ed. (New York: Simon & Schuster/Touchstone, 1984). Also see Arthur M. Okun, *The Political Economy of Prosperity* (New York: W. W. Norton, 1970).

4. See Alan S. Blinder, *Economic Policy and the Great Stagflation*, student ed. (New York: Academic Press, 1981).

5. On the history and politics surrounding the negative income tax, see Daniel P. Moynihan, *The Politics of a Guaranteed Income: The Nixon Administration and the Family Assistance Plan* (New York: Vintage Books, 1973). On the experiments with such a plan, see Alice M. Rivlin, *Systematic Thinking for Social Action* (Washington, DC: Brookings Institution, 1971), pp. 94–108.

6. See John E. Schwarz, *America's Hidden Success: A Reassessment of Public Policy from Kennedy to Reagan*, rev. ed. (New York: W. W. Norton, 1988), p. 24.

7. See Rose Gutfeld, "IRS Faces Pressure to Raise Collections — But Not Get Tough," *Wall Street Journal*, 24 December 1987, pp. 1, 4.

8. See Frank S. Levy, Arnold J. Meltsner, and Aaron Wildavsky, *Urban Outcomes: Schools, Streets, and Libraries* (Berkeley: University of California Press, 1974), pp. 240–45.

9. See James A. Maxwell, *Financing State and Local Governments*, rev. ed. (Washington, DC: Brookings Institution, 1969), chap. 6.

10. Some governments go through the budgetary process once every two years (e.g., the state of Minnesota).

11. See Thomas D. Lynch, *Public Budgeting in America* (Englewood Cliffs, NJ: Prentice-Hall, 1979).

12. See Frank S. So, "Finance and Budgeting," in *The Practice of Local Government Planning*, ed. by Frank S. So et al. (Washington, DC: International City Management Association, 1979), pp. 122–25; and Lynch, *Public Budgeting in America*, chap. 4.

13. See E. J. Mishan, *Cost-Benefit Analysis*, expanded ed. (New York: Praeger, 1976).

14. For a critical introduction to the development of planning-programming-budgeting, see Ida R. Hoos, *Systems Analysis in Public Policy: A Critique*, rev. ed. (Berkeley: University of California Press, 1983).

15. Richard P. Nathan et al., *Reagan and the States* (Princeton, NJ: Princeton University Press, 1987), pp. 40–41.

16. See ibid., pp. 38–41; and Lawrence Brown, James W. Fossett, and Kenneth T. Palmer, *The Changing Politics of Federal Grants* (Washington, DC: Brookings Institution, 1984).

17. General revenue sharing was carefully monitored and reported on in a number of studies; see, for example, Richard P. Nathan et. al., *Monitoring Revenue Sharing* (Washington, DC: Brookings Institution, 1975); and Richard P. Nathan et. al., *Revenue Sharing: The Second Round* (Washington, DC: Brookings Institution, 1977).

18. See Aaron Wildavsky, *The New Politics of the Budgetary Process* (Glenview, IL: Scott, Foresman/Little, Brown, 1988).

19. See John L. Mikesell, "Administration and the Public Revenue System: A View of Tax Administration," *Public Administration Review* 34 (November/December 1974): 615–24, esp. 618–20; and John L. Mikesell, *Fiscal Administration: Analysis and Applications for the Public Sector* (Homewood, IL: The Dorsey Press, 1982), chap. 9.

20. See Mikesell, *Fiscal Administration*, pp. 60–61.

21. Ibid., pp. 62–64.
22. Bureau of the Census, *Statistical Abstract of the United States, 1989* (Washington, DC: Government Printing Office, 1989), table 489.
23. Ibid., table 455.
24. See Mikesell, *Fiscal Administration*, chap. 12.
25. These figures are drawn from data provided in *City & State*, 1 February 1988, p. 11.
26. These bankers and brokers often act as underwriters; see Mikesell, *Fiscal Administration*, pp. 345–49.
27. See Robert W. Bailey, *The Crisis Regime: The MAC, the EFCB, and the Political Impact of the New York Financial Crisis* (Albany, NY: State University of New York Press, 1984).

CHAPTER 14

PUBLIC

ADMINISTRATION

IN THE FUTURE

Managing Continuity and Change in Public Administration

Continuities

Americans of the last half of the twentieth century accept change as a fact of life. As a dynamic society thriving on progress and challenge, we are constantly facing new circumstances. Nonetheless, there are some basic aspects of our system of public administration that are not likely to change in the near future.

First, public bureaucracies will continue to exist. Our political system will continue to rely on public administration as the way to implement the policies decided by our democratic institutions. Indeed, we are likely to become even more dependent on the public sector for both basic services and a growing list of amenities.

Second, we can expect continuing tension between the basic social and political values of our society and the requirements of the administrative state. The expectations generated by our commitment to a democratic government will continue to emphasize citizen sovereignty, participation, equality, and responsiveness to legitimate authority. The expectations and values of the administrative state will continue to emphasize efficiency and effectiveness. In short, public administration, with its reliance on bureaucratic forms of organization, will continue to face pressures and tendencies toward undemocratic processes. This fact will influence our concerns about and color our vision of public administration in the United States.

Third, and most important, the operations of American government will continue to be influenced by a strong concern for the accountability of public administrators. On the one hand, public administrators will continue to find themselves in positions that require them to exercise discretion—from the police officer deciding whether to issue a ticket or a warning to a driver speeding on a turnpike to the top administrator of the EPA deciding on the guidelines to use in disbursing money from the Superfund. On the other hand, the American public, as consumers of public administration, will continue to be concerned about whether public administrators are doing their jobs.

The fundamental challenge of American public administration will continue to be that of being responsive to the diversity of expectations confronting public administrators. Further, the wide range of sources of these expectations will not diminish. Public administrators will continue to face the expectation that they live up to the standards of the Constitution and the laws enacted by relevant legislative bodies. They will continue to confront pressures to use their exercise of administrative discretion in ways that serve the public interest, their agency's clientele, and the general public. Public administrators will continue to face the expectations that they be responsive to the concerns of elected officials, their employing agencies, and the professions to which they belong. Finally, public administrators will continue to face the challenge of fulfilling their own expectations as employees, U.S. citizens, family members, and human beings.

Public administrators will continue their efforts at managing these diverse and sometimes incompatible expectations. Although the nature of the expectations may change over time, neither their sources nor the processes by which administrators manage them are likely to change.

Divergent and Changing Expectations

Whether public administrators succeed in meeting the fundamental challenge of managing diverse expectations can have profound effects on the quality of our lives as Americans. Sometimes these effects are dramatic, as was the case when the space shuttle *Challenger* exploded on January 28, 1986. More often, the successes and failures of public administrators influence our lives in less dramatic but profound ways.

NASA and the Shuttle *Challenger*.   In many respects, the National Aeronautics and Space Administration (NASA) is a unique government agency. Its history and technical mission differ greatly from those of agencies that deliver more basic public services (e.g., highway construction or trash collection). Yet NASA shares with all public agencies the need to face and respond to divergent expectations.

After the 1986 *Challenger* accident, President Ronald Reagan appointed a special commission to investigate the disaster. Headed by former Secretary of State William Rogers, the commission investigated the technical design of the space shuttle and NASA's decision-making procedures leading up to its launch. The commission discovered that the explosion was caused, in part, by a technical failure in a joint located between two segments of the launch vehicle's rocket motor. Upon closer investigation, however, the Rogers Commission also concluded that administrative procedures at NASA contributed to the accident. In other words, the way NASA was operating at the time of the shuttle explosion was a "contributing cause" of the tragedy.

At the time of the *Challenger* accident, NASA was not operating as it had in the past. Changes had occurred in NASA's operations over the preceding decade as the agency responded to changes in its environment. During the 1960s, for example, NASA's engineers and technicians were expected to make key judgment calls on whether a space vehicle was ready to launch. Such decisions were not left to upper-level management alone. This was possible, in part, because the agency enjoyed widespread public and congressional support for its missions of landing an American on the moon by 1970 and of remaining ahead of the Soviet Union in the "race for space." Under these supportive conditions, NASA's leaders faced few significant financial constraints or other external pressures. Thus, there was little need to impose unnecessary rules and restrictive regulations on the agency's engineers and scientists. Although a public bureaucracy, the early NASA did not have to operate bureaucratically. Rather, it was a more open organization in which those "on the line" — the space agency's experts — had considerable influence over a wide range of decisions.

In the late 1960s and early 1970s, however, NASA was forced to respond to significant changes in the thinking of American policymakers. For example, the Soviets were no longer a threat to the American lead in space, and the American public became less willing to spend money on space exploration. As a result, NASA was expected to minimize its costs and even to justify its existence. The agency responded to these expectations by developing a program that gives top priority to establishing regularly scheduled shuttle launchings. In this program, reusable shuttles are cost effective and serve the interests of the military and the private sector in launching satellites into space. NASA also had to respond to cuts in its budget. It did so through internal reorganization, such as relying more on outside contractors to reduce costs and placing more decision-making authority in the hands of top-level agency management. Thus, the responsibility of making critical decisions about spacecraft design, launch safety, and flight readiness became less that of the agency's technical experts and more that of higher-level managers and contractors with a proprietary interest in the shuttle program's success.

Such was the situation at NASA when the decision to launch the *Challenger* was made on that fateful January morning. Hours before the launch, a cross-country teleconference was held involving the launch managers at NASA and the engineers in Utah who worked for Morton Thiokol, the manufacturer of the shuttle's booster rocket. Questions were being raised about the advisability of launching the *Challenger* in temperatures hovering around the freezing point. The discussion among Thiokol's engineers was intense but inconclusive, leading NASA's Houston-based launch managers to express frustration with their Utah colleagues. Thiokol's managers put the NASA personnel on hold, and an even more heated debate took place among the engineers. Eventually the managers at Thiokol took control of the discussion by announcing that the decision about what to recommend to NASA was a managerial matter, not a technical one to be left to the engineers. Getting back on-line to Houston, Thiokol's managers gave their endorsement to a launch decision. With this recommendation in hand, NASA's managers decided to launch the *Challenger* that morning. Reflecting on the events of that day, some analysts have argued that the tragedy could have been avoided had the engineers (that is, the expert technicians), rather than the managers, had the final say on the launch decision. In this way, the changing circumstances and expectations surrounding NASA may have contributed to the *Challenger* tragedy.[1]

The Changing Needs of Veterans. While the *Challenger* tragedy is a highly visible example of how an agency's responses to divergent expectations can affect our lives, it is not a unique one. Most other public agencies in this country also face divergent expectations. Many times the divergence reflects differences between the expectations of individuals within the agency and expectations deriving from external sources.

The Department of Veterans Affairs (known as the Veterans Administration, or the VA, until 1989) is expected to provide high-quality medical care to veterans with service-related disabilities. At the same time, however, it faces the growing expectation that it contain costs. This dilemma is manifested in the policy debate over what the agency should do to deal with two new challenges: the incidence of post-trauma syndrome among those who served in the Vietnam War and the growing number of homeless veterans.

Post-trauma syndrome is an illness that emerged during the 1970s and early 1980s among military personnel who served in Southeast Asia. It is a delayed reaction to the trauma of combat, often occurring as long as ten years after the event. To deal with the illness, the VA considered setting up store-front clinics and walk-in counseling centers to serve veterans. By providing counseling centers, the agency believed it could treat veterans suffering from post-trauma syndrome before the illness progressed to extreme psychosis, and thereby minimize the need for hospitalization. However, this approach conflicted with the expectations that others have of the agency—that it treat only veterans requiring hospitalization. According to this perspective, if veterans are not sick enough to require hospitalization, then they do not need the agency's medical services.

In 1988, the agency faced similar difficulties when it proposed opening shelters for homeless veterans. This program was intended to work with other programs dealing with counseling and drug and alcohol abuse. The idea was that the combined services would give homeless veterans a better start toward self-sufficiency. However, the agency was criticized for getting involved in activities that go beyond its traditional responsibilities and obligations.[2]

Schools and Latch-key Children. While the *Challenger* accident and the difficulties faced by the Veterans Affairs department may seem far removed from our daily experiences, similar dilemmas facing public agencies influence our lives much more directly. One such issue involves the pressures on local school administrators to provide more after-school programs to deal with the problems of latch-key children.

In the past, school administrators often limited such programs to student participation in bands, athletics, debate teams, and other extracurricular activities. The selection of students for these programs was based on competition. Some schools even required students to maintain certain grade-point averages before they could participate in the programs. Today, there is increasing pressure for school boards to establish after-school programs—such as intramural sports and special interest clubs in photography, computers, and science fiction—that do not restrict student participation. These expectations come from a growing number of working parents who need after-school adult supervision of their children. An increasing trend toward the two-income family means that fewer parents are able to care for their children at the end of the school day. Thus, the school is expected to fill the vacuum created by this changing social situation.

The Management Challenge

Juggling Acts

Public administrators face complex challenges because of the diversity and multiplicity of the expectations they face. Chapters 4 through 9 detailed many of these sources of expectations. Administrators cannot possibly satisfy everybody's expectations. For example, local residents who want city workers to collect their trash daily instead of twice a week are not likely to receive lower tax bills or lower trash-collection user charges no matter how much they argue for such reductions. Meeting contrasting expectations of increased services and lower taxes often poses a no-win situation for public-sector agencies, and yet they face such demands all the time. Public administrators cannot be responsive to all expectations, especially when they are contradictory. Consequently, even under the best conditions, public administrators find themselves trying to juggle diverse and possibly incompatible expectations.

Managing public agencies during times of change is an especially difficult challenge. This task involves thinking about the future, which is risky in a time of rapid change because the projections may not always be accurate.

"Easy" and "Hard" Changes

Changes that are merely continuations of existing trends are not so difficult to project, such as the aging of the American population. That change is a logical conclusion drawn from projected changes in population birth and death patterns. In recent years, America's birthrate has slowly declined from its high during the baby-boom era of the 1950s. As the baby boomers age, the general population of this country ages. In addition, longer life spans due to advances in medicine and increasing concern for personal health will encourage this trend toward an aging population. In turn, this will influence the expectations that Americans have for government services toward meeting the needs of the elderly.

The changes that are hardest to anticipate are those representing disjunctions or dramatic breaks with the past. For example, it is difficult to estimate the degree of change that we will face as a nation in the future or to judge the nature and direction of those changes accurately. Who would have guessed twenty years earlier that by 1990 the United States would have staggering trade imbalances, a trillion-dollar federal budget, and huge budget deficits that seem to grow uncontrollably? Or that we would be struggling with administrative guidelines to govern the introduction of genetically engineered organisms into the environment? Or that the federal government would be funding research to develop drug treatments for AIDS, a deadly disease unknown to the medical and scientific communities just a decade earlier?

Threats

In addition to the constant challenges facing public administration as a result of a complex and changing environment, some public agencies must deal with infrequent but direct threats to their existence. During a period of budget cutbacks, many agencies are challenged to do more with fewer resources and others are subject to proposals for their elimination. Agency responses to such threats can range from resistance to cutbacks and termination to complete capitulation.[3] It is in the face of such direct threats that we can learn much about how American public administrators view their obligations.

In 1981, for example, the Reagan administration ordered the Bureau of Health Planning (BHP) in the Department of Health and Human Services to prepare for its own termination by 1983. The BHP originally employed three hundred public servants, who administered a federal grant program for local health systems agencies (HSAs) whose primary function was to improve local community access to quality health care. Under the termination orders it received, the BHP was to reduce its staff to ten workers by 1982, and then completely disappear from the federal budget by 1983. BHP personnel could have resisted these orders by mobilizing their supporters in and out of Congress. Alternatively, they could have done nothing at all—that is, sat on their hands and effectively abandoned the local HSAs. Instead, during the period of 1981 to 1983, BHP personnel spent much of their time trying to locate alternative funding to help strengthen the local HSAs that they had served for many years. These efforts were not taken without risk. According to one observer, the bureau's activities on behalf of HSAs violated the spirit of what the Reagan administration intended when it ordered the agency to begin terminating its operations. In the end, the BHP was not eliminated but rather reorganized and significantly reduced in size. By 1984, however, thanks to BHP efforts, the HSAs were in better shape than the agency that served them so well during its critical hours.[4]

A more positive outcome was in store for the federal Bureau of Alcohol, Tobacco, and Firearms (BATF). Formed in 1919 as the Bureau of Prohibition, this agency had a famous employee in Eliot Ness, a federal law-enforcement official whose exploits have been featured in television programs and movies. Although often confused with the FBI, the BATF never achieved the same visibility and popularity. Nevertheless, by the early 1970s, it employed over four thousand people. In the 1980s, however, it became the target of Reagan administration budget cutters who felt that the BATF staff was too large. Its work force was significantly reduced—to 1,600 employees in 1988. Nonetheless, the agency survived by de-emphasizing its role in enforcing alcohol and cigarette tax collections and stressing instead its efforts against terrorist bombings, gun control, and other matters under its firearms jurisdiction.[5] This strategy kept BATF in operation despite Reagan administration efforts to shrink it significantly.

Achieving the "Higher" Standard

Public administration continues to face pressures from cutbacks in the resources available for administrators to do their jobs. But this situation may turn out to be just another phase in the long history of American governmental growth and contraction. More constant are the pressures that come from the inconsistent, often contradictory, and sometimes unrealistic expectations concerning public agencies and administrators.[6]

Consider, for example, the commonly shared belief that those who work for government should follow standards that are not merely *different* from but also *higher* than those required in the private sector. The call for higher standards of behavior for public servants is rarely accompanied by descriptions or explanations of what that higher standard entails.

To understand the problems this situation can produce, consider the dilemma posed for public administrators. The four accountability systems discussed in Chapter 3—legal, bureaucratic, political, and professional—may be regarded as a reflection of four distinctive versions of the "higher standard" to which public servants are held. Sometimes that higher standard is defined in legal terms, in which the administrator is urged to follow the precept that this is a nation of laws, not people. At other times, the higher standard involves putting aside personal ambitions and biases and deferring to the wishes of the chief executive or supervisor. In contrast to this bureaucratic perspective, other public employees are urged to follow a politically responsive standard, through which they do their best to serve their constituency or clientele. In still other instances, the higher standard is linked to some professional code of behavior. In all cases, however, the higher standard of government service remains an ambiguous and perhaps impossible ideal to achieve.

The greatest difficulty emerges when a public administrator is under pressure to meet two or more of these higher standards. It may not be possible to be simultaneously legally correct, bureaucratically obedient, politically responsive, and professionally responsible if the demands of one standard are incompatible with one or more of the others. A city manager who feels strongly obliged to uphold his or her professional integrity might run into significant conflicts in a community where political responsiveness is given priority as the standard for government work. This kind of situation poses a dilemma for public servants: When faced with a choice among alternative standards, public servants may inadvertently (or invariably) subject themselves to criticism by those who view governing standards in a different light.

The pressures of public-sector work are enormous in this regard and should not be underestimated. Thus, government administrators have much more than multiple expectations to contend with—they must also face constant complaints from various groups and individuals who believe they are not performing according to some higher standard.

Administrators for the Future

Who would want to be a public administrator in such a setting? Public administrators must be able to manage change and complexity. They must be able to adapt to both predictable and unpredictable changes in the environment. They must be capable of managing government agencies in an ambiguous, turbulent, and uncertain environment. The kind of person who seeks to be a public administrator is one who thrives on and can handle the continuing challenges of ambiguity, complexity, and rapid change.

Public administrators' jobs are never completed. They cannot rest on the laurels of past accomplishments. This situation can be a tremendous source of frustration for public administrators who prefer tidy solutions to problems. It is more rewarding to those who view these ambiguous, complex, and changing situations as challenges and opportunities to derive a tremendous sense of accomplishment. It all depends on how the administrator views the existence of the many, diverse, and possibly incompatible expectations.

Two Scenarios

To understand who the public administrator of the future should be, we must consider two alternative scenarios for the future of the public service. The first scenario allows us to anticipate the future from the past. The expectations and performance of past public administration will influence our future administrative expectations and responses. In the second scenario, the future is viewed as one of constant change. Here there is so much shifting and changing that we cannot necessarily project from the past. Thus, future public administrators must be able to shift gears quickly to accommodate these changes.

What kind of people do we need for these different futures of public administration? If our first scenario holds true, the challenge will be to recruit administrators who understand the past, appreciate the present, and can project future patterns. These people should be capable of coping with the crosscurrents and divergent expectations characteristic of public administration. If, however, the second scenario holds true, the administrators of the future must be flexible, able to learn new things, and willing to relearn when circumstances require it. In an era of constant change, the successful public administrators will be consummate contingency managers, adapting their strategies to the unique circumstances of the moment rather than applying the same strategies to all situations.

Problem of Recruitment

At the present time, U.S. governments are finding it difficult to recruit responsible and qualified people to public office, whether as elected officials or public employees. Bureaucrat bashing, which occurs when elected officials are too quick to blame public policy shortcomings on the people who administer those programs, has diminished the attractiveness of public employment for young people entering the work force.[7] Miserly reward systems and career prospects, compared to private-sector opportunities, further hamper recruitment to the public sector.

It will not be easy to recruit future public administrators. We need to find people who derive a sense of reward from doing something for the community. In all probability, we will need to change our thinking about the rewards appropriate to people who are willing to make such a contribution.

Developing Relevant Ethics

Beyond the issue of recruitment, we need to consider the related issue of promoting public service ethics. Scholars in this area argue that public service must be founded on a knowledge of and belief in democratic values and that the primary motivation of public servants in the United States should be benevolence toward all citizens.[8] Public administrators have an obligation to democratic values because they have a permanence that elected officials do not. One particular problem we face in trying to inculcate public service ethics is the tendency for professional education to emphasize value-free education.[9]

One way to deal with such concerns is to articulate our expectations for ethical behavior in codes of ethics. Many professional associations have codes of ethics, such as the American Medical Association and the American Bar Association. In the public sector, the International City Management Association (ICMA) and the American Society for Public Administration both have devoted a great deal of attention to developing and updating codes of ethics (see Chapter 3).

One problem with codes of ethics is that they tend to be retrospective, reflecting past experiences rather than recent ones. Today's ethical standards for behavior may not be useful guides for tomorrow's needs and challenges. Codes of ethics are often unable to address ethical dilemmas that arise because of changes in the environment within which the individual works.

Another problem with codes of ethics is that they are often mostly symbolic; that is, they are rarely used as the basis for imposing sanctions on individuals who violate the standards of behavior. One notable exception is the code of the ICMA, which actively investigates charges of unethical behavior on the part of its members (see Chapter 3). The ICMA uses its ultimate sanction—expulsion from the organization—when the breach of ethics is serious.

Without ethical norms and standards of behavior for public-sector employees, we run the risk of having administrators who base their behavior on purely personal standards. Instead, what is needed are standards of behavior that recognize public employees' obligations to the public interest, to democratically derived mandates, and to co-workers who share responsibility for preserving and enhancing the practice of public administration.[10]

New Changes, New Challenges

Beyond the issues of who will be the public administrators of the future and how they will conduct themselves on the job, there are new and unique changes facing public-sector agencies that will affect the expectations that administrators confront. These changes generate political activity leading to policy changes, which, in turn, create new challenges for public administration.

As indicated in Chapter 6, our shifting population brings with it changes in expectations for government involvement in our lives. As the American population ages, we expect government to adapt its services to our needs. Some elderly Americans are organized into special interest groups, such as the American Association of Retired People and the Gray Panthers. These groups are flexing their muscle in political arenas and changing the priorities of government by forcefully articulating their expectations.

The increasing cultural diversity of the American population also has generated new expectations for public administrators. This situation is highlighted in the recent immigration of refugee groups. The integration of non-Western cultures into the American community is, in part, an administrative problem. For example, law-enforcement officials in central California face problems involving the Hmong tribespeople, who relocated from southeast Asia and have traditions of opium use and marriage rituals that look more like kidnaping and rape under American law.[11] How do public administrators enforce the laws of the state of California and at the same time remain sensitive to the cultural beliefs of these residents?

Another important cultural change and one that is a logical extension of earlier trends is the increasingly litigious nature of American society.[12] Public administrators once enjoyed immunity from civil suits for damages to others occurring as a result of their actions on the job. Today, however, public administrators face increasing liability in their jobs as public servants. Now they can be sued for their actions if they violate the constitutional rights of a citizen (e.g., denying residents equal access to a city service or entering private property without a search warrant or other authorization). They even can be sued for what they have *not* done, such as failing to provide a safe or adequate service. For example, parents can sue city officials if their child falls off a slide at a city park. Children falling off playground equipment is not new, but the expectation that city officials are responsible for providing accident-proof playground equipment is new. Oftentimes individual public employees, such as the city manager and the parks director, are also named in such lawsuits. This means that public employees have the potential to contribute more to their communities than private-sector employees do, but they also face greater risk of legal liability in an increasingly litigious American society.

Advances in technology have also had significant impacts on public administration. The widespread use of computers that process credit-card purchases can also provide access to consumer credit records. How are the potential abuses and misuses of this new technology going to be limited or controlled? At the same time, computer technology can make government operations more efficient. Computers can be used to cross-check information on income taxes and Social Security contributions to find absentee parents who are behind in their child-support payments. These and other changes in our environment represent new challenges for American public administration. They are central to what makes public-sector work both frustrating and rewarding.

The Challenge and the Opportunity

Public administration has a pervasive role in American society, and Americans need to understand it for that reason alone. An understanding of public administration is also important for its value as a survival skill. In order to work your way through the system of public bureaucracies to get some problem resolved, it helps to understand the dynamics of public administration and the perspectives of the people who staff government agencies.

Finally, it is worth understanding public administration so that you can better judge whether you are interested in working in the public sector. If you are attracted to a job in an environment that is unfailingly complex and where the expectations may change with a fair degree of regularity, then you may want to consider a career in public administration. The arena is not for the weak spirited, the faint of heart, or the thin-skinned. Success in public administration requires flexibility and a willingness to defer to democratic bosses. It is, however, as rewarding as it is demanding.

Summary

1. American public administration will continue to exist, as will the tensions it creates in our democratic system and its susceptibility to the influence of expectations.
2. What will change are the expectations themselves, for they are constantly shifting and becoming more diverse.
3. This change poses the greatest challenge to public administrators, especially those in managerial positions. The key concern is how to handle the challenge.
4. Public administration must deal with several major problems, including the recruitment of the best and brightest people to serve in government, the development of ethical standards of behavior and ways to enforce them, and meeting the changing expectations of demographic, cultural, technological, and other factors. These are the challenges—and the opportunities—of future public administrators.

Notes

1. See Barbara S. Romzek and Melvin J. Dubnick, "Accountability in the Public Sector: Lessons from the Challenger Tragedy," *Public Administration Review* 47 (May/June 1987): 227–38.
2. See Michael H. Lang, *Homelessness Amid Affluence: Structure and Paradox in the American Political Economy* (New York: Praeger Publishers, Inc., 1989), esp. Part IV.
3. See Charles H. Levine, ed., *Managing Fiscal Stress: The Crisis in the Public Sector* (Chatham, NJ: Chatham House, 1980).
4. See Irene S. Rubin, *Shrinking the Federal Government: The Effect of Cutbacks on Five Federal Agencies* (New York: Longman, 1985), chap. 3.
5. Wayne King, "A Bureau That Battled Bootleggers Is Tough Target for Budget-Cutters," *New York Times*, 1 February 1988, p. 12.
6. See Charles Goodsell, *The Case for Bureaucracy* (Chatham, NJ: Chatham House, 1983), esp. chap. 4.
7. See the Report of the National Commission on the Public Service, *Leadership for America: Rebuilding the Public Service* (Washington, DC: Government Printing Office, 1989).
8. H. George Frederickson and David K. Hart, "The Public Service and the Patriotism of Benevolence," *Public Administration Review* 45 (September/October 1985): 547–54.
9. See Frederick C. Mosher, *Democracy and the Public Service*, 2d ed. (New York: Oxford University Press, 1982), esp. chap. 2.
10. Terry L. Cooper, "Hierarchy, Virtue, and the Practice of Public Administration: A Perspective for Normative Ethics," *Public Administration Review*, 47 (July/August 1987): 320–28.
11. Katherine Bishop, "Asian Tradition at War with American Laws," *New York Times*, 10 February 1988, p. 10.
12. See Jethro K. Lieberman, *The Litigious Society* (New York: Basic Books, 1981).

INDEX